ARTICLE 370

ARTICLE 370

A Constitutional History of Jammu and Kashmir

A.G. Noorani

OXFORD
UNIVERSITY PRESS

OXFORD
UNIVERSITY PRESS

Oxford University Press is a department of the University of Oxford.
It furthers the University's objective of excellence in research, scholarship,
and education by publishing worldwide. Oxford is a registered trademark of
Oxford University Press in the UK and in certain other countries

Published in India by
Oxford University Press
22 Workspace, 2nd Floor, 1/22 Asaf Ali Road, New Delhi 110002

First Edition published in 2011
Oxford India Paperbacks 2014
27th impression 2024

ISNB-13 (print edition): 978-0-19-945526-3
ISNB-10 (print edition): 0-19-945526-0

ISNB-13 (eBook): 978-0-19-908855-3
ISNB-10 (eBook): 0-19-908855-1

Typeset in Adobe Garamond Pro 11/13.3
by Excellent Laser Typesetter, Pitampura, Delhi 110 034
Printed in India by Manipal Technologies Limited, Manipal

Dedicated to the memory of Mridula Sarabhai
who gave her all for Kashmir and
received little recognition from the ones she had helped

Contents

Documents

Preface

This collection of documents on Article 370 of the Constitution of India, which contains 'temporary provisions' with respect to the State of Jammu and Kashmir, provides documents on the five-month long negotiations which preceded its enactment on 17 October 1949; explains the significance of the article; describes how it was eroded, and traces the Constitutional evolution of the State and its relationship with the Union of India thereafter. It covers the period from 1946 to 2010.

The Third Group set up by the Prime Minister Dr Manmohan Singh, as a result of the three Round Table Conferences on Kashmir was devoted to this aspect. Justice Saghir Ahmad, a retired judge of the Supreme Court, drew up a report of this group. It is no more than a resume of various viewpoints expressed in the Conference by the political parties. All political parties in Kashmir are agreed on the restoration of the State's autonomy.

This, of course, requires qualification. The BJP's predecessor the Bhartiya Jan Sangh's founder, Shyama Prasad Mookerjee, endorsed Article 370 when he was a member of the Union Cabinet. If he had considered it disruptive of national unity, he would have resigned from the Cabinet. In a letter of 4 February 1953 Sheikh Abdullah tellingly reminded Mookerjee 'This arrangement (Art. 370) has not been arrived at now but as early as 1949 when you happened to be a part of the Government' (*Integrate Kashmir: Mookerjee–Nehru & Abdullah Correspondence*, Publicity Department, Bhartiya Jan Sangh, p. 37).

It is hoped that this collection of pertinent documents will assist in resolving the impasse on Article 370 and in providing a solution to the wider Kashmir problem. A draft of a revised Article 370, embodying proper safeguards, is included to assist in the discussions.

I would like to record my gratitude to Mr Iqbal Ganai, Secretary, Legislative Assembly of the State of Jammu and Kashmir for furnishing me with copies of the two volumes of the Official Record of the State's Constituent Assembly and the Record of the Legislative of the Assembly debates on the Autonomy Report in 2000.

I am particularly grateful to four Kashmiri friends for their invaluable assistance in this work. They are Mr Saifuddin Soz, former Union Minister, Mr Abdul Rahim Rather, Finance Minister in the Government of Jammu and Kashmir and the moving spirit behind the State's Autonomy Committee, Mr Naeem Akhtar, Chief Spokesman of Jammu & Kashmir Peoples Democratic Party and Mr Iftikhar Gilani, Special Correspondent of the Tehelka group. Responsibility for the selection of documents is entirely mine.

Last but not least, I would like to thank my friends Mr Manzar Khan, Managing Director of Oxford University Press for his constant encouragement in the project and the interest he took throughout and Mr Shashank Sinha, Senior Commissioning Manager of Oxford University Press for his enormous pains and editorial skills.

May 2011   **A.G. Noorani**

Introduction

Article 370 of the Constitution of India relating to the State of and Kashmir is now sixty years old. The Constitution came into force on 26 January 1950 and with it, this unique provision. All other provisions were debated in the Constituent Assembly of India after deliberations in its Drafting Committee and, sometimes, discussions in the Congress Parliamentary Party.

Article 370 was discussed for five months by the Prime Minister of India, Jawaharlal Nehru and his colleagues with the Prime Minister of Jammu and Kashmir, Sheikh Mohammad Abdullah, and his colleagues; from May to October 1949 (Chapter 2, Doc. Nos 1–9). The State of Jammu and Kashmir is the *only* State in the Union of India which *negotiated* the terms of its membership with the Union. The Constituent Assembly merely put the imprimatur of its approval, on 17 October 1949, to a draft agreed between the Union and the State. Article 370 records a solemn compact. Neither side can amend or abrogate it unilaterally, except in accordance with the terms of that provision.

The Union Home Minister P. Chidambaram acknowledged in the Rajya Sabha on 6 August 2010 that Jammu and Kashmir had acceded to India in 'unique circumstances' (*Indian Express*, 7 August 2010). He added that the State poses a 'unique problem' which requires a 'unique solution'. It is not very evident, however, that the dimensions of the uniqueness and its implications are fully realized. It is one thing to say that 'it is important to win the hearts and minds of the people of Jammu and Kashmir'. It is another to admit precisely what led to the *grim* situation which called for this resolve and to define realistically the measures which will accomplish the objective which the Minister mentioned.

A little over a decade after the enactment of Article 370, its co-architect, Prime Minister Nehru, declared in the Lok Sabha on 27 November 1963 that Article 370

has been eroded, if I may use the word, and many things have been done in the last few years which have made the relationship of Kashmir with the Union of India very close. There is no doubt that Kashmir is fully integrated... We feel that this process of gradual erosion of article 370 is going on. Some fresh steps are being taken and in the next month or two they will be completed. We should allow it to go on. We do not want to take the initiative in this matter and completely put an end to Article 370 (Chapter 9, Doc. No. 1).

There was no need for that, as the Union Home Minister Gulzari Lal Nanda explained in the Lok Sabha on 4 December 1964: 'the only way of taking the Constitution (of India) into Jammu & Kashmir is through the application of Article 370... It is a tunnel. It is through this tunnel that a good deal of traffic has already passed and more will' (Chapter 9, Doc. No. 2).

He pointed out that 'while the normal process of (constitutional) amendment is subject to stringent conditions, the process of amendment made available to [sic.] Article 370 are very simple'—by a Presidential Order. In regard to the rest of India, if a state's powers are to be curbed, and correspondingly those of the Union enlarged, the elaborate procedure laid down in Article 368 will have to be followed. In regard to the State of Jammu and Kashmir, Nanda argued, a mere executive order made by the President under Article 370 would suffice. His successors in office accepted this interpretation of Article 370.

Nanda concluded: 'What happens is that only the shell is there. Article 370, whether you keep it or not, has been completely emptied of its contents. Nothing has been left in it' (Ibid.).

This is the reality of 'the special status' of the State of Jammu and Kashmir. Nehru was conscious of the indelicacy of the metaphor. Article 370 was not 'eroded' by efflux of time or ravages of the elements. It was denuded of content by conscious executive acts on his advice through one Presidential Order after another. Of no other constitutional provision can the metaphor ('eroded') be thus used. It is important to trace the steps by which this result was accomplished.

The Indian Independence Act, 1947 empowered the Governor General of India (Section 8(2)) to adapt the Government of India Act, 1935 as the interim constitution till the enactment of a Constitution by the Constituent Assembly of India. The Act, as adapted, served as a Constitution from 15 August 1947 to 25 January 1950.

Section 6(1) of the Act enabled 'an Indian State', a formerly princely state, to accede to India by its ruler executing an Instrument of Accession. It is important to note that no specific form was prescribed by the Act itself. All it required was that the Instrument declare the act of accession and specify its terms. As a matter of convenience the Government of India used the Draft Instrument which was drawn up after the Act of 1935 became law. The federation it envisaged did not come into being. In the case of Jammu and Kashmir, the Instrument of Accession which the Ruler executed on 26 October 1947 was accompanied, uniquely, by a letter of the same date signed simultaneously with the Instrument. In law, such a document is a collateral document and the two form an integral whole. The letter has the same legal effect as does, indeed, the Governor General's letter of acceptance dated 27 October 1947 (Chapter 1, Doc. Nos 5 and 6). Acceptance is a legal prerequisite under Section 6(1) of the Act. The Governor General's letter stipulated that 'as soon as law and order have been restored in Kashmir and her soil cleared of the invader; the question of the State's accession should be settled by a reference to the people'. Accordingly, the *White Paper on Jammu & Kashmir* published by the Government of India early in 1948 recorded: 'In accepting the accession, the Government of India made it clear that they would regard it as purely provisional until such time as the will of the people of the State could be ascertained' (Chapter 1, Doc. No. 7).

Clause 7 of the Instrument of Accession said, 'Nothing in this instrument shall be deemed to commit me in any way to acceptance of

any future Constitution of India or to fetter my discretion to enter
into arrangements with the Government of India under any such future
Constitution' (Chapter 1, Doc. No. 5). Except Jammu and Kashmir,
every state accepted Part B of the Constitution of India which contained provisions uniformly for the governance of the former princely
states. Jammu and Kashmir was the only state to declare its intention
to have its own Constitution drafted by its own Constituent Assembly.
That was as far back as 5 March 1948, by the Maharaja's Proclamation,
which is why it negotiated the terms of Article 370 to protect those
rights (Chapter 1, Doc. No. 9).

The State had acceded to India in 1947 in respect only of defence,
foreign affairs, and communications. Negotiations were held on 15 and
16 May 1949 at the Deputy Prime Minister Vallabhbhai Patel's residence in New Delhi on Kashmir's future set-up. Nehru and Abdullah
were present. Foremost among the topics were 'the framing of Constitution' for the State and 'the subjects in respect of which the State should
accede to the Union of India'. On the first, Nehru recorded in a letter
to the Abdullah (on 18 May) that both Patel and he agreed that it was a
matter for the State's Constituent Assembly. 'In regard to (ii) the Jammu
and Kashmir State now stands acceded to the Indian Union in respect
of three subjects; namely, foreign affairs, defence and communications.
It will be for the Constituent Assembly of the State when convened,
to determine in respect of which other subjects the state may accede'
(emphasis added, throughout) (Chapter 2, Doc. No. 1(a)). Article 370
embodies this basic principle which was reiterated throughout.

On 16 June 1949, Sheikh Abdullah, Mirza Mammad Afzal Beg,
Maulana Mohammed Saeed Masoodi, and Moti Ram Baigra joined
the Constituent Assembly of India (Chapter 2, Doc. No. 1(e)): Ne-
gotiations began in earnest on Article 370 (Article 306A in the draft).
N. Gopalaswamy Ayyangar tried to reconcile the differences between
Patel and Abdullah. A text, agreed on 16 October, was moved in the
Constituent Assembly the next day, but was unilaterally altered by
Ayyangar. It was 'A trivial change,' he claimed in a letter to the Sheikh
on 18 October (Chapter 2, Doc. No. 4). Patel confirmed it to Nehru
on 3 November on his return from the United States (Chapter 2, Doc.
No. 5). Beg had withdrawn his amendment after the accord. Abdullah

and he were in the lobby, and rushed to the House when they learnt of the change. In its original form the draft would have made the Sheikh's ouster in 1953 impossible. It was an unfortunate breach which created distrust.

Article 370 embodies six special provisions for Jammu and Kashmir. First, it exempted the State from the provisions of the Constitution providing for the governance of all the states. Jammu and Kashmir was allowed to have its own Constitution.

Second, Parliament's legislative power over the State was restricted to three subjects—defence, foreign affairs, and communications. The President could extend to the State other provisions of the Constitution so as to provide a federal constitutional framework if they related to the matters specified in the Instrument of Accession. For this, only 'consultation' with the State government was required since the State had already accepted them by the Instrument. But, thirdly, if other 'constitutional' provisions or other Union powers were to be extended to Kashmir, the prior 'concurrence' of the State government was required.

The fourth feature is that this concurrence was strictly provisional. It had to be ratified by the State's Constituent Assembly. Article 370(2) says clearly: 'If the concurrence of the Government of the State ... be given before the Constituent Assembly for the purpose of framing the Constitution of the State is convened, it shall be placed before such Assembly for such decision as it may take thereon.'

The fifth feature is that the 'State Government's' authority to give the 'concurrence' lasts only till the State's Constituent Assembly is 'convened'. It is an 'interim' power. Once the Constituent Assembly met, the State government could not give its own 'concurrence'; still less, after the Assembly met and dispersed. Moreover, the President cannot exercise his power to extend the Indian Constitution to Jammu and Kashmir indefinitely. The power has to stop at the point the State's Constituent Assembly drafted the State's Constitution and decided finally what additional subjects to confer on the Union, and what other provisions of the Constitution of India it should get extended to the State, rather than having their counterparts embodied in the State Constitution itself. Once the State's Constituent Assembly had finalized the scheme and dispersed, the President's extending powers ended completely.

The sixth special feature, the last step in the process, is that Article 370(3) empowers the President to make an order abrogating or amending it. But for this also 'the recommendation' of the State's Constituent Assembly 'shall be necessary before the President issues such a notification'.

Article 370 cannot be abrogated or amended by recourse to the amending provisions of the Constitution of India which apply to all the other states; namely, Article 368. For, in relation to Jammu and Kashmir, Article 368 has a proviso which says that no constitutional amendment 'shall have effect in relation to the State of Jammu and Kashmir' unless applied by order of the President under Article 370. That requires the concurrence of the State's government and ratification by its Constituent Assembly.

Jammu and Kashmir is mentioned among the states of the Union in the First Schedule as Article 1(2) requires. But Article 370(1)(c) says: 'The provisions of Article 1 and of this Article shall apply in relation to that State.' Article 1 is thus applied to the State through Article 370.

Ayyangar's exposition of Article 370 in the Constituent Assembly of India on 17 October 1949 is authoritative.

We have also agreed that the will of the people, through the instrument of a Constituent Assembly, will determine the Constitution of the State as well as the sphere of Union jurisdiction over the State. ... You will remember that several of these clauses provide for the concurrence of the Government of Jammu and Kashmir State. Now, these relate particularly to matters which are not mentioned in the Instrument of Accession, and it is one of our commitments to the people and Government of Kashmir that no such additions should be made except with the consent of the Constituent Assembly which may be called in the State for the purpose of framing its Constitution (Chapter 2, Doc. No. 3).

Ayyangar explained:

the provision is made that when the Constituent Assembly of the State has met and taken its decision both on the Constitution for the State and on the range of federal jurisdiction over the State, the President may, on the recommendation of that Constituent Assembly, issue an Order that this Article 306A (370 in the draft) shall either cease to be operative, or shall be operative only subject to such exceptions and modifications as may be specified by him. But before he issued any order of that kind, the recommendations of the Constituent Assembly will be a condition precedent (Chapter 2, Doc. No. 2).

In plain words, Article 370 cannot be invoked after the State's Constituent Assembly has 'taken its decision' on the Constitution 'and on the range of federal jurisdiction over the State'.

The unique process of Presidential Orders altering constitutional provisions by a mere executive order ends with the final decision of the State's Constituent Assembly. Ayyangar repeatedly said that the State government's concurrence alone will not do. 'That concurrence should be placed before the Constituent Assembly when it meets and the Constituent Assembly may take whatever decisions it likes on those matters.' It was, as he put it, 'only an interim arrangement'.

In 1949, no one knew when Kashmir's Constituent Assembly would be elected. Ayyangar therefore said:

The idea is that even before the Constituent Assembly meets, it may be necessary... that certain items which are not included in the Instrument of Accession would be appropriately added to that list in the Instrument... and as this may happen before the Constituent Assembly meets, the only authority from whom we can get consent for the addition is the Government of State.

This was explicitly only for that interim period.

Article 370(1)(b) is clear. 'The power of Parliament to make laws for the said State shall be limited to' (i) matters in the Union and Concurrent Lists corresponding the broad heads specified in the Instrument of Accession and (ii) such other matters in the said Lists as, with the concurrence of the Government of the State the President may by order specify. An Explanation defined 'the Government of the State'. Similar 'concurrence' was required when extending provisions regarding Union institutions *beyond* the agreed ones. But Article 370(2) stipulated clearly that if that concurrence is given 'before the Constituent Assembly... is convened, it shall be placed before such Assembly for such decision as it may take thereon.'

Once Kashmir's Constituent Assembly was 'convened' on 31 October 1951, the State government lost all authority to accord any 'concurrence' to the Union. With the Assembly's dispersal on 17 November 1956, after adopting the Constitution of Jammu and Kashmir, vanished the only authority which alone could vide: (i) more powers to the Union and (ii) accept Union institutions other than those specified in the Instrument of Accession. All additions to Union powers since then are unconstitutional. This understanding informed decisions right until 1957. It was abandoned thereafter.

The Constituent Assembly of India adopted the Constitution of India on 26 November 1949. A day earlier, the ruler of Kashmir made a Proclamation declaring that it 'shall in so far as it is applicable to the State of Jammu and Kashmir, govern the constitutional relationships between this State and the contemplated Union of India' (Chapter 2, Doc. No. 6). On 26 January 1950, the President made his first order under Article 370, extending specified provisions of the new Constitution to the State (Chapter 2, Doc. No. 8).

On 20 April 1951, the ruler made a Proclamation for convening the State's Constituent Assembly. It first met on 31 October 1951. Two issues came to the fore. Nehru was eager to secure Kashmir's 'closer integration' with India; the Sheikh was as eager to preserve its autonomy. The Delhi Agreement that followed was announced at a press conference in Delhi on 24 July 1952 by both. This Union–State accord had no legal force by itself. Only an Order under Article 370 could confer that after the State's Constituent Assembly gave its concurrence, as it alone could, the State government having lost the power on 31 October 1951 when the Assembly was convened.

The Sheikh, meanwhile, pressed for an order to redraft 'the Explanation' in Article 370 redefining the State government as one headed by an elected 'Sadar-i-Riyasat (State President) ... acting on the advice' of his ministers.

Nehru himself wrote on 29 July 1952: 'It is not a perfectly clear matter from the legal point of view how far the President can issue notifications under Article 370 several times' (Chapter 4, Doc. No. 8). On 6 September 1952, President Rajendra Prasad pointed out the illegality of such a course in a closely reasoned note. He questioned 'the competence of the President to have repeated recourse to the extraordinary powers conferred on him' by Article 370. He added: 'Any provision authorizing the executive government to make amendments in the Constitution' was an incongruity and endorsed Ayyangar's views on the finality of a single order under Article 370. 'I have little doubt myself that the intention is that the power is to be exercised *only once*, for then alone would it be possible to determine with precision which particular provisions should be excepted and which modified' (Chapter 5, Doc. No. 6).

The President concluded: 'The conclusion: therefore, seemed to me to be irresistible that Clause (3) of Article 370 was not intended to be used from time to time as occasion required. Nor was it intended to be used without any limit as to time. The correct view appears to be that recourse is to be had to this clause only when the Constituent Assembly (sic.) (Constitution) of the State has been fully framed' (Ibid.).

But he yielded to Nehru's pressure and made the Order on 15 November 1952 (Chapter 5, Doc. No. 10). Seeds of distrust were sown on 17 November 1949. At the time of the Delhi Agreement, distrust between Nehru and Abdullah was palpable. This was reflected in Sheikh Abdullah's warning in the State's Constituent Assembly on 11 August 1952 while explaining the terms of the Delhi Agreement: 'I would like to make it clear that any suggestions of altering arbitrarily the basis of our relationship with India would not only constitute a breach of the spirit and letter of the Constitution, but it may invite serious consequences for a harmonious association of our State with India' (Chapter 4, Doc. No. 12; vide also Doc. No. 11).

Nehru and Abdullah viewed the Agreement differently. To Nehru it was a step towards a closer integration of the State with India as well as a prelude to the finalization of its accession. This alarmed Sheikh Abdullah. On 14 May 1948 Indira Gandhi wrote to her father from Srinagar: 'They say that only Sheikh Saheb is confident of winning the plebiscite…' (Sonia Gandhi (ed.)) *Two Alone, Two Together*, Penguin, New Delhi, 2004, pp. 512–18). Five years later even Sheikh Abdullah had abandoned hope as President Rajendra Prasad reported to Prime Minister Nehru on 14 July 1953 after the Vice-President S. Radhakrishnan's visit to Kashmir (Valmiki Choudhari (ed.), *Dr. Rajendra Prasad's Correspondence and Select Documents*, Allied Publishers, New Delhi, 1987, Volume 16, p. 91).

Sheikh Abdullah sensed the popular mood and the popular desire for finality. He set up a Committee of eight of his close colleagues in the National Conference to devise alternatives. They included men like Bakshi Ghulam Mohammed and G.M. Sadiq who favoured plebiscite in various forms as late as on 9 June 1953 (Chapter 6, Doc. No. 2). Abdullah kept Nehru as well as Maulana Abul Kalam Azad fully informed. He could not have derived much comfort from a confidential note which Nehru wrote to him from Sonemarg in Kashmir on 25 August 1952 (Chapter 5, Doc. No. 5).

It reflected Nehru's desire for finality but through a course diametrically opposite to that which his friend favoured. The Sheikh sought finality by an agreement on Kashmir between India and Pakistan. Nehru sought finality by a unilateral finalization of accession by the State's Constituent Assembly to the exclusion of Pakistan, with which he had been negotiating since the accession. The plan could not have been absent from his mind when he concluded the Delhi Agreement with Abdullah only a month earlier. To Abdullah, the course Nehru recommended spelt his political suicide. Nehru panicked at the course on which his erstwhile interlocutor had set himself and decided to act ruthlessly. As Abdullah explained to Maulana Azad on 16 July 1953, 'If I fail to gain in the confidence of the people here, I will not be able to render any service to my friends' (in New Delhi). This letter was in reply to Nehru's offer, conveyed through Azad, 'that the special position given to Kashmir will be made permanent. If such a declaration had been made at an appropriate time it would have helped. Events in India had alarmed Kashmiris' (Chapter 6, Doc. No. 4). Nehru's Note of 25 August 1952 ran contrary to this belated offer.

The Note which the Prime Minister dictated to his Private Secretary M.O. Mathai on 31 July 1953 clinches the long debated question whether he knew and approved of his former friend's arrest (Chapter 6, Doc. No. 5). It records to the last detail—dismissal of Sheikh's government; take 'prominent members of the executive of the Party (the National Conference) into confidence'; render 'such assistance as may be considered necessary for the maintenance of law and order should be available; (the army had been put on alert); and officers 'whose loyalty is doubted' should be removed. It was to be a swift work followed by a thorough purge.

The unconstitutionality of the Sheikh's dismissal is now universally recognized. The ground stated in the Sardar-i-Riyasat's letter to the Premier on 8 August and repeated in his order of dismissal on the same day is manifestly, demonstrably irrelevant; namely 'the divergence within your Cabinet' (Chapter 6, Doc. Nos 6 and 7). No government in India, Central and State, is free from this 'divergence'. The Sheikh was not asked to demonstrate his majority in the House. He was put in prison. His Deputy Bakshi Ghulam Mohammed, who had agreed with him, on the record, till as late as on 9 June 1953, was made Prime Minister. He presided over a regime of corruption till 1964 and was censured by a Commission of Inquiry headed by a former Judge of the Supreme Court, Justice N. Rajagoplala Ayyangar (Report of the Commission of Inquiry, J&K Government, Srinagar 30 June 1967).

As for the Sheikh, he was released from prison on 6 January 1958, rearrested on 29 April 1958; belatedly implicated on 23 October 1958 in a case of conspiracy filed on 17 May 1958 and released from prison only on 8 April 1964 when the case was withdrawn (vide A.G. Noorani, *The Kashmir Question*, Manaktalas, Bombay, 1964, pp. 79, 80, and 86). He was detained in May 1965 and released on 2 January 1968; interned in New Delhi in December 1970 and freed only on 5 June 1972 (Sheikh Muhammed Abdullah, *Aatish-e-Chinar*, 1982, Srinagar, p. 836).

Documents in Chapter 3 show the earnest with which Kashmiri's Constituent Assembly undertook its task from 1951 to 1952. Chapter 7 contains documents which record the new turn its proceedings took with the Sheikh and his colleagues, especially the principal colleague, Mirza Muhammad Afzal Beg, behind the bars. Beg was the moving figure in the Assembly's proceedings in 1951–2; in the negotiations on Article 370 and the Delhi Agreement; and in the talks in 1974.

During the 'internal emergency' proclaimed by the Government of India on 25 June 1975, a large number of opposition leaders were put in prison. This raised a question as to the legality of Parliament's decisions thereafter. The matter was not pursued since the Government was defeated and lost the General Election of March 1977. It is, however, of more than academic interest in the proceedings of Kashmir's Constituent Assembly after the events of 8 August 1953. *In re: K. Anandan*

(AIR 1952 Madras 117), the Madras High Court rejected the detained Member of Legislative Assembly (MLA), K. Anandan Nambiar's plea to attend the House. Justice Somasundaram's observations are however pertinent to the arrest in Kashmir in 1953 and in the rest of India in 1975:

We, however, readily concede the contention of Mr S. Mohan Kumaramangalam that if a party in power detains a political opponent or continues his detention with the mala fide object of stifling opposition and prejudicing the party to which he belongs in a forthcoming election, there would be an undermining of the basis of the Constitution, putting in jeopardy the second pillar to which we have adverted ('honesty, character and integrity in the component organs of the Constitution') (Para 7 of Judgement Appadurai, p. 119).

Even while the State's Constituent Assembly was still at work, the President made an Order under Article 370 on 14 May 1954; presumably in implementation of the Delhi Agreement. It is regarded to this day as the basic order (Chapter 7, Doc. No. 5). The Constituent Assembly had given its concurrence, three months earlier, in a quaint manner on 15 February 1954 while adopting the Report of the Drafting Committee.

This volume contains proceedings, and documents of the Constituent Assembly of Jammu and Kashmir which are not easy of access now. Two features are particularly noteworthy. One, reflected in Doc. Nos 6, 11, and 12 of Chapter 7—the latter two on 14 November 1956—testify to the Assembly's consciousness of the fact that its hurried ratifications of amendments to the Constitution of India, enacted by Parliament, was indispensable to their legal efficacy. The other is the solemn, very formal character of its dissolution on 26 January 1957 after adopting the State's Constitution on 17 November 1956 (Chapter 7, Doc. No. 13).

The Constituent Assembly of India adopted the Constitution of India on 26 November 1949 and resolved to 'adjourn till such date before the 26th of January 1950 as the President may fix' (*Constituent Assembly Debates*, Volume 12, p. 996). It met again on 24 January 1950 when Dr Rajendra Prasad was elected the first President of India and members signed three copies of the Constitution. The President of the Constituent Assembly, Dr Rajendra Prasad, declared: 'The House will stand adjourned now *sine die.*' The proceedings record: 'The Constituent Assembly is adjourned, *sine die*' (Ibid., p. 7).

The contrast with the end of the deliberations of the Constituent Assembly of Jammu and Kashmir could not have been more glaring. It formally, solemnly resolved to dissolve itself by considered, deliberate moves. On 17 November 1956 it adopted Mir Qasim's resolution that 'this Assembly resolves that it should stand dissolved on the 26th day of January 1957, which is the date of the commencement of the Constitution' (Chapter 7, Doc. No. 14). On 25 January 1957, the President, G.M. Sadiq declared: 'Today this historic session ends and with this the Constituent Assembly is dissolved according to the resolution passed on 17th November, 1956.' The record of the proceedings contains this Note: 'The Clock struck 12 P.M. and the Constituent Assembly was dissolved by the President, Hon'ble G.M. Sadiq, according to the resolution passed by the Constituent Assembly on 17th November, 1956' (Chapter 7, Doc. No. 16).

These were deliberate and considered actions and their legal significance brooks no evasion—the sole ratificatory authority to the extension of the Centre's powers over the State on the extension of additional provisions of the Constitution of India was gone. The State Government's 'concurrence', valid only till the Assembly first met on 31 October 1951, and then also subject to the Constituent Assembly's ratification, was no substitute for the Assembly's ratification. No executive can usurp the powers of a legislature, still less those of a constituent assembly. All the more so if the executive had come to power through one rigged poll after another. 'From 1953 to 1975, Chief Ministers of that State had been nominees of Delhi. Their appointment to that post was legitimized by the holding of farcical and totally rigged elections in which the Congress party led by Delhi's nominee was elected by huge majorities.' This authoritative description of a blot on the record, which most overlook, was written by B.K. Nehru, who was Governor of Jammu and Kashmir from 1981 to 1984, in his memoirs published in 1997 (*Nice Guys Finish Second,* Viking Books, 1997, New Delhi, pp. 614–15).

Chapter 11, Doc. No. 1 is a compilation of texts of the President's Orders under Article 370 made from 1954 to 1994. In all, ninety-four of the ninety-seven entries in the Union List were extended to Jammu and Kashmir as were 260 of the 395 Articles of the Constitution.

Worse, the State's Constitution itself was overridden by those Orders. Its basic structure was altered. The head of state elected by the State legislature was replaced by a Governor nominated by the Centre. Article 356 (imposition of President's rule) was applied despite a provision in the State's Constitution for Governor's rule (Section 92). This was done on 21 November 1964. On 24 November 1966, the Governor replaced the Sadar-i-Riyasat after the State's Constitution had been amended on 10 April 1965 by the Sixth Amendment in violation of Section 147 of the Constitution. Section 147 makes itself immune to amendment. It referred to the Sadar-i-Riyasat and required his assent to constitutional amendments. He was elected by the Assembly (Section 27[2]). To replace him by the Centre's nominee was unconstitutionally to alter the basic structure of the Constitution (Chapter 10, Doc. No. 1(a) and (b)).

Article 370 was used freely not only to amend the Constitution of India but also of the State. On 23 July 1975 an order was made debarring the State legislature from amending the State Constitution on matters in respect of the Governor, the Election Commission, and even the composition of the Upper House, the Legislative Council.

It would be legitimate to ask how all this could pass muster when there existed a Supreme Court of India. Three cases it decided tell a sorry tale. In *Prem Nath Kaul* v *State of J&K*, decided in 1959, a Constitution Bench consisting of five judges unanimously held that Article 370(2) 'shows that the Constitution-makers attached great importance to the final decision of the Constituent Assembly, and the continuance of the exercise of powers conferred on the Parliament and the President by the relevant temporary provisions of Article 370(1*) is made conditional on the final approval by the said Constituent Assembly in the said matters.*' It referred to Clause (3) and said that 'the proviso to Clause (3) also emphasizes the importance which was attached to the final decision of Constituent Assembly of Kashmir in regard to the relevant matters covered by Article 370.' The Supreme Court ruled that '*the Constitution-makers were obviously anxious that the said relationship should be* *finally determined by the Constituent Assembly of the State itself* (Chapter 11, Doc. No. 2 (a) and (b)).

But, in 1968, in *Sampat Prakash* v *the State of J&K*, another Bench ruled to the contrary without even referring to the 1959 case. Justice M. Hidayatullah sat on both Benches. The Court held that Article 370 can still be used to make Orders thereunder despite the fact that the State's Constituent Assembly had ceased to exist.

Four basic flaws stand out in the judgement. First, the Attorney General cited Ayyangar's speech only on the India-Pakistan war of 1947, the entanglement with the United Nations, and the conditions in the State. On the basis, the court said, in 1968, that 'the situation that existed when this article was incorporated in the Constitution has not materially altered,' twenty-one years later. It ignored completely Ayyangar's exposition of Article 370 itself; fundamentally, that the Constituent Assembly to Kashmir alone had the final say.

Secondly, it brushed aside Article 370(2) which lays down this condition, and said that it spoke of 'concurrence given by the Government of State before the Constituent Assembly was convened and makes no mention at all of the completion' of its work or its dissolution.

The supreme power of the State's Constituent Assembly to ratify any change, or refuse to do so, was clearly indicated. Clause (3) on the cessation of Article 370 makes it clearer still. But the Court picked on this clause to hold that since the Assembly had made no recommendation that Article 370 be abrogated, it should continue. It, surely, does not follow that after that body dispersed the Union acquired the power to amass powers by invoking Article 370 when the decisive ratifying body was gone.

Thirdly, the Supreme Court totally overlooked the fact that on its interpretation, Article 370 can be abused by collusive State and Central governments to reduce Article 370 to a nought. Lastly, the Court misconstrued the State Constituent Assembly's recommendation of 17 November 1952, which merely defined in an Explanation 'the Government of the State'. To the Supreme Court this meant that the Assembly had 'expressed its agreement to the continued operation of this Article by making a recommendation that it should be operative with this modification only.' It had made no such recommendation.

The Explanation said no more than that 'for the purposes of this Article, the Government of the State means...' It does not, and indeed, cannot, remove the limitations on the State government's power of concurrence imposed by Clause (2); namely, ratification by the Constituent Assembly.

The Supreme Court laid down no limit whatever whether as regards the time or the content. 'We must give the widest effect to the meaning of the word "modification" used in Article 370(1)'. The net result of this ruling was to give a *carte blanche* to the Government of India to extend to Jammu and Kashmir such of the provisions of the Constitution of India as it pleased.

In 1972, in *Mohammed Maqbool Damnoo* v *the State of J&K*, another Bench blew sky high the tortuous meaning given to the explanation. It was a definition which had become 'otiose'. But this Bench also did not refer to the 1959 ruling (1972) 2 SC 735). Cases there are, albeit rare, when courts have overlooked a precedent. But that is when there is a plethora of them. Article 370 gave rise only to three cases. The first was studiously ignored in both that followed. The Supreme Court found no difference between an elected Sadar-i-Riyasat and an appointed Governor. 'There is no question of such a change being one in the character of that government from a democratic to a non-democratic system.' If the Constitution of India is amended to empower the Prime Minister to nominate the President, as Sri Lanka's 1972 Constitution did, would it make no difference to its democratic character? To this Bench, the essential feature of Article 370(1)(b) and (d) is the necessity of the concurrence of the State government, not the Constituent Assembly. This case was decided before the Supreme Court formulated in 1973 the doctrine of the unamendable 'basic structure' of the Constitution.

Sheikh Abdullah had no cards to play when he concluded an accord with Indira Gandhi and became Chief Minister on 24 February 1975 (Chapter 11, Doc. No. 3). At the outset, on 23 August 1974, he had written to G. Parthasarathi: 'I hope that I have made it abundantly clear to you that I can assume office only on the basis of the position as it existed on 8 August 1953.' Judgement on the changes since will be deferred until the newly elected Assembly comes into being. On 13 November 1974, G. Parthasarathi and M.A. Beg signed 'Agreed Conclusions': Article 370 remained; so did the residuary powers of legislation (except in regard to anti-national acts); constitutional provisions extended with changes can be 'altered or repealed'; the State could review Central laws on specified topics (welfare, culture, and so on) counting on the Centre's 'sympathetic consideration'; and a new bar on amendment to the State Constitution regarding the Governor and the Election Commission. Differences on *'nomenclature'* of the Governor and Chief Minister were 'remitted to the principles'. Differences persisted on the Election Commission, Article 356, and other points. On 25 November, Abdullah sought a meeting with Prime Minister Indira Gandhi. Her reply not only expressed doubt on the usefulness of talks but also on his commitment to the basic features of the State's Constitution and to the democratic functioning of the Government. Hurt, he wrote back ending the parleys. They met at Pahalgam. An exchange of letters, on 13 February 1975, clinched the deal on the basis of the Agreed Conclusions.

This was a political accord between an individual, however eminent, and the Government of India, like the Punjab Accord (24 July 1985); the Assam Accord (15 August 1985); and the Mizoram Accord (30 June 1986)—each between the Government and the opposition. It cannot override Article 370; still less sanctify constitutional abuse. It bound the Sheikh alone and only until 1977.

This was explicitly an accord on 'political cooperation between us', as Indira Gandhi wrote (16 December 1974). On 12 February 1975, Abdullah recorded that it provided 'a good basis for my cooperation at the political level'. In Parliament, on 3 March 1975, she called it a 'new political understanding'. He was made Chief Minister on 24 February, backed by the Congress's majority in the Assembly and on the understanding of a fresh election soon. Sheikh Abdulah's memoirs *Aatish-e-Chinar* (Urdu) record her backtracking on the pledge in March 1977 when she lost the Lok Sabha elections. The Congress withdrew support and staked a claim to form a government. Governor's rule was imposed. The Sheikh's National Conference won the elections with a resounding majority on a pledge to restore Jammu and Kashmir's autonomy. The 1975 accord had collapsed.

It was, I can reveal, based on gross error. The Agreed Conclusions said (Para 3): 'But provisions of the Constitution already applied to the State of J&K without adaptation or modification are unalterable'. This preposterous assertion was made in the teeth of the *Sampat Prakash* case. One Order can always be rescinded by another. All the orders since 1954 can be revoked; they are a nullity anyway. Beg was precariously ill and relied on advice which Parthasarathi's 'expert' had given him. He was one S. Balakrishnan whom R. Venkataraman refers to as 'Constitutional Adviser in the Home Ministry' in his memoirs. It is no disrespect to point out that issues of such complexity and consequence are for counsel's opinion; not from a solicitor, still less a bureaucrat even if he had read the law. Even the Law Secretary would have insisted on the Attorney General's opinion. Amazed at what Beg had told me in May 1975, I pursued the matter and eventually met Balakrishnan in 1987. He confirmed that he had, indeed, given such advice. It was palpably wrong. The 1975 accord, based or a fundamental error of law, is worse than useless. It is harmful to Kashmir's rights and interests. It has neither legal efficacy nor moral worth.

The Beg–Parthasarathi Agreed Conclusions of 13 November 1974, on which the Indira Gandhi–Sheikh Abdullah Accord of February 1975 was based provided in Para 5:

As an arrangement reciprocal to what has been provided under Article 368, a suitable modification of that Article as applied to the State should be made by Presidential order to the effect that no law made by the legislature of the State of Jammu and Kashmir, seeking to make any change in or in the effect of any provision of the Constitution of the State of Jammu and Kashmir relating to any of the under mentioned matters shall take effect unless the Bill, having been reserved for the consideration of the President receives his assent.

The matters are: (a) the appointment, powers, functions, duties, privileges and immunities of the Governor; (b) The following matters relating to elections, namely, the superintendence direction and control of elections by the Election Commission of India, eligibility for inclusion in the electoral rolls without discrimination, adult suffrage, and composition of the Legislative Council, being matters specified in Sections 138, 139, 140 and 50 of the Constitution of the State of Jammu and Kashmir (Chapter 11, Doc. No. 3).

The reference to reciprocity is farcical. Shortly after Sheikh Abdullah assumed office, now as Chief Minister of Jammu and Kashmir, the

President made an Order under Article 370(1), on 23 July 1975 (CQ 101) avowedly 'with the concurrence' of the State Government. It overrode the State's Constitution and laid down '(b) After Clause (3) of Article 368, the following shall be added, namely:

(4) No law made by the Legislature of the State of Jammu and Kashmir seeking to make any change in or in the effect of any provision of the Constitution of Jammu and Kashmir relating to:

(a) appointment, powers, functions, duties, emoluments, allowances, privileges, or immunities of the Governor, or

(b) superintendence, direction, and control of elections by the Election Commission of India, eligibility for inclusion in the electoral rolls without discrimination, adult suffrage and composition of the legislative Council, being matters specified in Sections 138, 139, 140, and 50 of the Constitution of Jammu and Kashmir.

Shall have any effect unless such law has, after having been reserved for the consideration of the President, received his assent.

However, Article 147 of the Constitution of Jammu and Kashmir does not require the President's assent for any amendment to the Constitution; only the assent of the Governor. It says:

an amendment of this Constitution may be initiated only by the introduction of a Bill for the purpose in the Legislative Assembly, and when the Bill is passed in each House by a majority of not less than two-thirds of the total membership of that House, it shall be presented to the Governor for his assent and, upon such assent being given to the Bill, the Constitution shall stand amended in accordance with the terms of Bill. ... (Chapter 11, Doc. No. 1)

The Order of 23 July 1975 is manifestly unconstitutional for two reasons. First the State Government lacked the legal competence to accord any such 'concurrence' after the Constituent Assembly was convened on 31 October 1951. Once that sole consenting body, the Assembly, was dissolved on 17 November 1956, the President can make no Order under Article 370. Secondly and fundamentally, Article 370 envisages extension of the Constitution of India to the State. It cannot be invoked to amend the State's Constitution. Such an order is an abuse of Article 370 and, therefore, void.

Jammu and Kashmir has been put in a status inferior to that of other states. One illustration suffices to demonstrate this. Parliament had to amend the Constitution four times, by means of the Fifty-ninth, Sixty-fourth, Sixty-seventh, and Sixty-eighth Constitution amendments, to extend President's rule imposed in Punjab on 11 May 1987. For the State of Jammu and Kashmir, the same result was accomplished, from 1990 to 1996, by mere executive orders under Article 370.

Another gross case illustrates the capacity for abuse. On 30 July 1986, the President made an Order under Article 370, extending to Kashmir Article 249 of the Constitution in order to empower Parliament to legislate even on a matter in the State List on the strength of a Rajya Sabha resolution. 'Concurrence' to this was given by the Centre's own appointee, Governor Jagmohan. G.A. Lone, a former Secretary, Law and Parliamentary Affairs to the State Government, described how the 'manipulation' was done 'in a single day' against the Law Secretary's advice and in the absence of a Council of Ministers (Chapter 11, Doc. No. 3A).

The Nehru–Abdullah Agreement in July 1952 (the Delhi Agreement) confirmed that the residuary powers of legislation (on matters not mentioned in the State List or the Concurrent List), which Article 248 and Entry 97 (Union List) confer on the Union, will not apply to Kashmir. The Order of 1986 purported to apply to the State Article 249, which empowers Parliament to legislate even on a matter in the State List if a Rajya Sabha resolution so authorizes it by a two-thirds vote. But it so amended Article 249 in its application to Kashmir as in effect to apply Article 248 instead—'any matter specified in the resolution, being a matter which is not enumerated in the Union List or in the Concurrent List' (Chapter 11, Doc. No. 1).

The Union thus acquired the power to legislate not only on all matters in the State List, but others not mentioned in the Union List or the Concurrent List—the residuary power. In relation to other states, an amendment to the Constitution would require a two-thirds vote by both Houses of Parliament plus ratification by the states (Article 368). For Kashmir, executive orders have sufficed since 1953 and can continue till doomsday. 'Nowhere else, as far as I can see, is there any provision authorizing the executive government to make amendments in the Constitution,' President Rajendra Prasad pointed out to Prime

Minister Nehru on 6 September 1952. Is this the state of things we wish
to perpetuate?

The State Assembly adopted, on 26 June 2000, a resolution recording
its acceptance of the Report of the State Autonomy Committee and asked
the Union government and the Government of Jammu and Kashmir to
take positive and effective steps for the implementation of the same
(Doc. Nos 90 and 91). On 4 July 2000, the Union Cabinet said that the
'resolution was unacceptable ... would set the clock back and reverse the
natural process of harmonizing the aspirations of the people of Jammu
& Kashmir with the integrity of the State' (*The Hindu*, 5 July 2000, for
the text).

This was understandable. The National Democratic Government was
headed by the Bharatiya Janata Party which was pledged to the repeal of
Article 370. In May 2004, the United Progressive Alliance, headed by
the Indian National Congress, came to power at the Centre.

Prime Minister Manmohan Singh convened three Round Table
Conferences (RTCs) on the Kashmir problem. At the second RTC,
in Srinagar on 24 and 25 May 2006, five Working Groups were set
up. The Chairman of four groups presented their Reports to the
third RTC in New Delhi on 24 April 2007—N.C. Saxena on good
governance; C. Rangarajan on economic development; M.K. Rasgotra
on strengthening relations across the Line of Control; and Mohammad
Hamid Ansari (now Vice-President) on confidence-building measures
across segments of society in the State. All, particularly the last two,
were able documents. It is another matter they were pigeonholed.

The Report of the fifth group, headed by Justice (retd) S. Saghir
Ahmad, former Chief Justice of the Jammu and Kashmir High Court
and judge of the Supreme Court, on Centre–State relations was the most
sensitive. If wisely written, the report could have served as a basis for
an all-party dialogue and invested the RTCs with success. The Working
Group was formed to find a common ground on self-rule, autonomy,
and regional aspirations. More than any other report, this was eagerly
awaited. The Group held five meetings between 1 December 2006
and 3 September 2007. He submitted the Report suddenly on 18
December 2009.

The issues under the purview of the Working Group V were as follows: strengthening relations between the State and the Centre and to deliberate on (i) matters relating to the special status of Jammu and Kashmir within the Indian Union; (ii) methods of strengthening democracy, secularism, and the rule of law in the State; (iii) effective devolution of powers among different regions to meet regional, sub-regional, and ethnic aspirations. The central issue was erosion of Article 370, a fact admitted by Jawaharlal Nehru in the Lok Sabha on 27 November 1963.

Each of the three unionist parties presented its case through its advocate—the National Conference, through Abdul Rahim Rather, Finance Minister, the People's Democratic Party through Muzaffar Hussein Baig, former Deputy Chief Minister; and the Congress, through Prof. Saifuddin Soz, former Union Minister. The State's Autonomy Report, an excellently documented expose of the Centre's abuse of Article 370, did not refer to the external dimension. The PDP's concept of 'Self Rule' supplies this vital component—the links between the two parts of Jammu and Kashmir (vide Jammu & Kashmir: The Self-Rule Framework for Resolution; Srinagar, October 2008).

Saghir Ahmad recorded all the parties' submissions, including those of the Bharatiya Janata Party and hinted at the outset that the job was beyond him. 'In order to find out an answer to these questions, it would be necessary to delve into the archives of old records which would reveal the historical and political background of Article 370 of the Constitution of India.'

The published material, including the debates in the Constituent Assembly and the Nehru–Sheikh Abdullah correspondence, which he ignores, provide enough material. In any case, two years were more than enough for archival research.

The entire debate on Article 370 in the Constituent Assembly on 17 October 1949, and N. Gopalaswamy Ayyangar's authoritative exposition were completely omitted.

There are but two main judgements of the Supreme Court on Article 370: *Premnath v. State of J&K* (AIR 1959 S.C. 749) and Sampat Prakash vs. State of J&K AIR 1970 1118, which, he rightly notes, took a contrary view to the first case. Justice M. Hidayatullah was on both Benches but did not refer to the earlier case. The first case ruled in favour of autonomy; the second, against it. A former judge of the Supreme Court charged with the task that he was, should have analysed both. Both were dismissed in a single laconic paragraph.

In the same spirit, the Delhi Agreement of 1952 and the Indira Gandhi–Sheikh Abdullah Accord of 1975 are also set out, so is a list of forty-three orders under Article 370, after the major one of 14 May 1954; a list of the Chief Ministers from 1952 to 2008; and the periods of Governor's and Central Rule. The purpose of the exercise emerges on page 64 of the 101-page report: 'Article 370(1)(D)(II) provides that an addition to the matters in the Union List and the Concurrent List as set out in Clause 1(b), the Right of Parliament to make laws will also extend to such other matters in that list as with the concurrence of the government of the State, the President may by Order specify. The list of Chief Ministers given above indicates that *there was always a popular government in power* and, therefore, the Presidential orders were apparently issued with the concurrence of that government.' Governor B.K. Nehru held a different view.

The State Government's power to accord its concurrence was subject to ratification by the Constituent Assembly of Jammu and Kashmir as Clause (2) of Article 370 makes clear and both Gopalaswamy Ayyangar and Sheikh Abdullah emphasized. On page 16 he himself records Abdul Rahim Rather's unanswerable argument that the government's power to accord concurrence ended once the State's Constituent Assembly met in 1951 and the Assembly's ratificatory authority ended on its dissolution in 1956.

Clearly, Saghir Ahmad was out to deny the erosion of Article 370 and the State's autonomy. The Explanation to Article 370(1) defining the government of the State does not and cannot override the explicit bar in Clause (2) of Article 370. But read this:

Under Governor's Rule, there is, obviously, no Council of Ministers and the Governor acts on his own without any advice being tendered to him by the Council of Ministers. If any entry in the Union List which did not pertain to three items, namely, Defence, External Affairs and Communication was extended to the State of Jammu & Kashmir during Governor's Rule, can it be said that such entry was properly and legally extended. This is a query which naturally arises in the mind but it cannot be finally decided, as this question, as stated by the present law Secretary in his report quoted earlier, a Writ Petition *Dr. Mohd Amin Andrabai and another (Rakesh Kumar)* v. *Union of India and two others*, namely, State of J&K, and Mr Jagmohan, Governor is pending in the Delhi High Court since 1988 (Chapter 12, Doc. No. 4).

A case pending for over twenty years cannot debar a body like Group V or, for that matter, anybody else from expressing an opinion on the law.

But where he does opine, it is in favour of the Union, not the State.

It is clear that legislative fields had already been indicated between the Centre and the State in the Document of Accessories which was also incorporated in the Indian Constitution in the form of Article 370 and, therefore, the Parliament, to begin with, could make laws for the State of Jammu and Kashmir only on the topics indicated in the Schedule attached with the document of Accession but also on the topics subsequently applied to the State of J&K.

Justice Saghir Ahmad concludes:

The question of Autonomy and its demand can be examined in the light of the Kashmir Accord or in some other manner or on the basis of some other formula as the present Prime Minister may deem fit and appropriate so as to restore the Autonomy to the extent possible. This is also a long pending demand which requires to be settled once for all to usher in a brighter relationship between the Centre and the State. The question of appointment of the Governor and dismissal of popular Government by the Governor may be considered and resolved.

What help does such a report render to a Government of India that seeks sincerely to resolve the problem? What help this counsel?: 'A period of about 60 years is a long period and the Working Group recommends that the question of Article 370 should be settled once for all and the state of uncertainty in respect of this article should be given a final shape.' He does not suggest even vaguely how this should be done. What is plain is his acknowledgement that there is a problem to be solved to give Article 370 'a formal shape'.

The Parliamentary Delegation which visited Kashmir on 20–21 September 2010 returned with strong impressions. One of its most senior

members, Sitaram Yechury, member of the Politburo of the Communist
Party (Marxist), said in a press interview:

The intensity of the alienation surprised me. We believe that Article 370
has constantly been diluted and is not being implemented. ... Article 370
is a historic commitment we made to Kashmiris. How can you nullify that?
An order passed in 1954—the Constitution (Application to Jammu &
Kashmir) Order—*circumscribed* the provisions of Article 370. The starting
point for any discussion on Kashmir should be the pre-1953 status (*Tehelka*,
16 October 2010).

This 'pre-1953 status' is a shorthand for the status the State enjoyed
before Sheikh Abdullah's dismissal from office and his arrest on 8–9
August 1953 and long imprisonment thereafter.

As well as Article 370, certified by Nehru and Nanda to have been
set at nought as back as in 1963–4, the Delhi Agreement of 1952 is also
a total wreck as, in deed, is the Accord of 1975. A new Constitutional
Settlement which enjoys popular support and is negotiated freely with
their leaders by representatives of the Government of India is necessary.
The mechanism for investing the Settlement with legal force and efficacy
is ironically, Article 370 itself.

A Memorandum submitted by the National Conference to the Prime
Minister of India, P.V. Narsimha Rao on 4 November 1995, establishes,
with copious references to Constitutional provisions and judicial pronouncements that 'Article 370 (1) (d) is not and cannot just be a one-
way stream. ... There is no legal impediment, as is evident from the
pronouncements of the Supreme Court, in reversing the dilution made
to the autonomy of the state' (Chapter 12, Doc. No. 1).

A final order can be made by the President of India under Article 370
to wipe out all the patently unconstitutional orders made earlier, from
1954 to 1994, and give the new Constitutional Settlement legal force
under this Order. In the unique historical circumstances genuine/popu-
lar support will make do for the Constituent Assembly ratification. It
must meet two tests, besides popular acceptance. First it, must provide
cast-iron guarantees against recurrence of the abuse perpetrated in the
teeth of Article 370. Its safeguards have proved of no avail. This is best
done by terminating the President's power to make any further orders

under Article 370. Its Clause (3) empowers the President to make an order to 'declare that this Article shall cease to be operative'. This will also put an end to the anachronism of constitutional amendment by executive fiat which President Rajendra Prasad trenchantly criticized as far back as on 6 September 1952 (Chapter 5, Doc. No. 6).

The present position is palpably absurd based as it is on a record of admitted abuses stretching over five decades. There is another aspect. Article 253 of the Constitution of India reads thus: 'Notwithstanding anything in the foregoing provisions of the Chapter, Parliament has power to make any law for the whole or any part of the territory of India for implementing any treaty, agreement or convention with any other country or countries or any decision made at any international conference, association or other body'.

It has been applied to Jammu and Kashmir with this proviso: 'Provided that after the commencement of the Constitution (Application to Jammu and Kashmir) Order 1954, no decision *affecting the disposition of the State of Jammu and Kashmir* shall be made by the Government of India without the consent of the Government of that State'.

Agreements on a plebiscite in the State were reduced to irrelevance decades ago. Secession of the State has long ceased to be part of any realistic discussion of the Kashmir problem. This Introduction and the documents in the volume are confined to the internal aspect of the problem. As far as the external aspect is concerned, it is well known that discussions between India and Pakistan since 2005 have centred on a Four-Point formula. Its elements are: reduction of the Line of Control in the State to irrelevance; demilitarization of the State; self-governance or self-rule in both parts of the State; and a joint management mechanism whose members will be drawn from both sides.

Article 370, when revised as an agreed final provision, denuding the President, and, therefore, the Central Government of the power to alter it, will fit the Four-Points like a glove by guaranteeing self-rule.

Chapter 12, Doc. No. 5 is the writer's tentative contribution to that effort. It is a draft of Article 370 which guarantees an agreed quantum of self-rule.

It, however, omits the second and indispensable guarantee of autonomy, namely, a Head of State elected by the State itself and not one imposed upon it by the Centre. The office of an elected Sardar-i-Riyasat, of Jammu and Kashmir, established in 1952, was abolished in 1965 and replaced by that of the Governor appointed by the Centre.

The record bears recalling. On 12 June 1952, Kashmir's Constituent Assembly accepted the recommendation of its Basic Principles Committee, headed by Mirza Mohammad Afzal Beg, that 'the office of the head of state shall be elective'. On 20 July in New Delhi, the Sheikh had to accept a change that made a mockery of the Assembly's decision. It was agreed that 'the head of state shall be a person recognized by the President on the recommendation of the legislature of the state'. Worse, he could be sacked any time, without cause, by the Centre—'he shall hold office during pleasure of the President' (Chapter 4, Doc. No. 6), that is, the Government of India.

Article 310 (22) of India's Constitution defined 'ruler' *inter alia* as one 'who for the time being is recognized by the President as the ruler of the State'. It was outrageous to apply a rule governing hereditary princes to a head of state elected by its Assembly. Nehru explained the Delhi Agreement in Lok Sabha on 24 July: 'They recommend and then it is for the President to recognize.' He has the veto (Chapter 4, Doc. No. 6). However, in a Note for Sheikh Abdullah dated 14 August 1952, Nehru said 'In practice, the recommendation of the Constituent Assembly or the Legislative Assembly will naturally he accepted by the President' (Chapter 5, Doc. No. 1, Para 5).

Kashmir's Constituent Assembly amended the old Constitution to abolish monarchy from 17 November 1952. On 9 August 1953, Sheikh Abdullah, co-author of the Delhi Accord, was sacked as premier. Article 27 of the State's Constitution, enacted by the rump Assembly in his absence Delhi's says: 'The Sardar-i-Riyasat shall be the person who for the time being is recognized by the President.' Only a proviso provided for his election. But Article 28 said that he shall hold office 'during the pleasure of the President', that is, Government of India. The Constitution 6th Amendment Act, 1965, of Kashmir provided for appointment of the State's Governor by the President. On 23 July 1975, by a mere executive order under Article 370, the Constitution of India was amended to bar the State Assembly from correcting the wrong and restoring the pre-1965 position. The Delhi Agreement was wrecked repeatedly.

The integrity and independence of the office of head of State are crucial to any scheme of autonomy. In 1937, the Congress insisted on assurances of disavowal of the Governor's special responsibilities before accepting office in the Provinces granted autonomy by the Government of India Act, 1935. The Autonomy Statute of South Tyrol provides for election of the Region's President and Vice-President from among its own members, with a member each of the Italian and German language groups to serve rotationally in both posts. The President of Italy cannot veto their elections. Another is the accord of 27 June 1921 between Sweden and Finland on autonomy for the Aaland Islands. The Governor is appointed by agreement between the President of Finland and Aaland's legislature. If they differ, the legislature recommends a panel of five for Finland's President to choose from.

Obviously, as well as redrafting of Article 370, a review of the Constitution of Jammu and Kashmir, drafted in abnormal circumstances, to say the least, will be necessary. The amendments must be based on agreement between all the major parties in Kashmir. They must meet Jammu's concerns as well.

Under the regional formula of Punjab in 1956, two regional committees of the Assembly were set up, comprising MLAs of the Punjabi- and Hindi-speaking regions. Each enjoyed a virtual veto on fourteen specified topics dealing with social and economic development.

In 1970, the Steering Committee of the Jammu and Kashmir State People's Convention, convened by Sheikh Abdullah drew up a scheme for 'internal constitutional set-up' providing for devolution of power to the village level.

Given the political will, sincerity of purpose, and a spirit of compromise, it is not difficult to retrieve from the wreckage of Article 370 a Constitutional Settlement which satisfies the aspirations of the people of Jammu and Kashmir.

* * *

This book presents a collection of rare materials—most of which are not easily accessible—letters, memoranda, white papers, proclamations, and amendments. No stylistic or substantive change has therefore been made to the documents to maintain authenticity.

Chapter 1

Accession to India

1. The British Cabinet Mission's Statement on 16 May 1946 (Extracts)

Papers Relating to the Cabinet Mission to India 1946, Manager of Publications, Delhi, 1946, p. 3

Paragraph 14. Before putting forward our recommendation we turn to deal with the relationship of the Indian States to British India. It is quite clear that with the attainment of independence by British India, whether inside or outside the British Commonwealth, the relationship which has hitherto existed between the Rulers of the States and the British Crown will no longer be possible. Paramountcy can neither be retained by the British Crown nor transferred to the new Government. This fact has been fully recognised by those whom we interviewed from the States. They have at the same time assured us that the States are ready and willing to co-operate in the new development of India. The precise form which their co-operation will take must be a matter for negotiation during the building up of the new constitutional structure, and it by no means follows that it will be identical for all the States.

We have not therefore dealt with the States in the same detail as the Provinces of British India in the paragraphs which follow.

2. The Cabinet Mission's Memorandum on Indian States, Treaties, and Paramountcy (Extracts)

Cmd. 6835, HMSO London

[...]

Prior to the recent statement of the British Prime Minister in the House of Commons an assurance was given to the Princes that there was no intention on the part of the Crown to initiate any change in their relationship with the Crown or the rights guaranteed by their treaties and engagements without their consent. It was at the same time stated that the Princes' consent to any changes which might emerge as a result of negotiations would not unreasonably be withheld. The Chamber of Princes has since confirmed that the Indian States fully share the general desire in the country for the immediate attainment by India of her full stature. His Majesty's Government have now declared that if the Succession Government or Governments in British India desire independence, no obstacle would be placed in their way. The effect of these announcements is that all those concerned with the future of India wish to attain a position of independence within or without the British Commonwealth. The Delegation have come here to assist in resolving the difficulties which stand in the way of India fulfilling this wish.

2. During the interim period, which must elapse before the coming into operation of a new constitutional structure under which British India will be independent or fully self-governing, paramountcy will remain in operation. But the British Government could not and will not in any circumstances transfer paramountcy to an Indian Government.

3. In the meanwhile, the Indian States are in a position to play an important part in the formulation of the new constitutional structure for India, and His Majesty's Government have been informed by the Indian States that they desire, in their own interests and in the interests of India as a whole, both to make their contribution to the framing of the structure, and to take their due place in it when it is completed. In order to facilitate this they will doubtless strengthen their position by

doing everything possible to ensure that their administrations conform to the highest standard. Where adequate standards cannot be achieved within the existing resources of the State they will no doubt arrange in suitable cases to form or join administrative units large enough to enable them to be fitted into the constitutional structure. It will also strengthen the position of States during this formulative period if the various Governments which have not already done so take active steps to place themselves in close and constant touch with public opinion in their State by means of representative institutions.

4. During the interim period it will be necessary for the States to conduct negotiations with British India in regard to the future regulation of matters of common concern, especially in the economic and financial field. Such negotiations, which will be necessary whether the States desire to participate in the new Indian constitutional structure or not, will occupy a considerable period of time, and since some of these negotiations may well be incomplete when the new structure comes into being, it will, in order to avoid administrative difficulties, be necessary to arrive at an understanding between the States and those likely to control the succession Government or Governments that for a period of time the then existing arrangements as to these matters of common concern should continue until the new agreements are completed. In this matter, the British Government and the Crown Representative will lend such assistance as they can should it be so desired.

5. When a new fully self-governing or independent Government or Governments come into being in British India, His Majesty's Government's influence with these Governments will not be such as to enable them to carry out the obligations of paramountcy. Moreover, they cannot contemplate that British troops would be retained in India for this purpose. Thus, as a logical sequence and in view of the desires expressed to them on behalf of the Indian States, His Majesty's Government will cease to exercise the powers of paramountcy. This means that the rights of the States which flow from their relationship to the Crown will no longer exist and that all the rights surrendered by the States to the paramount Power will return to the States. Political arrangements between the States on the one side and the British Crown and British India on the other will thus be brought to an end. The void will have to

be filled either by the States entering into a federal relationship with the successor Government or Governments in British India, or failing this, entering into particular political arrangements with it or them.

The following explanatory note was issued by the Cabinet Mission in New Delhi on the date of publication (22 May 1946):

The Cabinet Delegation desire to make it clear that the document issued today entitled 'Memorandum on States' Treaties and Paramountcy presented by the Cabinet Delegation to His Highness the Chancellor of the Chamber of Princes' was drawn up before the Mission began its discussions with party leaders and represented the substance of what they communicated to the representatives of the States at their first interviews with the Mission. This is the explanation of the use of the words 'succession Government or Governments of British India', an expression which would not of course have been used after the issue of the Delegation's recent statement.

[...]

3. The Indian Independence Act, 1947 (Extracts)

Be it enacted by the King's most Excellent Majesty, by and with the advice and consent of the Lords Spiritual and Temporal, and Commons, in this present Parliament assembled, and by the authority of the same as follows:–

1. *The new Dominions*:—(1) As from the fifteenth day of August, nineteen hundred and forty-seven, two independent Dominions shall be set up in India, to be known respectively as India and Pakistan.

(2) The said Dominions are hereafter in this Act referred to as 'the new Dominions', and the said fifteenth day of August is hereafter in this Act referred to as 'the appointed day'.

2. *Territories of the new Dominions*:—(1) Subject to the provisions of sub-sections (3) and (4) of this section, the territories of India shall be the territories under the sovereignty of His Majesty which, immediately before the appointed day, were included in British India except the territories which under sub-section (2) of this section, are to be the territories of Pakistan.

(2) Subject to the provisions of sub-sections (3) and (4) of this section, the territories of Pakistan shall be:—

(a) the territories which, on the appointed day, are included in the Provinces of East Bengal and West Punjab, as constituted under the two following sections;

(b) the territories which, at the date of the passing of this Act, are included in the Province of Sind and the Chief Commissioner's Province of British Baluchistan; and

(c) if, whether before or after the passing of this Act but before the appointed day, the Governor-General declares that the majority of the valid votes cast in the referendum which, at the date of the passing of this Act, is being or has recently been held in that behalf under his authority in the North-West Frontier Province are in favour of representatives of that Province taking part in the Constituent Assembly of Pakistan, the territories which, at the date of the passing of this Act, are included in that Province.

(3) Nothing in this section shall prevent any area being at any time included in or excluded from either of the new Dominions, so, however, that:—

(a) no area not forming part of the territories specified in sub-section (1) or, as the case may be, sub-section (2), of this section shall be included in either Dominion without the consent of that Dominion; and

(b) no area which forms part of the territories specified in the said sub-section (1) or, as the case may be, the said sub-section (2), or which has after the appointed day been included in either Dominions, shall be excluded from that Dominion without the consent of that Dominion.

(4) Without prejudice to the generality of the provisions of sub-section (3) of this section, nothing in this section shall be construed as preventing the accession of Indian States to either of the new Dominions.

[...]

7. *Consequences of the setting up of the new Dominions:*—(1) As from the appointed day:—

(a) His Majesty's Government in the United Kingdom have no responsibility as respects the government of any of the territories

which, immediately before that day, were included in British
India;

(b) the suzerainty of His Majesty over the Indian States lapses, and
with it, all treaties and agreements in force at the date of the
passing of this Act between His Majesty and the rulers of Indian
States, all functions exercisable by His Majesty at that date with
respect to Indian States, all obligations of His Majesty existing at
that date towards Indian States or the rulers thereof, and all powers, rights, authority or jurisdiction exercisable by His Majesty at
that date in or in relation to Indian States by treaty, grant, usage,
sufferance or otherwise; and

(c) there lapse also any treaties or agreements in force at the date
of the passing of this Act between His Majesty and any persons having authority in the tribal areas, any obligations of
His Majesty existing at that date to any such persons or with
respect to the tribal areas, and all powers, rights, authority or
jurisdiction exercisable at that date of His Majesty in or in
relation to the tribal areas by treaty, grant, usage, sufferance or
otherwise:

Provided that, notwithstanding anything in paragraph (b) or paragraph (c) of this sub-section, effect shall, as nearly as may be continued
to be given to the provisions of any such agreement as is therein referred
to which relate to customs, transit and communications, posts and
telegraphs, or other like matters, until the provisions in question are
denounced by the ruler of the Indian State or person having authority
in the tribal areas on the one hand, or by the Dominion or Province or
other part thereof concerned on the other hand, or are superseded by
subsequent agreements.

[...]

8. *Temporary provision as to government of each of the new
Dominions*:—(1) In the case of each of the new Dominions, the powers
of the Legislature of the Dominion shall, for the purpose of making
provisions as to the constitution of the Dominion, be exercisable in
the first instance by the Constituent Assembly of that Dominion,
and references in this Act to the Legislature of the Dominion shall be
construed accordingly.

(2) Except in so far as other provision is made by or in accordance with a law made by the Constituent Assembly of the Dominion under sub-section (1) of this section, each of the new Dominions and all Provinces and other parts thereof shall be governed as nearly as may be in accordance with the Government of India Act, 1935; and the provisions of that Act, and of the Orders in Council, rules and other instruments made thereunder, shall, so far as applicable, and subject to any express provisions of this Act, and with such omissions, additions, adaptations, and modifications as may be specified in orders of the Governor-General under the next succeeding section, have effect accordingly:
[...]

4. The Government of India Act, 1935, as Adapted on 15 August 1947 by the India Order (Provisional Constitution), 1947 (Extracts)

No. GGO 14, Dated 14 August 1947, Gazette of India, 1947, Extraordinary, p. 834

[As amended by the India Provisional Constitution and Provincial Legislatures (Amendment) Order, 1947, and the India Provisional Constitution (Second Amendment) Order, 1947]

Whereas by sub-section (2) of section 8 of the Indian Independence Act, 1947 (hereafter in the recitals to this Order referred to as the said Act), it is provided that except in so far as other provision is made by or in accordance with a law made by the Constituent Assembly of the Dominion under sub-section (1) of the said section, each of the new Dominions and all Provinces and other parts thereof shall be governed as nearly as may be in accordance with the provisions of the Government India Act, 1935, and that the provisions of the Act shall, so far as applicable and subject to any express provisions of the said Act and with such omissions, additions, adaptations and modifications as may be specified in orders of the Governor-General under the next succeeding section of the said Act have effect accordingly:

And whereas by paragraph (c) of sub-section (1) of section 9 of the said Act it is provided that the Governor-General shall by order make such provision as appears to him to be necessary or expedient for making omissions from, additions to, and adaptations and modifications of, the Government of India Act, 1935, in its application to the separate new Dominions;

And whereas by sub-section (4) of section 19 of the said Act it is provided that in the said Act, except so far as the context otherwise requires, references to the Government of India Act, 1935, include references to any enactments amending or supplementing that Act and in particular references to the India (Central Government and Legislature) Act, 1946;

Now therefore in exercise of the powers conferred by the said provisions of the said Act, the Governor-General is pleased to make the following Order:—

1. (1) This Order may be cited as the India (Provisional Constitution) Order, 1947.

(2) It shall come into force on the fifteenth day of August 1947, which day is hereinafter referred to as 'the appointed day.'

[...]

6. For this section substitute:—

6. *Accession of Indian States:*—

(1) An Indian State shall be deemed to have acceded to the Dominion if the Governor-General has signified his acceptance of an Instrument of Accession executed by the Ruler thereof whereby the Ruler on behalf of the State:—

(a) declares that he accedes to the Dominion with the intent that the Governor-General, the Dominion Legislature, the Federal Court and any other Dominion authority established for the purposes of the Dominion shall, by virtue of his Instrument of Accession, but subject always to the terms thereof, and for the purposes only of the Dominion, exercise in relation to the State such functions as may be vested in them by order under this Act; and

(b) assumes the obligation of ensuring that the effect is given within the State to the provisions of this Act so far as they are applicable therein by virtue of the Instrument of Accession.

(2) An Instrument of Accession shall specify the matters which the Ruler accepts as matters with respect to which the Dominion Legislature may make laws for the State, and the limitations, if any, to which the power of the Dominion Legislature to make laws for the State, and the exercise of the executive authority of the Dominion in the State, are respectively to be subject.

(3) A Ruler may, by a supplementary Instrument executed by him and accepted by the Governor-General vary the Instrument of Accession of his State by extending the functions which by virtue of that Instrument are exercisable by any Dominion authority in relation to his State.

[...]

5. Instrument of Accession of the State of Jammu & Kashmir Signed by Maharaja Hari Singh on 26 October 1947

White Paper on Jammu & Kashmir, Government of India, 1948, pp. 17–19

Whereas the Indian Independence Act, 1947, provides that as from the fifteenth day of August, 1947, there shall be set up an independent Dominion known as India, and that the Government of India Act, 1935, shall, with such omissions, additions, adaptations and modification as the Governor-General may by order specify be applicable to the Dominion of India;

And whereas the Government of India Act, 1935, as so adapted by the Governor-General provides that an Indian State may accede to the Dominion of India by an Instrument of Accession executed by the Ruler thereof:

Now Therefore

I ... Ruler of ... in the exercise of my sovereignty in and over my said State Do hereby execute this my Instrument of Accession, and

1. I hereby declare that I accede to the Dominion of India with the intent that the Governor-General of India, the Dominion Legislature, the Federal Court and any other Dominion authority established for

the purposes of the Dominion shall, by virtue of this my Instrument of Accession, but subject always to the terms thereof, and for the purposes only of the Dominion, exercise in relation to the State of ... (hereinafter referred to as 'this State') such functions as may be vested in them by or under the Government of India Act, 1935, as in force in the Dominion of India on the 15th day of August 1947 (which Act as so in force is hereinafter referred to as 'the Act').

2. I hereby assume the obligation of ensuring that due effect is given to the provisions of the Act within this State so far as they are applicable therein by virtue of this my Instrument of Accession.

3. I accept the matters specified in the Schedule hereto as the matters with respect to which the Dominion Legislature may make laws for this State.

4. I hereby declare that I accede to the Dominion of India on the assurance that if an agreement is made between the Governor-General and the Ruler of this State whereby any functions in relation to the administration in this State of any law of the Dominion Legislature shall be exercised by the Ruler of this State, then any such agreement shall be deemed to form part of this Instrument and shall be construed and have effect accordingly.

5. The terms of this my Instrument of Accession shall not be varied by any amendment of the Act or of the Indian Independence Act, 1947, unless such amendment is accepted by me by an Instrument supplementary to this Instrument.

6. Nothing in this Instrument shall empower the Dominion Legislature to make any law for this State authorising the compulsory acquisition of land for any purpose, but I hereby undertake that should the Dominion for the purposes of a Dominion law which applies in this State deem it necessary to acquire any land, I will at their request acquire the land at their expense or if the land belongs to me transfer it to them on such terms as may be agreed, or, in default of agreement, determined by an arbitrator to be appointed by the Chief Justice of India.

7. Nothing in this Instrument shall be deemed to commit me in any way to acceptance of any future constitution of India or to fetter my discretion to enter into arrangements with the Government of India under any such future constitution.

8. Nothing in this Instrument affects the continuance of my sovereignty in and over this State, or, save as provided by or under this Instrument, the exercise of any powers, authority and rights now enjoyed by me as Ruler of this State or the validity of any law at present in force in this State.

9. I hereby declare that I execute this Instrument on behalf of this State and that any reference in this Instrument to me or to the Ruler of the State is to be construed as including a reference to my heirs and successors.

Given under my hand this... day of August, Nineteen hundred and forty seven.

...

I do hereby accept this Instrument of Accession.

Dated this... day of August Nineteen hundred and forty seven.

(Governor-General of India)

Schedule

The matters with respect to which the Dominion Legislature may make laws for this State.

Defence

1. The naval, military and air forces of the Dominion and any other armed force raised or maintained by the Dominion; any armed forces, including forces raised or maintained by an Acceding State, which are attached to, or operating with, any of the armed forces of the Dominion.

2. Naval, military and air force works, administration of cantonment areas.

3. Arms; firearms; ammunition.

4. Explosives.

External Affairs

1. External affairs; the implementing of treaties and agreements with other countries; extradition, including the surrender of criminals and accused persons to parts of His Majesty's dominions outside India.

2. Admission into, and emigration and expulsion from, India, including in relation thereto the regulation of the movements in India of persons who are not British subjects domiciled in India or subjects of any acceding State; pilgrimages to places beyond India.

3. Naturalisation.

Communications

1. Posts and telegraphs, including telephones, wireless, broadcasting, and other like forms of communication.

2. Federal railways; the regulation of all railways other than minor railways in respect of safety, maximum and minimum rates and fares, station and service terminal charges, interchange of traffic and the responsibility of railway administrations as carriers of goods and passengers; the regulation of minor railways in respect of safety and the responsibility of the administrations of such railways as carriers of goods and passengers.

3. Maritime shipping and navigation, including shipping and navigation on tidal waters; Admiralty jurisdiction.

4. Port quarantine.

5. Major ports, that is to say, the declaration and delimitation of such ports, and the constitution and powers of Port Authorities therein.

6. Aircraft and air navigation; the provision of aerodromes; regulation and organisation of air traffic and of aerodromes.

7. Lighthouses, including lightships, beacons and other provisions for the safety of shipping and aircraft.

8. Carriage of passengers and goods by sea or by air.

9. Extension of the powers and jurisdiction of members of the police force belonging to any unit to railway area outside that unit.

Ancillary

1. Elections to the Dominion Legislature, subject to the provisions of the Act and of any Order made thereunder.

2. Offences against laws with respect to any of the aforesaid matters.

3. Inquiries and statistics for the purposes of any of the aforesaid matters.

4. Jurisdiction and powers of all courts with respect to any of the aforesaid matters but, except with the consent of the Ruler of the Acceding State, not so as to confer any jurisdiction or powers upon any courts other than courts ordinarily exercising jurisdiction in or in relation to that State.

[...]

6. The Maharaja's Letter to the Governor-General of India, Lord Mountbatten, on 26 October 1947 and the Governor-General's Letter in Reply Dated 27 October 1947

White Paper on Jammu & Kashmir, Government of India, 1948, pp. 46–7

26th October 1947

My Dear Lord Mountbatten,

I have to inform Your Excellency that a grave emergency has arisen in my State and request immediate assistance of your Government.

As Your Excellency is aware the State of Jammu and Kashmir has not acceded to either the Dominion of India or to Pakistan. Geographically my State is contiguous to both the Dominions. It has vital economically and cultural links with both of them. Besides my State has a common boundary with the Soviet Republic and China. In their external relations the Dominion of India and Pakistan cannot ignore this fact.

I wanted to take time to decide to which Dominion I should accede, whether it is not in the best interest of both the Dominions and my State to stand independent, of course with friendly and cordial relations with both.

I accordingly approached the Dominions of India and Pakistan to enter into a standstill agreement with my State. The Pakistan Government accepted this arrangement. The Dominion of India desired further discussion with representatives of my Government. I could not arrange this is view of the developments indicated below. In fact the Pakistan Government under the standstill agreement are operating Post and Telegraph system inside the State.

Though we have got a standstill agreement with the Pakistan Government, that Government permitted steady and increasing strangulation
of supplies like good, salt and petrol to my State.

Afridis, Soldiers in plain clothes, and desperadoes, with *modern*
weapons, have been allowed to infilter into the State at first in Poonch
area, then in Sialkot and finally in mass in the area adjoining Hazara
district on the Ramkote side. The result has been that the limited
number of troops at the disposal of the State had to be dispersed and
thus had to face the enemy at several points simultaneously that is has
become difficult to stop the wanton destruction of life and property and
looting. The Mahoora Power House which supplies the electric current
to the whole of Srinagar has been burnt. The number of women who
have been kidnapped and raped makes my heart bleed. The wild forces
thus let loose on the State are marching on with the aim of capturing
Srinagar, the Summer Capital of my Government, as a first step to
overrunning the whole State.

The mass infiltration of tribesmen drawn from the distant areas of the
N.-W.F. Province coming regularly in Motor Trucks using Mansehra-
Muzaffarbad road and fully armed with up-to-date weapons cannot
possibly be done without the knowledge of the Provincial Government
of the N.-W.F. Province and the Government of Pakistan. In spite of
repeated appeals made by my Government no attempt has been made
to check these raiders or stop them from coming to my State. In fact
both the Pakistan Radio and Press have reported these occurrences. The
Pakistan Radio even put out a story that a Provisional Government has
been set up in Kashmir. The people of my State both the Muslims and
non-Muslims generally have taken no part at all.

With the conditions obtaining at present in my State and the great
emergency of the situation as it exists I have no option but to ask for
help from the Indian Dominion. Naturally they cannot send the help
asked for by me without my State acceding to the Dominion of India.
I have accordingly decided to do so and I attach the Instrument of
Accession for acceptance by your Government. The other alternative
is to leave my State and my people to freebooters. On this basis no
civilised Government can exist or be maintained. This alternative I will

never allow to happen so long as I am the Ruler of the State and I have life to defend my country.

I may also inform Your Excellency's Government that it is my intention at once to set up an Interim Government and ask Sheikh Abdulla to carry the responsibilities in this emergency with my Prime Minister.

If my State has to be saved immediate assistance must be available at Srinagar. Mr. Menon is fully aware of the situation and he will explain to you if further explanation is needed.

In haste and with kindest regards.

Hari Singh

Reply from Governor-General, India, Delhi, Dated 27 October 1947

My Dear Maharaja Sahib,

Your Highness's letter, dated the 26th October has been delivered to me by Mr. V.P. Menon. In the special circumstances mentioned by Your Highness, my Government have decided to accept the accession of Kashmir State to the Dominion of India. Consistently with their policy that, in the case of any State where the issue of accession has been the subject of dispute, the question of accession should be decided in accordance with the wishes of the people of the State, it is my Government's wish that, as soon as law and order have been restored in Kashmir and her soil cleared of the invader, the question of the State's accession should be settled by a reference to the people. Meanwhile, in response to Your Highness's appeal for military aid, action has been taken today to send troops of the Indian Army to Kashmir to help your own forces to defend your territory and to protect the lives, property and honour of your people.

My Government and I note with satisfaction that your Highness has decided to invite Sheikh Abdulla to form an Interim Government to work with your Prime Minister.

Mountbatten of Burma

[...]

7. White Paper on Jammu and Kashmir, Government of India (Extracts)

White Paper on Jammu & Kashmir, Government of India, February 1948, pp. 2–3

Jammu and Kashmir, until August 15th, 1947, was an autonomous State in treaty relations with, and subject to the Paramountcy of, the Crown of England. Like other Indian States, it had, however, no international existence. On that date, the Indian Independence Act came into force, and the new Dominions of India and Pakistan came into being. The Indian States became free to decide whether they would accede to one or the other of the two Dominions. The position of the Indian States on the transfer of power was made clear in His Majesty's Government's Declaration of June 3rd, 1947, supplemented by the Statement issued by the British Cabinet Mission on May 16th, 1946. A large number of States acceded to the Dominion of India, and copies of the Instrument of Accession, as well as of the Standstill Agreement governing the administrative arrangements between the States and the Government of India until the new Constitution should come into force in India, are appended. The State of Jammu and Kashmir announced its intention of negotiating Standstill Agreements with both India and Pakistan. In fact, however, the State signed a Standstill Agreement only with Pakistan and entered into no agreement with the Government of India, prior to its accession on October 26th, 1947.

The object of the Standstill Agreement was to provide for the continuance of economic and administrative relations between the State and Pakistan on the same basis as had existed before the creation of the new Dominions. Nevertheless, in an effort to coerce the State into accession to Pakistan, the Pakistan authorities cut off supplies to Kashmir of food, petrol and other essential commodities, and hindered the free transit of travellers between Kashmir and Pakistan. Economic pressure was thus applied simultaneously with military pressure in the form of border raids. Conditions in the State were made more difficult by the communal disturbances which broke out in the two Punjabs after the announcement of the partition. There was a large influx of refugees into the Southern districts of the State, and the State became a channel for the passage of Muslim refugees moving from East Punjab to West Punjab and for non-Muslims moving in the opposite direction. [...]

On the 20th of October, the Wazir of Mirpur sent a message that armed men were gathering opposite Chechiam and Mangla. On the 22nd, he reported that raids on Owen were being methodically carried out. On the 23rd of October, heavy fighting was reported from Kotli which had, by now, been completely cut off from Poonch by road blocks put up by the 'raiders'.

On the 24th of October, 1947, the Government of India received the first request for military aid from the Government of the Jammu and Kashmir State. At that time the Government of India had no agreement, military or political, with the State. A document signed by the British Chiefs of Staff of the Indian Armed Forces states that on the 24th of October information of the capture of Muzaffarabad was received by the Commander-in-Chief in India. No plans for sending troops to Kashmir had up to that time been considered by the Indian Army. On the 25th the Government of India directed the preparation of plans for sending troops to Kashmir by air and road. Indian troops were sent to Kashmir by air on the 27th, following the signing of the Instrument of Accession on the previous night.

The accession was legally made by the Maharaja of Kashmir, and this step was taken on the advice of Sheikh Abdullah, leader of the All-Jammu and Kashmir National Conference, the political party commanding the widest popular support in the State. Nevertheless, in accepting the accession, the Government of India made it clear that they would regard it as purely provisional until such time as the will of the people of the State could be ascertained.

8. The Maharaja's Emergency Administration Order on 30 October 1947 Appointing Sheikh Mohammad Abdullah as the Head of the Administration

Press Information Bureau, Government of Jammu & Kashmir

We are hereby pleased to command that pending the formation of the Interim Government as agreed upon and in view of the emergency that has arisen I charge Sheikh Mohammad Abdullah to function as the Head of Administration with power to deal with the emergency.

Sheikh Mohammad Abdullah be sworn in by the Chief Justice or any other Judge of the High Court at Srinagar.

Hari Singh,
Maharaja

Emergency Council

1. The Hon'ble Sheikh Mohammad Abdullah, Head of Emergency Administration.

2. The Hon'ble Bakshi Ghulam Mohammad, Deputy Head of Administration.

3. The Hon'ble Mirza Mohd. Afzal Beg, Emergency Officer, Anant-nag District.

4. The Hon'ble G.M. Sadiq, Emergency Officer, Internal Security, Home Guards, Cultural Front.

5. The Hon'ble Sham Lal Saraf, Emergency Officer, Trade and Supplies.

6. The Hon'ble Girdhari Lal Dogra, Emergency Officer, Kathua.

7. The Hon'ble Sardar Budh Singh, Emergency Officer (Goodwill Mission to Jammu).

8. The Hon'ble Pt. Jia Lal Kilam, Emergency Officer, Food.

9. Maulana Mohd. Syed, Emergency Officer, Publicity.

10. Kh. Gulam Moni-ud-din, Emergency Officer, Communications.

11. Kh. Abdul Ahad, Emergency Officer. (Firewood, Fuel).

12. Soofi Mohd. Akbar, Emergency Officer, Baramulla.

13. Peer Mohd. Maqbool, Emergency Officer, Muzaffarabad.

14. Pt. Kashapa Bandhu, Emergency Officer, Refugees & Rehabilitation.

15. Mr. Mohi-ud-Din Hamdani, Emergency Officer, Peace Brigade.

16. Mr. D.P. Dhar, Secretary, Internal Security & Law and Order.

17. Mr. J.N. Zutshi, Private Secretary to the Head of Administration and Secretary to the Emergency Council.

18. Kh. Ahsan Ullah, Emergency Officer, Transport.

19. Mr. Mohd. Amin, Emergency Officer, Banihal.

20. Col. Ram Lal, Emergency Officer, Home Guards.

21. Col. Baldev Singh Pathania, Chief Emergency Officer, Jammu.

22. Col. Adalat Khan, Chief Administrative Officer, Bhadarwah.

23. Col. Baldev Singh Samval, Emergency Officer, Border Scouts, Jammu.

9. The Maharaja's Proclamation on 5 March 1948 Appointing a Popular Interim Government

Press Information Bureau, Government of Jammu & Kashmir

In accordance with the traditions of my dynasty I have, from time to time, provided for increasing association of my people with the administration of the State with the object of realising the goal of full Responsible Government at as early a date as possible and in pursuance of that object have, by the Jammu and Kashmir Constitution Act of 1996 (xiv of 1996) established a Constitutional Government with a Council of Ministers, a Legislature with a majority of elected members and an independent Judiciary;

I have noted with gratification and pride the progress so far made and the legitimate desire of my people for the immediate establishment of a fully democratic constitution based on adult franchise with a hereditary Ruler from my dynasty as the Constitution Head of an Executive responsible to the legislature;

I have already appointed the popular leader of my people Sheikh Mohammad Abdullah as the Head of the Emergency Administration;

It is now my desire to replace the Emergency Administration by a Popular Interim Government and to provide for its powers, duties and functions, pending the formation of a fully democratic Constitution.

I accordingly Hereby Ordain as Follows:—

1. My Council of Ministers shall consist of the Prime Minister and such other Ministers as may be appointed on the advice of the Prime Minister. I have by Royal Warrant appointed Sheikh Mohammad Abdullah as the Prime Minister with effect from today.

2. The Prime Minister and other Ministers shall function as a Cabinet and act on the principle of joint responsibility. A Dewan appointed by me shall also be a member of the Cabinet.

3. I take this opportunity of giving once again a solemn assurance that all sections of my people will have opportunities of service, both civil and military, solely on the basis of their merits and irrespective of creed or community.

4. My Council of Ministers shall take appropriate steps, as soon as restoration of normal conditions has been completed, to convene a National Assembly based upon adult suffrage, having due regard to the principle that the number of representatives from each voting area should, as far as practicable, be proportionate to the population of that area.

5. The Constitution to be framed by the National Assembly shall provide adequate safeguards for the minorities and contain appropriate provisions guaranteeing for the freedom of conscience, freedom of speech and freedom of assembly.

6. The National Assembly shall, as soon as the work of framing the new constitution is completed, submit it through the Council of Ministers for my acceptance.

7. In conclusion I repeat the hope that the formation of a popular Interim Government and the inauguration, in the near future, of a fully Democratic Constitution will ensure the contentment, happiness and the moral and material advancement of my beloved people.

10. Proclamation Entrusting Yuvaraj Karan Singh with all the Maharaja's Powers on 9 June 1949

Press Information Bureau, Government of Jammu & Kashmir

Whereas I have decided for reasons of health to leave the State for a temporary period and to entrust to the Yuvaraj Shree Karan Singh Ji Bahadur for that period all my powers and functions in regard to the Government of the State.

Now, therefore, I hereby direct and declare the all powers and functions, whether legislative, executive or judicial which are exercisable by me in relation to the State and its Government, including in particular my right and prerogative of making Laws, of issuing Proclamations, Orders and Ordinances, of remitting, commuting or reducing sentences and of pardoning offenders, shall during the period of my absence from the State be exercisable by Yuvaraj Shree Karan Singh Ji Bahadur.

Hari Singh
Maharajadhiraj

Chapter 2

Kashmir–Union Negotiations
on Article 370
May–October 1949

1(a). Letter Dated 17 May 1949 by N. Gopalaswami Ayyangar to Vallabhbhai Patel Enclosing Jawaharlal Nehru's Draft Letter to Sheikh Abdullah for his Approval

Durga Das (ed.), *Sardar Patel's Correspondence 1945–50*, Navajivan Publishing House, Ahmedabad, 1971, pp. 275–309

(The chapter Article 306A was not enclosed...)

New Delhi
17 May 1949

My dear Sardarji,

Herewith the draft. Jawaharlalji has seen and approved of it.

2. Will you kindly let Jawharlalji know direct as to your approval of it? He will issue the letter to Sheikh Abdullah only after receiving your approval.

Yours sincerely,

N. Gopalaswami

The Hon'ble Sardar Vallabhbhai Patel

New Delhi

Enclosure

New Delhi

18 May 1949

My dear Sheikh Sahib,

In the course of the talks at Sardar Patel's residence on 15 and 16 May 1949 between some of my colleagues and me and you and your colleagues, important issues raised by you in regard to the future of Jammu and Kashmir State were discussed.

2. Among the subjects that were discussed were: (i) the framing of a constitution for the State; (ii) the subjects in respect of which the State should accede to the Union of India; (iii) the monarchical form of government in the State; (iv) the control of the State Forces, and (v) the rights of the citizens of the State to equality of opportunity for service in the Indian Army.

3. As regards (i) and (iii), it has been the settled policy of the Government of India, which on many occasions has been stated both by Sardar Patel and me, that the constitution of Jammu and Kashmir State is a matter for determination by the people of the State represented in a Constituent Assembly convened for the purpose. In the special circumstances of the State of Jammu and Kashmir, the Government of India have no objection to the Constituent Assembly of the State considering the question of the continuance of the association of the State with a constitutional monarchy.

4. In regard to (ii), Jammu and Kashmir State now stands acceded to the Indian Union in respect of three subjects, namely, Foreign Affairs, Defence and Communications. It will be for the Constituent Assembly of the State, when convened, to determine in respect of what other subjects the State may accede.

5. Regarding (iv), both the operational and administrative control over the State Forces has already, with the consent of the Government of Jammu and Kashmir State, been taken over by the Indian Army.

The final arrangements in this connection, for the duration of the present emergency, including financial responsibility for the expenditure involved, were agreed to between us on the 16th inst.

6. As regards (v), the citizens of the State will have equality of opportunity for service in the Indian Army. Under Article 10 of the draft of the new Constitution, as passed by the Constituent Assembly of India, equality of opportunity for employment under the State, including employment in the Indian Army, is declared to be amongst the fundamental rights of all Indian citizens.

7. I trust that the Government of India's position, as stated above, will give you the clarification that you have asked for.

Yours sincerely,
Jawaharlal Nehru

The Hon'ble Sheikh Mohammed Abdullah
Srinagar

1(b). Draft Article 306A as Proposed by the Government of Jammu & Kashmir

Indian Constitutional Document, Munshi Papers, Bharatiya Vidya Bhavan, Bombay, 1967, Volume II, pp. 519–20

306A. Notwithstanding anything contained in this Constitution, until on the recommendation of the Constituent Assembly constituted for the purpose of framing the Constitution of the Jammu and Kashmir State (hereinafter referred to as the State in this Article) the President may, by public notification, alter, modify or amend this Article,

(a) Only such provisions of this Constitution shall apply in relation to the State as are declared by the President, in consultation with the Government of the State, to relate directly to the matters specified in the Instrument of Accession governing the accession of the State to the Dominion of India;

(b) The power of Parliament to make laws for the State shall be limited to:—

those matters in the Union List and the Concurrent List which are declared by the President, in consultation with the Government of the State, to correspond to matters specified in the Instrument of Accession governing the accession of that State to the Dominion of India as the matters with respect to which the Dominion Legislature may make laws for the State.

Explanation:—

The Government of the State in this Article means the person for the time being recognised as the Maharaja of the State by the Union acting on the advice of the Council of Ministers as at present constituted and not acting in his discretion or in his individual judgment.

1(c). Amendments Proposed by the Ministry of States of the Government of India

Amendment Proposed to be Incorporated in the Law Constitution by the Ministry of States, *Indian Constitutional Document, Munshi Papers*, **Bharatiya Vidya Bhavan, Bombay, 1967, Volume II, pp. 473 and 476–7**

The Government of India have also carefully considered the position of Jammu and Kashmir State in the context of their international commitments. Ordinarily, they would have liked to treat this State like other States in the category of Part III States. The main difficulty in adopting this procedure is that the Premier of this State has definitely expressed his inability to extend the content of the accession of the State till the Constituent Assembly of the State has taken a decision in the matter. Against the present background, he is most anxious that the accession of the State should continue in respect of three subjects of Defence, Foreign Affairs and Communications only. During the course of the discussion at the Drafting Committee meeting, it was pointed out that the scheme embodied in the Draft Constitution visualised that all States in Part III would accept List I and List II and in addition accept all provisions relating to fundamental rights and the provisions relating to High Courts and Supreme Court. It was further pointed out that if the quantum of accession of Kashmir State was not extended, difficulties would arise in respect of the citizenship of the subjects of Kashmir State as also in connection with the operation of the provisions regarding fundamental rights and Supreme Court in respect of this State. The

Government of India have considered the matter in its various aspects and are of the opinion that in the view of the present peculiar situation in respect of Jammu and Kashmir State it is desirable that the accession of the State should be continued on the existing basis till the State could be brought to the level of other States. A special provision has therefore to be made in respect of this State on the basis suggested above as a transitional arrangement. It may be added that 'naturalisation' is already covered by the existing Instrument of Accession signed by the Ruler of the State and this may perhaps meet the requirements in respect of citizenship of the subjects of this State.

The Ministry of States suggest for the consideration of the Drafting Committee the following approach to this question:—

1. Jammu and Kashmir State may be treated as part of the Indian territory and shown in States specified in Part III of Schedule I.

2. A special provision may be made in the Constitution to the effect that until the Parliament provides by law that all the provisions of the Constitution applicable to the States specified in Part III will apply to this State, the power of the Parliament to make laws for the State will be limited to the items specified in the Schedule to the Instrument of Accession governing the accession of this State to the Dominion of India or to the corresponding entries in List I of the new Constitution. [...]

1(d). Revision of Rules for Admission of J&K's Representatives to the Constituent Assembly on 27 May 1949

Constituent Assembly Debates (hereafter *CAD*), 27 May 1949, Volume 8, p. 357

N. Gopalaswami Ayyangar (Madras: General): Mr. President, Sir, I rise to move:

That after paragraph 4 of the Schedule to the Constituent Assembly Rules, the following paragraph be inserted, namely:—

4-A. Notwithstanding anything contained in paragraph 4, all the seats in the Assembly allotted to the State of Kashmir may be filled by nomination and the representatives of the State to be chosen to fill such seats may be nominated by the Ruler of Kashmir on the advice of his Prime Minister.

Sir, very few words are really needed from me to commend this motion to the House. Kashmir is one of the States which under the rules framed for the composition of this Assembly have to be represented in the House. Rules have been framed as to how this representation could be secured. But though Kashmir acceded to the Indian Dominion so far back as the end of October 1947, this representation has not materialised. Honourable Members will remember that the conditions in Kashmir have been in a fluid state all these months. [...] The question may now be put.
[...]

Replying to the debate N. Gopalaswami Ayyanagar said:[1] Sir, I have really very little to say. But I think a few words have to be said about one or two observations that were made by my honourable Friend, Maulana Hasrat Mohani. He doubted whether the Prime Minister's description of this accession as being complete is altogether correct. I maintain that it is perfectly correct. The accession was offered by the Maharaja and it was accepted by the Governor-General of the time. I have a copy of that document before me. It is an absolutely unconditional offer. But my honourable Friend referred to what has happened since and I know my other honourable Friend Prof. Shah also seemed to imply what the Maulana contended. Now the correct position is this. The accession is complete. No doubt, we have offered to have a plebiscite taken when the conditions are created for the holding of a proper, fair and impartial plebiscite. But that plebiscite is merely for the purpose of giving the people of the State the opportunity of expressing their will, and the expression of their will, will be only in the direction of whether they would ratify the accession that has already taken place—not ratify in the sense that that act of ratification is necessary for the completion of the accession, but if the plebiscite produces a verdict which is against the continuance of accession to India of the Kashmir State, then what we are committed to is simply this, that we shall not stand in the way

[1] *CAD*, Volume 8, p. 373.

of Kashmir separating herself away from India. In this connection, I should like to draw the attention of the House to the Provisions of the Indian Independence Act under which, when a State accedes and subsequently wished to get out of the act of accession, thus separating itself from the main Dominion, it cannot do so except with the consent of the Dominion. Our commitment is simply this, that if and when a plebiscite comes to be taken and if the verdict of that plebiscite is against India, then we shall not stand in the way of the wishes of the people of Kashmir being given effect to, if they want to go away from us. That is all that it means. So I maintain that the statement that the accession at present is complete is a perfectly correct description of the existing state of things.

Then he asked why should representatives be brought in at this stage. We are not bringing them into this House for the purpose of placing their seal on the act of accession. We are giving them an opportunity for the exercise of the rights which they have obtained by virtue of the fact that accession has already taken place. We are making a new constitution which affects not merely the Union as a whole but affects the units of the Union, and Kashmir, on account of the fact of accession, is at present a unit of that Union. In fashioning the constitution for the whole Union it is only right that representatives of all units should find seats in this Assembly.

[...]

1(e). J&K's Representatives Join the Constituent Assembly on 16 June 1949

CAD, Volume 8, p. 915

The following Members took the pledge and signed the Register:—
    1. Sheikh Mohd. Abdullah.
    2. Mirza Mohd. Afzal Beg.
    3. Maulana Mohd. Syeed Masoodi.
    4. Shri Moti Ram Bagda.
[...]

1(f). Letter of 26 September 1949 to the Drafting Committee of the Constituent Assembly Forwarding the Ministry's Draft

Indian Constitutional Documents, Munshi Papers
Bharatiya Vidya Bhavan, Bombay, 1967, Volume II, p. 461

The 26th September, 1949

Dear Sir,

A meeting of the Drafting Committee will be held at 3 p.m. on Tuesday, the 4th October 1949, in Room No. 25 Ground Floor, Council House, New Delhi.

I enclose a copy of the revised New Part VI-A containing provisions as to the Constitution of the States in Part III of the First Schedule as circulated to the various States Unions and States by the Ministry of States.

Yours truly,
S.N. Mukherjee
Joint Secretary

List of Amendments which will be Necessary if the Constitution of States in Part III of the First Schedule is Incorporated in the Constitution of India

New Part VI-A Containing Provisions as to the Constitution of the States in Part III of the First Schedule
Part VI-A The States in Part III of The First Schedule

Application of Provisions of Part VI to States in Part III of the First Schedule

211-A. The provisions of Part VI of this Constitution shall apply in relation to the States for the time being specified in Part III of the First Schedule as they apply in relation to the States for the time being specified in Part I of that Schedule subject to the following modifications and omissions, namely:—(Kashmir was listed in Part III)

[...]

Articles 306A and 306B (New). After Article 306, the following new articles be inserted:—

Temporary Provisions with Respect to the State of Jammu & Kashmir

306A. Notwithstanding anything contained in this Constitution, until such date as the President may by public notification announce to be the date on which this article shall cease to be operative:—

(a) the power of Parliament to make laws for the State of Jammu and Kashmir shall be limited to those matters in the Union List which the President, in consultation with the Government of that State, may by order specify;

(b) the provisions of Article 211A of this Constitution shall not apply in relation to that State; and

(c) the provisions of Part V and Parts IX to XVII of this Constitution shall apply in relation to that State subject to such exceptions and modifications as the President may by order specify.

Temporary Provisions with Respect to States in Part III of the First Schedule

306B. Notwithstanding anything contained in this Constitution, during a period of ten years from the commencement thereof, or during such longer or shorter period as Parliament may by law provide in respect of any State, the Government of every State for the time being specified in Part III of the First Schedule shall be under the general control of, and comply with such particular directions, if any, as may from time to time be given by, the President, and any failure to comply with such directions shall be deemed to be a failure to carry out the Government of the State in accordance with the provisions of this Constitution.

Provided that the President may by order direct that the provisions of this article shall not apply to any State specified in the order.

1(g). Correspondence on Redraft of Article 306(A)

(g) (i). Letter by Ayyangar to Patel on 15 October 1949 Enclosing the Redraft and Letter to Abdullah of Same Date

New Delhi
15 October 1949

My dear Sardarji,

Sheikh Abdullah and two colleagues of his had a talk with me for about an hour and a half this morning. It was a long drawn out argument, and, as I told you this morning, there was no substance at all in the objections that they put forward to our draft. At the end of it all, I told them that I had not expected that, after having agreed to the substance of our draft both at your house and at the party meeting, they would let me and Panditji down in the manner they were attempting to do. In answer, Sheikh Abdullah said that he felt very grieved that I should think so but that in the discharge of his duty to his own people he found it impossible to accept our draft as it was. I told him thereafter to go back and think over all that I had told them and hoped that he would come back to me in a better frame of mind in the course of the day or tomorrow.

I have since thought over the matter further and dictated a draft which, without giving up the essential stands we have taken in our original draft, readjusts it in minor particulars in a way which I am hoping Sheikh Abdullah would agree to.

I discussed this draft with the Drafting Committee in the evening and one or two small suggestions which they made have been incorporated in it. I enclose a copy of this redraft as also of my letter to Sheikh Abdullah for your information.

I trust that this will meet with your approval.

Yours sincerely,
N. Gopalaswami

The Hon'ble Sardar Vallabhbhai Patel
New Delhi
Encl.: 2

Enclosure I
Redraft of Article 306-A

Provisions with Respect to the State of Jammu and Kashmir   306-(A)
(1) Notwithstanding anything contained in this Constitution:—

    (a) the provisions of Article 211-A of this Constitution shall not apply in relation to the State of Jammu and Kashmir;

    (b) the power of Parliament to make laws for the State shall be limited to

        (i) those matters in the Union List and the Concurrent List which are declared by the President to correspond to matters specified in the Instrument of Accession governing the accession of that State to the Dominion of India as the matters with respect to which the Dominion legislature may make laws for that State, and

        (ii) such other matters in the said lists as with the concurrence of the Government of that State, the President may, by order, specify

    (c) the provisions of Article I and Part II of this Constitution shall apply in relation to that State;

    (d) the other provisions of this Constitution shall apply in relation to that State subject to such exceptions and modifications as the President may, by order, specify

        (i) after consultation with the Government of that State, in cases where such exceptions or modifications are necessary by reason of, or, are incidental to, or are consequential upon, the provisions of clause (a) or clause (b) of this article; and

        (ii) with the concurrence of that Government, in other cases,

(2) not withstanding anything in the preceding clause of this article, from such date as he may specify, the President may, on the recommendation of the Constituent Assembly, constituted for the purpose of framing the Constitution for the State, direct that this article shall cease to be operative, or shall be operative only with such exceptions and modifications as may be agreed on.

N. Gopalaswami
15 October 1949

Enclosure II

New Delhi
15 October 1949

My dear Sheikh Abdullah,

Our discussion this morning, as I indicated to you, left me even more distressed than I have been since I received your last letter from Srinagar.

But this personal reaction of mine is irrelevant when I feel weighted with the responsibility of finding a solution for the difficulties that, after Panditji left for America and within the last few days, have been created, from my point of view, without adequate excuse.

In spite of this personal feeling, I am as anxious and keen now as ever I have been to see that you are not given any cause for genuine or even imagined grievance in regard to the policy that the Government of India are following in relation to Kashmir. I have, therefore, since you left me this morning, tried to find a way out of the present situation in regard to Article 306-A.

I enclose a draft of Article 306-A with the language of it readjusted so as to meet practically all your main points.

I do not wish to write a thesis on the changes that I have made. You will be able to recognise them easily. If you wish to have any further elucidation in the matter, I would request you to come over and discuss it frankly with me.

I do hope you will appreciate the gesture I am making. If you are agreeable to this new draft being substituted for the one of which the Drafting Committee has already given notice, I shall ask the Drafting Committee to give notice of this draft in substitution of the other one. Personally, I should like you to move this draft yourself in the House. We shall be there to support you, and I hope the debate would be maintained at such a high level that a report of it, when cabled to America, will have an effect on the discussions of the Kashmir problem, that may there be going on, which will be of the maximum help to Panditji.

I am looking forward to you rising to the occasion.

Yours sincerely,
N. Gopalaswami

The Hon'ble Sheikh Mohd. Abdullah
New Delhi

1(g) (ii). Patel's Reply on 16 October 1949

New Delhi
16 October 1949

My dear Gopalaswami,

Thank you for your letter of 15 October, which I received only this afternoon on my return from the Constituent Assembly.

I find there are some substantial changes over the original draft, particularly in regard to the applicability of fundamental rights and directive principles of State policy. You can yourself realise the anomaly of the State becoming part of India and at the same time not recognising any of these provisions.

I do not at all like any change after our party has approved of the whole arrangement in the presence of Sheikh Sahib himself. Whenever Sheikh Sahib wishes to back out, he always confronts us with his duty to the people. Of course, he owes no duty to India or to the Indian Government, or even on a personal basis, to you and the Prime Minister who have gone all out to accommodate him.

In these circumstances, any question of my approval does not arise. If you feel it is the right thing to do, you can go ahead with it.

Yours sincerely,
Vallabhbhai Patel

The Hon'ble Shri N. Gopalaswami Ayyangar
New Delhi

1(h). Final Agreed Draft of Article 306A

Indian Constitutional Document, Munshi Papers, Bharatiya Vidya Bhavan, Bombay, 1967, Volume II, pp. 518–19

306A. (1) Notwithstanding anything contained in this Constitution,
 (a) the provisions of article 211A of this Constitution shall not apply in relation to the State of Jammu and Kashmir;
 (b) the power of Parliament to make laws for the State shall be limited to
  (i) those matters in the Union List and the Concurrent List which, in consultation with the Government of the State,

are declared by the President to correspond to matters specified in the Instrument of Accession governing the accession
of the State to the Dominion of India as the matters with
respect to which the Dominion Legislature may make laws
for the State; and

(ii) such other matters in the said Lists as, with the concurrence of the Government of the State, the President may by
order specify;

Explanation:—For the purposes of this article, the Government of the
State means the person for the time being recognised by the Union as the
Maharaja of Jammu and Kashmir acting on the advice of the Council of
Ministers appointed under the Maharaja's Proclamation dated the 5th
March 1948.

(c) the provisions of Article 1 of this Constitution shall apply in
relation to the State;

(d) such of the other provisions of this Constitution and subject to
such exceptions and modifications shall apply in relation to the
State as the President may by order specify:—

Provided that no such order which relates to the matters specified in
the Instrument of Accession of the State aforesaid shall be issued except
in consultation with the Government of the State;

Provided further that no such order which relates to matters other
than those referred to in the preceding proviso shall be issued except
with the concurrence of that Government;

2. If the concurrence of the Government of the State referred to in
sub-clause (b) (ii) or in the second proviso of sub-clause (d) of clause (1)
was given before the Constituent Assembly for the purpose of framing
the Constitution of the State is convened, it shall be placed before such
Assembly for such decision as it may take thereon;

3. Notwithstanding anything in the preceding clauses of this article,
the President may, by public notification, declare that this article shall
cease to be operative or shall be operative only with such exceptions and
modifications and from such date as he may specify;

Provided that the recommendation of the Constituent Assembly
of the State shall be necessary before the President issues such a
notification.

2. Ayyangar's Detailed Exposition of Article 370 (306-A in the Draft) in the Constituent Assembly on 17 October 1949 (Extracts)

CAD, Volume X, pp. 422–7

[...]

Mr. President: We take up article 306A now. Mr. Gopalaswami Ayyangar.

The Honourable Shri N. Gopalaswami Ayyangar (Madras: General): Sir, before I read out the motion, I would request your permission, Sir, not to move item 379, but to move item 451 instead.

Sir, I move:

'That with reference to Amendment No. 379 of List XV (Second Week), after article 306, the following new article be inserted:—

"306A. (1) Notwithstanding anything contained in this Constitution,

(a) the provisions of Article 211A of this Constitution shall not apply in relation to the State of Jammu and Kashmir;

(b) the power of Parliament to make laws for the State shall be limited to

(i) those matters in the Union List and the Concurrent List which, in consultation with the Government of the State, are declared by the President to correspond to matters specified in the Instrument of Accession governing the accession of the State to the Dominion of India as the matters with respect to which the Dominion Legislature may make laws for the State; and

(ii) such other matters in the said List as, with the concurrence of the Government of the State, the President may by order specify;

Explanation:—For the purposes of this article, the Government of the State means the person for the time being recognised by the Union as the Maharaja of Jammu and Kashmir, acting on the advice of the Council of Ministers.'

I am making, Sir, with your permission, a change here. Instead of the word 'appointed' I am substituting the words, 'for the time being in office'—'under the Maharaja's Proclamation, dated the fifth day of March, 1948.'

Pandit Hirday Nath Kunzru: We could not hear the honourable Member, correctly.

The Honourable Shri N. Gopalaswami Ayyangar:

'*Explanation*:—For the purposes of this article, the Government of the State means the person for the time being recognised by the Union as the Maharaja of Jammu and Kashmir, acting on the advice of the Council of Ministers, for the time being in office, under the Maharaja's Proclamation, dated the fifth day of March, 1948.'

I have there substituted the words 'for the time being in office,' for the word 'appointed'.

'(c) the provisions of Article 1 of this Constitution shall apply in relation to the State.

(d) such of the other provisions of this Constitution and subject to such exceptions and modifications shall apply in relation to the State as the President may by order specify;

Provided that no such order which relates to the matters specified in the Instrument of Accession of the State aforesaid shall be issued except in consultation with the Government of the State;

Provided further that no such order which relates to matters other than those referred to in the last preceding proviso shall be issued except with the concurrence of that Government.

(2) If the concurrence of the Government of the State referred to in sub-clause (b) (ii) or in the second proviso to sub-clause (1) was given before the Constituent Assembly for the purpose of framing the Constitution of the State is convened, it shall be placed before such Assembly for such decision as it may take thereon.

(3) Not withstanding anything in the preceding clauses of this article, the President may, by public notification, declare that this article shall cease to be operative or shall be operative only with such exceptions and modifications and from such date as he may specify:—

Provided that the recommendation of the Constituent Assembly of the State shall be necessary before the President issues such a notification.'

Sir, this matter, the matter of this particular motion, relates to the Jammu and Kashmir State. The House is fully aware of the fact that State has acceded to the Dominion of India. The history of this accession is also well-known. The accession took place on the 26th October, 1947. Since then, the State has had a chequered history. Conditions are not yet normal in the State. The meaning of this accession is that at present that State is a unit of a federal State, namely, the Dominion of India. This Dominion is getting transformed into a Republic, which will be inaugurated on the 26th January, 1950. The Jammu and Kashmir State, therefore, has to become a unit of the new Republic of India.

As the House is aware, accession to the Dominion always took place by means of an instrument which had to be signed by the Ruler of the State and which had to be accepted by the Governor-General of India. That has taken place in this case. As the House is also aware, Instruments of Accession will be a thing of the past in the new Constitution. The States have been integrated with the Federal Republic in such a manner that they do not have to accede or execute a document of Accession for the purpose of becoming units of the Republic, but they are mentioned in the Constitution itself; and, in the case of practically all States other than the State of Jammu and Kashmir, their constitutions also have been embodied in the Constitution for the whole of India. All those other States have agreed to integrate themselves in that way and accept the Constitution provided.

Maulana Hasrat Mohani: Why this discrimination, please?

The Honourable Shri N. Gopalaswami Ayyangar: The discrimination is due to the special conditions of Kashmir. That particular State is not yet ripe for this kind of integration. It is the hope of everybody here that in due course even Jammu and Kashmir will become ripe for the same sort of integration as has taken place in the case of other States. (*Cheers*) At present it is not possible to achieve that integration. There are various reasons why this is not possible now. I shall refer again to this a little later.

In the case of the other Indian States or Unions of States there are two or three points which have got to be remembered. They have all accepted the Constitution framed for States in Part I of the new Constitution and those provisions have been adapted so as to suit conditions of Indian States and Unions of States. Secondly, the Centre, that is the Republican Federal Centre will have power to make laws applying in every such State or Union to all Union and Concurrent Subjects. Thirdly, a uniformity of relationship has been established between those States and Unions and the Centre. Kashmir's conditions are, as I have said, special and require special treatment.

I do not want to take much of the time of the House, but I shall briefly indicate what the special conditions are. In the first place, there has been a war going on within the limits of Jammu and Kashmir State.

There was a cease-fire agreed to at the beginning of this year and that cease-fire is still on. But the conditions in the State are still unusual and abnormal. They have not settled down. It is therefore necessary that the administration of the State should be geared to these unusual conditions until normal life is restored as in the case of the other States.

Part of the State is still in the hands of rebels and enemies.

We are entangled with the United Nations in regard to Jammu and Kashmir and it is not possible to say now when we shall be free from this entanglement. That can take place only when the Kashmir problem is satisfactorily settled.

Again, the Government of India have committed themselves to the people of Kashmir in certain respects. They have committed themselves to the position that an opportunity would be given to the people of the State to decide for themselves whether they will remain with the Republic or wish to go out of it. We are also committed to ascertaining this will of the people by means of a plebiscite provided that peaceful and normal conditions are restored and the impartiality of the plebiscite could be guaranteed. We have also agreed that the will of the people, through the instrument of a constituent assembly, will determine the constitution of the State as well as the sphere of Union jurisdiction over the State.

At present, the legislature which was known as the Praja Sabha in the State is dead. Neither, that legislature nor a constituent assembly can be convoked or can function until complete peace comes to prevail in that State. We have therefore to deal with the Government of the State which, as represented in its Council of Ministers, reflects the opinion of the largest political party in the State. Till a constituent assembly comes into being, only an interim arrangement is possible and not an arrangement which could at once be brought into line with the arrangement that exists in the case of the other States.

Now, if you remember the viewpoints that I have mentioned, it is an inevitable conclusion that, at the present moment, we could establish only an interim system. Article 306A is an attempt to establish such a system.

I shall now proceed to take the House through the provisions of this article. As honourable Members will remember, the constitution of Indian States is mainly governed by article 211A of this Constitution which applies the Constitution to Indian States, subject to the modifications contained in Part VI-A read with the Schedule. So far as that provision is concerned, I have already indicated to you that the provisions regarding the Constitution of other States could not at present be applied to Jammu and Kashmir. Therefore, clause (1) (a) of this article says that the provisions of article 211A of this Constitution shall not apply to the State of Jammu and Kashmir.

The Second portion of this article relates to the legislative authority of Parliament over the Jammu and Kashmir State. This is governed primarily by the Instrument of Accession. Broadly speaking, that legislative power is confined to the three subjects of defence, foreign affairs and communications, but as a matter of fact these broad categories include a number of items which are listed in the Instrument of Accession. I believe they number some twenty to twenty-five. Now, these items have undergone a change in description, in numbering, in arrangement, as amongst themselves, in List I and List III of the new Constitution. It is therefore necessary that the items mentioned in the Instrument of Accession should be brought into line with the changed designations of entries in Lists I and III of the new Constitution. So, clause (1) (b) of article 306A says that this listing of the items as per the terms of the new Constitution should be done by the President in consultation with the Government of the State.

Clause (b)(ii) refers to possible additions to the List in the Instrument of Accession, and these additions could be made according to the provisions of this article with the concurrence of the Government of the State. The idea is that even before the Constitution Assembly meets, it may be necessary in the interests of both the Centre and the State that certain items which are not included in the Instrument of Accession would be appropriately added to the List in that Instrument so that administration, legislation and executive action might be furthered, and as this may happen before the Constituent Assembly meets, the only authority from whom we can get consent for the addition is the Government of the State. That is provided for.

Then, there is the Explanation, which defines what the Government of the State means. The Government of the State is defined both in the Constitution which is now supposed to be in force in the Jammu and Kashmir State as well as in the Proclamation which the Maharaja issued on the 5th March 1948. The terms of the Proclamation, to the extent that they are inconsistent with the provisions of the Constitution Act of the State, will prevail over that Constitution Act, and therefore it is that in this Explanation it is the Proclamation which is referred to. Under the terms of that Proclamation the Maharaja constituted an interim popular Government, and he said,

I hereby ordain as follows:—

(1) My Council of Ministers shall consist of the Prime Minister and such other Ministers as may be appointed on the advice of the Prime Minister. I have by Royal Warrant appointed Sheikh Mohd. Abdullah as the Prime Minister with effect from the 1st day of March 1948.

He proceeds:—

The Prime Minister and other Ministers would function as a Cabinet and act on the principle of joint responsibility.

Then there was no Legislature functioning, and so he instituted a kind of responsible Government with a Prime Minister and colleagues who would own collective responsibility for their acts and regard themselves as jointly responsible for all the acts of the Government. Now, that is brought out in this Explanation.

The Honourable Shri K. Santhanam: The Explanation says that the Maharaja will be recognised by the Union instead of by the President.

The Honourable Shri N. Gopalaswami Ayyangar: Perhaps we may leave it to the Third Reading. As you know the scheme of the

Constitution Act is that the Rajpramukh must be recognised by the President. So, this also says that the Maharaja of Jammu and Kashmir should be a person recognised for the time being by the Union.

As regards the Council of Ministers, this Proclamation set up a system under which this Council was to be established, *viz.*, that the Maharaja first finds the Prime Minister and then on his advice appoints his colleagues, and the Explanation as now amended by me says that whatever Council of Ministers is in being at the time will, along with the Maharaja to whom they are responsible, give their concurrence or give their advice on such matters as are referred to them under this article.

Clauses (c) and (d) refer to the provisions of the Constitution other than the matters listed in Lists I and III. These various provisions have been divided into certain categories. The first according to this draft is that article 1 of the Constitution will automatically apply. As you know, it describes the territory of India, and includes amongst these territories all the States mentioned in Part III, and Jammu and Kashmir is one of the States mentioned in Part III. With regard to the other provisions in the Constitution, these will apply to the Jammu and Kashmir State with such exceptions and modifications as may be decided on when the President issues an Order to that effect. That Order can be issued in regard to subjects mentioned in the Instrument of Accession only after consultation with the Government of the State. In regard to other matters, the concurrence of that Government has to be taken.

Now, it is not the case, nor is it the intention of the members of the Kashmir Government whom I took the opportunity of consulting before this draft was finalised—it is not their intention that the other provisions of the Constitution are not to apply. Their particular point of view is that these provisions should apply only in cases where they can suitably apply and only subject to such modifications or exceptions as the particular conditions of the Jammu and Kashmir State may require. I wish to say no more about that particular point at the present moment.

Then we come to clause (2). You will remember that several of these clauses provide for the concurrence of the Government of Jammu and Kashmir State. Now, these relate particularly to matters which are not mentioned in the Instrument of Accession, and it is one of our commitments to the people and Government of Kashmir that no such additions should be made except with the consent of the Constituent Assembly which may be called in the State for the purpose of framing its Constitution. In other words, what we are committed to is that these additions are matters for the determination of the Constituent Assembly of the State.

Now, you will recall that in some of the clauses of this article we have provided for the concurrence of the Government of the State. The Government of the State feel that in view of the commitments already entered into between the State and the Centre, they cannot be regarded as final authorities for the giving of this concurrence, though they are prepared to give it in the interim periods but if they do give this concurrence, this clause provides that that concurrence should be placed before the Constituent Assembly when it meets and the Constituent Assembly may take whatever decisions it likes on those matters.

The last clause refers to what may happen later on. We have said article 211A will not apply to the Jammu and Kashmir State. But that cannot be a permanent feature of the Constitution of the State, and hope it will not be. So the provision is made that when the Constituent Assembly of the State has met and taken its decision both on the Constitution for the State and on the range of federal jurisdiction over the State, the President may on the recommendation of that Constituent Assembly issue an order that this article 306A shall either cease to be operative, or shall be operative only subject to such exceptions and modifications as may be specified by him. But before he issues any order of that kind the recommendation of the Constituent Assembly will be a condition precedent. That explains the whole of this article.

The effect of this article is that the Jammu and Kashmir State which is now a part of India will continue to be apart of India, will be a unit of the future Federal Republic of India and the Union Legislature will get jurisdiction to enact laws on matters specified either in the Instrument of Accession or by later addition with the concurrence of the Government of the State. And steps have to be taken for the purpose of convening a Constituent Assembly in due course which will go into the matters I have already referred to. When it has come to a decision

on the different matters it will make a recommendation to the President
who will either abrogate article 306A or direct that it shall apply with
such modifications and exceptions as the Constitutent Assembly may
recommend. That, Sir, is briefly a description of the effect of this article,
and I hope the House will carry it.

(Amendments Nos. 459, 460 and 461 were not moved.) Draft Article
306A was adopted without a vote.

3. Sheikh Abdullah's Letter to N. Gopalaswami Ayyangar on 17 October 1949 Complaining of Unilateral Alteration of Article 370

Durga Das (ed.), *Sardar Patel's Correspondence 1945–50*,
Navjivan Publishing House, Ahmedabad, 1971, p. 306

17 October 1949

The events that took place this morning in the Constituent Assembly
have deeply distressed me and my three colleagues, representing Kashmir
in the Constituent Assembly.

2. In my letter of 12 October 1949 I had told you that the draft
Article 306-A handed over by you to Mr. Beg [Mirza Afzal Beg][1] was
not acceptable to us, as it failed to implement the pledges given to us by
Panditji on behalf of the Government of India and was totally opposed to
the stand taken up by the National Conference in this matter right from
the beginning and approved by Panditji and Sardar Patel in a number of
public speeches, and we submitted our alternative draft, which restricted
the power of Parliament to make laws for the State and the application
of the provisions of the Constitution in relation to the State in matters
which directly related to the three subjects specified in the Instrument
of Accession in accordance with the assurances given to us by Panditji.
After that, the position was discussed several times with you by my
representatives, and during the night of 15 October, I received another
draft from you along with the letter of that date. In reply, on the 16th
morning, I informed you that it was not possible to accept your revised

[1] Member of Abdullah Ministry.

draft, and, in order to accommodate your viewpoint to the maximum extent possible, I submitted another draft to you, which, as I stated in my letter dated 15 October, went far beyond the sphere in respect of which we had *it* acceded to India. I clearly told you in that letter that it was not possible for me to go beyond this draft and requested you to accept it. You further discussed the matter with my representatives, and another draft, prepared by you in consultation with them, was sent to me by you through them. Yesterday afternoon this draft was finalised, and, on the assurance given by you to Mr. Beg that this finally revised draft will be put up before the Constituent Assembly on behalf of the Drafting Committee, he withdrew his amendment, about the moving of which in the Constituent Assembly he had given notice to the Secretary of the Assembly. I also wrote to you a letter expressing my gratefulness to you for the pains you had taken in the matter and for the final draft, which had been accepted by you on behalf of the Government, and I informed you therein that Mr. Beg had written to the Secretary of the Constituent Assembly for withdrawing his amendment.

3. This morning when we expected the final draft, which had appeared in the List of Amendments circulated by the Secretary of the Constituent Assembly, to come up before the Assembly, you and Maulana [Azad] Sahib came to me and asked me if I could accept an important change in the Explanation to Sub-clause (b) of Clause (I) of the draft Article 306-A, as appearing in the List of Amendments. After careful consideration of the proposed amendment in the Explanation, my colleagues and I told you both in the lobby that it was not possible for us to accept this change in the final draft and you and Maulana Sahib left us. While we were still discussing the matter in the lobby amongst ourselves, the draft Article 306-A was moved by you in the Constituent Assembly, and, when part of your speech was over, we were told by someone that the draft Article had been taken up by the Assembly, and, therefore, we took our seats in the Assembly Hall. We could not conceive that any amendment in the final draft, as circulated in the List of Amendments, would be made by you without conveying your final decision in the matter to us, and so we took it for granted that the final draft Article 306-A was presented before the Assembly in the form in which it had our consent; and, therefore, when it was passed by the

Assembly, we did not take part in the debate. While Maulana Sahib and you came to us to discuss the matter with us in the lobby, I clearly told you that, in the event of any change in the finalised draft Article 306-A, we should be at liberty to move the amendment, of which notice had been given by Mr. Beg and his two other colleagues and which had been withdrawn on the express assurance given by you yesterday. In these circumstances, it was not possible for us to move any amendment and we did not get an occasion to express our views on the matter before the open House.

4. As I have told you before, I and my colleagues have been extremely pained by the manner in which the thing has been done, and, after careful consideration of the matter, we have [arrived] at the conclusion that it is not possible for us to let the matter rest here. As I am genuinely anxious that no unpleasant situation should arise, I would request you to see if even now something could be done to rectify the position. In case I fail to hear from you within a reasonable time, I regret to say that no course is left open for us but to tender our resignation from the Constituent Assembly.

4. Ayyangar's Reply to Abdullah on 18 October 1949

Durga Das (ed.), *Sardar Patel's Correspondence 1945–50*,
Navjivan Publishing House, Ahmedabad, 1971, p. 308

New Delhi
18 October 1949

My dear Sheikh Abdullah,
I opened and read your letter dated 17 October 1949 when I returned home after the close of the prolonged sitting of the Constituent Assembly yesterday.

2. It would be too mild a description of my first reaction to your letter if I said that it was a painful surprise to me that you should have chosen to write to me in the terms you have done. It is clear that behind all that you have said in the letter there is an undercurrent of feeling that the only person that has, and could have, a sense of grievance in connection with this matter is yourself. Nothing could be farther away from a correct, balanced appreciation of the facts.

3. You have ended up your letter with a sentence which reads like an ultimatum. I am sure that, after you had slept over what you had written to me yesterday evening, you have yourself come to realise that you should not have written to me in that way.

4. I do not propose to deal with the history of the drafting of Article 306-A which, in its final form the Assembly adopted unanimously and without a single dissentient voice and without a speech from anybody raising any note of criticism. It is true that after having unsuccessfully attempted, along with Maulana Azad, to persuade you to agree willingly to the substitution of the words 'for the time being in office' for the word 'appointed', I did move the article with that amendment after obtaining the permission of the President to do so. The whole House accepted this. I am sorry that you could not move any amendment of your own as against the one I moved. There was, however, nothing to prevent you or any of your colleagues from opposing the amendment that I did move, and as a matter of fact, we were looking forward to your making a speech on the whole of the article, and believe the President waited for a minute or two for Members to rise for making speeches before he put the draft article to the House.

5. Article 306-A, as finalised in the agreement between us, was given notice of on the evening of the 16th after I got your letter of that date and it was immediately circulated to the Members of the House. The attempt made by me and Maulana Azad the next morning, when the House was sitting, to persuade you to accept a trivial change was due to the desire expressed by a large number of the leading Members of the House. All of us, including myself, Maulana Azad and Sardar Vallabhbhai Patel, were of the opinion that it was necessary from many points of view that the change suggested should be accepted. Personally, having agreed with you to the language of the original draft, I felt a special responsibility in agreeing to this change. And I may tell you at once that I agreed to it because I was, and am, convinced that the change in the actual words used in that particular connection did not alter the meaning of the draft agreed to between us.

6. I should think that it is impossible to escape the correctness of what I have just now said. The words in the Explanation as agreed to between us are 'Council of Ministers appointed under the Maharaja's

Proclamation dated 5 March 1948.' The words appearing in the Article as passed yesterday are 'the Council of Ministers for the time being in office under the Maharaja's Proclamation dated 5 March 1948.' Under the Article, the Council of Ministers has to be consulted on certain matters and its concurrence has to be obtained in other matters. It is obvious that members of this Council appointed under the Maharaja's Proclamation cannot give their advice or concurrence unless they happen to be functioning, that is, in office, at the time when such advice or concurrence has to be given. Nor can there be any members of the Council competent to give their advice or concurrence unless they were persons appointed under the Maharaja's Proclamation. I hope you will, on reflection, realise that the change of words does not constitute the slightest change in sense or substance.

7. In the circumstances, I am unable on the merits to appreciate your suggestion that something should be done 'to rectify the position.' There is nothing, so far as I can see, which needs rectification. But if you think otherwise, you and your colleagues, who are Members of the Assembly, might take such steps as the rules of the House may allow for carrying out any rectification that you may desire and, if any concrete proposal is made, I can assure you, on behalf of the Government of which I am a Member, that your proposal would receive our best consideration on its merits. I am bound to add, however, that there was nothing in the manner in which the Article was moved and passed which laid itself open to any criticism. It was both politically and parliamentarily unexceptionable.

8. I do not consider, therefore, that there is any justification for your entertaining any idea of resignation from the Constituent Assembly. The step, if taken, would produce the most unwelcome and serious repercussions in Kashmir, India and the world, and I must ask you to communicate with the Prime Minister before you decide on anything like it. For myself, I shall pass on to him your letter and this reply of mine to it.

With very kind regards,

Yours sincerely,
N. Gopalaswami

The Hon'ble Sheikh Mohammed Abdullah
New Delhi

5. Patel's Letter to Nehru on 3 November 1949 Justifying the Alteration

Durga Das (ed.), *Sardar Patel' Correspondence 1945–50*, Navjivan Publishing House, Ahmedabad, 1971, p. 310

New Delhi
3 November 1949

My dear Jawaharlal,

There was some difficulty about the provision relating to Kashmir. Sheikh Sahib went back on the agreement which he had reached with you in regard to the provision relating to Kashmir. He insisted on certain changes of a fundamental character which would exclude in their application to Kashmir the provisions relating to citizenship and fundamental rights and make it necessary in all these matters as well as others not covered by the accession to three subjects to seek the concurrence of the State Government which is sought to define as the Maharaja acting on the advice of the Council of Ministers appointed under the proclamation of 8 March 1948. After a great deal of discussion, I could persuade the party to accept all the changes except the last one, which was modified so as to cover not merely the first Ministry so appointed but any subsequent Ministries which may be appointed under that proclamation. Sheikh Sahib has not reconciled himself to this change, but we could not accommodate him in this matter and the provision was passed through the House as we had modified. After this he wrote a letter to Gopalaswami Ayyangar threatening to resign from the membership of the Constituent Assembly. Gopalaswami has replied asking him to defer his decision until you returned.

Yours sincerely,
Vallabhbhai Patel

The Hon'ble Pandit Jawaharlal Nehru
Prime Minister

6. Proclamation by Yuvaraj Karan Singh on 25 November 1949 Accepting the New Constitution as Drafted by the Constituent Assembly

White Paper on Indian States, Ministry of States, Government of India, Manager of Publications, Delhi, 1950, pp. 371–2

Dated the 25th November, 1949

Whereas with the inauguration of the new Constitution for the whole of India now being framed by the Constituent Assembly of India, the Government of India Act, 1935, which now governs the constitutional relationship between this State and the Dominion of India will stand repealed;

And whereas, in the best interests of this State, which is closely linked with the rest of India by a community of interests in the economic, political and other fields, it is desirable that the constitutional relationship established between this State and the Dominion of India, should be continued as between this State and the contemplated Union of India; and the Constitution of India as drafted by the Constituent Assembly of India, which includes duly appointed representatives of this State, provides a suitable basis for doing so;

I now hereby declare and direct:—

That the Constitution of India shortly to be adopted by the Constituent Assembly of India shall in so far as it is applicable to the State of Jammu and Kashmir, govern the constitutional relationship between this State and the contemplated Union of India and shall be enforced in this State by me, my heirs and successors in accordance with the tenor of its provisions;

That the provisions of the said Constitution shall, as from the date of its commencement, supersede and abrogate all other constitutional provisions inconsistent therewith which are at present in force in this State.

Karan Singh
Yuvaraj,
Regent of Jammu & Kashmir

7. Temporary Provisions with Respect to the State of Jammu & Kashmir

370. (i) Notwithstanding anything in this Constitution:—

   (a) the provisions of article 238 shall not apply in relation to the State of Jammu and Kashmir;

   (b) the power of Parliament to make laws for the said State shall be limited to:—

      (i) those matters in the Union List and the Concurrent List which, in consultation with the Government of the State, are declared by the President to correspond to matters specified in the Instrument of Accession governing the accession of the State to the Dominion of India as the matters with respect to which the Dominion Legislature may make laws for that State; and

      (ii) such other matters in the said Lists as, with the concurrence of the Government of the State, the President may by order specify.

Explanation:—For the purposes of this article, the Government of the State means the person for the time being recognised by the President as the Maharaja of Jammu and Kashmir acting on the advice of the Council of Ministers for the time being in office under the Maharaja's Proclamation dated the fifth day of March, 1948;

   (c) the provisions of article I and of this article shall apply in relation to that State;

   (d) such of the other provisions of this Constitution shall apply in relation to that State subject to such exceptions and modifications as the President may by order specify:

Provided that no such order which relates to the matters specified in the Instrument of Accession of the State referred to in paragraph (i) of sub-clause (b) shall be issued except in consultation with the Government of the State:

Provided further that no such order which relates to matters other than those referred to in the last preceding proviso shall be issued except with the concurrence of that Government.

(2) If the concurrence of the Government of the State referred to in paragraph (ii) of sub-clause (b) of clause (I) or in the second proviso to sub-clause (d) of that clause be given before the Constituent Assembly for the purpose of framing the Constitution of the State is convened, it shall be placed before such Assembly for such decision as it may take thereon.

(3) Notwithstanding anything in the foregoing provisions of this article, the President may, by public notification, declare that this article shall cease to be operative or shall be operative only with such exceptions and modifications and from such date as he may specify.

Provided that the recommendation of the Constituent Assembly of the State referred to in clause (2) shall be necessary before the President issues such a notification.

8. The President of India's First Order under Article 370 Applying the Constitution to J&K on 26 January 1950

The Constitution (Application to Jammu and Kashmir) Order, 1950

C.O. 10, dated the 26th January, 1950:—In exercise of the powers conferred by clause (1) or Article 370 of the Constitution of India, the President, in consultation with the Government of the State of Jammu and Kashmir, is pleased to make the following order, namely:—

1. (1) This Order may be called the Constitution (Application to Jammu and Kashmir) Order, 1950.

(2) It shall come into force at once.

2. For the purpose of sub-clause (b) (i) of clause (1) of Article 370 of the Constitution, the matters specified in the First Schedule to this Order being matters in the Union List, are hereby declared to correspond to matters specified in the Instrument of Accession governing the accession of the State of Jammu and Kashmir to the Dominion of India as the matters with regard to which the Dominion Legislature may make laws for that State, and accordingly, the powers of Parliament to make laws for the State shall be limited to the matters specified in the said First Schedule.

3. In addition to the provisions of Articles 1 and Article 370 of the Constitution, the only other provisions of the Constitution which shall apply in relation to the State of Jammu and Kashmir shall be those specified in the Second Schedule to this order, and shall so apply subject to the exceptions and modifications specified in the said Schedule.

The First Schedule

(See Paragraph 2)

[Note:—The number of each entry in the Schedule is the number of the corresponding entry in the Union List.]

1. Defence of India and every part thereof including preparation for defence.

2. Naval, military and air forces work, and other armed forces of the Union.

3. Delimitation of cantonment areas, local self-Government in such areas, the Constitution and powers within such areas of Constitution and powers within such areas of cantonment authorities and the regulations of house accommodation (including the control of rents) in such areas.

4. Naval, military and air force works.

5. Arms, firearms, ammunition and explosives.

6. Atomic energy for the purpose of defence and mineral resources necessary for its production.

9. Preventive detention for reasons connected with defence, Foreign affairs or the security of India.

10. Foreign Affairs; all matters which bring the Union into relation with any foreign country.

11. Diplomatic, consular and trade representation.

12. United Nations Organisation.

13. Participation in international conferences, associations and other bodies and implementing of decisions made there at.

14. Entering into treaties and agreements with foreign countries and implementing of treaties, agreements and conventions with foreign countries.

15 . War and peace.

16. Foreign jurisdiction.

17. Naturalisation and aliens.

18. Extradition.

19. Admission into, and emigration and expulsion from, India, passport and visas.

20. Pilgrimages to places outside India.

21. Piracies and crimes committed on the high seas or in the air offence against the law of nations committed on land or on the high seas or in the air.

22. Railways, but as respects any railway owned by the State of Jammu and Kashmir, and either operated by that State or operated on its behalf otherwise than in accordance with a contract with the State by the Government of India, limited to the regulation thereof in respect of safety, maximum and minimum rates and fares, station and service terminal charges, interchange of traffic and the responsibility of the railway administration as carriers of goods and passengers and as respects any railway which is wholly situate within the State and does not form a continuous line of communication with a railway owned by the Government of India, whether of the same gauge or not, limited to the regulation thereof in respect of safety and the responsibility of the railway administration as carriers of goods and passengers. [...][1]

25. Maritime shipping and navigation, including shipping and navigation on tidal waters, provision of education and training for the mercantile marine and regulation of such education and training provided by States and other agencies.

26. Lighthouses, including Lightships, beacon and other provision for the safety of shipping and aircraft.

27. Ports declared by or under law made by Parliament or existing law to be major ports, including their delimitation, and the Constitution and powers of port authorities therein.

28. Port quarantine, including hospitals, connected there with, seamen's and marine hospitals.

---

[1] Omitted in the original.

29. Airways, aircraft and air navigation, provision of aerodromes, regulation and organisation of air traffic and of aerodromes, provision for aeronautical education and training and regulation of such education and training provided by States and other agencies.

30. Carriage of passengers and goods by railway, sea or air.

31. Posts and telegraphs, telephones, wireless, broadcasting and other like forms of communication.

41. Trade and commerce with foreign countries.

72. To Parliament, and the offices of President and Vice-President, the Election Commission.

73. Salaries and allowances of members of Parliament, the Chairman and Deputy Chairman of the Council of States, and the Speaker and Deputy Speaker of the House of the people.

74. Powers, privileges and immunities of each House of Parliament and of the members and the communities of each house, enforcement of attendance of persons for giving evidence or producing documents before committee of Parliament or commissions appointed by Parliament.

75. Salaries and allowances of the Ministers for the Union, the salaries, allowances and right in respect of leave of absence and other conditions of service of the Comptroller and Auditor-General.

76. Audit of the accounts of the Union.

77. Constitution and organisation of the Supreme Court and the fees taken therein, persons entitled to practice before the Supreme Court.

80. Extension of the powers and jurisdiction of members of a police force belonging to any State to railway areas outside the State.

93. Offences against laws with respect to any of the matters aforesaid.

94. Inquiries and statistics for the purpose of any of the matters aforesaid.

95. Jurisdiction and powers of all Courts, except the Supreme Court with respect to any of the matter aforesaid, but, except with the consent of the State Government not so as to confer any jurisdiction or powers upon any Courts other than Courts ordinarily exercising jurisdiction in, or in relation to, the State, admiralty jurisdiction.

96. Fees in respect of any of the matters aforesaid but not including fees taken in any Court.

The Second Schedule

Published in the Gazette of India, Extraordinary, Part II
Section 3, No. III, Dated the 14th May, 1954

Provision of the Constitution Applicable	Exception	Modifications
Part V	Article 72(1) (c), 72(3), 133, 134, 135, 136, 138, 145(1) (c) and 152(2)	1. Articles 80 and 81 shall apply subject to the modification that the representatives of the State in the Council of States and the House of the people respectively, shall be chosen by the President in consultation with the Government of the State. 2. Article 149 and 150 shall apply subject to the modification that the references therein to the State shall be construed as not including the State of Jammu and Kashmir.
Part XI	Articles 247 to 252, clauses (3) and (4) of Articles 257 and Articles 260, 262 and 263	1. Clause (1) of Article 246 shall apply subject to the provisions of paragraph 2 of this order and clauses (2) and (3) of Article 246 shall not apply in relation to the State. 2. Clause (1) of Article 259 shall apply subject to the modification that after the words 'until parliament by law otherwise provides' the words 'and the concurrence of the State to such law has been obtained' shall be deemed to be inserted.
Part XI	Articles 264, and 265, clause (2)	1. Article 266 shall apply only so far as it relates to the consolidated

	of Article 267, clause (2) of Article 283, Articles 286 to 291, 293, 295, 296 and 297	Fund of India and the public account of India. 2. Articles 282 and 284 shall apply only in so far as they relate to the Union or the public account of India. 3. Articles 298, 299 and 300 shall apply only in so far as they relate to the Union or Government of India.
Part XV	Articles 325 to 329	Article 324 shall apply only in so far as it relates to elections to Parliament and to the offices of the President and Vice-President.
Part XVI	Articles 332, 333, and 337 to 342	1. Article 330 shall apply only in so far as it relates to seats reserved for Scheduled Castes. 2. Article 334 shall apply only in so far as it relates to the House of the People. 3. Article 335 shall apply only in so far as it relates to the Union.
Part XVII	Nil	The provisions of this part shall apply only in so far as they relate to the official language of the Union and to proceedings in the Supreme Court.
Part XIX	Articles 362, 363 and 365.	1. Article 361 shall apply in so far as it relates to the President. 2. Article 364 shall apply only in so far as it relates to the laws made by Parliament.
Part XX	Nil	Article 368 shall apply subject to the additional proviso: 'Provided further that no such amendment shall have effect in relation to the

		State of Jammu and Kashmir unless applied by order of the President under clause (1) of Article 370'.
Part XXI	Articles 369, 371, and 373, clause (4) of Articles 374 and 378 and clause 2 of Article 388.	1. In clause (3) of Article 379 after the words 'Minister for any such State' the words 'other than the State of Jammu and Kashmir' shall be deemed to be inserted. 2. Article 389 shall apply only in so far as it relates to Bills pending in the Dominion Legislature. 3. Article 390 shall apply only in so far as it relates to the Consolidated Fund of India.
Part XXII	Nil	Nil
First Schedule	Nil	Nil
Second Schedule	Paragraph 6	Nil
Third Schedule	Forms V, VI, VII, and VIII	Nil
Fourth Schedule	Nil	Nil
Eighth Schedule	Nil	Nil

9. Special Provisions Regarding the State of Jammu & Kashmir (Extracts)

White Paper on Indian States, Ministry of States, Government of India, Manager of Publications, Delhi 1950, pp. 111–13

221. The State of Jammu and Kashmir acceded to India on October 26, 1947. The form of the Instrument of Accession executed by the Ruler of the State is the same as that of the Instruments executed by the Rulers of other acceding States. Legally and constitutionally therefore

the position of this State is the same as that of the other acceding States. The Government of India, no doubt, stand committed to the position that the accession of this State is subject to confirmation by the people of the State. This, however, does not detract from the legal fact of accession. The State has therefore been included in Part B States. In view of the special problems arising in respect of this State and the fact that the Government of India have assured its people that they would themselves finally determine their political future, the following special provision has made in the Constitution:

[...]

Article 370 is reproduced.

The effect of this provision is that the State of Jammu and Kashmir, continues to be a part of India. It is a unit of the Indian Union and the Union Parliament will have jurisdiction to make laws for this State on matters specified either in the Instrument of Accession or by later additions with the concurrence of the Government of the State. An order has been issued under Article 370 specifying (1) the matters in respect of which the Parliament may make laws for the Jammu and Kashmir States and (2) the provisions, other than Article 1 and Article 370, which shall apply to that State (Appendix LVI). Steps will be taken for the purpose of convening a Constituent Assembly which will go into these matters in detail and when it comes to a decision on them, it will make a recommendation to the President who will either abrogate Article 370 or direct that it shall apply with such modifications and exceptions as he may specify.

Chapter 3

Jammu & Kashmir's Constituent Assembly

1951–2

1. Resolution of the All J&K National Conference on Convening a Constituent Assembly for the State

M.K. Teng, R.K. Kaul Bhatt, and Santosh Kaul (eds),
Kashmir: Constitutional History and Documents,
Light & Life Publishers, New Delhi, 1977, p. 548

This meeting of the General Council of the All Jammu and Kashmir National Conference views with great concern the repeated failure of the UN to redress the wrongs of aggression of which the people of the State continue to be victims. This failure in its opinion is due to the continued concessions given to Pakistan by placing a premium on her intransigence.

The indecision and unrealistic procedure adopted so far has condemned the people of the State to a life of agonizing uncertainty. The All Jammu and Kashmir National Conference is gravely concerned and cannot any longer afford to ignore the perpetuation of these conditions of doubt and frustration. In the opinion of the General Council, time has come when the initiative must be regained by the people to put an end to this indeterminate State of drift and indecision.

The General Council recommends to the Supreme National Executive of the people to take immediate steps for convening a Constituent Assembly based upon adult suffrage and embracing all sections of the people and all the Constituents of the State for the purpose of determining the future shape and affiliations of the State of Jammu and Kashmir. In this sovereign Assembly embodying the supreme will of the people of the State, we shall give ourselves and our children a constitution worthy of the traditions of our freedom struggle and in accordance with the principles of New Kashmir.

2. Sheikh Abdullah's Letter to Ayyangar on 16 January 1951 and Ayyangar's Marginal Comments

Top Secret.
Jammu
16th January 1951

D.O. No. CPM-1/5-51
My Dear Gopalaswami Ji,
    Kindly refer to your secret letter dated 9th January 1951.

Please see my marginal comments. Re: my remarks on p. 2, I doubt whether we should correspond with Sheikh Abdullah further. This should be processed further so that the proclamation may issue early. (ltd.) N.G.A. 12.1.51

2. I placed a copy of my D.O. letter CPM-1/51 dated 4th January, 1951 addressed to Panditji, the substance of my discussions which I had with Rajaji, Maulana Sahib and yourself in a meeting held in New Delhi on 9th January 1951 and the draft proclamation enclosed by you with your secret letter dated 9th January 1951 before my colleagues. I told them that while you appreciated the stand taken by me and my colleagues in this matter, you felt that in view of the complexities of the international situation and the Government of India's entanglement with the United Nations in regard to Indo-Pakistan dispute

over Kashmir, it would be expedient that the draft proclamation for convening the Constituent Assembly should be as short and simple as possible and should avoid specific reference to matters which might later on involve the Government of India in controversy with the United Nations. I have also told them that at the meeting which I had with Rajaji, Maulana Sahib and yourself all three of you had given me an assurance that there was no disagreement between the views expressed in my D.O. letter addressed to Panditji and those of the Government of India in regard to the subject which would come up for discussion and decision before the Constituent Assembly, namely, the question of accession of the State, the question of retention or abolition of the Ruler as the Constitutional Head of the State and the question of framing a constitution for the State including the question of defining the sphere of Union jurisdiction over the State and that there was no dispute as regards the sovereign powers of the Assembly to take whatever decision it liked on the subjects that would come up before it. I also told them that you considered it both unnecessary and inexpedient that the Proclamation should be issued* over the signatures of the Maharaja who has practically ceased to have anything to do with the State. After careful consideration of all these matters placed before my colleagues, they have arrived at the unanimous conclusion that while they fully endorse the views expressed in my D.O. letter No. CPM-1/51 dated 4th January, 1951 to Panditji, in view of the difficulties that the Government

Should really be 'whose powers, jurisdiction, etc. have really been delegated to the Regent'. (Itd.) N.G.A.

of India might encounter vis-à-vis the United Nations in regard to the Kashmir dispute and in view of the assurances held out by Rajaji, Maulana Sahib and yourself on behalf of the Government of India, to which reference has been made above, they accept the draft proclamation, as now proposed by you, provided that certain drafting changes are made in the proclamation—as would be indicated in the next paragraph—on the clear understanding that the Government of India accept the position that the Constituent Assembly thus set up would be able to take decisions on all issues specified above and that the Government of India would treat these decisions as binding on all concerned and fully back them up.

This is perhaps going beyond what we said. Itd. N.G.A.

3. After careful consideration of the draft proclamation it appears to us that sub-para 3 of the preamble is liable to be misconstrued. There is no question of abrogating the whole of the Proclamation dated March 5, 1948 under which the present Government has come into office as it has been given statutory recognition in the explanation appended to sub-clause (b) of clause (1) of article 370 of the Constitution. In connection with the setting up of the Constituent Assembly all that is necessary is to render ineffective clauses 4 to 6 of the operative part of the Proclamation in which reference has been made to the convening of a National Assembly and certain provisions have been made therefore. It is, therefore, suggested that the following words, namely, 'in regard to the convening of the National Assembly as contained in

clauses 4 to 6 of the operative part thereof' be inserted between the words and figures '5th March 1948' and the words 'do not meet the requirements of the present situation'. Sub-para 3 of the preamble would thereafter read as follows:—

Prima facie I have no objection to this suggestion.
Itd. N.G.A.

'And whereas terms of Proclamation of His Highness the Maharaja dated the 5th March 1948 in regard to the convening of the National Assembly as contained in clauses 4 to 6 of the operative part thereof do not meet the requirements of the present situation.'

(ii) So far as paragraph 2 of the Proclamation is concerned we feel that in certain cases it may be necessary to delimit a constituency having a population slightly exceeding 40,000.—It is, therefore, proposed that in paragraph 2 of the Proclamation for the words and figures 'each containing a population not exceeding 40,000' the words and figures 'each containing a population of 40,000 or as nearly thereto as possible' may be substituted.

I accept the amendment; only yet the words I have underlined.
Itd. N.G.A.

(iii) It further appears that some action has already been taken by the Franchise Office in the matter of preparing provisional electoral rolls. It is, therefore, considered desirable that a clause validating these acts on the lines of section 29 of the Representation of the People Act, 1950 may be added to the Proclamation as clause 8 which will read as follows:—

'8. All things done and all steps taken before the issue of this Proclamation with a view to facilitating the provisional preparation of electoral rolls for the purpose of elections to the Constituent Assembly shall in so far as

they are in conformity with the provisions of this Proclamation be deemed to have been done or taken under this Proclamation as if it
I accept this also.   was in force at the time such things were done
Itd. N.G.A.   ·   or such steps were taken.'
I am sure that you will have no objection to these minor drafting changes. A copy of the Proclamation embodying these changes is enclosed.

Yours sincerely,
S.M. Abdullah

The Hon'ble
Shree Gopalaswami Ayyangar,
Minister for States,
Government of India,
5, Queen Victoria Road,
New Delhi

3(a). Union Home Minister C. Rajagopalachari's Comments on the Letter in His Letter to Ayyangar on 20 January 1951

C. Rajagopalachari Papers (IV Instalment) Subject File No. 62, No. 212/51, Nehru Memorial Museum and Library, New Delhi

Top Secret

1, York Place,
New Delhi.
20th January 1951
I have seen the papers sent with Vishnu Sahay's note dated the 20th January. I shall not be here, but I agree with you and you might hold a Foreign Affairs Committee meeting in my absence and dispose of the letter from Shaikh Abdullah. It is really unsatisfactory that Shaikh Abdullah has taken for granted what he has put at the end of paragraph 2

of his letter dated the 16th January and which go beyond what we said.

C. Rajagopalachari.

The Hon'ble
Shri N. Gopalaswami Ayyangar,
Minister for Transport,
5, Queen Victoria Road,
New Delhi

3(b). Bakshi Ghulam Mohammed in the Constituent Assembly of Kashmir, 25 October 1956

J&K Constituent Assembly Debates (Official Report), Part II, pp. 1057–8

Before convening the Constituent Assembly there was a good deal of correspondence between the Government of India and the State Government regarding the power and sovereignty of this House and Mr. Beg knows everything about it. In 1950, the question of convening the Constituent Assembly and the functions of this body were discussed. I read out the following passages from the records of this correspondence:—

In the autumn of 1950, the question of convening Constituent Assembly of the State of which mention had been made before in the letter of the Prime Minister of India dated 18th May, 1949, and in Article 370, was mooted. The main functions which the Constituent Assembly was to discharge were:—

(i)   the question of the Accession of the State;
(ii) retention or abolition of the Ruler as the Constitutional Head of the State;
(iii) the question of framing a Constitution for the State including the question of defining the Union sphere of jurisdiction over the State; and
(iv) the question of awarding compensation to the landlords whose lands had been expropriated under the Big Landed Estates Abolition Act.

There was a good deal of correspondence between the State Government and the Government of India on the question of the scope of the

Constituent Assembly and eventually Mr. Rajagopalacharia, Maulana Abdul Kalam Azad and Mr. Gopalaswami Ayyangar on behalf of the Government of India assured the Prime Minister of Kashmir that there was no disagreement with the views expressed by the State Government and those of the Government of India in regard to the subjects which would come up for discussion and decision before the Constituent Assembly (vide Kashmir Prime Minister's letter to Mr. Gopalaswami Ayyangar dated 16th January, 1951). The same view had been expressed by the Prime Minister of India in his letter dated 9th February, 1951, which he had addressed to the Prime Minister to Kashmir from London. It was said therein:—'I have no doubt that the will of the Kashmir people must prevail in regard to every matter and it is they who will decide ultimately every question affecting the State.'

After December 29, 1950 it was further stated:—'Normally the very idea of a Constituent Assembly is that it has the power to decide the question before it. We must presume this power and go ahead.' [...]

4. Proclamation Dated 1 May 1951 Convening Jammu & Kashmir's Constituent Assembly

Whereas it is the general desire of the people of the State of Jammu and Kashmir that a Constituent Assembly should be brought into being for the purpose of framing a Constitution for the State;

Whereas it is commonly felt that the convening of the Assembly can no longer be delayed without detriment to the future well-being of the State;

And whereas terms of the proclamation of the Maharaja dated 5 March, 1948 in regard to the convening of a national assembly as contained in clauses 4 to 6 of the operative part thereof do not meet the requirements of the present situation;

I, Yuvraj Karan Singh, do hereby direct as follows:

1. A Constituent Assembly consisting of representatives of the people, elected on the basis of adult franchise, shall be constituted forthwith for the purpose of framing a constitution for the State of Jammu and Kashmir;

2. For the purpose of the said elections the State shall be divided into a number of territorial constituencies, each containing a population of 40,000 or as near thereto as possible, and each electing one member. A delimitation Committee shall be set up by the Government to make recommendations as to the number of constituencies and the limits of each constituency;

3. Elections to the Constituent Assembly shall be on the basis of adult franchise, that is to say, every person who is a State subject of any class, is not less than twenty-one years of age on the first day of March, has been a resident in the constituency for such period as may be prescribed by the rules, shall be entitled to register in the electoral rolls of that constituency, provided that any person who is of unsound mind or has been so declared by a competent court, shall be disqualified for registration;

4. The vote at the election shall be direct and by secret ballot;

5. The Constituent Assembly shall have power to act not withstanding any vacancy of the Membership thereof;

6. The Constituent Assembly shall frame its own agenda and make rules for the governing of its procedure and the conduct of its business;

The Government shall make such rules and issue such instructions and orders as may be necessary to give effect to the terms of this proclamation.

[...]

5. Sheikh Abdullah's Speech to the Constituent Assembly on 5 November 1951

Jammu and Kashmir Constituent Assembly Official Report, Volume 1 (1951–5), pp. 55–81

After centuries, we have reached the harbour of our freedom, a freedom, which, for the first time in history, will enable the people of Jammu and Kashmir, whose duly elected representatives are gathered here, to shape the future of their country after wise deliberation, and mould their future organs of Government. No person and no power stand between them and the fulfilment of this—their historic task. We are free, at last to shape our aspirations as people and to give substance to the ideals which have brought us together here.

We meet here today, in this palace hall, once the symbol of unquestioned monarchial authority, as free citizens of the New Kashmir for which we have so long struggled. I see about me in this hall, many companions—Hindus, Muslims, Buddhists, Harijans and Sikhs, who first trod with me that path which has brought us to this Constituent Assembly of 1951. We fought as one, against tyranny and oppression. We survived privations and bitter struggles—the jails of Hari Parbat, Bahu, Badarwah and those other jails which only imprisoned our bodies but could not crush our spirit.

When we I took back on these years, we see how our footsteps have taken us not among the privileged, but into the homes of the poor and downtrodden. We have fought their battle against privilege and oppression and against these darker powers in the background which sought to set man against man on the ground of religion. Our movement grew and thrived side by side with the Indian National Congress and gave strength and inspiration to the people of the Indian States.

I may be forgiven if I feel proud that once again in the history of this State, our people have reached a peak of achievement through what I might call the classical Kashmiri genius for synthesis, born of toleration and mutual respect. Throughout the long tale of our history, the highest pinnacles of our achievement have been scaled when religious bigotry and intolerance ceased to cramp us, and we have breathed the wider air of brotherhood and mutual understanding.

Our movement to freedom has been enacted against the background of this same old struggle. We stood for the brotherhood of men of all creeds and strengthened our union on the basic of common work and sacrifice. Against us were ranged the forces of religious history centred in the Muslim League and its satellites, and the Hindu communalists from within and without the State. Ranged against us, and often in alliance with communalism were the forces of the autocratic States, backed up on the one hand by British Imperialism, the paramount power, and on the other, by the rich landowners and other beneficiaries of Court patronage.

We must remember that our struggle for power has now reached
its successful climax in the convening of this Constituent Assembly.
It is for you to translate the vision of New Kashmir into reality, and
I would remind you of its opening words, which will inspire our
labours.
[...]
You are the sovereign authority in this State of Jammu and Kashmir;
what you decide has the irrevocable force of law. The basic democratic
principle of sovereignty of the nation, embodied ably in the American
and French Constitution, is once again given shape in our midst.
[...]
What then are the main functions that this Assembly will be called
upon to perform?
One great task before this Assembly will be to devise a Constitution
for the future governance of the country, Constitution-making is a
difficult and detailed matter. I shall only refer to some of the broad
aspects of the Constitution, which should be the product of the labours
of this Assembly.
Another issue of vital importance to the nation involves the future
of the Royal Dynasty. Your decision will have to be taken both with
urgency and wisdom for on that decision rests the future form and
character of the State.
The third major issue awaiting your deliberations arises out of the
Land Reforms which the Government carried out with vigour and
determination. Our 'land to the tiller' policy brought light into the dark
homes of the peasantry; but, side, by side, it has given rise to the problem of the landowner's demand for compensation. The nation being the
ultimate custodian of all wealth and resources, the representatives of the
nation are truly the best jury for giving a just and final verdict on such
claims. So in your hands lies the power of this decision.
Finally, this Assembly will after full consideration of three alternatives that I shall state later, declare its reasoned conclusion regarding
accession. This will help us to canalise our energies resolutely and with
greater zeal in direction in which we have already started moving for the
social and economic advancement of our country.
[...]

You are no doubt aware of the scope of our present constitutionalities with India. We are proud to have our bonds with India, the goodwill of whose people and Government is available to us in unstinted and abundant measure. The Constitution of India has provided for a federal union and in the distribution of sovereign powers has treated us differently from other constitutional units. With the exception of the items grouped under Defence, Foreign Affairs and Communication in the Instrument of Accession, we have complete freedom to frame our Constitution in the manner we like. In order to live and prosper as good partners in a common endeavour for the advancement of our peoples, I would advise that, while safe guarding our autonomy to the fullest extent so as to enable us to have the liberty to build our country according to the best traditions and genius of our people, we may also by suitable constitutional arrangements with the Union establish our right to seek and compel Federal co-operation and assistance in this great task, as well as offer our fullest co-operation and assistance to the Union.

[...]

New Kashmir contains a statement of the objectives of our social policy. It gives broadly a picture of the kind of life that we hope to make possible for the people of Jammu and Kashmir and manner in which the economic organisation of the country will be geared to the purpose. These ideals you will have to integrate with the political structure which you will devise.

The future political set-up which you decide upon for Jammu and Kashmir must also take into consideration the existence of various subnational groups in our State. Although culturally diverse, history has forged an uncommon unity between them; they all are pulsating with the same hopes and aspirations, sharing in each other's joys and sorrows. While guaranteeing this basic unity of the State, our Constitution must not permit the concentration of power and privilege in the hands of any particular group or territorial region. It must afford the fullest possibilities to each of these groups to grow and flourish in conformity with their cultural characteristics, without detriment to the integral unity of the State or the requirements of our social and economic policies.

[...]

This event in the history of the State had catastrophic consequences for the people. The old feudal order, which was bad enough, gave way to more exacting rule, in which the Maharaja assumed all proprietary rights over land. The entire State was plunged into a chaotic economic condition, aggravated by a heavy state of taxation, tributes and levies which were required to make up for the money given by the Maharaja to the British. This unrelieved despotism reduced the bulk of the people to the level of serfs. There was general impoverishment. In 1948, some 4,000 artisans started on a trek to Lahore, with the object of permanently settling there. Even the British counselled the Maharaja to loosen his grip so as to avoid a total collapse of his administration. Perhaps the forefathers of the great poet-philosopher son of Kashmir, Iqbal, were also part of the same trail of migrants who left the State at this time. When his agony over the fate of the people of his homeland burst out in immortal verse, his feelings are echoed in the heart of every Kashmiri:

O Wind, if you pass through Geneva, give this message to the comity of the people of the world. They sold the peasant, his field, his property and the roof over his head, in fact, they sold the entire nation and for what a paltry price!

Invested with this absolute authority acquired in 1846, the present ruling dynasty was in power for one hundred years. This sad and stern century of servitude has stultified the growth of our people, leaving them in the backwaters of civilisation. While in British India, and even in some of the Indian States, many a measure of reform was introduced to alleviate the misery of the people, in this State the unenlightened absolutism of the Rulers drove them deeper and deeper into poverty and degradation. When conditions became increasingly intolerable they made determined efforts to wrest power from the hands of the Ruler.

By 1947, India had achieved independence and reached one of her historical watersheds. It was clear that with the withdrawal of the Paramount Power, the treaty rights of the Indian Princes would cease. Sovereignty in that case should revert to the people; they wished, therefore, to be consulted about the arrangements to be made with regard to the transfer of power. But a strange situation arose. The Cabinet Mission, while admitting the claims of the Indian National Congress and the Muslim League in British India, completely refused a similar representation of the States people, who would not allow the right of the Princes to speak on their behalf.

In our own State the National Conference had made it clear as early as February 10, 1946 that it was against any further continuance of the treaty rights of the Princes which had been 'made in times and under circumstances which do not obtain now and which have been framed without seeking the consent of the State peoples. Under such circumstances no treaties or engagements which act as a dividing wall between their progress and that of their brethren in British India, can be binding on the people.'

It was in this connection that I invited the attention of the Cabinet Mission to the standing inquiry of the Treaty of Amritsar, and sought its termination. I wrote to the Cabinet Delegation that:

as the mission is at the moment reviewing the relationship of the Princes with the Paramount Power with reference to treaty rights, we wish to submit that for us in Kashmir re-examination of this relationship is a vital matter because a hundred years ago in 1846, the land and people of Kashmir were sold away by the British for 50 lakhs of British Indian Rupees. The people of Kashmir are determined to mould their destiny and we appeal to the Mission to recognise the justice and strength of our cause.

In the Memorandum submitted to the Cabinet Mission later by the National Conference, the demand for independence from autocracy was reiterated:

Today the national demand of the people of Kashmir is not merely the establishment of responsible Government, but their right to absolute freedom from autocratic rule. This immensity of the wrong done to our people by the sale deed to 1646 can only be judged by looking into the actual living conditions of the people. It is the depth of our torment that has given strength to our protest.

The indifferent attitude of the Cabinet Mission to the claims of the State's people convinced us that freedom would not be given to a hundred million people who were to be left to groan under the heel of autocratic rulers. Consequently the National Conference gave a call to the people to prepare themselves for fresh ordeals and new responsibilities in the final bid for the capture of power from the hands of autocracy. This call came on the eve of the transfer of power in India and was therefore in keeping with the spirit of the times.

[...]

It is clear that this dynasty can no longer exercise authority, on the basis of an old discredited Treaty. During my trial for sedition in the 'Quit Kashmir' movement I had clarified the attitude of my partly when I said:

The future constitutional set-up in the State of Jammu and Kashmir cannot derive authority from the old source of relationship which was expiring and was bound to end soon. The set-up could only rest on the active will of the people of the State, conferring on the Head of the State the title and authority drawn from the true and abiding source of sovereignty, that is the people.

On this occasion, in 1946, I had also indicated the basis on which an individual could be entrusted by the people with the symbolic authority of a Constitutional Head: 'The State and its Head represent the constitutional circumstance and the centre of this sovereignty respectively, the Head of the State being the symbol of the authority with which the people may invest him for the realization of their aspirations and the maintenance of their rights.'

In consonance with these principles, and in supreme fulfilment of the people's aspirations, it follows that a Constitutional Head of the State will have to be chosen to exercise the functions which this Assembly may choose to entrust to him.

So far as my party is concerned, we are convinced that the institution of monarchy in incompatible with the spirit and needs of modern times which demand an egalitarian relationship between one citizen and another. The supreme test of a democracy is the measure of equality of opportunity that it affords to its citizens to rise to the highest point of authority and position. In consequence, monarchies are fast disappearing from the world picture, as something in the nature of feudal anachronisms. In India, too, where before the partition, six hundred and odd princes exercised rights and privileges of rulership, the process of democratisation has been taken up and at present hardly ten of them exercise the limited authority of constitutional heads of State.

After the attainment of complete power by the people, it would have been an appropriate gesture of goodwill to recognize Maharaja Hari Singh as the first Constitutional Head of the State. But I must say with regret that he has completely forfeited the confidence of every section of the people. His incapacity to adjust himself to changed conditions and his antiquated views on vital problems constitute positive disqualifications for him to hold the high office of a democratic Head of the State. Moreover, his past actions as a ruler have proved that he is not capable of conducting himself with dignity, responsibility and impartiality. The people still remember him with pain and regret this failure to stand by them in times of crisis, and his incapacity to afford protection to a section of his people in Jammu.

[...]

The next issue before us is that of the compensation which we should or should not grant to those landowners who have been expropriated during the putting into operation of the 'land to the tiller' legislation, under which land was given, or given back, to the man who actually cultivates it.

[...]

We, therefore, thought it best to call upon our own people to declare what future they seek. At last we, in October, 1950 decide to convoke a Constituent Assembly which would pronounce upon the future affiliations of our State. We were, and are, convinced that whatever some groups or individuals in the world outside might have to say about this decision of ours, there are in every country many people who have faith in justice and straightforward dealing.

[...]

Under the Indian Independence Act of the British Parliament, the Paramountcy of the British Crown, against which the Princes had been leaning, lapsed, and it was made clear that it would not be transferred to either of the succeeding Dominions. There were three alternative courses open to them. They could accede to either of the two Dominions or remain independent. This gave the Prince, themselves the option to decide the fate of their States.

Following the announcement of the 'Mountbaten Plan' on June 3, some of the Indian States acceded to Pakistan and some to India by means of Instruments of Accession executed through their Princes. There were also some who entered into Stand Still Agreements with either or both pending finalization of their decisions.

The betrayal of the interests of the States people had been expected following the rejection of the Memorandum of the National Conference, and so we in Kashmir decided to place the issue before the people themselves.

[...]

Immediately on my release from imprisonment, I clarified the issue at a mass meeting in Srinagar. The first and fundamental issue before us was the establishment of a popular Government. Our objective might be summarised a 'Freedom First'. Then alone could we as a free people decide our future associations through accession. I also made it clear that the National Conference would consider this issue without prejudice to its political friends and opponents, and strictly in accordance with the best interests of the country as a whole. I said that, in the state of tension and conflict that obtained both in India and Pakistan, it was difficult for the people here and now to predict what the final shape of both would be.

You will realise, therefore, that we could not be accused of being partial to one side or the other. During that period we openly discussed the matter with representatives of the Muslim League who had come to Srinagar for this purpose. We even sent one of our representatives to Lahore to acquaint the authorities in Pakistan, with our point of view. We were thus still struggling against autocracy and for freedom when the State was suddenly invaded from the side of Pakistan.

[...]

Legally the instrument of Accession had to be signed by the Ruler of the State. This the Maharaja did. While accepting that accession, the Government of India said that she wished that 'as soon as law and order have been restored in Kashmir and her soil cleared of the invader, the question of the State's accession should be settled by reference to the people.'

[...]

As a realist I am conscious that nothing is all black or all white, and there are many facts to each of the propositions before us. I shall first speak on the merits and demerits of the State's accession to India. In the final analysis, as I understand it, it is the kinship of ideals which determines the strength of ties between two States. The Indian National Congress has consistently supported the cause of the State's peoples' freedom. The autocratic rule of the Princes has been done away with and representative governments have been entrusted with the administration. Steps towards democratisation have been taken and these have raised the people's standard of living, brought about much needed social reconstruction, and, above all built up their very independence of spirit. Naturally, if we accede to India there is no danger of a revival of feudalism and autocracy. Moreover, during last four years, the Government of India has never tried to interfere in our internal autonomy. This experience has strengthened our confidence in them as a democratic State.

The real character of a State is revealed in its Constitution. The Indian Constitution has set before the country the goal of secular democracy based upon justice freedom and equality for all without distinction. This is the bedrock of modern democracy. This should meet the argument that the Muslims of Kashmir cannot have security in India, where the large majority of the population are Hindus. Any unnatural cleavage between religious groups is the legacy of Imperialism, and no modern State can afford to encourage artificial divisions if it is to achieve progress and prosperity. The Indian Constitution has amply and finally repudiated the concept of a religious State, which is a throwback to medievalism, by guaranteeing the equality of rights of all citizens irrespective of their religion, colour, caste and class.

[...]

I shall refer now to the alleged disadvantages of accession to India. To begin with, although the land frontiers of India and Kashmir are contiguous, an all-weather road-link as dependable as the one we have Pakistan does not exist. This must necessarily hamper trade and commerce to some extent, particularly during the snowy winter months. But we have studied this question, and with improvements in modern engineering, if the State wishes to remain with India the establishment of an all weather stable system of communication is both feasible and easy. Similarly, the use of the State rivers as a means of timber transport is impossible if we turn to India, except in Jammu where the river Chenab still carries logs to the plains. In reply to this argument, it may be pointed out that accession to India will open up possibilities of utilising our forest wealth for industrial purposes and that, instead of lumber, finished goods which will provide work for our carpenters and labourers, can be exported to India where there is a ready market for them. Indeed in the presence of our fleets of timber-carrying trucks, river transport is a crude system which inflicts a loss of some 20% to 35%.

Still another factor has to be taken into consideration. Certain tendencies have been asserting themselves in India which may in the future convert it into a religious State wherein the interests of Muslims will be jeopardised. This would happen if a communal organisation had a dominant hand in the Government, and Congress ideals of the equality of all communities were made to give way to religious intolerance. The continued accession of Kashmir to India should, however, help in defeating this tendency. From my experience of the last four years, it is my considered judgement that the presence of Kashmir in the Union of India has been the major factor in stabilising relations between the Hindus and Muslims of India. Gandhiji was not wrong when he uttered words before his death which para-phrase; 'I lift up mine eyes unto the hills, from whence cometh my help.'

As I have said before, we must consider the question of accession with an open mind, and not let our personal prejudices stand in the way of balanced judgement. I will now invite you to evaluate the alternative of accession to Pakistan.

The most powerful argument which can be advanced in her favour is that Pakistan is a Muslim State, and a big majority of our people being Muslim the State must accede to Pakistan. This claim of being a Muslim State is of course only a camouflage. It is a screen to dupe the common man, so that he may not see clearly that Pakistan is a feudal State in which a clique is trying by these methods to maintain itself in power. In addition to this, the appeal to religion constitutes a sentimental and a wrong approach to the question. Sentiment has its own place in life, but often it leads to irrational action. Some argue, as supposedly natural corollary to this that our acceding to Pakistan our annihilation or survival depends. Facts have disproved this, Right thinking men would point out that Pakistan is not an organic unity of all the Muslims in this sub-continent. It has on the contrary, caused the dispersion of the Indian Muslims for whose benefit it was claimed to have been created. There are two Pakistans at least a thousand miles apart from each other. The total population of Western Pakistan which is contiguous to our State, is hardly 25 million, while the total number of Muslims resident in India is as many as 40 million. As one Muslim is as good as another, the Kashmiri Muslim if they are worried by such considerations should choose the forty millions living in India.

[…]

We have another important factor to consider, if the State decides to make this the predominant consideration. What will be the fate of the one million non Muslims now in our State? As things stand at present, there is no place for them in Pakistan. Any solution which will result in the displacement or the total subjugation of such a large number of people will not be just or fair, and it is the responsibility of this House to ensure that the decision that it takes on accession does not militate against the interests of any religious group.

[…]

The third course open to us has still to be discussed. We have to consider the alternative of making ourselves an Eastern Switzerland, of keeping aloof from both States, but having friendly relations with them. This might seem attractive in that it would appear to pave the way out of the present deadlock. To us as a tourist country it could also have certain obvious advantages. But in considering independence we must not ignore practical considerations. Firstly, it is not easy to protect sovereignty and independence in a small country which has not sufficient to strength defend itself on our long and difficult frontiers bordering so many countries. Secondly, we must have the good-will of all our neighbours. Can we find powerful guarantors among them to pull together always in assuring us freedom from aggression? I would like to remind you that from August 15 to October 22, 1947, our State was independent and the result was that our weakness was exploited by the neighbour with whom we had a valid Standstill Agreement. The State was invalid. What is the guarantee that in future too we may not be victims of a similar aggression?

I have now put the pros and cons of the three alternatives before you. It should not be difficult for men of discrimination and patriotism gathered in this Assembly to weigh all these in the scales of our national good and pronounce where the true well being of the country lies in the future.

[...]

On this historic day, we remember the Prime Minister of India, our cherished friend and never failing comrade on this difficult journey, and, besides, an illustrious son of Kashmir, the many friends in India and some even in Pakistan, who in the years before partition, helped us forward. We remember the Ahrars who went to jail in their thousands for us; Badshah Khan and our friends of the frontier, now in jails and fighting for their own freedom. Nor can we ever forget our kith and kin across the cease-fire line who are at present living under the heel of the enemy. There welfare is always dear to us and we shall continue to regard them as an integral part of ourselves. For twenty years, Mr. President, we have journeyed to this day and our criterion in all we do must be the welfare of our people. This consideration alone must guide our decision. Now again, I have put my deepest thoughts before you and may God, in His mercy, lead us all forward on the right path.

[...]

6. Appointment of an Advisory Committee on Fundamental Rights and Citizenship on 7 November 1951

Jammu and Kashmir Constituent Assembly Official Report, **Volume 1, pp. 119–21**

Hon'ble M.A. Beg: (Revenue Minister): Sir, I beg to move:—

This Assembly resolves:

1. That an Advisory Committee regarding Fundamental Rights and citizenship be appointed consisting of:—

    (a) the mover as Chairman, and

    (b) Ten other members noted below:—

        1. Mr. G.M. Hamdani

   2. Mr. Chuni Lal
   3. Mr. Abdul Gani Goni
   4. Mrs. Maini
   5. Mr. Mubarak Shah
   6. Sardar Kulbir Singh
   7. Mr. Mansukh Raj
   8. Mr. Kashuk Baqula
   9. Mr. Mir Qasim and
  10. Mr. Assad Ullah Mir

2. That the Committee shall make recommendations as regards the qualifications necessary for the State citizenship and the fundamental rights of the citizens of the State. In making recommendations, the Committee shall keep in view the definition of the 'State Subject' as contained in Notification No. I-L/84 dated the 20th April, 1927.

3. That the Committee may invite any other person to take part in its deliberations.

4. That the quorum for the Committee shall be one third of the total number of members for the time being of the Committee.

5. That the Committee shall submit this report to the Assembly within four months from this date.

6. That Mr. Mubarak Shah will function as the Secretary of the Committee.

* Mr. President, before I proceeded to speak on the merits of the Resolution, I beg to move an amendment with regard to the personnel of the Committee of which I have given notice this morning. In view of the short time at my disposal and in view of requests which came from certain quarters and which could be easily accommodated. I am sorry I could not submit my notice. It is, therefore, requested that my notice may be admitted. I propose that in clause I sub-clause (b) instead of the names of items Nos. 9 and 10 the names of Kh. Abdul Gani Trali and Mr. Habibullah of Sopore be substituted.

Hon'ble President: No notice to this effect was received in this office in time.

Hon'ble M.A. Beg: Sir, permission may be given now.

Hon'ble President: I am afraid, I cannot give permission at this time.

* Hon'ble Mr. M.A. Beg: Before the draft of this resolution is taken up by this Assembly it is necessary for this Assembly to make a detailed enquiry on different subjects which concern its very basic principles: These subjects involve two questions viz. the Fundamental rights and the Citizenship rights which stand in need of a thorough investigation. There are different rules in different countries for granting civic rights to citizen of a country. In some countries continuous residence for a specific period entitles an individual to the civic rights. For instance if a person resides somewhere or twenty five, twenty or ten years the law of the land treats him as a citizen of that country and this renders him eligible to the same political social, economic and other rights as are possessed by other citizens of that country. In some countries the principle of birth is current and the civic right of the country is possessed only by such people as are born within the country. Somewhere residence and birth both form the conditions precedent to the grant of civic rights.

Now the question arises as to who is called a citizen and what rights are possessed by a citizen? A citizen of a country can take part in its economic, social and political activities and also in all matters that are calculated to keep up or change its destiny. What rights should a citizen of our country have in the new set up is one of the many important questions before this Assembly for the solution of which it is intended to constitute this Committee. For becoming a citizen of the Jammu and Kashmir State a specific date was fixed twenty four years back under the Law I-L/48 issued on 20th April, 1927. This law was given the importance of a notification and under it the limit of S. year 1942 was prescribed i.e. those who had been residing in the State on or before that date were granted the Status of first class State Subject. For the second class residence and immovable property were prescribed as necessary conditions and for the third class the condition of ten years continuous residence was prescribed. The notification formed the basis for the definition of citizenship.

It would be irrelevant to discuss as to what benefit or harm resulted from this definition. For the preservation of a country's rights whether social, economic or political it is necessary to define citizenship. The Dominion constitution of India also embodies the definition of a citizen to show who is a citizen of India. They instituted a detailed enquiry in the matter and after sufficient consideration [sic.] on decided this important question. Now as the State of Kashmir is acceding to the Dominion Centre and has to find the solution for various pressing problems we have to see how the local citizenship and the Indian Citizenship will affect us and how the principles governing the two kinds of citizenship can be reconciled. These are the two complicated questions which will come up before the Committee and on the solution of which it has to bestow its thoughtful consideration. This Committee will have to examine the definitions of citizenship prescribed in the U.S.A. Britain Russia and China and think over it. This is an international and complicated question and needs detailed investigation. This Committee has to frame laws after careful consideration and in framing the constitution it should not be swayed by any narrow mindedness or prejudice. As remarked by the Quaid-i-Azam yesterday that in framing the constitution of our country we should not entertain any kind of malice or jealousy but we have to scrutinise the constitutions and the laws of the world and keep in view all that is good in them.

The second thing on which the Committee has to deliberate and present its report in this Assembly relates to fundamental rights. What are the fundamental rights and what provisions are necessary to be made in the constitution to preserve them. This work has to be accomplished by this committee in framing the constitution.

[...]

7. Appointment of a Basic Principles Committee on 7 November 1951

Jammu and Kashmir Constituent Assembly Official Report,
Volume 1, pp. 135–6

Sheikh Mohammad Abdullah (Prime Minister): This Assembly resolves:—

    1. That a Basic Principles Committee be appointed consisting of:—
    (a) the mover as Chairman, and
    (b) Seventeen other Members named below:–
        1.   Hon'ble Bakshi Ghulam Mohd.

2. Maulana Mohd. Saeed
3. Hon'ble Mirza M.A. Beg
4. Hon'ble Pt. Girdhari Lal Dogra
5. Mr. D.P. Dhar
6. Hon'ble Pt. Shyam Lal Saraf
7. Mr. Bhagat Ram Sharma
8. Mr. Mir Qasim
9. Sardar Harbans Singh Azad
10. Major Piar Singh
11. Mr. G.M. Hamdani
12. Mr. Moti Ram Baigra
13. Mrs. Rajinder Singh
14. Mr. Ram Pira Saraf
15. Mr. Abdul Gani Goni
16. Mr. Mubarik Shah and
17. Mr. Assad Ullah Mir

2. That the Committee shall evolve basic principles for framing a Constitution for the State keeping in view the board outlines of the statement of the Hon'ble Sheikh Mohammad Abdullah made in the Assembly on the 4th November, 1951.

3. The Committee may invite any other person to take part in its deliberations.

4. That the Chairman may delegate his functions to any other member of the Committee during his absence.

5. That the quorum for the Committee shall be one third of the total number of members for the time being of the Committee.

6. That the Committee shall submit its report to the Assembly within four months from this date.

7. That Mr. Mir Qasim will function as the Secretary of the Committee.

Sir, I need not go into the details of the objectives of this Committee. I have already indicated in my statement on the 5th of November the aims and objectives and other principles which should guide us while framing the constitution of the Jammu and Kashmir State. I would only like to reiterate those relevant passages so that the Hon'ble members who have been proposed on this committee may take due note of these passages. As a matter of fact the organisation to which we have the honour to belong and which has sent us here has laid down the basic principles for our future constitution in a booklet named New Kashmir. This was done in the year 1938 or 1939. I would again like to remind the Hon'ble members of this House and particularly those whom I have proposed or this committee to fully keep in view the words contained in the 'New Kashmir' which are as follows: (reads out extracts).

[...]

8. Election of Jammu & Kashmir's Representatives to Both Houses of Parliament on 25 March 1952

Jammu and Kashmir Constituent Assembly Official Report,
Volume 1, pp. 168–9

Hon'ble S.M. Abdullah (Prime Minister): Sir, I beg to move the following resolution:—

This Assembly proposes the names of the following persons for being chosen as representatives of the State of Jammu and Kashmir in the two Houses of the Parliament of India and authorises the Government of Jammu and Kashmir to make a recommendation to the President of the Indian Republic in accordance therewith.

Council of States

1. S. Budh Singh
2. Col. Pir Mohd. Khan
3. Rai Bahadur Pt. Anant Ram
4. Aga Syed Moh'd. Shah Jalali

House of the People

1. Maulana Moh'd Saeed Masoodi
2. Major Lachhman Singh Charak
3. Sofi Moh'd Akbar
4. Pt. Shiv Narain Fotedar
5. Ch. Moh'd Shaffi
6. Kh. Ghulam Qadir

9. Resolution on the State's Flag: 7 June 1952

Jammu and Kashmir Constituent Assembly Official Report,
Volume 1, pp. 324, 354–6

Sheikh Mohd. Abdullah:

Sir, I rise to move the following resolution:

'Resolved that the National Flag of the Jammu and Kashmir State shall be rectangular in shape and red in colour with three equidistant vertical strip of equal width next to the staff and a white plough in the middle with its handle facing the strips. The ratio of width to the length of flag shall be 2:3.

Sir, while framing the constitution of the country the question of flag is of great importance. As a rule every nation of the world has its aspirations, ambitions, desires aims and objects. Similarly the four million people of Kashmir have their own aspirations, ambitions and desires and to achieve them they have fought continuously and have never hesitated to make any sacrifice. The struggle of Kashmiris has taken an obvious turn for the last twenty years especially and whatever their ambitions and aspirations were they have made it manifest to the world to a great extent.

It was the 13th July, 1931, when for the first time the people of Kashmir raised their voices against the system which had trampled upon their hopes and desires. This voice made their aspiration obvious and the sacrifices they had to undergo in raising this voice, from part of history now which I need not reiterate here. People marched on consistently and underwent various privations.

[…]

Mr. Mir Qasim: Sir, I propose to move the following amendment. 'That the words "National" occurring before the world "Flag" in the first line of the resolution be deleted'.

My submission is that the great historical importance attached to the change, from the old order to the new one, needs no elucidation. This flag represents the unity of the peasantry and the working class. The flag can help in scientifically analysing the history of the National movement and its various stages. The unity of the peasantry and the working class which is growing and strengthening every day is a best lesson for us. Besides, many other things which the flag symbolizes need to comment. Because this flag was first prepared by the National Conference, it runs by the name of National flag. The members of the very same National Conference who are now at the helm of affairs now present it as the State-Flag. Therefore, my submission is that the word 'National' occurring before the word 'Flag' be deleted.

Sardar Harbans Singh Azad: Sir, I second the amendment.

Hon'ble Prime Minister: Sir, I accept this amendment.

Hon'ble President: Before putting this question to the vote of the House, would the Hon'ble mover of the main resolution like to say anything?

Hon'ble Sheikh Mohammad Abdullah: Sir, the resolution I have moved in the House has been supported from different corners of the House. Hon'ble Members of the House threw sufficient light on those aims and objects which are connected with the flag. I do not want to prolong the discussion, but only like to reiterate the fact that the biggest aim of this national symbol is national unity and brotherhood which we have achieved under this flag. The sense of national unity and brotherhood prevalent in the State is the distinguishing feature of the flag. The freedom movement of the country sponsored by the people developed due to sentiments of national unity and brotherhood. People of Kashmir did not take rest until they had put the freedom movement on the path progress and achieved the same. Some of my respected friends have in their speeches observed that the main thing which has been kept in view is that this flag does not represent any particular class or country but it represents the four million people of Kashmir. The four million people of Kashmir. The four million people of the State mostly comprise peasants and workers and the symbol of plough in the flag is the symbol of workers and peasants.

[...]

Hon'ble President: The question before the House is:—

'That the flag of the Jammu and Kashmir State shall be rectangular in shape and red in colour with three white, equidistant, vertical stripes of equal width next to the staff and a white plough in the middle with its handle facing the stripes.

The ratio of width to the length of the flag shall be 2:3 inches.

Note: The motion was adopted prolonged Cheers.

Hon'ble President: I think it proper that the Hon'ble Members should rise for a moment to honour the flag.

Note: The Hon'ble Members accordingly rose for a minute or so.

10. Appointment of a Drafting Committee: 10 June 1952

Jammu and Kashmir Constituent Assembly Official Report,
Volume 1, pp. 358–9

Hon'ble Mr. M.A. Beg: Mr. President, Sir, this House, in its last Autumn Session set-up two Committees for purposes of determining what would be the basic principles or our future constitution and what rights would form the fundamental rights in the future constitution of this State. These matters allied with other matters had to be gone through by these two committees. After the findings of these committees are recorded by this House and necessary directives given, if it so chooses, the whole material will have to go back to the Drafting Committee for purposes of drafting the constitution for this State. Through an over-sight, we have not moved the House so far for setting up of a committee of that character which will after receiving the decisions of this House on the reports of the Basic Principles Committee and Fundamental Rights Committee, give them legal shape and perhaps fill up gaps here and there and also put in sympathic consequental [sic.] provisions. It is, therefore, necessary for the drafting of constitution that a committee of that character be set up. I have, therefore, reasons to request this House to accord sanction to the Resolution that I am moving:

'This Assembly resolves that a Drafting Committee be set up consisting of the mover as Chairman and the following members:

1. Mr. Girdhari Lal Dogra
2. Mr. D.P. Dhar
3. Mr. Mir Qasim and
4. Mr. Harbans Singh Azad

to prepare a Draft Constitution for the State of Jammu and Kashmir, in accordance with the directives given by this Assembly from time to time in the form of its Resolutions or otherwise and on the basis of the decision take by this House on the recommendations of the Basic Principles Committee and the Advisory Committee on Fundamental Rights and Citizenship.

2. The Committee may coopt any expert to render such assistance as may be required.

3. The presence of at least three members of the Committee (including the Chairman) shall constitute the quorum.

4. Mr. Mir Qasim shall function as the Secretary of the Committee' [...]

Hon'ble Mubarak Shah: Sir, I second the resolution.

Hon'ble President: Now the question is that the resolution presented by Mr. M.A. Beg be passed.

The Resolution was passed.

11. Interim Report of the Basic Principles Committee: 10 June 1952

Jammu and Kashmir Constituent Assembly Official Report, Volume 1, pp. 401–4, 10 June 1952

While proceeding with the task assigned to it, the Basic Principles Committee has felt it imperative to seek a clear directive from the Constituent Assembly with regard to the basic character and shape of the future constitution of the Jammu and Kashmir State. In order to determine its broad frame work it is essential to know whether it will be based on the total application of the Principles of democracy or whether the existing system of constitutional monarchy should continue. This naturally involves an immediate consideration of the future status of the Ruling dynasty of the Jammu and Kashmir State and only a decision on this fundamental issue will enable the Committee to proceed further with the task of finalising the principles of the draft constitution.

The Committee has carefully examined the nature of the title and claim of the Ruling Dynasty of the Jammu and Kashmir State, which it derived from the Treaty of 1846. The Committee has no doubt that the Treaty was the natural consequence of the British Imperial policy in the Indian sub-continent which perpetuated and intensified feudal and autocratic rule in certain territories of the sub-continent.

When the popular upsurge for independence compelled the British Government to withdraw from the sub-continent, the Paramountcy exercised by it over these States lapsed and it was obvious that the iniquitous relationships which the British Government had entered into with the Indian Princes would automatically terminate. But the failure of the British Government to recognise a status of equality and independence on par with the status conferred upon the people of the Provinces ruled by it directly, created an anomalous situation. While in the rest of India, sovereignty was restored to the people, in the Indian State, it continued to be vested in an individual who was all along functioning under the protection and suzerainty of the British Government.

The people of our State, alongwith those of other Indian States resisted this relationship which condemned them to bondage and feudal exploitation. Their resentment found expression in their organised struggles against this unjust and discriminatory treatment meted out to them. They sought repudiation of this ambiguous constitutional arrangement and demanded the right of self-determination for themselves, prompted by the same urges that had moved the people in other parts of India.

The outmoded and anachronistic character of the dynastic rule was brought to light sharply by the crisis with which the State was faced in 1947. The general feeling of resentment against this autocratic system had corroded it to such an extent as left no doubt in its futility and incompetence to render elementary functions of guaranteeing the security of life and property of the citizens in time of a severe crisis. It was, therefore, natural that this unpopular system should yield place to a representative form of Government; but the natural and magnitude of the emergency facing our State made it impossible to effect any drastic changes in the constitutional set up during these critical times. The peoples representatives while tackling the difficult task of administration under stress of abnormal conditions had to function within the same work of the existing constitutional set up.

There was a major change in the situation when in March 1948, the Maharaja had to entrust the work of day to day administration to a popular Ministry but it was soon obvious that this arrangement could not work smoothly and stood in the way of progress and development. Consequently, the Maharaja who was conscious of his erstwhile power and privileges, incapable of any adjustment to the changed conditions, was forced to retire and was succeeded by Yuvaraj Karan Singh, who assumed the functions of a constitutional Ruler acting on the advice and guidance of his Cabinet.

This was obviously an interim arrangement subject to examination and revision by a properly elected body of the people's representatives. Accordingly the Constituent Assembly came into being in October 1951, with sovereign powers.

The Basic Principle Committee feels that the time has come when a final decision should be taken in regard to the institution of hereditary rulership.

After due deliberation and careful thought, the Committee is of the opinion that the institution of monarchy is a relic of the feudal system which was based on mass exploitation of the resources of a country and the labour of its people for the self-aggrandisement of an individual and a limited class of his associates. As such, the Committee considers this system opposed to the aspirations of the people for an untrammelled democratic order, the spirit of which is surging throughout all countries of the world. It strongly feels that the continuance of a monarchical system would be the imposition of an anachronism particularly when these monarchies are disappearing fast in many parts of the world under the compelling forces of history and social change.

It is the considered view of the Committee that sovereignty does and must reside in the people and that all power and authority must flow from the expression of their free will. The State and its Head, respectively, symbolise this sovereignty and its centre of gravity. The Head of the State represents the authority vested in him by the people for the maintenance of their rights. The promotion of this vital principle of constitutional progress makes it imperative that this symbol of State power should be subject to the vote of the people. The Committee therefore strongly feels that, consistent with the democratic aspirations of the people of the State, the office of Head of the State should be based upon the elective principle and not upon the principle of heredity. This would afford opportunities to all citizens to rise to the highest point of authority and position, with the support and confidence of the people. The spirit of equality and fraternity required by democracy demands that in no sphere of the State activity should a citizen be debarred from participating in the progress of his country and the advancement of its ideals and traditions. It is clear that the hereditary principles in the appointment to any office of power curtails the people's choice and to that extent, restricts their right to elect suitable person of outstanding merit and personal qualities to that position. The process of democratisation will not be complete till the highest office of the State is thrown open to the humblest of the land and in this manner, the Head of the State will be repository of the unbounded respect, confidence and esteem of the people.

In view of these considerations of the Committee feels that there must be a sense of finality about the decisions in regard to this fundamental issue. Accordingly, the Committee recommends that:—

(a) the form of the future constitution of Jammu and Kashmir shall be wholly democratic,

(b) the institution of hereditary Rulership shall be terminated, and

(c) the office of the Head of the State shall be elective.

(Sd.) S.M. Abdullah.
  "   G.M. Bakshi.
  "   M.A. Beg.
  "   G.L. Dogra.
  "   S.L. Saraf.
  "   D.P. Dhar.
  "   Piar Singh.
  "   Harbans Singh.
  "   Mubarik Shah.
  "   G.M. Hamdani.
  "   Mir Qasim.
  "   Bhagat Ram Sharma.
  "   Abdul Gani Goni.

12. The Constituent Assembly Adopts the Report: 12 June 1952

Jammu and Kashmir Constituent Assembly Official Report,
Volume 1, pp. 479–80

S.M. Abdullah: Let me request only with your permission Sir, that we adopt that Interim Report of the Basic Principles Committee and accept the recommendations contained therein as under:—

'Sir, I move that this Interim Report of the Basic Principles Committee be adopted and the recommendations contained therein be accepted.'

Hon'ble Bakshi Ghulam Moh'd: Sir, I second the motion of the Leader of the House.

Hon'ble President: Now the question is that the recommendations contained in the Interim Report of the Basic Principles Committee:—

(a) the form of the future constitutions of Jammu and Kashmir State shall be wholly democratic.

(b) the institution of hereditary Rulership shall be terminated.

(c) the office of the Head of the State shall be elective, be adopted.

These Hon'ble Members would say 'Aye' and those who oppose may say 'No'.

Note: The report was adopted unanimously. (Prolonged Cheers)

Mr. D.P. Dhar: Permit me Sir, to move the following resolution:—

This Assembly resolves that the recommendations contained in the Interim Report of the Basic Principles Committee as adopted by the Assembly be implemented and that for this purpose the Drafting Committee be directed to place before this Assembly appropriate proposals in the form of resolution or otherwise, a period of one month from the date of passing of this resolution.

Mechanism has already been settled in the resolution according to which the Drafting Committee has been appointed by this House. This resolution Sir, is merely formal in character and seeks that this House may direct the Drafting Committee to place before this Assembly appropriate proposals which will contain appropriate recommendations of the Basic Principles Committee which have been adopted by the House today.

Mr. Mir Qasim: Sir, consequent upon the adoption of the Interim Report of the Basic Principles Committee by the Hon'ble Members of this House after due expression of their views the motion moved by Mr. D.P. Dhar regarding implementation of the recommendations of the Basic Principles Committee and directing Drafting Committee to submit appropriate proposals constitutionally is seconded.

Hon'ble President: The question is that the 'recommendations contained in the Basic Principles Committee as adopted by this House be implemented and for this purpose the Drafting Committee be directed to place before this Assembly appropriate proposals in the form of resolution or otherwise, within a period of one month from the date of passing of this resolution.'

The Hon'ble Members who support the resolution may say 'Aye' and those who oppose may say 'No'.

The resolution was adopted.

Chapter 4

Negotiating the Delhi Agreement
1952

1. Nehru's Note on Constituent Changes in Kashmir, Dated 3 June 1952

Selected Works of Jawaharlal Nehru (hereafter *SWJN*), Volume 18, pp. 394–7

The Kashmir Constituent Assembly, after functioning for some time as Legislative Assembly, will meet on Saturday next (7 June 1952) in Srinagar to resume its Constitution-making functions. We have been informed that the first question that it is going to consider is that of the Headship of the State. The present proposal is to remove Maharaja Hari Singh, to declare that in future there will be no hereditary or dynastic succession, but that there will be a chosen Head of the State, elected for five years. Further the proposal goes on to authorize the present Constituent Assembly to elect this Head of the State for the next five years. The second draft resolution proposes the election of Yuvaraj Karan Singh as Head of the State for five years.

2. All this is not entirely new, as Shaikh Abdullah, in his opening speech before the Constituent Assembly some months back, said that they wanted an elected Head of the State instead of dynastic succession. He also said then that they would like to have Yuvaraj Karan Singh as their first chosen President. No period was then mentioned.

[...]

6. Normally, the proper course for the Constituent Assembly would be to lay down some basic principles of the Constitution and then to proceed with drawing it up. When the Constitution has been finally passed, some date should be fixed for giving effect to it. It is not desirable to give effect to the Constitution piecemeal before it is finalized. The whole picture must be seen. I suppose there is no legal bar to this piecemeal change, but from the practical point of view it does not appear to be desirable. Therefore, it would have been better if the Constituent Assembly laid down some basic principles only now without giving effect to them. For instance, the Assembly might say, if it so chooses, that the Constitution should provide for an elective Head of the State. No other detail, such as period, manner of election, etc., need be mentioned at this stage. There is another advantage that it accustoms people to the idea of the proposed change, which otherwise might come as a shock to some.

[...]

9. The accession of Kashmir to India was an act, in law, of Maharaja Hari Singh. If he abdicates and his son succeeds him, no change takes place. If his son subsequently agrees to become the elective Head, presumably no break takes place, although the change is important. But if the Constituent Assembly deposes the Maharaja, then it is not quite clear to me what effect this would have on Kashmir's accession to India. Of course the Constituent Assembly can reaffirm at the same time the accession to India. Anyhow this is a matter for consideration, more especially the effect it would have on the proceedings in the United Nations.

[...]

11. If the Constituent Assembly is going to deal with this matter, it seems to me necessary that it should also deal with the accession to India.

12. It is rather unfortunate that this matter comes up at a moment when some strain has been caused in public feeling in India and among some people in Kashmir because of certain recent happenings. This necessitates a careful handling of the situation.

13. This note, which is being sent to members of the Foreign Affairs Committee of the Cabinet, is my first reaction to the proposal made. I might mention that the draft resolution that I have seen appears to me unfortunate even in its wording, apart from its contents.

2. Nehru's Letter to Abdullah on 5 June 1952

SWJN, Volume 18, pp. 397–401

New Delhi
June 5, 1952

My dear Shaikh Saheb,

Day before yesterday, D.P. Dhar came to see me. Maulana Saeed was also with him. He told me that your Constituent Assembly, functioning as a Legislative Assembly, was for the present finishing its labours, and that it would meet from Saturday next to resume its functions as a Constituent Assembly. At this meeting it was your intention to put forward a resolution, the draft of which he showed me. This related to the Headship of the State.

[…]

4. What you propose now in the draft resolution is meant to carry out that intention. Your reason for this at this stage is understandable. I could guess it even apart from D.P. telling us about it. This reason is that, on the one hand, by removing Hari Singh and laying down the elective rule for the Head of the State, you not only carry out your declared policy but create a good impression on large numbers of people in Kashmir as well as on people in 'Azad Kashmir' and, to some extent, even in Pakistan. At the same time, you consider it important simultaneously to elect the Yuvaraj in order to assure the minority communities, more especially in Jammu and Ladakh. I understand that.

5. The question is, how exactly you should give effect to your intentions and the manner and timing of doing so. Normally speaking, a new Constitution is not drawn up piecemeal and much less given effect

to piecemeal. The whole Constitution is drawn up by the Constituent Assembly. When it is completed, then the whole is considered afresh so that there are no lacunae or contradictions in it and then passed. A date is fixed for its application. In such a Constitution there are, inevitably, transitory provisions, because it is hardly possible suddenly overnight to give effect to it entirely.

[...]

7. If the resolution as drafted by you is passed by your Constituent Assembly, the question of Kashmir's accession to India is indirectly affected, because the person who, as Ruler and Head of the State, acceded to India is himself removed. What exactly the legal implications of this will be, we cannot immediately say. They have to be enquired into. The matter cannot be ignored and anyhow it would be the better part of wisdom not to do anything now which may come in our way in the Security Council.

8. But far more important is the question of how the proposed change in Kashmir would affect Kashmir's legal and constitutional connection with India, apart from of course other aspects of this question. According to our Constitution, the Maharaja of Kashmir is recognized by the President and thereupon is supposed to be the Rajpramukh of the State. Any change brought about by your Constituent Assembly unilaterally, and without our Constitution being changed, would bring about a certain legal conflict and disharmony. A very curious situation would arise and the whole question of Kashmir's accession to India would become one of acute debate and argument. There are of course some people in our Parliament who would try to make capital out of this legal disharmony, but apart from them, many others would also be troubled by it. In fact it might be interpreted as a breach of our Constitution by a constituent part and it is not clear to me immediately what the consequences would be.

[...]

10. You will appreciate that this will create any number of difficulties. The accession of Kashmir to India, though complete when it took place, has become somewhat undefined, except of course for the fact that the accession took place in regard to three subjects named. But the accession is not a unilateral thing. It entails mutual obligations. Indeed, the mere fact that our Constituent Assembly contained representatives

of Kashmir and our present Parliament contains them, is proof enough of Kashmir's accession. But there are other matters that flow from it, which have yet to be decided. If at this stage this new complication arises, it will undoubtedly lead to grave complications in law. It will of course also become a subject for heavy argument all over India and, to some extent, abroad.

[...]

15. I have sought to place before you some major issues involved in this business. I feel that, in the circumstances, the only right course is to postpone a decision by the Constituent Assembly of this issue and for a full consideration to be given to it by you and us, so that any step that might be taken should be fitting and in harmony with the wishes of the people and the Constitution of India. Shaikh Abdullah replied on 9 June 1952 that in order to enable the Government of India to affect corresponding adjustments necessitated by the decision of the Kashmir Constituent Assembly to terminate the system of hereditary rulership in the State, it had been decided to defer consideration of the proposed constitutional changes 'for nearly a month.' He added that in the meantime a delegation was being sent to New Delhi for discussions. Shaikh Abdullah, however, disagreed with Nehru that the repercussions of their decision 'will be either harmful or unpleasant. On the contrary, we are convinced that the effect of this decision will be positively wholesome and advantageous. It may even go a long way in stabilizing our position so far as international opinion is concerned.'

3. Nehru's Note on Jammu & Kashmir's Status in the Indian Union, Dated 19 June 1952

SWJN, Volume 18, pp. 402–3

I had an interview with Mr Afzal Beg, Maulana Saeed and Mr D.P. Dhar about Kashmir matters today. As I was talking to them, I was seeing a note from Shri Gopalaswami Ayyangar about his talks with the Kashmir Delegation. I glanced through this rapidly.

Mr Beg appeared to be very depressed and said that they were leaving tonight for Kashmir. No results had been achieved thus far by their talks. They were anxious to help in every way.

[...]

He then told me that he had discussed with Mr Gopalaswami
Ayyanagar the question of the Head of the State, the title, etc., and the
period for which he should be appointed.
[...]
I told him that I did not attach very much importance to these
matters.
[...]
But the real question before me was a wider one. What was the
position of the Jammu and Kashmir State in the Indian Union? Was it
a federal unit of that Union? Were Kashmiris citizens and nationals of
India, using Indian passports? What was the position of our President
who was the symbol of the entire Union? Where did the Supreme Court
come in and the flag?
If these matters were clarified, then it would not be difficult to find
ways and means to decide the other questions which had been raised
now.
Financial integration was an important matter, but even that is de-
pendent upon this larger issue. The small details of financial integration
could be considered at some leisure. But the major points need not take
long to decide if we were clear about the position of the Kashmir State
in the Union of India.
[...]
Thus the point I stressed was that even before they finalised their
Constitution, the relationship of Kashmir to India must be fully
clarified. Once this was done, the other matters would not offer much
difficulty.
[...]

4. Nehru's Letter to President Rajendra Prasad, Dated 19 June 1952

New Delhi
June 19, 1952

My dear Mr President,

Thank you for your letter of the 19th June sending me a note on
Kashmir. The Kashmir Ministers, after their preliminary talks with us,

have gone back tonight to Srinagar. Presumably they will return after some days.

[...]

In your note you have laid stress on strictly legal aspects of the case and the limited powers of the Constituent Assembly of Jammu and Kashmir State. Whatever the strict law may be, I imagine that it is difficult to limit the powers of the Constituent Assembly deriving its sanctions from the people.

[...]

I rather doubt if any argument, however sound in strict law, which is based on the Maharaja's autocratic power, can be advanced now. In dealing with other states, we got some kind of consent from the Rulers. But it is well-known that consent was due to the pressure of circumstances and not through any particular goodwill on their part. In any event, I do not see how we can take our stand on some innate authority of a hereditary autocratic Ruler.

What is important to me is not the Ruler but the President and the Constitution of India and anything that may be done should be in keeping with that Constitution and with the dignity and authority of our President. It must be remembered that the position of Kashmir has been very peculiar ever since its accession and, more especially, since the reference to the UN. We are committed to abide by the decision of the people of Kashmir, whatever it might be. We are committed secondly to a plebiscite. If the people of Kashmir decide to remove or do away with their old Ruler, we must accept that decision, in view of our repeated assurances to that effect. If they want to leave India, that also we have to accept, because of our assurance. We could of course want this done in the proper way and having due regard to constitutional proprieties. The Maharaja's wishes cannot come in the way.

Because of all this, a special provision was made in our Constitution in the transitory clause, so that we can give effect to changing circumstances without having recourse to a formal amendment of our Constitution. So far as Maharaja Hari Singh is concerned, he was put out of the picture a long time ago and he has no authority whatever now and there is not the least chance of his return to Kashmir as Ruler.

It is, however, perfectly true that the Kashmir Government or Constituent Assembly should not take any step affecting our Constitution without reference to India and without our concurrence. If they take such a step unilaterally, it means some kind of conflict with our Constitution, unless we are prepared to adapt our Constitution to meet their wishes.

Even the present situation in Kashmir is that the Maharaja or his son, the Regent, is a strictly constitutional Head and should abide by the advice of his Ministers. If he refuses to do so, he breaks a well-recognized convention.

We have to bear in mind also that, apart from Kashmir, there is strong feeling in India, and in our Parliament, against all hereditary Rulers. Even the present position of Rajpramukhs and other pensioned Rulers is criticized and not accepted willingly. An argument based on hereditary right will not be agreeable except to very few in India.

The important questions that arise are mentioned in paragraph 9 of your note. In my talks with the Kashmir Ministers, I told them that the first question to decide and clarify was the position of Jammu and Kashmir State vis-à-vis India. In this connection, I mentioned some of the matters to which you have referred in paragraph 9.

Their answer was that of course Jammu and Kashmir State is a constituent unit of the Republic of India, that it has acceded in regard to three subjects and it is open to it to accede to more. That the Supreme Court undoubtedly exercises jurisdiction in regard to the subjects of accession. That the Union Parliament has full jurisdiction in regard to the subjects of accession, whatever they might be. They admit the necessity of financial integration of the State with India and are prepared to have talks on this. They are waiting for a note from the States Ministry on this subject. As regards the flag, they recognize the Flag of India and say that there is no conflict in having a separate flag of their own at the same time.

I told them that all this was rather vague and we should define our relationship precisely.

4(a) Nehru's Note of 3 July 1952 Recording His Plans for Kashmir's Integration

SWJN, Volume 18, pp. 423–5

Kashmir, like other states, acceded to India on three subjects in October 1947 under rather peculiar circumstances. Later, other states became more integrated in regard to additional subjects and they accepted the Constitution of India in its entirety.

2. This development did not take place in regard to Kashmir because of those special reasons—war with Pakistan, reference to UNO, etc., and therefore Kashmir's accession was continued to be limited to those three subjects. This was a fluid condition, which could not be finalized then. When our Constitution was taking its final shape, something had to be said about Kashmir and, therefore, some transitional provisions relating to Kashmir were added to it. The position remained fluid.

3. The Dominion of India became the Republic of India. That made no difference to Kashmir and its accession to the Republic of India was also in regard to those three subjects only.

4. In the normal course, more definite shape would have been given to the position of Kashmir in the Union of India and the transitory provisions would have been replaced by a more permanent arrangement. But, chiefly because of the reference to the UN, we did not take this matter up and allowed things to continue in the transitional and rather vague state. Even in the transitional clauses of our Constitution, reference was made to a future Constituent Assembly of Kashmir State, which was to draw up a Constitution for Kashmir.

5. Now that this Constituent Assembly of the J&K State has started functioning, we can no longer delay taking decisions in regard to some of these matters affecting the relation of Kashmir to India. This has been brought to a head by the desire of the Kashmir leaders to change the nature of the Headship of the State. In considering this particular matter, we cannot isolate it from other matters. Therefore, we have to define with some precision, though not necessarily with detail, the nature of this relationship.

6. The first question that arises is this: must all constituent units of the Republic of India have exactly the same relation to the Union, as embodied in our Constitution and various Lists of subjects, or can there be a variation?

7. If they must stand on exactly the same footing, then there is not much room for argument and Kashmir must line up with the others.

8. This is not a practical proposition and, even from the larger point of view, it is desirable to have a certain flexibility in our Constitution. Therefore, we must proceed on the basis of some special treatment of J&K State in this connection.

9. Whatever special treatment we may accord to that State, if the State is a constituent unit of the Union of India, then certain inevitable results flow from it.

10. We proceed on the assumption that J&K State is a constituent unit of the Union of India. For the present, the major Central subjects in regard to the State are three only, namely, Foreign Affairs, Defence and Communications. We accept that limitation for the present, but it must be made clear that these subjects can be added to. Even now certain additions will have to be made to bring out the inevitable consequences of J&K State being a part of India. These would not be major subjects, but rather corollaries of accession.

11. Accepting that J&K State is a constituent unit of the Union of India, it follows that there can only be one common nationality or citizenship, namely, that of the Republic of India. There cannot be any kind of separate citizenship for Kashmir or dual citizenship.

12. The authority of the President as given in our Constitution must be acknowledged. (The President has certain overriding powers of suspending the Constitution in a State.) It will have to be considered whether this power should remain in regard to J&K State.

13. Any Head of the J&K State must be recognized by the President.

14. The Supreme Court must function in the State in regard to anything connected with the subjects of accession as well as Fundamental Rights and other important clauses. The Fundamental Rights may be varied, with our consent, by the Constituent Assembly for Kashmir. There may be other variations too in the Kashmir Constitution. The

Supreme Court, however, should be the final authority to interpret the Kashmir Constitution, as it does our own.

15. The question to be considered is whether the Supreme Court should be the highest appellate tribunal for Kashmir also.

16. The National Flag must be the symbol of authority in Kashmir. The new State Flag might continue, but not as a rival of the National Flag.

17. There is to be financial integration. It does not necessarily follow that that integration should be exactly of the kind we have got with other States. In any event, it is to be remembered that customs revenue is the main source of income from Kashmir and if we take it, the whole State finances will collapse. It has to remain with the State for a number of years, which may be at least 10 and which might be 15.

18. The question of income-tax has to be considered in this connection also.

19. As regards the Head of the State, once it is acknowledged that the recognition of our President is essential, the rest, though important, does not vitally affect our Constitution. I think that, in the circumstances, we must accept that the Head of the State may be elected. The period has to be considered. I do not think a life term is feasible. It is not likely to please anyone really. Possibly a longer term than five years might be better, from all points of view.

5. Nehru's Note Recording Discussions with Kashmir's Delegation on 20 July 1952

SWJN, Volume 19, p. 211

The meeting began at 4.10 p.m. and lasted till 8.40 p.m.

The Members of the Foreign Affairs Committee of the Cabinet were present. The Prime Minister of Jammu and Kashmir, Shaikh Mohammad Abdullah was also present together with his colleagues, Bakshi Ghulam Mohammad, Mirza Afzal Beg, Shri Girdharilal Dogra and Shri D.P. Dhar.

The principal points in two notes, one by Shaikh Abdullah and the other by Shri Gopalaswami Ayyangar, both dated 19th July, were taken as a basis for discussion.

Head of the State

The following was agreed:—

1. The Head of the State shall be the person recognized by the President on the recommendation of the Legislature of the State.

2. He shall hold office during the pleasure of the President.

3. He may, by writing under his hand addressed to the President, resign his office.

4. Subject to the foregoing provisions of this Article, the Head of the State shall hold office for a term of five years from the date he enters upon his office:

Provided that he shall, notwithstanding the expiration of his term, continue to hold office until his successor enters upon his office.

Citizenship

It was agreed that, in accordance with Article 5 of the Constitution, persons who have their domicile in the Jammu and Kashmir State shall be the citizens of India, there being only one citizenship throughout the territory of India which included, in accordance with Article 1 of the Constitution, Jammu and Kashmir State.

The Kashmir delegation were anxious that the rights and privileges given to 'State subjects' (Jammu and Kashmir Notification dated 20th April 1927) should be preserved, subject to such variations as the Constituent Assembly of the State might decide upon. These rights and privileges relate more specially to the acquisition and holding of immovable property, appointment to services, etc.

It was pointed out that under Article 19(5) of the Constitution this was clearly permissible both in regard to the existing law or any subsequent legislation on the subject. It was admitted that, having regard to the special position of Kashmir, some such protection was necessary for the permanent residents of the State. There were in fact provisions in the Constitution giving special protection, such as in the tribal areas in Assam or in the land legislation in the Punjab and elsewhere, which prevented non-agriculturists from acquiring land. This was matter which could be dealt with by the State Legislature.

It was agreed therefore that:—

The State Legislature shall have power to define and regulate the rights and privileges of the permanent residents of the State, more especially in regard to the acquisition of immovable property, appointments to services and like matters. Till then, the existing State law would apply.

The use of the term 'State subject' should be avoided as this was not in keeping with present-day conditions.

Fundamental Rights

It was pointed out that Fundamental Rights should not come in the way of land reforms already undertaken or that might be undertaken in the State. In the Constitution of India, some form of compensation was provided for. Such compensation had not been provided for in the State legislation which had been recently passed and given effect to. This was agreed to.

It was further pointed out that, in view of the peculiar situation in the State because of the invasion of the State by Pakistan, subsequent war and ceasefire, very special precautions had to be taken against people infiltrating for espionage, sabotage, or to create trouble otherwise. If, by the full application of the Fundamental Rights in the Constitution, these persons could not be dealt with swiftly and effectively, the situation may well deteriorate and go out of hand. Therefore, the State Government required special powers to deal with this situation and the Fundamental Rights should not take away these powers. This principle was agreed to.

For the rest, there was general agreement about the application of Fundamental Rights to the State. It was stated, however, by the Kashmir delegation that they would like to include Fundamental Rights in their constitution in conformity with those in the Constitution of India. In reply it was stated that while there was no objection to a repetition of these Fundamental Rights in the State constitution, if they did not in any way conflict with the Fundamental Rights in the Constitution of India, it was not desirable to have a separate enumeration of these rights in the State constitution, as this might lead to some confusion in regard to interpretation.

The Kashmir delegation, while in general agreement, said that they would like to think over this matter as to how best to give effect to it.

On the part of the Government of India, it was stated that they would be prepared to apply the provisions of Part III of the Constitution of India to Jammu and Kashmir State with such modifications and exceptions as may be agreed upon to be necessary. Subject to this, Fundamental Rights attached to every Indian citizen, wherever he may be resident in the territory of India.

Supreme Court

It was agreed that the Supreme Court should have original jurisdiction in respect of disputes mentioned in Article 131 of the Constitution of India.

It was further agreed that the Supreme Court should have jurisdiction in regard to Fundamental Rights which are agreed to by the State.

The State delegation wanted to consider further as to additional Fundamental Rights being justiciable in the Supreme Court.

On behalf of the Government of India, it was recommended that the Advisory Tribunal in the State, designated 'His Highness's Board of Judicial Advisers' should be abolished and the jurisdiction exercised by it should be vested in the Supreme Court of India. That is to say that the Supreme Court should be final court of appeal in all civil and criminal matters as laid down in the Constitution of India.

The Kashmir delegation said that they had no objection to this, but would like some time to consider it further.

National Flag

Shaikh Abdullah had already made it clear in his public statements that the National Flag was the supreme flag and that it had the same status and position in the Jammu and Kashmir State as in the rest of India. The State flag was in no sense rival to this. But for historical and sentimental reasons, connected with the freedom struggle in Kashmir, they wanted this symbol to continue.

This was agreed to. It was stated, however, that it would be desirable to make this perfectly clear. As the Constituent Assembly of the State had passed a resolution in regard to the State flag, it would be desirable that the Assembly made it clear what the position of the National Flag was.

President of India

On behalf of the Government of India, it was stated that the powers to reprieve and commute death sentences etc., should also belong to the President of the Union. This was agreed to by the Kashmir delegation.

Financial Integration

The principle of financial integration was agreed to. The details would have to be worked out.

Emergency Powers

On behalf of the Government of India, it was stated that the application of Article 352 of the Constitution was necessary, as it related to vital matters affecting the security of the State. They did not press for the application of Article 356 or 360.

On behalf of the Kashmir delegation, it was stated that the application of Article 352 to the State was not necessary. In the event of war or external aggression, Item 1 of the Seventh Schedule, relating to the defence of India, applied and the Government of India would have full authority to take any step in connection, as even some petty internal disorder might be considered sufficient for the application of Article 352.

In reply it was pointed out that Article 352 could only be applied in a state of grave emergency and not because of some relatively small disorder or disturbance.

In order to meet the apprehensions of the Kashmir delegation, it was suggested on behalf of the Government of India that Article 352 might be accepted as it is with the addition at the end of the first paragraph (1) of the following words: 'but in regard to internal disturbances at the request or with the concurrence of the Government of the State' (the actual wording to be fitted in the proper place).

This was generally accepted by the Kashmir delegation, but they wanted some time to consider the implications and consequences as laid down in Articles 353, 358 and 359.

In regard to Article 354, they wanted to examine it further before expressing their opinion.

It was suggested that Shaikh Abdullah should address Members of Parliament or, at any rate, Members of the Congress Party in Parliament, before his departure from Delhi.

It was decided that a further meeting should take place on Monday, 21st July, at 4 p.m. at the Prime Minister's House in order to finalize the decisions.

The meeting dispersed at 8.40 p.m. No record of the further discussions is available. Nehru announced the agreement on 24 July in the House of the People and on 5 August 1952 in the Council of States. Shaikh Abdullah placed the agreement in the Kashmir Constituent Assembly on 11 August 1952.

6. Nehru's Statement in the Lok Sabha on 24 July 1952 on the Delhi Agreement

Statement on Kashmir in the House of the People, New Delhi, 24 July 1952, *Parliamentary Debates, House of the People Official Report*, Part II, Volume III, No. 16, cols 4501–21; *SWJN*, Volume 19, p. 219

Sir, I am grateful to you for this opportunity to make a statement in regard to affairs relating to the Jammu and Kashmir State. The House has been interested, and the wider public is also interested, in these developments and, therefore, with your permission, Sir, I shall take a little time of the House to state not only the present position, but go somewhat into the background, because we are apt to forget what has happened in the recent past. Public memory is short and unless we remember that past it is sometimes a little difficult to understand the present.
[...]

Now, while that progress was going on in regard to other states, it did not go on in regard to Jammu and Kashmir state deliberately, for a variety of reasons. Well, reason number one was that the whole matter was in a fluid state, before the United Nations, etc. Reason number two, equally important, that from the very beginning, for obvious factors, we had recognized that the position of Kashmir was somewhat different. Thirdly, that from the very beginning we had repeated that from even before the Partition, I may inform the House that no step will be taken about Jammu and Kashmir state without the concurrence and consent of the people of Kashmir. So, deliberately, Kashmir remained with those three subjects, and those subjects only. Of course, when I say three subjects like Defence, Communications and Foreign Affairs, please remember that each subject itself is a category of subjects. It is a category, if you go into detail. We did not touch that. And Sardar Patel was all this time dealing with these matters.

This came to an end in November, I think, of 1949 when we were designing our Constitution in the Constituent Assembly. Well, we could not leave everything quite vague and fluid there. Something had to be stated in our Constitution about Jammu and Kashmir state. That problem had to be faced by Sardar Patel. Now, he did not wish to say very much, he wanted to leave it, we all wanted to leave it in a fluid condition because of these various factors and gradually to develop those relations, those legal and constitutional relations, and not to force the pace in any way. As a result of this, a rather unusual provision was made in our Constitution relating to Jammu and Kashmir. That provision is now in Article 370 in Part XXI, temporary and transitional provision.

Now, that Article if you will look into it—I will not trouble you by reading it—if you refer to it, if you are interested, you will see the position that emerged at the time of our finalizing our Constitution. And I might say that Article 370, although it is by no means a final Article, nevertheless, it defined more precisely the relationship of that unit—that constituent unit, with the Union of India. After that, on the 26th of January, the President issued an Order in terms of that Article 370, a President's Order defining the categories of subjects and parts of the Constitution that should be applicable to the Jammu and Kashmir State.

The position since the Constitution was framed is thus contained in Article 370 and in the President's Order following it. Article 370 was obviously of a transitional nature, and it allowed the President to make any additions to it, any variations to it, later on, the object being that if any change or addition was required, we need not have to go through the cumbrous process of amending our Constitution, but the President was given authority to amend it in the sense of adding a subject, part of a subject, whatever, it was to the other subjects, in regard to Kashmir. But in Article 370, the old principle was repeated and emphasized that all these changes or any change, required the approval of the Constituent Assembly of the Jammu and Kashmir State.

When this was put down in our Constitution, there was no Constituent Assembly of Jammu and Kashmir State, but we envisaged it. We had envisaged it for a long time. And if the Constituent Assembly was not there, then it required the consent of the Jammu and Kashmir Government. So that was the position.

The House will appreciate that throughout our position has been, from before Partition, that we will not take any step which might be considered a step in the nature of compulsion or coercion, that everything should flow with the consent of the people concerned. That was the basic position. In addition to that fact, when this became an international issue, we did not wish to do anything which might be thought as if we were trying to override or bypass any assurance that we had given to the United Nations. This rather fluid condition continued, and our relationship was fluid in this sense, namely legally fluid; otherwise there was no difficulty and we carried on.

[...]

Now, in regard to the talks we have had, the position, obviously the admitted position, is that the Jammu and Kashmir State is a constituent part or unit of the Indian Republic. It is a unit of India and is, therefore, a part of the territory of India. That is the basic position.

The question of citizenship arose obviously. Full citizenship applies there. But our friends from Kashmir were very apprehensive about one or two matters. For a long time past, in the Maharaja's time, there had been laws there preventing any outsider, that is, any person from outside Kashmir, from acquiring or holding land in Kashmir. If I may mention it, in the old days the Maharaja was very much afraid of a large number of Englishmen coming and settling down there, because the climate is delectable, and acquiring property. So, although most of their rights were taken away from the Maharaja under the British rule, the Maharaja stuck to this that nobody from outside should acquire land there. And that continues. And in the state subjects notification by the Maharaja, they have defined four grades of subjects, Class number one,

Class two, Class three and Class four.[1] And unless you come in one of these classes, you just cannot acquire land there, or any immovable property. So the present Government of Kashmir is very anxious to preserve that right because they are afraid, and I think rightly afraid, that Kashmir would be overrun by people whose sale qualification might be the possession of too much money and nothing else, who might buy up, and get the delectable places. Now they want to vary the old Maharaja's laws to liberalize it, but nevertheless to have checks on the acquisition of lands by persons from outside. So far as we are concerned, I agree that under Article 19, clause (5), of our Constitution, we think it is clearly permissible both in regard to the existing law and any subsequent legislation. However, we agreed that this should be cleared up. The old state's subjects definition gave certain privileges regarding this acquisition of land, the services, and other minor things, I think, State scholarships and the rest. So, we agreed and noted this down:

The State Legislature shall have power to define and regulate the rights and privileges of the permanent residents of the State, more especially in regard to the acquisition of immovable property, appointments to services and like matters. Till then the existing State law should apply.

Then there was another matter relating to citizenship, because owing to these troubles in Kashmir since 1947, and a little before and after, there have been large numbers of people who have gone out of Kashmir but want to return. In fact in our own Constitution, some provision has been made, and I might inform the House that this question was raised early this year or last year about the inclusion of a large number of

[1] A notification of 20 April 1927 classified the state subjects as follows: Class I included persons who were born and residing in the state before the reign of Maharaja Gulab Singh and also those who had settled and been permanently residing there before 1885; Class II included those, other than belonging to Class I, who had settled in the state before 1911 and also acquired immovable property; Class III included those permanently residing in the state and who had acquired any immovable property or who might have acquired such property after ten years of continuous residence; Class IV included those not covered under the Classes I, II, and III.

migrants from East Bengal. We could not include them in our electoral rolls, because they came too late. We are including them now. Those that fulfil the conditions will all come in. So those, who had gone away from Kashmir into Pakistan or elsewhere, and who normally speaking might not be eligible for citizenship, should be provided for, if they want to return. So we said:

Special provision should be made in the laws governing citizenship for the return of those permanent residents of Jammu and Kashmir State, who went to Pakistan in connection with the disturbances of 1947 or earlier in fear of them, and could not return. If they return they should be entitled to the rights and privileges and obligations of citizenship.

Then came the question of Fundamental Rights. Now there was general agreement that there should be Fundamental Rights and these Fundamental Rights should apply to the State. But again there were great apprehensions in the minds of our friends from Kashmir. First of all, the question was how far these Fundamental Rights might come in the way of their land legislation now or any later development of it. Certainly, we did not want them to come in the way of their land legislation. We like their land legislation. We thought it was very good. In fact, it is quite impossible to upset a thing that has been done, but we said the matter should be cleared.

The second thing was this. Owing to all this business of invasion of Kashmir State, war, ceasefire, all kinds of continuing tensions, difficulties due to infiltration etc., constant attempts are made by infiltration, espionage cases are repeatedly heard, there is sabotage and the rest, but if you go to that State, you find normalcy there, that is to say, the State functioning normally, but behind that normalcy there is this tension, constant tension of an enemy trying to come in to create trouble, to disturb, and all that. The State Government has to be wary and watchful all the time, and so we were told that it was possible that some part of the Fundamental Rights provisions might very well hamper the activities of the State Government from taking these precautions and these measures. We agreed that it was essential and in the interests of Kashmir, situated as the State is now, that the State Government should have that authority. So subject to this, further consideration can be given to it as to how this could be done, so that a fuller consideration of this and like matters was necessary, so that the Fundamental Rights might be applied with such modifications and exceptions as might be considered necessary from this point of view, and agreed upon.

Then in regard to the Supreme Court, it was agreed that the Supreme Court should have original jurisdiction in respect of disputes mentioned in Article 131 of the Constitution of India. It was further agreed that the Supreme Court should have jurisdiction in regard to Fundamental Rights which are applied to that State. On behalf of the Government of India we recommended that the Advisory Tribunal in the State which is designated as His Highness's Board of Judicial Advisers should be abolished, and the jurisdiction exercised by it should be vested in the Supreme Court of India, that is to say, that the Supreme Court should be the final Court of Appeal in all civil and criminal matters as laid down in the Constitution of India. The Kashmir Government delegation had no objection to this. They were prepared to agree, but they said they would like to consider the matter in some detail further.

Now I come to the question which has been much discussed and referred to in the newspapers, the question of the Head of the State.

I might mention that, apart from past history, when this Constituent Assembly met in Kashmir, the inaugural address to that Assembly stated quite clearly some of the policies that they were going to pursue, and among these policies was the election, by democratic process, of the Head of the State. That has been the declared policy of the National Conference organisation in Kashmir for a long time. We had no objection with regard to the enunciation of that principle then.

Now, after careful consideration—because we have always had to consider two matters: firstly to give effect to the wishes of the people of the State and secondly to give effect to our own Constitution—we have come to an agreed formula. Of course, you will not attach too much importance to the language—a word here or there. For legal and constitutional purposes the words may be changed, but it describes the way we have been thinking and what we have agreed to. Now it was agreed:—

1. That the Head of the State shall be the person recognized by the President on the recommendation of the legislature of the State

(How the legislature of the State recommends is a matter for the legislature. Whether it is by the process of election or not, it is for them to decide; it may be by the process of a majority, or two-thirds majority; it is entirely for them to decide. Anyhow they recommend and then it is for the President to recognize).

2. He, that is, the Head of the State, shall hold office during the pleasure of the President.

3. He—the Head of the State—may by writing under his hand addressed to the President, resign his office.

4. Subject to the foregoing provisions of the Article, the Head of the State shall hold office for a term of five years from the date he enters upon his office, provided that he shall, notwithstanding the expiration of his term, continue to hold office until his successor enters upon his office. That is so far as the Head of the State is concerned.

Then there has been a good deal of misunderstanding in regard to the National Flag. This has been cleared up, I think, adequately by public statements made. Nevertheless, we thought that this should be further cleared up. Shaikh Abdullah, the Prime Minister of Jammu and Kashmir State, had stated publicly that the question did not arise so far as they were concerned, because the National Flag was the supreme flag and it had exactly the same status and position in the Jammu and Kashmir State as in any other part of India. The State flag was in no sense a rival to the National Flag, but for historical and sentimental reasons connected with their struggle for freedom in Kashmir, they wanted this State symbol to continue. This was agreed to. It was added that this should be made clear in a formal manner, preferably by the Constituent Assembly of the State.

Then in regard to the President of India, it was agreed that the powers to reprieve and commute death sentences, etc. should belong to the President of India.

There has been some talk about financial integration. It was decided that such financial arrangements between the State and the Government of India should be considered further and details worked out. The position, as I said, is a dynamic, changing one. Matters have to be gone into in some detail; so whatever the financial arrangements might be, we shall gradually make them out.

Then there is the question of emergency powers contained in our Constitution, more especially in our Article 352 of the Constitution. It was agreed to. I will remind the House what Article 352 is: in case of invasion, external danger or internal disturbances, the President has power to declare a state of emergency, and then various consequences flow from it. This Parliament is then seized of the position. Now this was agreed to; but the friends from Kashmir were slightly apprehensive of what 'internal disturbances' meant there. For the rest they have said, of course if there is a grave emergency this should happen. So, with regard to adding some words to clear up, not to clear up that matter but rather to bring in the fact that in the case of internal disturbances any action taken should be with the concurrence of the Government of the State. It was agreed that Article 352 of the Constitution should apply to the State with the addition at the end of the first paragraph of the following words:

but in regard to internal disturbances, at the request or with the concurrence of the Government of the State.

That is, the State of emergency will be declared with the concurrence of the Government of the State.

These are the principal things that have been discussed and I think that we have arrived at very satisfactory decisions—agreements which are in consonance with the wishes of the people of Kashmir and in consonance with our Constitution. I would repeat that there is nothing final about this and gradually we can fill in other details later. I presume that at the present moment, as I said, the relationship of Kashmir with the Union of India is governed more or less by Article 370 of our Constitution. Now the accession has been complete. There is a certain confusion in people's minds. The accession is complete in law and, in fact, Jammu and Kashmir State is a constituent unit like any other. It is a part of the territory of India, the people of Jammu and Kashmir are citizens of India like any other. But the fact that the subjects to which Jammu and Kashmir has acceded are limited, or less than those applying to other States, that fact produces this misunderstanding as if there was partial accession. That is not so. Accession is quite complete. In fact, all the states acceded only in regard to these three subjects to begin with; it may be that we may have more subjects later, but we are proceeding, and we propose to proceed always in such matters with the consent of the other parties concerned. Now, presumably the President of the Union will have to issue some order under Article 370 of the Constitution to give effect to any of these modifications or changes that we have suggested.

[...]

7. Nehru's Letter to Karan Singh on 26 July 1952

SWJN, Volume 19, pp. 254–5

My dear Yuvaraj,

[...]

Many things were decided by this agreement which knit the Jammu and Kashmir State closer to India and which make our Constitution applicable in a greater measure to the State. At the same time, we recognized the special position of the State and gave it greater autonomy in many matters than our other States of the Indian Union possess.

You will, of course, be chiefly interested in the decisions arrived at in regard to the Head of the State. Perhaps you may not like some part of them, but I had indicated to you, in the course of our talks when you were here, that it seemed inevitable to me that some such change must take place. Circumstances had so developed and they could not be denied without causing injury to all concerned and the cause we have at hand. I think that the decision and the form of words we have used are satisfactory and a fair compromise. Whatever law or Constitution might say, in the last analysis we have to pay heed to the wishes of the people. That indeed has often been declared by us in regard to the Jammu and Kashmir State. But really the principle applies everywhere in India.

[...]

In effect now, this means that at the proper moment the Constituent Assembly of Jammu and Kashmir State will make a recommendation to the President by election of a person who is to be the Head of the State. Although this is called a recommendation, the President will naturally agree. There is no doubt that your name is going to be recommended.

The period is five years. It is quite likely that at the end of the period, you might be re-elected.

[...]

I hope, therefore, that you will make it clear to Shaikh Abdullah and others that you willingly accept the changes suggested by agreement with the Government of India and that you will abide by any decisions that the Constituent Assembly of the Jammu and Kashmir State takes.

[...]

Yours sincerely,
Jawaharlal Nehru

8. Nehru's Letter to Abdullah on 29 July 1952

SWJN, Volume 19, p. 257

New Delhi
July 29, 1952

My dear Shaikh Saheb,

I have just received your letter of the 29th July about the Head of the State.[1]

I do not see how we can go through all the various processes about this matter before the 16th August. It is not a perfectly clear matter from the legal point of view how far the President can issue notifications under Article 370 several times. In any event, it would be desirable to include in one notification such present changes that we have decided to make. To have repeated notifications following one another in fairly quick succession would be odd, apart from the possible difficulty about their legality. We are having this matter examined.

There is also the question of how the present Maharaja should be dealt with. The obviously easy and decorous course is for him to abdicate. I hope he will do so. If not, then it may become necessary for the President to take some step. All this has to be thought out.

---

[1] Shaikh Abdullah had written that as the Kashmir Constituent Assembly was to elect the Head of the State on 16 August 1952, he wished that the necessary notification under Article 370 of the Indian Constitution be issued by the President in time.

In this matter you will appreciate that we have to proceed with the concurrence of the President. The final decision, no doubt, is that of the Government. But we cannot hustle the President.

[...]

Yours sincerely,
Jawaharlal Nehru

9. Nehru's Letter to Sheikh Abdullah on 1 August 1952

SWJN, Volume 9, pp. 260–1

New Delhi
August 1, 1952

My dear Shaikh Saheb,
I have just received your letter of July 30th.

[...]

The question of implementation, however, is more important and difficult because this involves action not only by the Constituent Assembly of the Jammu and Kashmir State, but by the President here. As I have written to you, there is doubt here as to whether we can issue a succession of President's orders dealing with these questions piecemeal. Apart from the legality, there is also the question of propriety.

[...]

Yours sincerely,
Jawaharlal Nehru

10. Nehru's Letter to Sheikh Abdullah on 7 August 1952

SWJN, Volume 19, pp. 312–13

New Delhi
August 7, 1952

My dear Shaikh Saheb,
[...]
There are any number of other points that arise in regard to the draft resolution that D.P. Dhar has brought. I am not for the moment dealing with them.

There is one aspect, however, which I should like to put before you. We have argued at great length in Parliament here about the actual terms of the agreement we arrived at. I have justified the language we used, and I have justified that language from various points of view. If that language is changed in any resolution of yours, then my argument in Parliament here will fall to the ground and that, you can well understand, would be exceedingly embarrassing, and would give a big handle to our critics and even disconcert our friends.

The whole position that I took up in Parliament does not fit in with the draft resolution you have sent.

You will remember the wording that we arrived at after much discussion about the Head of the State that he should be recognized by the President of India on the recommendation of the Constituent Assembly. This wording has been changed, and the change will immediately be noticed by all those who have carefully argued this point in Parliament here.

Again, the State President is supposed to hold office during the pleasure of the President of India. What exactly does this mean? It has no meaning in the context of the resolution.

In the First Schedule, among the qualifications for the State President is that he should be a State subject of Class I. Thereby you are perpetuating in your constitution the various divisions of State subjects and classes which were made many years ago, and which you said were out of date and were going to be revised.

The procedure for impeachment is also rather singular. The trial of the State President is to be by a tribunal, which is appointed by this impeaching authority itself. I am not aware of any such procedure anywhere. The State High Court Judge is to be its chairman. The State High Court is supposed to be subordinate to the Supreme Court. Where does the Supreme Court or the President of India come into the picture? I am putting to you some of my immediate reactions, even before I have considered this matter carefully, because I shall have to deal with these matters here, and I do not know how I shall be able to explain them or justify them.

Yours sincerely,
Jawaharlal Nehru

11. White Paper of the Government of J&K on the Delhi Agreement Entitled 'India and Kashmir— Constitutional Aspect'

It has been observed that of late efforts have been renewed by certain interested parties here in the State as well as in India to bring into question the validity of the constitutional relationship which exists at present between the State and India. In the past too when similar attempts had been made, they found sympathetic echoes in many international circles. With a view to create confusion in the public mind, the Praja Parishad has in particular put mischievous and misleading interpretations on the agreements arrived at recently between the State Government and the Government of India with the approval of the people's representatives. There can be no doubt that this mutually agreed basis of our relationship has the support and goodwill of the people here as well as in India. As it is likely that this misrepresentation of facts may create wrong impressions in the minds of some people, a re-statement of the State's constitutional position *vis-à-vis* India is necessary. The following is a factual and objective appraisal of this position:

2. In May 1946 with the failure of the Indian National Congress and the All India Muslim League to reach agreement upon the fundamental issue of unity or division of India, the British Government presented what is known as the Cabinet Mission Plan. It was clearly laid down in that Plan that 'paramountcy could neither be retained by the Crown nor transferred to the new Government'. It affirmed that the rights of the States which flowed from the relationship with the Crown would no longer exist and that the rights surrendered by the States to the Paramount Power would revert to the States. The Cabinet Mission, however, made it clear that the void thus created will have to be filled up by co-operation between the States and the new Government which would be a matter for negotiations during the building up of the new constitutional structure 'and this need not be identical for all the States.'

3. The Cabinet Mission Plan, however, did not fructify and eventually the British Government made a further statement on June 3, 1947, which in the end brought about the partition of India. In this

statement which became the basis of the partition of India, the British Government reaffirmed their policy towards the Indian States which had been unfolded in the Cabinet Mission Plan of 12th May 1946. This statement was accepted both by the Congress and the League. Under this Plan on the partition of India, the British Paramountcy was to lapse and it was to revert to the States. They could either accede to either succeeding Dominion or if they chose, they could remain independent. But while the States became completely free and independent, they were in their own interests advised by Lord Mountbatten, the Viceroy, in his address to the Chamber of Princes on the 25th July 1947 to link their future with either of the two Dominions they liked subject to certain geographical compulsions. Lord Mountbatten in his address made it quite clear that according to the Cabinet Mission Plan of 1946, which remained unchanged so far as the Indian States were concerned, the States had to accede to the Central Government in three subjects only, namely: Defence, External Affairs and Communications. Lord Mountbatten in his speech mentioned the apprehensions of some of the rulers that the Central Government might attempt to impose financial liability upon States or encroach in other ways upon their sovereignty. He, however, considered these apprehensions baseless and pointed out:

The draft Instrument of Accession provides that the States accede to the appropriate Dominion on three subjects *only without any financial liability*. Further that Instrument contains an explicit provision that in no other matters has the Central Government any authority to encroach on the internal autonomy or the sovereignty of the States.

He, therefore, advised the States to accede to either succeeding Dominion before the power was transferred to them, namely: 15th August 1947. On the advice of Lord Mountbatten, a large number of rulers feeling relieved of their misapprehensions joined the Indian Dominion but the then Maharaja of Kashmir took no heed of the warning given by Lord Mountbatten and allowed the sands of time to run out. Lord Mountbatten, as a matter of fact, did not more than re-echo the policy set forth by Sardar Patel on behalf of the Government of India in his statement of 5th July 1947. His appeal to the Indian States to accede in relation to Defence, Foreign Affairs and Communications was couched in the following words:

We ask no more of them than accession on these three subjects in which common interests of the country are involved. In other matters we would scrupulously respect their autonomous existence.

4. The Instrument of Accession which was signed by some of the States was the same as was supplied to the Indian States under the Government of India Act, 1935, though some of the States later on executed supplementary Instruments of Accession. On 26th October 1947, when the State had become an independent sovereign State, the then Maharaja of Kashmir signed the Instrument of Accession which confined the accession to the three subjects referred to above, the details of which were set forth in the Instrument of Accession. The residuary sovereignty of the State was fully safeguarded under clause 8, and under clause 7 the State did not commit itself to the acceptance of any future Constitution of India, nor fettered its discretion to enter into agreement with the Government of India under any such future Constitution. The Centre which was to be Constituted under the Cabinet Mission Plan was necessarily to be entrusted with minimum number of powers in order to preserve the fullest autonomy of the different cultural units constituting the Union. After the partition, it was felt that the Centre should have larger number of powers and the powers given to the Provinces envisaged under the Cabinet Mission Plan should be curtailed. A large number of the Indian States were represented in the Indian Constituent Assembly right from the beginning and took full share in the framing of the Constitution of India. While the Indian Constituent Assembly was passing through its final stages, four representatives from Jammu and Kashmir were nominated to it in June 1949. Before this, the right of the Kashmir State to draft its own constitution was fully recognized by the leaders of India including Panditji and Sardar Patel. A reference may in this connection be made to the letter addressed by Panditji to the Prime Minister of Kashmir on 18th May 1949 in which it had been stated:

It has been the settled policy of the Government of India which on many occasions has been stated both by Sardar Patel and by me that the constitution of Jammu and Kashmir State is a matter for determination by the people of the State represented in a Constituent Assembly convened for the purpose.

The Kashmir Constituent Assembly was perfectly free to accede or not to accede to India on any subject on which the State had not already acceded to India by virtue of the Instrument of Accession executed by it.

5. When the Indian Constituent Assembly was about to finalize its labours, it was felt that some provision in regard to Kashmir should find place in the Indian Constitution. The question of drafting Article 370, then Article 306-A, was then negotiated. In these negotiations it was made perfectly clear by the State Government that it was for the Constituent Assembly of the State to frame the constitution of the State and that in any provision that may be made in the Constitution of India regarding Kashmir, the basis should be the Instrument of Accession and that till the Constituent Assembly of the State consented to accede in any other subject to the Union, the relationship between India and the State should be limited to the subjects specified in the Instrument of Accession. A lengthy correspondence took place between the State Government and the Government of India on this subject and in the end the position taken up by the State was agreed to and Article 370, which is clearly based on the Instrument of Accession, found place in the Constitution of India. Article 370 is nothing more than a device to continue the relationship of the State with the Union on the basis of the Instrument of Accession under which the State had acceded to the Dominion of India before the inauguration of the Republic. This is fully borne out by what Sardar Patel had said in this matter in his speech in the Constituent Assembly on October 12, 1949:

In view of the special problem with which the Jammu and Kashmir Government is faced, we have made special provision for the continuance of the relationship of the State with the Union on the existing basis.

It has been shown above what the existing basis was before the Republic came into being.

6. In the autumn of 1950, the question of convening Constituent Assembly of the State of which mention had been made before in the letter of the Prime Minister of India dated 18th May, 1949 and in

Article 370, was mooted. The main functions which the Constituent Assembly was to discharge were:—

(i) The question or the accession of the State;

(ii) Retention or abolition of the Ruler as the Constitutional Head of the State;

(iii) The question of framing a constitution for the State including the question of defining the Union sphere of jurisdiction over the State; and

(iv) The question of awarding compensation to the landlords whose lands had been expropriated under the Big Landed Estates Abolition Act.

There was a good deal of correspondence between the State Government and the Government of India on the question of the scope of the Constituent Assembly and eventually Mr. Rajgopalachariar, Maulana Abul Kalam Azad and Mr. Gopalaswami Ayyangar on behalf of the Government of India assured the Prime Minister of Kashmir that there was no disagreement with the views expressed by the State Government and those of the Government of India in regard to the subjects which would come up for discussion and decision before the Constituent Assembly (vide Kashmir Prime Minister's letter to Mr. Gopalaswami Ayyangar dated 16th January 1951). The same view had been expressed by the Prime Minister of India in his letter dated 9th February 1951 which he had addressed to the Prime Minister of Kashmir from London. It was said therein:

I have no doubt that the will of the Kashmir people must prevail in regard to every matter and it is they who will decide ultimately every question affecting the State.

In another letter dated December 29, 1950, he had been pleased to observe:

Normally the very idea of a Constituent Assembly is that it has the power to decide the question before it. We must presume this power and go ahead.

7. That these were the objects for which the Constituent Assembly was convened will be clear from the following extract from the Opening Address delivered by the Prime Minister of Kashmir at the Constituent

Assembly meeting held on 5th November, 1951, which had been drafted by him in consultation with the Government of India:

What then are the main functions that this Assembly will be called upon to perform?

One great task before this Assembly will be to devise a Constitution for the future governance of the country. Constitution-making is a difficult and detailed matter. I shall only refer to some of the broad aspects of the Constitution, which should be the product of the labours of this Assembly.

Another issue of vital import to the nation involves the future of the Royal Dynasty. Your decision will have to be taken both with urgency and wisdom, for on that decision rests the future form and character of the State.

The third major issue awaiting your deliberations arises out of the Land Reforms which the Government carried out with vigour and determination. Our 'Land to the Tiller' policy brought light into the dark homes of the peasantry; but side by side, it has given rise to the problem of the landowners' demand for compensation. The nation being the ultimate custodian of all wealth and resources, the representatives of the nation are truly the best jury for giving a just and final verdict on such claims. So in your hands lies the power of this decision.

Finally, this Assembly will after full consideration of the three alternatives that I shall state later, declare its reasoned conclusions regarding accession. This will help us to canalise our energies resolutely and with great zeal in directions in which we have already started moving for the social and economic advancement of our country.

8. In June 1952, the Constituent Assembly adopted the report of the Basic Principles Committee recommending termination of the hereditary rulership in the State and its replacement by an elected head of the State. To give effect to this resolution, a drafting committee was set up to suggest appropriate measures for giving effect to the recommendations of the Basic Principles Committee. As the matter required consultation with the Government of India, because of the steps to be taken by them to amend certain provisions of the Constitution of India, especially Article 370, a delegation of the State representatives headed by Mr. M.A. Beg visited New Delhi. While the delegation was there, the Government of India also discussed with it certain other matters pertaining to the constitutional relationship of the State with the Union and broad understandings on some of the matters were arrived

at between the representatives of the Government of India and the State Government. These are contained in the statement that the Prime Minister of Kashmir made before the Constituent Assembly on 11th August 1952. The following passages from that statement may be aptly quoted here:

Since a good deal of confused thinking and uninformed criticism is indulged in by some interested people, I would like to point out here that the Constitution has confined the scope and jurisdiction of the Union Powers to the terms of the Instrument of Accession with the proviso that they may be extended to such other matters also as the President may by order specify with the concurrence of the Jammu and Kashmir Constituent Assembly. The special problems facing the State are thus taken into account and under the Constitution the relationship approximated to that subsisting under the Instrument of Accession.

The Constitution of the Indian Union, therefore, clearly envisaged the convening of a Constituent Assembly for the Jammu and Kashmir State which would be finally competent to determine the ultimate position of the State in respect of the sphere of its accession which would be incorporated in the shape of permanent provisions of the Constitution.

This, briefly, is the position which the Constitution of India has accorded to our State. I would like to make it clear that any suggestions of altering arbitrarily this basis of our relationship with India would not only constitute breach of the spirit and letter of the Constitution, but it may invite serious consequences for a harmonious association of our State with India. The formula evolved with the agreement of the two Governments remaining as valid today as it was when the Constitution was framed and reasons advanced to have this basis changed seem completely devoid of substance.

In arriving at this agreement, the main consideration before our Government was to secure a position for the State which would be consistent with the requirements of maximum autonomy for the local organs of State Power which are the ultimate source of autonomy in the State while discharging obligations as a unit of Federation.

9. A further reference to the above-mentioned statement of 11th August 1952 would show that as a result of the Delhi talks agreement on the points enumerated below was arrived at between the Governments of India and the State:—

    (i)   In view of the uniform and consistent stand taken up by the Jammu and Kashmir Government that sovereignty in all matters

other than those specified in the Instrument of Accession continues to reside in the State, the Indian Government agreed that
while the residuary powers of legislature vested in the Centre in
respect of all States other than Jammu and Kashmir, in the case
of the latter they vested in the State itself.

(ii) With regard to the President of India, he commands the same
respect in the State as he does in other units of the Union. All the
relevant articles in Part V. Chapter I of the Indian Constitution
relating to the President are applicable to the State of Jammu and
Kashmir. During the Delhi negotiations, it was further agreed
that the power to grant reprieves, pardons and remission of
sentences etc., would also vest in the President of India.

(iii) With regard to the State Flag, it was made clear by the State
Government that it was in no sense a rival of the Union Flag. It
was also recognized that the Union Flag had the same status and
position in the Jammu and Kashmir State as in the rest of India,
but for historical and other reasons connected with the freedom
struggle in the State need for the continuance of the State flag
was recognized.

(iv) In the same way certain conclusions were reached with regard
to citizenship, fundamental rights, jurisdiction of the Supreme
Court of India, financial integration and application of emergency provisions to the State. With regard to each of these points
certain principles accepted by the parties were enunciated and
the details were to be worked out later. In relation to some,
provision was to be made in the Indian Constitution and with
regard to others in the State Constitution. It was agreed that
the people of the State will have their fundamental rights but
it was recognized that the whole chapter relating thereto in the
Indian Constitution could not be applied to them. The point
that remained to be determined was whether the chapter on
Fundamental Rights should form part of the State Constitution
or the Indian Constitution.

(v) With regard to the position of the Sadar-i-Riyasat, complete
agreement was reached between the Union and the State Governments. Though the Sadar-i-Riyasat is elected, he has got to be

recognized by the President of the Union of India before his installation as such. His position is merely that of a Constitutional Head of the State and it does not in any way affect the position or authority of the President of the Indian Union. In each of the Indian States, whether prior to the inauguration of the Republic it was a Province or a State, there is a Head of the State who is known as Governor or Rajpramukh. Even in Part A States where Governors are formally appointed by the President, the Governor has to be a person acceptable to the Government of that State. No person who is not acceptable to the State Government can be thrust on the State as Governor. The difference in the case of our State lies only in the fact that the Sadar-i-Riyasat will in the first place be elected by the State itself instead of being purely a nominee of the State Government.

10. The facts analysed above make it perfectly clear that the State of Jammu and Kashmir enjoys a special position *vis-à-vis* the Union of India and this position has been accepted by all concerned. The residuary sovereignty of the State remains intact. It is for the State Constituent Assembly to frame a Constitution for the State. The agitation carried on to coerce the Constituent Assembly to take any particular line of action will harm the very purpose which the leaders of the agitation profess to serve. They are seeking to undo solemn pledges given to the people of Jammu and Kashmir by responsible Indian leaders that 'their autonomous existence will be scrupulously respected'.

12. Sheikh Abdullah's Statement on the Delhi Agreement in the State's Constituent Assembly on 11 August 1952

Jammu & Kashmir Constituent Assembly Official Report; pp. 485–99

Sir,

I crave permission to make a statement before the House in regard to the constitutional relationship between the Jammu and Kashmir State and the Indian Union. As the Hon'ble Members are aware, during the

last session of the Constituent Assembly, the Basic Principles Committee had submitted a report making certain specific recommendations
about the future Head of the State. The House, while accepting these
recommendations, had charged the Drafting Committee to present for
the consideration of the Assembly, a draft resolution incorporating the
proposed principles for the election of the Head of the State. The Drafting Committee will, no doubt, submit its report to the House during
this session.

Since the changes proposed by this Assembly involved corresponding
adjustments in the Indian Constitution, the Government of India desired that it should have time to discuss with our representatives the
proposals pending in this Assembly. Accordingly, a delegation headed
by Hon'ble M.A. Beg was sent by us to Delhi. The Government of
India also availed of this opportunity to discuss with our representatives
other matters pertaining to the constitutional relationship of our State
with the Union. During the last stage of these discussions, it became
necessary for me and some of my other colleagues in the Government
to participate in the talks. I am now in a position to inform the House
that certain broad principles have been laid down and certain decisions
have been tentatively arrived at between the two Governments.

Before I apprise this House of the details of these tentative decisions,
I wish to review briefly the background of our relationship with India.
For sometime past, there has been a good deal of discussion on this
important question both here as well as outside. In the heat of public
controversy, which this question aroused, the points at issue were sometimes obscured.

May I mention here the developments which led to the establish-
ment of our relationship with India in October 1947? After the
Independence Act, of 1947 was passed by the British Parliament, the
Dominion Status was conferred on India and Pakistan; and the British
Paramountcy having lapsed, the Indian States became independent.
They were, however, advised to join either of these two Dominions. It
is a tragic commentary on these arrangements proposed by the British
Government that the position of these Indian States, comprising one-
fourth of the total population of the entire Indian sub-continent, was
left absolutely vague and nebulous with the result that the future of the

States' people came to be subjected to the vagaries of their respective rulers. Many of them acceded to either of the two Dominions after a good deal of procrastination while others hesitated and delayed the final decision to the detriment of the interests of the people living in those States.

The Jammu and Kashmir State was one of the States whose ruler had not taken a decision in regard to accession. While the State was in the condition of uncertainty and indecision and while the national movement was seeking transfer of complete power to the representatives of the people and the then State Government was indulging in repression in certain areas of the State particularly in Poonch, the State was suddenly invaded. Thousands of tribesmen from Pakistan, as well as Pakistan nationals, launched a savage attack against the people of this State. The administration then in charge of its affairs proved singularly ineffective to cope with the grave emergency and consequently it collapsed all of a sudden. At that critical moment in the history of the State, the National Conference stepped in to avert what looked like total annihilation at the hands of raiders from Pakistan who were later proved to have been abetted by the Pakistan Government. The National Conference mobilised all sections of the population in an effort to prevent conditions of chaos and dislocation from spreading to the entire State. This factor was mainly responsible for the splendid morale displayed by the people of Kashmir who were inspired to heroic deeds in their resistance against the invaders.

It was, however, obvious that in face of the overwhelming number of the well-armed raiders, the unarmed people of Kashmir could not hold out for long. Consequently, it became urgently necessary for us to seek the assistance of a friendly neighbour which alone would enable us to throw back the invaders. In that critical moment, we could turn only to India where the Government and the people had demonstrated their sympathies for the ideals for which we were fighting the raiders.

But legal complications came in the way of India rendering the State any immediate help for its defence against aggression. The Government of India could send their army only if the State would accede to that Dominion. In accordance with the Indian Independence Act of 1947, the Instrument of Accession had to be executed by the Ruler of the State in order to make it legally valid. Consequently, with the backing of the most popular organization in the country, the Maharaja signed the deed of Accession on the 26th of October, 1947, and the State of Jammu and Kashmir became part of the Indian Dominion.

The basis of our relationship with India is the Instrument of Accession which enabled our State to enter into a union with India. In accordance with the terms of the Instrument, certain powers were transferred to the Centre. The principal matters specified for this purpose in respect to which the Dominion Legislature could make laws for this State were:

(a) Defence,

(b) External Affairs, and

(c) Communications.

This arrangement involved a division of sovereignty which is the normal feature of a Federation. Beyond the powers transferred by it to the Dominion, the State enjoyed complete residuary sovereignty.

These terms of the association of our State with the Dominion of India were maintained; and, subsequently, when the Constituent Assembly of India was charged with the task of framing a Constitution, this over-riding consideration was kept in view in determining the position of this State in the proposed Constitution. Earlier to this, it had been agreed between the two Governments that 'in view of the special problems arising in respect of this State and the fact that the Government of India have assured its people that they would themselves finally determine their political future', a special position should be accorded to Jammu and Kashmir in the future Constitution so that a limited field of the Union over the State is ensured. Four representatives were nominated from the Jammu and Kashmir State to the Constituent Assembly of India. These representatives participated in the deliberations of the Constituent Assembly of India at a time when the bulk of the Indian Constitution had already been adopted. It was at this stage that the constitutional position of this State was determined in the Constitution of India. The representatives of the Jammu and Kashmir State reiterated their view that our association with India should be based on the terms of the Instrument of Accession. It was also made clear that while the accession of the Jammu and Kashmir State with India was complete in fact and law to the extent of the subjects enumerated in this Instrument, the autonomy of the State with regard to all other subjects outside the ambit of the Instrument of Accession should be preserved.

Taking into account the special circumstances in which this State was placed, a special constitutional arrangement was evolved and provided in Article 370 of the Constitution which defines the position of Jammu and Kashmir as follows:—

'Notwithstanding anything in the Constitution,

(a) the provisions of Article 238 shall not apply in relation to the State of Jammu and Kashmir;

(b) the power of Parliament to make laws for the said State shall be limited to

    (i) those matters in the Union list and the Concurrent list which, in consultation with the Government of the State, are declared by the President to correspond to matters specified in the Instrument of Accession governing the accession of the State to the Dominion of India as the matters with respect to which the Dominion Legislature may make laws for that State; and

    (ii) such other matters in the said lists as, with the concurrence of the Government of the State, the President may by order specify.

Explanation:—For the purposes of this Article, the Government of the State means the person for the time being recognized by the President as the Maharaja of Jammu and Kashmir acting on the advice of the Council of Ministers for the time being in office under the Maharaja's Proclamation dated the fifth day of March, 1948;

(c) the provisions of Article 1 and of this Article shall apply in relation to that State;

(d) such of the other provisions of this Constitution shall apply in relation to that State subject to such exceptions and modifications as the President may by order specify:

    provided that no such order which relates to the matters specified in the Instrument of Accession of the State referred to in paragraph (i) of sub-clause (b) shall be issued except in consultation with the Government of the State:

Provided further that no such order which relates to matters other than those referred to in the last preceding proviso shall be issued except with the concurrence of that Government.

2. If the concurrence of the Government of the State referred to in paragraph (ii) of the sub-clause (b) of clause (1) or in the second proviso to sub-clause (d) of that clause be given before the Constituent Assembly for the purpose of framing the Constitution of the State is convened, it shall be placed before such assembly for such decision as it may take thereon.

3. Notwithstanding anything in the foregoing provisions of this Article, the President may, by public Notification, declare that this Article shall cease to be operative or shall be operative only with such exceptions and modifications and from such date as he may specify:

Provided that the recommendations of the Constituent Assembly of the State referred to in clause (2) shall be necessary before the President issues a Notification.

While the State of Jammu and Kashmir is included in the list of States in Part B of Schedule 1 of the Constitution, it is apparent from a perusal of this Article that the provisions of Article 238 relating to the constitution of the States in Part B shall not apply to the State of Jammu and Kashmir. In view of the special position and character of the State and with a view to regulate the relationship of the State with the Union of India, Article 370 was devised.

The other important feature of this constitutional set-up is that the matters specified in the Instrument of Accession shall apply in relation to the Jammu and Kashmir State in consultation with the Government of the Jammu and Kashmir State and all other matters which do not fall within the terms of the Instrument of Accession shall not apply in relation to our State except with the final concurrence of the Jammu and Kashmir Constituent Assembly.

Here I would like to point out that the fact that Article 370 has been mentioned as a temporary provision in the Constitution does not mean that it is capable of being abrogated, modified or replaced unilaterally. In actual effect, the temporary nature of this Article arises merely from the fact that the power to finalise the constitutional relationship between the State and the Union of India has been specifically vested in the Jammu and Kashmir Constituent Assembly. It follows that whatever modifications, amendments or exceptions that may become necessary either to Article 370 or any other Article in the Constitution of India in their application to the Jammu and Kashmir State are subject to the decisions of this sovereign body.

Since a good deal of confused thinking and uninformed criticism is indulged in by some interested people, I would like to point out here that the Constitution has confined the scope and jurisdiction of the Union Powers to the terms of the Instrument of Accession with the proviso that they may be extended to such other matters also as the President may by order specify with the concurrence of the Jammu and Kashmir Constituent Assembly. The special problems facing the State were thus taken into account and under the Constitution the relationship approximated to that subsisting under the Instrument of Accession.

The Constitution of the Indian Union, therefore, clearly envisaged the convening of a Constituent Assembly for the Jammu and Kashmir State which would be finally competent to determine the ultimate position of the State in respect of the sphere of its accession which would be incorporated as in the shape of permanent provisions of the Constitution.

This, briefly, is the position which the Constitution of India has accorded to our State. I would like to make it clear that any suggestions of altering arbitrarily this basis of our relationship with India would not only constitute a breach of the spirit and letter of the Constitution, but it may invite serious consequences for a harmonious association of our State with India. The formula evolved with the agreement of the two Governments remains as valid today as it was when the Constitution was framed and reasons advanced to have this basis changed seem completely devoid of substance.

In arriving at this arrangement, the main consideration before our Government was to secure a position for the State which would be consistent with the requirements of maximum autonomy for the local organs of State Power which are the ultimate source of authority in the State while discharging obligations as a unit of the Federation.

I would, therefore, plead that the validity of such constitutional arrangement should not be appraised academically but in the proper context of the extraordinary circumstances through which the State has been passing for the last five years or so. Since the State was invaded in 1947, the situation here has been bristling with such compelling urgencies as needed drastic administrative and economic changes. The revolutionary conditions prevailing in our State could be coped with only through extraordinary measures. The Government of the State was, therefore, called upon to take vital decisions which could not wait. Accordingly, it enacted laws which were calculated to transform the social and economic fabric of the common people. With the improvement in the internal situation of the country, the necessity for a legislature became obvious. Consequently, it was decided to convene a Constituent Assembly for the State elected on the basis of adult franchise. This Assembly accordingly came into being in October, 1951.

The Hon'ble Members are aware that as the leader of the National Conference party, I indicated in my inaugural address the scope of the decisions which I felt the Constituent Assembly would have to take. I listed the four main issues as pertaining to the main functions of the Assembly, viz., the future of the Ruling Dynasty, payment of compensation for the land transferred to cultivators under the Big Landed Estates Act, Ratification of the State's accession to India as well as the framing of a Constitution for the State. While discussing these issues in my address to this House, I had given clear indications of my party's views in regard to them. I had also an occasion to place my point of view on these issues before the representatives of the Government of India and I had the satisfaction that they approved of it.

When the Constituent Assembly commenced its labours, it had to tackle these issues in course of time. It took decisions in regard to payment of compensation to landlords and it came to the conclusion that no compensation was justified.

The Constituent Assembly has, at present, under its consideration the future of the Ruling Dynasty. In this connection the Basic Principles Committee recommended that the institution of hereditary rulership in the State should be abolished and in future the office of the Head of State should be elective. While accepting the recommendations of the Basic Principles Committee, this Assembly charged the Drafting Committee to place before this House appropriate proposals for the implementation of these recommendations.

As I said in the beginning of my statement, such a fundamental decision involved corresponding adjustments in the Indian Constitution and in order to finalise the position in respect of this issue and other matters pertinent to it, I and my colleagues had discussions with the representatives of the Government of India as a result of which we arrived at some tentative agreement, the details of which I wish to place before the House.

The Government of India held the view that the fact that the Jammu and Kashmir State was a constituent unit of the Union of India led inevitably to certain consequences in regard to some important matters, namely:—

(a) Residuary Powers,
(b) Citizenship,
(c) Fundamental Rights,
(d) Supreme Court of India,
(e) National Flag,
(f) The President of India,
(g) The Headship of the State,
(h) Financial Integration,
(i) Emergency Provisions, and
(j) Conduct of Elections to Houses of Parliament.

Permit me, Mr. President, now to deal with each one of these items and also the agreements arrived at between the Jammu and Kashmir Government and the Government of India in relation to them.

Residuary Powers

It was agreed that while under the present Indian Constitution, the Residuary Powers vested in the Centre in respect of all the States other than Jammu and Kashmir, in the case of our State, they rested in the State itself. This position is compatible with Article 370 of the Indian Constitution and the Instrument of Accession on which this Article is based. We have always held that the ultimate source of sovereignty resides in the people. It is, therefore, from the people that all powers can flow. Under these circumstances, it is upto the people of Kashmir through this Assembly to transfer more powers for mutual advantage to the custody of the Union Centre.

Citizenship

It was agreed that in accordance with Article 5 of the Indian Constitution persons who have their domicile in the Jammu and Kashmir State shall be the citizens of India. It was further agreed that the State legislature shall have power to define and regulate the rights and privileges of the permanent residents of the State, more especially in regard to acquisition of immovable property, appointments to services and like matters. Till then the existing State law would apply. It was also agreed that special provision should be made in the laws governing citizenship to provide for the return of those permanent residents of Jammu and Kashmir State, who went to Pakistan in connection with the disturbances of 1947 or in fear of them as well as of those who had left for Pakistan earlier but could not return. If they returned, they should be entitled to the rights, and privileges and obligations of citizenship.

There are historic reasons which necessitate such constitutional safeguards as for centuries past, the people of the State have been victims of exploitation at the hands of their well-to-do neighbours. The Hon'ble Members are perhaps aware that in the late twenties, the people of Jammu and Kashmir agitated for the protection of their bona fide rights against the superior competing interests of the non-residents of the State. It was in response to this popular demand that the Government of the day promulgated a Notification in 1927 by which a strict definition of the term 'State Subject' was provided. I am glad to say that the Government of India appreciated the need for such a safeguard. No definition of the special rights and privileges of the residents of the State can afford to remain static. The need may arise at one stage or the other to liberalize such a definition. The importance of the fact that State Legislature shall retain powers to be able to effect such modifications becomes obvious in this context.

There is yet another class of State Subjects whose interests had to be safeguarded. The Hon'ble Members of this House are aware that on account of the disturbances of 1947 and also as a consequence of the invasion of this country by Pakistan, large numbers of the residents of this State suffered dislocation. We have, therefore, to visualize the possibility of their return to their homes and hearths as soon as normal conditions are restored. It has been suggested in certain quarters that this protection has been provided only for those residents of the State who are at present stranded in Pakistan. I would like to make it clear, as I have stated earlier, that this protection will operate only when the conditions are normal and such conditions naturally presume that the resettlement of the dislocated population, whether Muslim or non-Muslim, cannot be one-sided or unilateral.

Fundamental Rights

It is obvious that while our constitution is being framed, the fundamental rights and duties of a citizen have necessarily got to be defined. It was agreed, however, that the Fundamental Rights, which are contained in the Constitution of India could not be conferred on the residents of the Jammu and Kashmir State in their entirety taking into account the economic, social and political character of our movement as enunciated in the New Kashmir Plan. The need for providing suitable modifications, amendments and exceptions as the case may be in the Fundamental Rights Chapter of the Indian Constitution in order to harmonize those provisions with the pattern of our principles was admitted. Particular care would have to be taken to preserve the basic character of the decisions taken by this House on the question of land compensation as well as the laws relating to the transfer of land to the tiller and other matters. The main point to be determined is whether the Chapter of our Fundamental Rights should form a part of the Kashmir Constitution or that of the Union Constitution.

Supreme Court

It was agreed that the Supreme Court should have original jurisdiction in respect of disputes mentioned in Article 131 of the Constitution of India. It was further agreed that the Supreme Court should have jurisdiction in regard to Fundamental Rights which are agreed to by the State.

On behalf of the Government of India, it was recommended that the Advisory Board in the State, designated 'His Highness's Board of Judicial Advisors' should be abolished and the jurisdiction exercised by it should be vested in the Supreme Court of India. That is to say that the Supreme Court should be the final Court of appeal in all civil and criminal matters as laid down in the Constitution of India.

We, however, felt that this would need a detailed examination and consequently it was agreed that we should have time to consider it further.

National Flag

We agreed that in view of the clarifications issued by me in my public statements while interpreting the resolution of this House according to which the old State flag was substituted by a new one, it was obvious that the new State flag was in no sense a rival of the National flag. But for historical and other reasons connected with the freedom struggle in the State, the need for the continuance of this flag was recognized. The Union flag to which we continue our allegiance as a part of the Union will occupy the supremely distinctive place in the State.

President of India

It was agreed that the powers to grant reprieve and commute death sentences, etc. should also belong to the President of the Union.

Headship of the State

I am glad to inform this House that the Government of India have appreciated the principle proposed by the Basic Principle Committee as adopted by this Assembly in regard to the abolition of the hereditary rulership of the State. In order to accommodate this principle, the following arrangement was mutually agreed upon:

(i) The Head of the State shall be the person recognized by the President of the Union on the recommendation of the Legislature of the State.

(ii) He shall hold office during the pleasure of the President.

(iii) He may, by writing under his hand addressed to the president, resign his office.

(iv) Subject to the foregoing provisions, the Head of the State shall hold office for a term of five years from the date he enters upon his office.

(v) Provided that he shall, notwithstanding the expiration of his term, continue to hold the office until his successor enters upon his office.

Financial Integration

In regard to this subject, we agreed that it would be necessary to evolve some sort of financial arrangement between the State and the Indian Union. But as this involved far-reaching consequences, it was felt that a detailed and objective examination of this subject would be necessary.

Emergency Powers

On behalf of the Government of India, it was stated that the application of Article 352 of the Constitution was necessary as it related to vital matters affecting the security of the State. They did not press for the application of Articles 356 or 360.

On behalf of the Kashmir Delegation, it was stated that the application of Article 352 to the State was not necessary. In the event of war or external aggression, item I in the Seventh Schedule relating to the defence of India applied and the Government of India would have full authority to take any steps in connection with defence, etc. In particular, we were averse to internal disturbance being referred to in this connection, as even some petty internal disorder might be considered sufficient for the application of Article 352.

In reply it was pointed out that Article 352 could only be applied in a state of grave emergency and not because of some small disorder or disturbance.

In order to meet our viewpoint, it was suggested on behalf of the Government of India that Article 352 might be accepted as it is with the addition at the end of the first paragraph (1) of the following words:

'but in regard to internal disturbance at the request or with the concurrence of the Government of the State'.

We generally accepted this position, but wanted some time to consider the implications and consequences as laid down in Articles 353, 358 and 359 which on the whole we accepted. In regard to Article 354, we wanted to examine it further before expressing our opinion.

Conduct of Elections to Houses of Parliament

Article 324 of the Indian Constitution already applies to the State in so far as it relates to elections to Parliament and to the offices of the President and the Vice-President of India.

I have put before this House the broad indications of the agreements arrived at between us and the Government of India. As the Hon'ble Members will, no doubt, observe, the attitude of the Government of India has been most helpful. A satisfactory position has emerged and we are now able to assess the basic issues of our constitutional relationship with India in clearer terms. There has been a good deal of accommodation of our respective points of view. Both the representatives of the Government of India and the Kashmir Delegation, have been impelled by the desire to strengthen further the existing relationship to remove all obscurity and vagueness. We are convinced, as ever before, that we have the full support both of the Government and the people of India in the fulfilment of our democratic ideals and the realization of our objectives.

This goodwill and amity, I am sure, will result in the consolidation of freedom and democracy in our country. I may, however, emphasize that the supreme guarantee of our relationship with India is the identity of the democratic and secular aspirations, which have guided the people of India as well as those of Jammu and Kashmir in their struggle for emancipation and before which all constitutional safeguards will take a secondary position.

It is, of course, for the Constituent Assembly, which is seized of these matters, to determine the extent and scope of the State's accession to India. The Assembly may agree to continue this relationship on the present basis or extend its scope as it might like and consider feasible and proper. In the course of framing the constitution for the State, the Hon'ble Members of this Assembly will have an opportunity of discussing these agreements and expressing their views thereon.

I thank you, Sir, for affording me this opportunity to place before the Hon'ble Members of this House the result of our recent talks with the representatives of the Government of India.

Chapter 5

Post-Delhi Agreement
1952

1. Nehru's Note for Sheikh Abdullah, Dated 14 August 1952

Selected Works of Jawaharlal Nehru (hereafter *SWJN*),
Volume 19, p. 319

This is a hurried note about the proposal regarding the Head of the State and the resolution now being discussed in the Jammu and Kashmir Constituent Assembly (since 11 August 1952). Regarding the resolution before the Constituent Assembly now, there is one rather important matter which deserves attention.

2. In our agreement in regard to the Supreme Court, after stating the views of the Government of India, it was said that the Kashmir delegation had no objection to the proposal made but that they would like to consider it further. As stated in Shaikh Saheb's speech before the Constituent Assembly, the part that 'the Kashmir delegation had no objection to the proposal' has been left out, and it is merely stated that this would need a detailed examination and further consideration. This

omission has attracted attention and it is desirable to rectify it. Importance was attached to the Supreme Court exercising normal appellate
jurisdiction in regard to civil and criminal matters as laid down in the
Constitution of India and thus becoming a final court of appeal for the
State. Naturally the Supreme Court would in doing so apply the laws
of the State. This was considered to be a vital link between the Jammu
and Kashmir State and the Union, and as such, it was stressed in the
Parliament of India. It has also been emphasized to the Yuvaraj. If some
doubt arises about this matter, then difficulties might be created.

3. In regard to the National Flag, it was agreed that it would be desirable to have a formal declaration by the Constituent Assembly. There is
no reference to this in the resolution.

4. The new draft is different in many ways from the old draft that was
sent here and to a large extent conforms to suggestions made here when
D.P. Dhar came. But it is felt that it would be better at this stage not to
have the schedules attached to the resolution. The schedules related to
the manner of election and to the emoluments, etc. Both these matters
could easily be dealt with a little later after the main proposal has been
passed. This need not involve any marked delay. This procedure of taking the schedule separately would make it easier for the President of
India to deal with this matter and will also probably make it easier to
get the consent of the Yuvaraj.

5. I am not dealing with the details in the schedules. But I think
it would be desirable, even keeping the main content as it is, to word
them differently in order not to make it appear that the President
of India's function is merely to rubber-stamp a decision. In practice,
the recommendation of the Constituent Assembly or the Legislative
Assembly will naturally be accepted by the President. But the wording
should be such as not to lessen the dignity of the President of India
and the importance of his recognition. This approach could involve a
certain amount of redrafting of these schedules.

6. While this part of the constitution deals with the permanent
method of choosing the Head of the State by the Legislative Assembly,
in effect the first choice will be made by the Constituent Assembly. It
is not, therefore, necessary for all these details and qualifications to be
laid down for this first choice though many of them might of course

be observed, just as the President of India was at first elected by the Constituent Assembly. Later he was elected by the more complicated procedure laid down in the Constitution.

7. Thus the proper course appears to be to pass the main proposal about the Headship of the State, and to add that the procedure etc., will be contained in schedules to be hereafter framed, and further to say that the first President shall be recommended to the President of India by the Constituent Assembly itself in such manner and by such procedure as that Assembly may think fit and proper. Thus this matter is left a little flexible for this first choice, and the Constituent Assembly can determine the method whenever it feels like it without any great delay. It need not at all have a complicated procedure for that.

8. This has the additional advantage of making it easier for the President of India to function in this matter, as well as for any step to be taken which might appear necessary a little later. In any event this appears to be the normal procedure for the first choice by a special body like the Constituent Assembly.

9. Coming to the main proposal about the Headship of the State, I would suggest that the identical language used in the agreement should be used here also. Any change in that gives the appearance of departing from that agreement. I would suggest, therefore, that the main body of the resolution should consist of the four sub-heads which were agreed upon in that very language. Another sub-head should be added after the fourth 'that the Head of the State should be designated as the Sadar-i-Riyasat.'

10. Further sub-heads might be added, as indicated above, relating to emoluments and other matters which should be prescribed in the constitution, and until these are so prescribed, shall be set out in the rules to be framed for the purpose by the Constituent Assembly later.

11. Para 3 of the resolution, relating to the Head of the State exercising such powers and performing such functions etc., might remain as it is.

12. Para 5, dealing with gross misconduct, should be left out. It is totally unnecessary at this stage. It may come in the fuller constitution. It is always open to the State legislature to make the recommendation to the President for withdrawal of recognition. Putting this in here at this stage is not at all helpful, and indeed has the reverse effect.

13. Part 6, about a casual vacancy, also appears to me to be unneces-sary at this stage. We are dealing with a brief period. If by mischance any such contingency arises during this brief period and before the con-stitution is finalized, it can easily be dealt with in the manner suggested, even without making any special provision for it.

14. I think that some slight changes in this would be desirable to keep it in line with rest of the resolution. Thus, for instance, it may run as follows:—

Whereas this Constituent Assembly adopted the recommendations contained in the interim report of the Basic Principles Committee in regard to the office of the Head of the State;

And whereas by its resolution dated the 12th June 1952 this Assem-bly directed that the above-mentioned directions be implemented and for that purpose charged the Drafting Committee to submit appropri-ate proposals;

This Assembly having now considered the report of the Drafting Committee, resolves...

15. As I have said above, this is a very hurried note giving some first reactions for consideration.

2. Sheikh Abdullah Asks Constituent Assembly to Endorse the Delhi Agreement on 14 August 1952

Jammu and Kashmir Constituent Assembly Official Report,
Part I, Volume 1 (1951–5), p. 500

Hon'ble S.M. Abdullah: Sir, I beg to move:—

'That the statement made by me in this House on the 11th of August 1952 in regard to the agreement reached between the Government of India and the Kashmir Government be taken into consideration'.

Mr. Harbans Singh Azad: Sir, I second the motion.

[...]

Mr. Assadullah Mir: Sir, I beg to move the following amendment:[1]

That at the end of the motion the following words should be added:—

---

[1] *Jammu & Kashmir Constituent Assembly Official Report,* p. 507.

and having considered the same the House approved the statement and resolves that the fundamental rights of the citizens of Jammu and Kashmir should be framed by Constituent Assembly of the State and embodied in the Jammu and Kashmir Constitution'.

[...]

3. Sheikh Abdullah's Reply to the Debate on 19 August 1952

Jammu and Kashmir Constituent Assembly Official Report,
Part 1, Volume 1 (1951–5), pp. 571–89

Hon'ble Sheikh Moh'd Abdullah: Sir, the statement which I place before the House on 11th August has been under discussion for two days. I have tried to follow the argument of all those speakers who have expressed their views in this connection. Some of the Hon'ble Members have suggested certain amendments Mr. Abdul Gani Goni has put forward this amendment:—

That the words 'During the pleasure of the President' appearing in clause (ii) under 'Headship of the State' in the statement be deleted and be substituted by the words, as long as he commands the confidence of the Legislature of the State.

In this connection, perhaps, the Hon'ble Member apprehends that the expression 'during the pleasure of the President' means that when we have elected the Head of the State, the President has powers to extend his term of office, or, to remove him from the office, when he is no more considered to be worthy of the confidence. As far as this expression goes. I would like to inform the Hon'ble Member that when the Head of the State is to be elected and, as has been clearly admitted by the Government of India, when the Legislature is the only authorised body to elect him, it is quite clear that he can also be removed by the body electing him.

Regarding the Headship of the State:—

The Head of the State shall be the person recognised by the President of the Union on the recommendation of the Legislature of the State.

How is the Legislature to recommend him for recognition as Head of the State? It is clear that a panel of names would be presented and a vote will be taken, and the successful candidate would be recommended. It is a kind of constitutional propriety that the party choosing its head can remove him from that office if he violates the constitution, or if he proves himself to be unworthy of that honour. Being a part of India, it is essential for us, like the people of other States, to honour and respect the President in a manner befitting his dignity and office. Coming again to the phrase 'during the pleasure of the President', it is applicable with regard to the formation of Cabinets. Elections are held, various persons fight them and try to be elected, and then, the President asks the leader of the majority party to form the cabinet. He cannot ask any other party to do so. So far as Council of Ministers is concerned, the Indian Constitution lays down:—

75 (i) The Prime Minister shall be appointed by the President and the other Ministers shall be appointed by the President on the advice of the Prime Minister. (ii) The Minister shall hold office during the pleasure of the President.

As you see this is the constitutional language. These apprehensions which are being expressed in this House, were placed before the Government of India and were thoroughly discussed. I am narrating all this in order to give you an insight into the matters discussed there. As I have submitted earlier, these are the intricacies of the constitutional language. When the President is authorised to appoint Ministers of the Cabinet, he can appoint anybody to or remove somebody from that office. But, in actual practice, he adopts the procedure related earlier by me, i.e. he calls upon the leader of the majority party to form the Government. He does not ignore the majority party and ask the minority party to form the Cabinet. The President has also to act according to certain procedure. Therefore, as far as this issue is concerned, we have entered into an agreement on the line that:

That the Head of the State shall be the person recognised by the President of the Union on the recommendation of the Legislature of the State.

How is the Legislature to recommend? What rules are to be framed in this connection? All this is to be examined by the Legislature. Our relations with India are quite natural, and the President of India is our President as well. The nomination papers would be sent to him formally. But, the question arises, what is the procedure when the President does not grant his sanction to our recommendation, or when the President advises us to reconsider the same. In that case, if the Legislature stands firmly by its first decision and the president is still unwilling to grant his sanction, a part of the Federation would break loose and drift away. But, as long as it is intended to keep the Federation intact, such a contingency would not be allowed to arise. I hope that Mr. Abdul Gani Goni would withdraw his amendment in view of my above submissions.

Another important point raised by him is to what would be the implications of Sub-clause 4 of the Clause 61, Clause 39 and Clause 96, dealing with the removal of President and the Speaker. So far as the 'no-confidence' motion against the Speaker is concerned, it is contained in the Clause 21 of our rules. Regarding the rest of the matters, we can remove the Head of the State, elected by us, in case he enters into any conspiracy with the enemy or if he does not act according to our wishes. But the point is that we have not reached that stage as yet. We are, at present, framing the Constitution and we will keep appropriate provisions in it and see that the Constitution is not devoid of these. We are moving forward gradually and cannot decide at once about all these matters. Some friends have raised the issue that the Kashmir Constituent Assembly is framing the Constitution by parts. But, Sir, there are specific reasons for doing so. Hon'ble Members are quite aware of the conditions through which we are passing, and these circumstances compel us to frame the Constitution by parts. We are taking up all the important issues one by one to avoid any hindrance in the path of our progress. Hon'ble Mr. Goni has drawn our attention to the procedure to be followed in case of non-availability of the Head of the State of our choice. I would like to say that the point is to be decided by the Constituent Assembly, after approving the agreement. We have taken up the task of framing the Constitution. Head of the State would be elected by us under the provisions of the Constitution. We shall make provision in the Constitution for the removal of the Head of the State by the representatives of the State, if he prove himself incompetent to retain the office, or if he goes against the provisions of the Constitution, or, if he enters into a conspiracy with our enemies. I would therefore express a hope that Hon'ble Mr. Goni would not press his amendment.

The second amendment, which comes from Mr. Ghulam Resool says:—

That in para 'Emergency Powers' the words at the end of the Ist para. 'But in regard to internal disturbance at the request or with the concurrence of the Government of the State' be substituted by the Words. But Section 352 of the Constitution of India may apply at the request or with the concurrence of the Jammu and Kashmir State.

This amendment has been dealt with at length by my colleague, Hon'ble Mr. Dogra. So far as we are concerned, we have acceded to the Union in full regarding Defence which is now the responsibility of the Centre. Regarding Section 352, we have declared that the President of the Union can apply this section only in the following two cases, i.e. danger of war or external aggression. But he cannot apply it in case of internal disturbances. Much has been said in this point and Mr. Ayyanger, while replying to the critics in the Council of the State, said:

There was nothing to prevent Parliament from making a low under Item No. 1 of the Union List which covered an aspect of defence and enabled the Centre to take a some what similar action when the peace or security of India was threatened by some disturbance inside the State.

The critics there had to be satisfied. An agreement has been reached between the representatives of the State and the Indian Union. We told them that Kashmir has acceded to India in the matter of Defence and that they can take necessary steps concerning this under Schedule 7 Item 1, and that there was no need of the application of section 352. In case of some specific happenings, the President can assume the powers for sometime and use them, but he has to get the sanction of the Parliament within two months of doing so. I would like to inform the Hon'ble Members that our discussions took place in a friendly atmosphere. As Hon'ble members know, discussions between two parties can take place in two ways only, firstly when the parties try to find excuse to avoid a settlement, and secondly when both the parties earnestly wish to come closer to each other. We, as well as our learned friends from India, wished to strengthen and smoothen our relations. They never wished that Kashmir should drift away from India and we never wished to severe our relations with India. Both the parties wished that the ties binding us should become stronger and lasting. When this be the spirit, some agreement on give and take basis is bound to be arrived at. Then there remains no need of stressing one's point of view. The basic point then is to come to an agreement. It is possible that we would not take the proper precautionary measures in case of a threat of war to India? Similarly India would help us in case of an invasion on Kashmir. We can not say, at that time, that we will think about it, make legislations, etc. etc. because it would be a lengthy procedure whereas, during a war every part of the country must be alert. There is no difference in that case among the different parts of the federation whether it be Bengal, the Punjab or Madras. At such critical times it is never thought as to how can one part of the country be saved if another is invaded, or how to save Kashmir if an attack on Madras has been made. Considering all these matters and in view of the fact the defence is in the hands of the Centre, we did not raise any objection as regards the application of Section 352. We limited its scope to the case of external aggression and threat of war and thus did not allow it to extend to the internal disturbances.

So far as internal disturbances are concerned we stated clearly that without our request or concurrence, this clause cannot be applied to us. They assured us, on the other hand, that they never meant that the President should take over the powers in case a disturbance of minor nature, what that really meant was that the President can apply the Emergency powers in case of a disturbance which tends to threaten the security and peace of the rest of the country. We submitted that we were not ignorant of all this and knew that the President would not exercise Emergency Powers in the case of a fight between two persons. But the point was that our agreeing to this clause would have given an excuse for creating disturbances to certain nefarious elements which include not only some friends from Jammu, but also Hindu, Muslim and Sikh friends from other parts of the State. If we once give way, these people would get an encouragement and would become a permanent source of menace to us, and so we expressed our unwillingness to agree to it. The Union President, therefore, cannot use Emergency Powers without the concurrence of the State Government. But, in the matters of External Aggression, we will be treated like the rest of India. I hope that the mover of the amendment, Mr. Ghulam Rasool, will withdraw the same in the light of the above observation. The fourth amendment stands in the name of Mr. Mir and reads:—

That at the end of the motion the following words should be added:

And having considered the same the House approves the Statement and resolves that the Fundamental Rights of the citizens of Jammu and Kashmir should be framed by the Constituent Assembly of the State and embodied in the Jammu and Kashmir Constitution.

In this connection I would like to inform my Hon'ble friend that so far as Fundamental Rights are concerned, a committee has been formed in the Constituent Assembly. This committee would present its report shortly and would recommend therein the Fundamental Rights to be enjoyed by the people of the State. Basically our Indian friends would like to have the Indian Constitution applied to our State in full, but we, on the other hand, are of the opinion that the fundamental principles under which Kashmir has acceded to India should not be interfered with while the efforts are being made to strengthen this relationship. We were asked as about the nature of fundamental rights in the State when there is no freedom of speech and the jails are packed with the political prisoners. Propagandists might say whatever they like, but the reality is that in spite of the fact that the country is in a state of war very few people are behind the prison bars. So much so that our Hon'ble Deputy Prime Minister who is in charge of the portfolio of Home Affairs informs us that there is only one political prisoner at present. In spite of all this, it is being alleged that the Government here is being run by the use of force and that this a Fascist Government. But when the State has been passing through warlike conditions for the last five years and the enemy has been sparing no pains to create internal disturbance, is it not creditable that there should be only one political prisoner behind the bars? This clearly shows that despite the fact that there are no specific Fundamental Rights, our people are enjoying more rights than the people of Pakistan or India.

[…]

It is clear that the citizens have got certain obligations towards the State, i.e. when they get certain rights from the State they have to fulfil certain duties towards her. But this is the work of the Committee formed by the Constituent Assembly and the Committee is bound to pay due regard to all these matters. But one thing must be kept in view, namely, that the fundamental rights of the State should not clash with the Fundamental Rights granted under the Indian Constitution by the Indian Government to the people of India. This question was also discussed and we assured them that we will try and see, that they are not contradictory. But we also told them that it was not necessary that we should frame the same Fundamental Rights which have been framed by them because there is a large difference between our respective Social Order. Our Social orders has got certain peculiar characteristics which can be retained only if we remain with India. There is no chance for the development of our social order, if we join Pakistan where feudal order obtains to the present day. Regarding Fundamental rights we have said:—

That the Fundamental Right which are contained in the Constitution of India could not be conferred on the People of Jammu and Kashmir State in their entirety taking into account the economic, social and political character of our movement as enunciated in the New Kashmir Plan. The need for providing suitable modifications, amendments and exceptions as the case may be in the Fundamental Rights Chapter of the Indian Constitution in order to harmonize those provisions with the pattern of our Principles was admitted.

It has also given rise to certain doubts and it is being said that the word 'confer' indicates that the citizenship rights would be bestowed on us by the centre. But I would like to make it clear that these are our basic rights and that there is no question of our receiving them from the Centre. It is unfortunate that I have not studied law and am not very much conversant with the legal terms. Legal terminology, however, was not the predominant factor in our talks and we were repeatedly assured that there was no legal snag in our discussions. They wanted only to understand our broad intentions, on which we are going to base our Constitution. The word 'confer' should not cause much worry to my Hon'ble friend. It is impossible that we would get our rights from the

Centre. Had it been so, it would have been useless to form Constituent Assembly and spend so much money. I affirm that the intentions were not as interpreted by my Hon'ble friend. It is, however, essential for the Fundamental Rights Committee to keep an eye on the Fundamental Rights in India and the other countries of the world, and then submit its recommendations to the House regarding the definition of Fundamental Rights and the duties of the people. It would also recommend whether the Fundamental Rights so framed are to be considered as a part of the Constitution of the State or of the Indian Union. The Fundamental Rights Committee has only to submit its considered opinion before the House and it would be for the House to take the final decision. Another issue, to which we have agreed is that of the Supreme Court.

It was agreed that the Supreme Court should have original jurisdiction in respect of disputes mentioned in Article 131 of the Constitution of India. Its was further agreed that the Supreme Court should have jurisdiction in regard to Fundamental Rights which are agreed to by the State.

As I have already stated, the Assembly has to decide whether the Chapter on the Fundamental Rights should form a part of Indian or the State Constitution. If it forms a part of the former then certain amendments will have to be made therein. We have got no objection to the Supreme Court's interpreting these rights but first we must frame these Fundamental Rights. The Fundamental Rights Committee has to make its recommendations after careful and thorough deliberations, as we have not taken any decision about it and as the issue is undecided as yet, I hope, that Mr. Assad Ullah Mir will not press his amendment.

Another amendment is that of S. Kulbir Singh. I accept it. This amendment has been supported by S. Harbans Singh Azad, Mr. Mubarak Shah, Mr. Chuni Lal and S. Kulbir Singh and it reads as follows:—

At the end of the motion the following be added:—

And having considered the same this House approves all the steps taken so far in the matter as indicated in the statement.

And further places on record its deep appreciation of the spirit in which the matters were discussed and agreed conclusions arrived at.

I have submitted my views regarding the statement and the amendments proposed thereto. The second part of my speech, I would deal with the remarks made by the Hon'ble Members while expressing their views on this Statement. S. Kulbir Singh drew our attention (if I remember rightly) in his speech to the Yuvraj's statement of 13th August, 1952. I do not wish to say anything about this statement which related to an interview. It was his look-out to give a statement to the press and he could understand fully its implications. I would, however, like to inform the House that we are not bound so far as constitution goes to select some particular person for the Headship of the State. But we are always of the opinion that we are fighting against a principle and not against any particular person or class. I suggested to the House, on the basis of my own personal experience, to bestow this honour on Yuvraj, but, in case the House does not consider him to be the right man for this honour it is unnecessary to act upon my suggestion. I would like to point out to a friend of mine who said that it is likely that we may remove the Yuvraj afterwards if we appoint him our Head for 5 years only that we cannot mould the public opinion. If, basically, Yuvraj is so fortunate as to win the favour of the Legislature and the people of all castes and creeds by dealing justly with everybody the masses would naturally adore him. Yuvraj Karan Singh's future is in his own hands and we cannot make any prediction about the principles which he is going to follow in future. But naturally he cannot win the confidence of the people, if he patronizes only a section of people, ignoring all others. Sheikh Abdullah possesses only one vote and so does every man in the street. Might is right, represents a principle of the by-gone days, but now the conditions have changed. The Government are formed and run on the basis of votes. The Government used to be run by force but now the times are not the same. It is possible for the Yuvraj to come to power again only if he breaks up with the reactionary elements and he can be popular with the masses only, if he understands clearly that his happiness and sorrow are linked up with the happiness and sorrow of the common-man. But, if he is under the delusion that he can retain his office with the help of his few supporters, he is mistaken. He can well understand the effect of the statement issued by him. But he can allow himself to be misguided at this stage only at the cost of his future. It is, however, not our function to worry about it, and all that I have submitted was said in a friendly spirit only.

Mr. Ram Piara Saraf remarked in his speech as to how was it that the Maharaja's Flag a symbol of autocratic rule, is still being hosted in Jammu while the people's Flag is flying in Kashmir. He said it give rise to certain misunderstandings. I submit that although we fought against the autocratic rule and suffered many hardships, we never insulted the Flag. As is known to House, efforts were made to crush down our movement by using baseless and shameful tactics but we never insulted the flag of the country because we did not like to stop to such means and baseless methods. The flag adopted by the Assembly would be for the whole of the State, but the decision regarding the Constitutional Head of the State is yet to be taken and till then the autocracy cannot be taken as abolished constitutionally. This interim report of the Basic Principles Committee would be coming in an official form before the House in a day or two and we will elect the Head of the State under its provisions. This move will establish a new order by putting an end to the old one. We do not lay much stress on minor matters as they cannot harm us in any way. We are following the constitutional path and want this new flag to be hoisted in places, where previously, the National Conference Flag was flown. It is our earnest desire that there should be only one flag for the whole of the State. Our attention was drawn to another issue referred to by Mr. Baigra also about the people who move about on either sides of the ceasefire line. I would request the Hon'ble Member to deal very carefully with these controversial matters. We should not align ourselves with world politics. We have to solve the problem of our own State … an issue which has become very complicated at present. It is the U.N. observers who cross the ceasefire line. Their duty, primarily, is to keep watch over the ceasefire line, and to settle any disputes connected therewith. It is altogether a different matter whether their decisions are based on justice and fairplay or not. Besides, the present day world is divided into two major groups, and we have to move very cautiously to avoid getting ourselves involved, lest we should be crushed. Nothing in our speeches should give any indication of partisanship. We want to live honourably. After all what power do we wield to interfere in world politics. We are already surrounded by so many dangers and should avoid further addition to our worries. We must tell the rest of the world that we need their help.

It is the basic policy of our Prime Minister to save the country from being a party in any war, because innumerable calamities would befall us if we get entangled in one. Hence we must try to create friendly relations with all other countries and try to save the world peace which is in the interests of our own country as well. Since our principle is the same as that of the Prime Minister of India it is essential that we do not give expression to any idea which may lead to confusion. I assure you, as Prime Minister, that I would not allow the Jammu and Kashmir State to align itself with either of the power blocks of the world and would follow the policy laid down by the Prime Minister of India. Some of our friends, instead or removing the old ones want to create more difficulties for us and thus hinder progress. In this speech Hon'ble Mr. Beg has remarked that Kashmir has acquired a special position.

[...]

I would quote from the instrument of accession i.e. the agreement which took place between India and Kashmir. I do not want to read out the whole of it but would only submit the following:—

'I hereby accede to the Dominion of India subject to the purposes of the Dominion Constitution and shall be always subject to the terms thereof'.

That is, I accede and do not want to go beyond that. And then again:—'I accept the matter specified in the schedule hereto ... and such other matter to which the Dominion Legislature may make laws for the state'.

The schedule is clear about everything and we are not responsible for the subsequent items and we are within our rights to refuse to accept them. Now under this schedule if any new item besides those contained in the instrument of accession crops up which make a mutual agreement. For such contingency it is provided:—

'Then any such agreement shall be deemed to form part of this instrument and shall be constituted to have effect accordingly'.

The terms of this instrument of ours shall not be varied by any amendment of the Act or of the Independence Act of 1947 unless such amendment is accepted by an instrument supplemented to this Instrument.

Since now we constitute the Government here, hence nothing can apply to us against our wishes or concurrence.

Nothing in this instrument shall be deemed to commit this House in any way in acceptance of any future constitution or form a party in any discussion with the Government of India under any such future constitution.

Now this is the basis of our relationship with the Government of India. Afterwards, when the Constitution of India was framed all the princes signed it. Sardar Patel convinced the Rulers that the Indian Constitution was their own Constitution, and persuaded them to agree to its application in their States. Some of the princes agreed to it and no untoward incident took place in any State whether it was Baroda, Hyderabad or Mysore. But we have nothing to do with them. They accepted the application of the Indian Constitution and that is all that can be said about it. But when we were asked about it, we told them that we could not agree to it in view of the special circumstances prevailing in Kashmir. The question was what position should Kashmir have in the Indian Constitution. It was evident that of all the States in India and Pakistan, the State of Kashmir was the only State which though having a Muslim majority preferred to join India and did not fall prey to communal frenzy. We also felt that Kashmir would not make such progress if it accedes to Pakistan by whom it would always be subjected to undue pressure.

As against this, we can make progress if we remain with India and thus the aspirations of the people of this State would be fulfilled. That is why we have acceded in three subjects only and kept the rest in our own hands. This issue was also discussed and it was agreed that Kashmir should not be forced against her wishes. The position, that with the exception of three subjects mentioned above we were independent in all matters, has been conceded in section 370 and others of the Indian Constitution and autonomy has been preserved. Now, when the Constituent Assembly has successfully arranged these matters with the Government of India, some friends are raising objections as to why Kashmir has been given a 'privileged position', but I fail to understand why these people who framed the Constitution, are creating fuss now. It is, however, entirely a different matter if the people of India want to have it changed, but I would like to ask Dr. S.P. Mukerjee (although I have a great respect for him, why did he not think of these matters at the time when he was one of the members of Government of India at the time of framing of Constitution. After all, one should have some trust. We have given assurance to the public of this country that it is only India which is free from the course of feudalism, secular in its outlook and where our dreams and aspirations can be realized. It is true that we have a great love for our religion but the States are not based on religions but on economic considerations. Therefore, we declared that out interests would be safe with India. But, if they want to cut at the very root of this assurance how can you keep Kashmir with India. It is true that nothing is static in this world and that everything is dynamic. Circumstances now are not the same as they were in 1947, and they would be different tomorrow. So, the representatives of this country or the Legislature may hand over some other matters to the Centre but it certainly cannot be effected by compulsion. Discussion took place in the light of all these considerations and they expressed their inclination to appreciate broad principles. Neither myself, nor the members of the delegation, had any authority to frame the Constitution. This authority rests with the House. They, however, wanted to understand our outlook with reference to our position. I have put forward this point of view in my statement and Mr. Beg has also shed sufficient light on it. All the residuary powers, excepting in three subjects, are in our hands; in fact, it is up to us whether we entrust, these matters to the centre or not. Under the provisions of International Agreement we can severe our relations with India even today if we wish to do so. This right is given to out State and not others. All this rests with India and we can say that we do not want to remain with India. It is up to us and we can declare that we want to go out of the Indian Union. There are provisions dealing with this aspect. The Hon'ble Members are aware that the Prime Minister of India has repeatedly said that although it would be painful to him if Kashmir does not want to remain with India, but it depends on the will of the people of this country. Those who are still trying to create this confusion seem to forget the basic principles under which we have acceded to India.

[...]

Regarding Head of the State, it was desired that the Head should be an elected one, and after his election, his name must be recommended for recognition to the Union President. The term of the office of the Head of the State should not exceed 5 years.

[...]

With these words I express my thanks to those who spoke in support of my motion, and further hope that Mr. Ghulam Rasool and Mr. Abdul Ghani would withdraw their amendments in view of my explanatory speech. I accept the amendment put forward by S. Kulbir Singh.

Hon'ble President: First of all, I place before you this resolution along with the amendment moved by S. Kulbir Singh which reads as follows:—

At the end of the motion the following be added:—

And having considered the same this House approves all the steps taken so far in the matter is indicated in the statement.

And further place on record its deep appreciations of the spirit in which the matters were discussed and agreed conclusions arrived at.

Now I put this amendment, along with the original resolution, to the House.

Mr. M.A. Beg: With your permission, Sir, may I understand that if this motion is put to vote along with the amendment moved by S. Kulbir Singh and if the motion is carried, all the other amendments will drop?

Hon'ble President: I shall put this amendment under Rule 32 clause (5) of the Rules of Business and I think if this motion is carried then automatically other amendments will drop.

Mr. Ghulam Rasool: Sir, I submit that before this statement.

Hon'ble President: I refer the Hon'ble Member to Rule 32 Clause (5) of the Rules of Business and Procedure and I think that will make the position clear.

Mr. Assadullah Mir: Sir, my submission is that all the amendments to the statement may be read out to the House and it would be better if the Movers of these amendments withdraw them before they are put to the House.

Hon'ble President: Now I will read Rule 32 Clause (5) of the Rules of Business and Procedure:—

'The Chairman may put amendments to the vote in any order he may choose.'

I think that the sense of the House is that the amendment in the name of S. Kulbir Singh may now be put to the vote.

Note: The motion along with the amendment of S. Kulbir Singh was put and passed unanimously. (Cheers)

* Hon'ble Bakshi Ghulam Moh'd.: Sir, have all other amendments proposed by other Hon'ble Members been dropped?

* Hon'ble President: Yes, all other amendments drop automatically.

4. The Drafting Committee's Report and the Assembly's Resolution on the Head of State, 20 August 1952

Jammu and Kashmir Constituent Assembly Official Report,
Part I, Volume 1 (1951–5), pp. 590–600

Hon'ble M.A. Beg: President, Sir, I and the Drafting Committee were directed by a resolution passed by this House on the 12th of June, 1952, to work out appropriate proposals in order to implement the resolution of this House regarding the termination of hereditary rulership in the State. I rise today. Sir, to present the report of that Committee for the consideration of this House.

Report

This Assembly unanimously adopted the recommendations contained in the Interim Report of the Basic Principles Committee with regard to the future Headship of the State on the 12th June, 1952, and directed the Drafting Committee to place within a period of one month. As it was necessary to have corresponding adjustments made in the Indian Constitution, it became essential to have consultations with the Government of India on this subject. Therefore, a Delegation headed by the Undersigned, the Chairman of the Drafting Committee, was deputed to Delhi for the purpose.

Drafting the course of consultations certain other matters cropped up besides the question of the future Headship of the State. All these matters and agreements arrived at between the Government of India and the representatives of the Kashmir Government have been placed before this House in a statement made by the Leader of the House and have been approved by the Assembly.

It was on account of these consultations at Delhi that the Drafting Committee could not submit its proposals within the period prescribed in the above mentioned resolution of this Assembly, and the Chairman requested you, Sir, for extension of the time limit in order to complete the task assigned to the Drafting Committee. I am extremely grateful to you, Sir, that you very kindly agreed to put my request before the House.

Accordingly, I now seek the permission to present this report with the resolution and the schedule attached to it.

Date   M.A. Beg
    19th August, 1952 (Sd.) All members of the Drafting Committee.

Resolution

Whereas this Assembly adopted the recommendations contained in the Interim Report of the Basic Principles Committee presented on the 10th of June, 1952.

And whereas by its resolution, dated the 12th June, 1952, this Assembly directed that the recommendations so adopted be implemented and for that purpose charged the Drafting Committee to submit appropriate proposals;

Now, therefore, in pursuance of the resolution dated the 12th June, 1952, and having considered the report of the Drafting Committee, this Assembly resolves:—

   1. (i) that the Head of the State shall be the person recognised
          by the President of the Union on the recommendations of the
          Legislative Assembly of the State;
       (ii) he shall hold office during the pleasure of the President;
       (iii) he may, by writing his hand, addressed to the President, resign
          his office;

(iv) subject to the foregoing provisions, the Head of the State shall hold office for a term of five years from the date he enters upon his office:

Provided that he shall, notwithstanding the expiration of his term, continue to hold the office until his successor enters upon his office;

2. that the recommendation of Legislative Assembly of the State in respect of the recognition of the Head of the State specified in sub-para (i) of paragraph 1, shall be made by election;

3. that the method of election to, qualifications for and all other matters pertaining to the office of the Head of the State shall be prescribed, in the Constitution, and until these are so prescribed, shall be as set out in the rules contained in the schedule annexed to this resolution;

4. that the Head of the State shall be designated as the Sadar-i-Riyasat;

5. that the Sadar-i-Riyasat shall be entitled to such emoluments, allowances and privileges as may be prescribed in the Constitution and pending the framing of the Constitution, to such emoluments, allowances and privileges as may be decided by this Assembly by separate resolution;

6. that the Sadar-i-Riyasat shall exercise such powers and perform such functions as may be prescribed in the Constitution to be framed by this Constituent Assembly, and until such Constitution is framed, he shall exercise such powers and perform such functions as have hitherto been exercised by His Highness under the Jammu and Kashmir Constitution Act, 1996, as amended by Act No. XVII of 2008.

7. that in the event of the occurrence of a casual vacancy in the office of the Sadar-i-Riyasat by reason of his death, resignation or otherwise, the powers and functions exercisable by the Sadar-i-Riyasat shall until the assumption of office by the newly elected Sadar-i-Riyasat in accordance with the procedure laid down in this resolution, be exercised and performed by the person recommended by the State Government for recognition as Officiating Sadar-i-Riyasat to the President of India; and

8. that this Assembly shall in due course provide a suitable remedy in respect of violation of the Constitution or gross misconduct by the person for the time being holding the office of the Sadar-i-Riyasat.

This Assembly further resolves:—

That the Prime Minister of Jammu and Kashmir State is authorised to communicate a copy of this resolution to 'the Government of India for favour of appropriate action to enable its being given effect to'.

Schedule (Para 3)

1. Qualifications:—(1) No person shall be eligible for election to the office of the Sadar-i-Riyasat, unless he:—
   (a) is a State Subject of Class I as defined in the State Subject Definition Notification No. I-L/84 dated 20th April, 1927;
   (b) has completed the age of 21 years, and
   (c) is not subject to any of the disqualifications specified in rule 4 of the Jammu and Kashmir Constituent Assembly Election (Part 1) Rulers, 2008, for being chosen as a member of the Constituent Assembly.

(2) A person shall not be eligible for election as the Sadar-i-Riyasat if he holds any office of profit under the Government or under any local or other authority subject to the control of the Government.

2. The Sadar-i-Riyasat shall not be a member of the Legislative Assembly of the State, or if a member of the Legislative Assembly of the State, he shall be deemed to have vacated his seat in the House on the date he enters upon his office as the Sadar-i-Riyasat.

3. The Sadar-i-Riyasat shall hold no other office of profit.

4. Method of Election:—(1) When election to the office of the Sadar-i-Riyasat becomes necessary, the Speaker of the State Legislative Assembly shall fix time and date for the holding of the election and shall cause a notice thereof to be sent to every member.

(2) At any time before noon on the date preceding the date so fixed, any member of the State Legislative Assembly may nominate another person for election by delivering to the Speaker or any officer authorised by the Speaker in this behalf, a nomination paper in the form prescribed in the annexure to this schedule signed by himself as proposer and by another member as seconder.

(3) Any person who has been so nominated may withdraw his candidature in writing addressed to the Speaker at any time before the Assembly proceeds to hold the election.

(4) At the time fixed for election under sub-clause (I), the Speaker or in his absence the person presiding shall read out to the Assembly the name of the persons who have been duly nominated and have not withdrawn their candidature together with those of their proposers and seconders and, if there is only one such candidate, shall declare him to be duly elected. If there is more than one such candidate the Assembly shall proceed to elect the Sadar-i-Riyasat by ballot.

(5) Where there are only two candidates for election, the candidate who obtains at the ballot the larger number of votes shall be declared elected. If they obtain an equal number of votes, the Speaker or in his absence the person presiding shall exercise his casting vote and the person in whose favour such vote is cast shall be declared elected.

(6) Where more than two candidates have been nominated and at the first ballot no candidate obtains more votes than the aggregate votes obtained by the other candidates, the candidate who has obtained the smallest number of votes shall be excluded from the election, and balloting shall proceed, the candidate obtaining the smallest number of votes at each ballot being excluded from the election, until one candidate obtains more votes than the remaining candidates, or than the aggregate votes of the remaining candidates, as the case may be, and such candidate shall be declared elected.

(7) Where at any ballot any of three or more candidates obtain an equal number of votes and one of them has to be excluded from the election under sub-clause (6), the determination as between the candidates whose votes are equal of the candidate who is to be excluded shall be by the casting vote of the Speaker or in his absence of the person presiding.

5. The Prime Minister of the State shall communicate the name of the person duly elected by the Assembly as the Sadar-i-Riyasat to the President of India for being recognized as the Sadar-i-Riyasat.

6. Oath.—The Sadar-i-Riyasat shall, before entering upon his office, make and subscribe in the presence of Chief Justice of the State High

Court or in his absence any Judge of the High Court available an oath or affirmation in the following form, namely:—

I, A.B., swear in the name of God/Solemnly affirm that I will faithfully execute the office of the Sadar-i-Riyasat, Jammu Wa Kashmir and will to the best of my ability preserve, protect and defend the Constitution of the State as by law established and that I will devote myself to the Service and well-being of the people of the State.

[...]

On 21 August 1952

Hon'ble President: Hon'ble member can make this suggestion after the consideration motion. The question is that the resolution enclosed with the report of the Drafting Committee prepared in pursuance of the resolution of the Constituent Assembly dated the 10th June, 1952 regarding the implementations of the recommendations contained in the Interim Report of the Basic Principles Committee be taken into consideration.

Note: The motion was put to the House and adopted unanimously.

21 August 1952

Hon'ble President: The question is that the discussion should be closed.

Note: The closure motion was unanimously agreed to by the House.

Hon'ble President:— Hon'ble Sheikh Mohammad Abdullah.

* Hon'ble Sheikh Mohammad Abdullah: Sir, the report placed before the House by the Drafting Committee is so exhaustive that it does not require any further elucidation. I would, however, like to draw the attention of the House to the principle, which has always been before us that if it the people alone who have the right to decide the fate of this country (Cheers). They have fought for the last 21 years and we have always endeavoured that the last word, in every matter, should remain with the people. The system which was thrust upon us gave all the powers to one person. Section 5 of the Constitution, under which we were being governed, lays down that:—

Notwithstanding anything contained in this Act, or any other Act, all the powers, Legislative, Executive and Judicial in relation to the State and its Government, are hereby declared to be and to have always been inherent in and possessed and retained by His Highness and nothing contained in this Order or any other Act shall effect or deemed to have effected the right and prerogative of His Highness to make laws, issue proclamations, orders and ordinances by virtue of this inherent authority.

This was the law under the provision of which one autocratic person controlled the destiny of 40 lac people of the State. The people of this country have been trying for the last 21 years to get rid of these chains. Hence, the House approved, after great deliberations, the recommendations contained in the report put forward by the Basic Principles Committee in the last session of this Constituent Assembly. The House directed the Drafting Committee to present the suitable proposals, in this connection, before it. The proposals put forward now by the Drafting Committee are, as I have already stated, so detailed as not to require any further elucidation.

[...]

As I explained yesterday that, having acceded to India, there is a legal link between Kashmir and 'India' which is explained in Article 370 of the Indian Constitution. This can be compared to a link of chain joining its different parts. I have nothing more to say about it as detailed speeches have already been delivered on this point. I would, however, like to repudiate a statement that the Maharaja served as a binding link between the different units of the State, and say that this is no more or less than a propaganda stunt on the part of enemy. Since, unfortunately, some simple-minded friends have been led away by it, the National Conference must at once take some action. The Maharaja, about whom it is being said that he served as a connecting link between different parts of the State, is none else than the person who helped the English to retain their hold on India for 150 years, and, further, who exploited the 40 lacs people of this State for centuries.

It is possible that this old system, like the English who divided India on the eve of their departure might give impetus to this storm. As is known to all, the English created such circumstances at the last movement which brought about the division of the sub-continent. Similarly it is to be feared that the dying system may try to bring about the partition of the State. I do not deny the possibilities of such a happening. The best counter-move in this connection lies in the unity of the people of this State i.e., residents of the whole of Jammu, Kashmir and Ladakh should collectively deliver such a below to these efforts of his lying-at-death-bed order that they are finished for ever, saving the country from further miseries. The proposal presented by me has received support from every quarter and I would, therefore, appeal for its unanimous adoption.

* Hon'ble President: I would place before the House the resolution along with the amendments admitted by the House and accepted by the Mover. The first amendment moved by Mr. Mubarik Shah is:—

(A) 'that sub-clause (2) clause 1 may be deleted and the figure (1) within the brackets be omitted.'

(B) 'that in sub-clause (b) of clause 1 so amended the words "on the data of filing the nomination paper" be added after the words "21 years".'

The second amendment accepted by the mover comes from Hakim Habib Ullah, and reads:—

'that in sub-clause (i) of para I of the resolution appended to the report of the Drafting Committee for the words "President of Union the words", "President of India" may be substituted.'

(The motion was adopted).

The amendments having been disposed of, I would now put the Resolution as amended by the House to the vote of the Assembly.

Note: The resolution as amended by the House was put to the House and adopted unanimously amidst prolonged cheers.

[...]

5. Nehru's Note for Sheikh Abdullah Written at Sonamarg, Kashmir, on 25 August 1952

I am writing this note to convey to you my own basic views about the situation in Kashmir. During the last five years or so, I have naturally given a great deal of thought to the various factors governing this situation—military, political, economic and others. I have tried to make my approach as objective as possible. Naturally, to some extent, I am influenced by my own personal feelings and attachment to Kashmir. Thus it may be said that I have two approaches—that of the Prime Minister of India and the personal one. As a matter of fact, however, I have not found any conflict between those two. Some difficulties have arisen occasionally in my mind, because I was not sure if my approach, personal or official, was completely in line with your approach. So far as I was concerned, you represented to me what the people of Kashmir wanted to be done, and as that was a paramount consideration for me, in the ultimate analysis I would accept that in preference to my own views. As a rule, there was no such conflict or difficulty.

2. My own view has been clear for the last four years or so and, in spite of changing circumstances, I have found no reason to alter it basically. Because of this, I have not been worried much on account of new developments. Being clear in my mind as to what should be done, it did not matter much to me what Pakistan did or what the United Nations might do. I was, however, sometimes a little surprised, and somewhat worried, to find that the leaders of Kashmir were not so clear in their minds about the present or the future and were, therefore, worrying a great deal. To give an instance, the present talks with Dr. Graham in Geneva do not appear to me to have any great importance. They do not alter my appraisal of the situation, or what we should do about it. I find, however, that much greater importance is attached to these Graham talks in Geneva, here in Kashmir, and there is some apprehension also about their result.

[...]

4. After some experience of the UN, I came to the conclusion that nothing substantial could be expected from it. It was clear that we would not give in on any basic point, whatever the UN might say. It seemed also clear that Pakistan would not simply walk out and revert to the *status quo ante*-war. Thus, towards the end of 1948 it seemed to me that there were only two possibilities open to us: (1) continuation of the war in a limited way; (2) some kind of a settlement on the basis of the then existing military situation.

5. I have not mentioned the plebiscite, because it became clear to me then that we would never get the conditions which were necessary for a

plebiscite.[1] Neither side would give in on this vital issue, and so I ruled out the plebiscite for all practical purposes.

6. ... Even that war, apart from foreign intervention, would not be a very easy or quick one. We had definite superiority from the military and industrial points of view, but that superiority was not so great as to overwhelm the enemy. And then, there was always the question of what foreign powers might do either in interfering or in aiding Pakistan in other ways.

7. The result of all this thought, and my own powerful inclination to avoid war on a big scale which brought disaster in its train, whatever the result, led me to certain definite conclusions towards the end of 1948. These conclusions were that the only possible way of putting an end to this conflict was by accepting, more or less, the *status quo* then existing. We were not prepared to give up any territory we possessed to Pakistan. But we might, for the sake of peace and a settlement, agree to their holding what they then had. I was doubtful if Pakistan would accept this. If not, then we continued where we were.

8. This conclusion was not a very pleasant one to me, but logically I could not help arriving at it. When I met Attlee and Bevin and Liaquat Ali Khan in London in the last quarter of 1948, I mentioned this briefly to them saying that it was entirely a personal suggestion because of my desire to end this conflict. I was not at all sure how far my own Government, or the Kashmir Government, would agree to it, because they felt strongly on this question of Pakistan aggression. Liaquat Ali Khan refused to consider this matter on this basis and there it ended.

9. At the end of 1948 we agreed to a ceasefire. I think it was a right move, but the question was not properly approached. We could have got the ceasefire on a somewhat better line if we had given more thought to it. However, that is a past mistake.

10. Since then, we have had the ceasefire, and all kinds of talks with the UN people have gone on without much result. Throughout this

[1] On the basis of the proposals of the United Nations Commission for India and Pakistan of 13 August 1948 and 5 January 1949, the future of Kashmir was to be decided by a plebiscite under the UN auspices. But the plebiscite was to be held when Pakistan and India had withdrawn their troops from the State territory.

period, my old conviction has taken root in my mind that the only feasible solution, short of resumption of war, was the acceptance of the *status quo*, more or less. War, I ruled out for a variety of reasons, unless it was thrust upon us by Pakistan.

[...]

13. As Prime Minister of India, I have to look ahead and consider the basic national interest of India. It is my duty to guard that interest. That interest fits in with ideas of world peace and the avoidance of war whether in the world or with Pakistan. But, of course, that does not mean that we should not be prepared for any contingency. That interest itself demands full preparation for war or peaceful effort. Fortunately, we have no troubles with any of our neighbours, or, for the matter of that, with any country in the world. Nor are we afraid of any country, however big it may be, invading India or compelling us by force to do something that we do not want to do. There is one present exception and that is Pakistan. We are superior to Pakistan in military and industrial power. But that superiority is not so great as to produce results quickly either in war or by fear of war. Therefore, our national interest demands that we should adopt a peaceful policy towards Pakistan and, at the same time, add to our strength. Strength ultimately comes not from the defence forces, but the industrial and economic background behind them. As we grow in strength, and we are likely to do so, Pakistan will feel less inclined to threaten or harass us, and a time will come when, through sheer force of circumstances, it will be in a mood to accept a settlement which we consider fair, whether in Kashmir or elsewhere. The only danger is that the Government of Pakistan, or some military clique there, might, in sheer desperation, launch on an adventure. That danger has to be faced and prepared for. Otherwise, our national interest demands that we should adopt a firm but non-provocative attitude towards Pakistan, and build up our economic strength, keeping our defence forces in good condition for any possibility. The world situation also demands that we should follow this policy.

14. What is the position of Jammu and Kashmir State *vis-à-vis* India? Looking at it objectively, this State is of importance, both from the strategic and other points of view, to both India and Pakistan. Hence,

the conflict between the two. We are not prepared to give in to Pakistan on that issue, even though it means war. The utmost we can do is to give in so far as that area is concerned which is occupied by Pakistan. That itself, strategically, is a disadvantage to us. But we are prepared to accept that disadvantage for the sake of peace. If the whole of the State went to Pakistan, it would be a danger to the north of India, and there would be continuous tension between us and the party controlling that State. Thus, purely from the point of view of India's national interest, we cannot agree, unless circumstances force us, to see this part of Kashmir State go to Pakistan. There are no circumstances visible that can force us to do this. Pakistan cannot. The United Nations cannot override our wishes in this matter.

15. This is an objective statement from the point of view of India's national interest. There is another aspect which we have stressed, and which is important. This is the wishes of the people of Kashmir. If the people of Kashmir clearly and definitely wish to part company from India, there the matter ends, however we may dislike it or however disadvantageous it may be to India. But, as I have stated above, I see no chance or whatever of any proper plebiscite determining this question, because the plebiscite itself raises highly controversial issues in regard to the conditions governing it and all that. So, ruling out the plebiscite we have to accept the present leadership of Kashmir and the Constituent Assembly there as representing the will of the people of Kashmir. If the Constituent Assembly told India to get out of Kashmir, we would get out, because under no circumstances can we remain here against the expressed will of the people. As far as I know, the Constituent Assembly will not do such a thing and therefore, the question does not arise for me.

16. Speaking now for a moment purely as a Kashmiri, I think that it would be the ruin of Kashmir if Pakistan took possession of it. I need not dilate on this issue, but I am convinced of it.

[...]

19. In fact, Jammu and Kashmir have to hold together. If Jammu is separated, Kashmir goes. If Kashmir goes, Jammu's position becomes precarious and the conflict does not end. Statesmanship therefore requires that Jammu and Kashmir should hold together. The people of

Jammu, therefore, should be made to feel the advantages of this union and the dangers of breaking. They should be won over and not irritated, because the safety and freedom of Kashmir is linked up with the retention of Jammu.

[...]

23. It must be remembered that the people of the Kashmir valley and roundabout, though highly gifted in many ways—in intelligence, in artisanship, etc.—are not what are called a virile people. They are soft and addicted to easy living. They are surrounded by hardy tribes in the north-west of Pakistan and even in the northern areas of the State. It will be difficult, and indeed hardly possible, for the people of Kashmir to survive by themselves, it left to their own resources. It was all very well when there was a strong suzerain power like that of England which could prevent harassment and raids. But if a strong suzerain power is absent, then Kashmir is likely to fall an easy prey to these depredations.

24. The result of all these considerations is that the only desirable future for the State is with a close association with India, retaining her autonomy in most ways; that Kashmir and Jammu should hold together; that we should consolidate our position in these areas and not care very much for what happens in the 'Azad Kashmir' areas. Most important of all is that we should have no doubts in our minds about these matters. Doubts in the minds of leaders percolate to their followers and to the people generally. The weakness of the situation in Kashmir is the constant discussion which go on between people holding different views. I do not know how many such groups there are, but obviously some people talk about a close association with India, others talk about a loose association with India, yet others think, if not talk, of an association with Pakistan, and yet others talk about independence. All this confusion in ideas and constant debate weakens the basic position. What is required is a firm and clear outlook, and no debate about basic issues. If we have that outlook, it just does not matter what the United Nations thinks or what Pakistan does.

25. Personally, I have that clear outlook and have had it for these years and it has surprised me that there should be so much discussion about obvious matters.

26. We have to consolidate the position in Kashmir, firstly, on the political plane by having this clear-cut idea about the future, and no nonsense tolerated, and, secondly, by improving the lot of the people, i.e., economic and other issues. Personally, I think that more important even than economic issues is an efficient administration. The common people are primarily interested in a few things—an honest administration and cheap and adequate food. If they get this, then they are more or less content. That is not enough, of course, and we have to go ahead. But there is far too much talk of going ahead, when we do not pay enough attention to basic things like administration and food policy. Slogans are good in their day, but slogans are dangerous companions when these basic problems have to be faced. It is dangerous to make promises which cannot be fulfilled, or to talk tall just to gain the good-will of the people for the moment. Facts cannot be ignored and have to be faced. The most important thing today in Kashmir is efficiency in administration and in food policy. [...]

27. Finally, I would repeat that there must be a clear-cut idea about what we want in Kashmir and about Kashmir, and that idea must be adhered to without debate or argument in future. I have indicated that the only possible course for Kashmir is for the State to be closely associated with India, that association not interfering with its autonomy in most respects. If that is so, then it is not wise to say or do things which imperil that association. Again, Jammu and Kashmir have to hold together for the sake of each other. They cannot be separated. If that is so, then every effort should be made to encourage that idea, and not to say or do anything which irritates people or makes them think of parting company.

28. Our general outlook should be such as to make people think that the association of Kashmir State with India is an accomplished and final fact, and nothing is going to undo it. I am not talking of speeches repeating this, but rather of other facts being mentioned which tend to make people believe it. For instance, I should stress the fact that a tunnel is going to be built under the Banihal or that trade etc. is developing with and through India or that development schemes are being undertaken.

29. [...] I would repeat that I have held these views concisely and precisely for the last four years, and nothing has happened during this period which has made me change them in the slightest. It is for this reason that meetings with Dr Graham or anyone else, or any developments in Pakistan, do not worry me in the least, in so far as Kashmir is concerned. What has sometimes worried me is what happens in Kashmir, because I have found doubt and hesitation there, and not clarity of vision or firmness of outlook.

6. President Rajendra Prasad's Note to the Prime Minister on Article 370, Dated 6 September 1952

Valmiki Chowdhary (ed.), *Dr. Rajendra Prasad: Correspondence and Select Documents*, Volume 15, Allied Publishers, New Delhi, 1991, pp. 104–8

To Jawaharlal Nehru

Rashtrapati Niwas
Simla
6th September 1952

My dear Prime Minister,

When you last saw me, I promised to send you a note on the legal and constitutional aspect of the proposal to substitute a system of elected head for the Jammu and Kashmir State in place of the existing Rajpramukh. I now enclose a note for your consideration. In view of the complexity and importance of the issue involved, I have no doubt that the Attorney-General and the Law Minister will be consulted.

I have received a memorial from the Maharaja, a copy of which, I understand, has also been received by you. Presumably, the Minister for States has also received a copy. I shall be glad in due course to have the comments of yourself and the Minister for States on this memorial.

I am leaving Simla on the morning of Sunday, the 7th Sept. for places in the interior of Himachal Pradesh, but will be back by the evening of Tuesday, the 9th September.

I am sending copies of this letter with enclosure to the Ministers for Education, Defence and States.

Yours sincerely,

Rajendra Prasad

Shri Jawaharlal Nehru
Prime Minister

Enclosure

The Prime Minister of Jammu and Kashmir has forwarded a copy of the resolution of the Constituent Assembly of the Jammu and Kashmir State relating to the substitution of a system of elected head of the State in place of Rajapramukh as at present with a request to the Government of India to take action to enable effect being given to the resolution. Along with the resolution, two draft notifications to be issued by the President, one under clause (1) of that Article, have also been received. The former draft involves amendment of a provision of the Constitution of India and the latter contemplates a modification of two other provisions of the Constitution in its application to the State of Jammu and Kashmir. The proposal raises questions of considerable importance concerning the constitutional scope of the proposed notifications and also about the competence of the President to have repeated recourse to the extraordinary powers conferred on him by the Article in question.

Before I take up this question it is very necessary to know whether any steps are being taken to amend the present constitution of the State of Jammu and Kashmir. It appears from paragraph 6 of the Resolution that there is already in existence the Jammu and Kashmir Constitution Act of 1996, which has been amended by Act No. XVII of 2008. Under this Constitution the Maharaja is presumably the head of the State, and it would obviously be necessary, as a first step, to amend that constitution if it is decided to give immediate effect to the proposal now under consideration. Not having a copy of the Jammu and Kashmir Constitution Act, I am not in a position to say whether provision exists in that constitution for its amendment, but inasmuch as it has been amended as recently as the Hindu year 2008, I believe such provision does exist. I suggest that this question needs looking into.

The first draft notification enclosed with the letter of the Prime Minister of Jammu and Kashmir purports to be issued under clause (3) of Article 370. This clause is of a peculiar and exceptional nature inasmuch as it authorises amendments of Constitution by an executive act of the Government of India as distinguished from Parliament. The Constitution of India contemplates and lays down, apart from this article, two methods for its amendment. An amendment proper of the Constitution can be effected by the special procedure laid down in Article 368. There are certain other provisions in the Constitution in regard to which it is specially and specifically laid down that Parliament, by ordinary legislation, can effect changes. In both these cases, it is the Parliament alone which can effect amendments. In the first case, even the power of Parliament to amend the Constitution is limited inasmuch as it can do so only if the special procedure in Article 368 is followed. In the second group of cases the Parliament is left free to pass legislation which may amount to amendment of the Constitution as laid down. Nowhere else, as far as I can see is there any provision authorising the executive government to make amendments in the Constitution, the temporary provisions contained in Article 391 and 392 having come to an end. There can be no doubt that Article 370, and particularly clause (3) thereof, is of an exceptional nature. While it safeguards in clause (2) the right of the Constituent Assembly of Jammu and Kashmir to revise or annul any action taken by the Government of that State in giving concurrence under clause 1(b)(ii) and the second proviso to clause 1(d) of Article 370, it excludes altogether the Parliament of India from having any say regarding the Constitution of Jammu and Kashmir and places full power in the hands of the government including the power to amend the Constitution of India. It is, therefore, necessary to examine the wording of this peculiar clause with some care for a correct appreciation of the intention underlying this provision. It is laid down in very wide and comprehensive terms that:—

Notwithstanding anything in the foregoing provisions of this article, the President may, by public notification, declare that this article shall cease to be operative or shall be operative only with such exceptions and modifications and from such date he may specify:—

Provided that the recommendation of the Constituent Assembly of the State referred to in clause (2) shall be necessary before the President issues such a notification.

Clause (1) of this Article lays down that
  (a) the provisions of Article 238 shall not apply in relation to the State of Jammu and Kashmir;
  (b) that the power of Parliament to make laws for the said State shall be limited to
      (i)   those matters in the Union list and the Concurrent list which, in consultation with the Government of State, are declared by the President to correspond to matters specified in the Instrument of Accession governing the accession of the State to the Dominion of India as the matters with respect to which the Dominion Legislature may make laws for that State; and
      (ii) such other matters in the said List as with the concurrence of the Govt. of the State the President may by order specify.

Then follows explanation of the term 'Government of the State' namely, the person for the time being recognised by the President as the Maharaja of Jammu and Kashmir acting on the advice under the Maharaja's proclamation dated the fifth day of March 1948.

The Article proceeds further to lay down in paragraphs (c) and (d) of clause (1) that the provisions of Article 1 and of the Article shall apply in relation to that State; and that such of the other provisions of the Constitution shall apply in relation to that State subject to such exceptions and modifications as the President may by order specify: Provided that no such order which relates to the matters specified in the Instrument of Accession of the State referred to in paragraph (i) of sub-clause (b) shall be issued except in consultation with the Government of the State; and provided further that no such order which relates to matters other than those referred to in the last preceding provision shall be issued with the concurrence of that Government.

The present proposal is to amend the Explanation in clause (1) by substituting for the words 'as the Maharaja of Jammu and Kashmir acting on the advice of the Council of Ministers for the time being in office under the Maharaja's Proclamation dated the fifth day of March, 1948', the words 'as the Sadar-i-Riyasat of Jammu and Kashmir acting on the advice of the Council of Ministers for the time being in office'.

It is worth noting that, while the proviso to clause (3) of Article 370 lays down that the recommendation of the Constituent Assembly of the State is a condition precedent to the issue of any notification by the President under the substantive provisions of the clause, it does not make it obligatory for the President to issue a notification to give effect to any recommendation that he may receive from the Constituent Assembly. Presumably it is deliberately so worded in order that the recommendation of the Constituent Assembly could be examined on its merits before the President is advised to issue a notification under that clause. It is also worth noting that the clause envisages two alternatives for the President, namely, either to declare that the whole of Article 370 shall cease to be operative or to declare that it shall be operative only with exceptions and modifications. In either case the President is further required to specify the date from which the notification is to take effect.

As I have already observed, the scope of this Article, if literally interpreted, is exceedingly wide. Suppose the first alternative is adopted and the whole of the Article is declared to be inoperative, what will be the result? One view would be that the Article being in the nature of an exception to the application of the Constitution to the State of Jammu and Kashmir, abrogation of that Article would result in the whole Constitution becoming applicable to the State of Jammu and Kashmir without any exception or modification. But the Article itself has been very peculiarly worded, for paragraph (c) of clause (i) of that Article expressly applies the provisions of Article 1 and of that Article to the State. In fact, it is because of this application of Article 1 to the State that the State is included within the territories of the Union. The abrogation of Article 370 abrogates along with it application of Article 1 to the State, with the result that the State ceases to be part of the territory of India. I do not think that this could have been the intention of the framers of the Constitution, for nowhere is the President empowered to exclude any portion of the territories of India from the Union. As a matter of fact, Article 2 contemplates the admission of fresh territories into the Union or the establishment of new States, but nowhere does the Constitution contemplate the exclusion of any territory from the territories of the Union.

Further, under the second alternative envisaged in clause (3), extensive power is conferred on the President to apply the Constitution to the State with such exceptions and modifications as may be specified in the notification, and the question at once arises whether such an extensive power is exercisable from time to time or is exhausted by a single exercise thereof. Judging by the language employed and by the very exceptional nature of the power conferred, I have little doubt myself that the intention is that the power is to be exercised only once, for then alone would it be possible to determine with precision which particular provisions should be excepted and which modified. The fact that President is also required to specify the date from which the notification is to take effect also tends to confirm this view. Although the phrase 'exceptions and modifications' is used, there can be no doubt that what is involved is really an amendment by executive order of the Constitution in relation to the State of Jammu and Kashmir. Parliament could never have intended that such an extraordinary power of amending the Constitution by executive order was to be enjoyed without any limitation as to the number of times on which it could be exercised or as to the period within which it was exercisable or as to the scope and extent of the modifications and exceptions that could be made. It cannot be seriously maintained that for all time to come the application of our Constitution to Jammu and Kashmir would derive its authority from Article 370, to the complete exclusion of Parliament. The marginal note to Article 370 itself describes the nature of the Article as 'Temporary Provisions with respect to the State of Jammu and Kashmir'. The conclusion, therefore, seems to me to be irresistible that clause (3) of Article 370 was not intended to be used from time to time as occasion required. Nor was it intended to be used without any limit as to time. The correct view appears to be that recourse is to be had to this clause only when the Constituent Assembly of the State has been fully framed.

7. Bill to Amend the State's Constitution, 3 November 1952

Valmiki Chowdhary (ed.), *Dr. Rajendra Prasad: Correspondence and Select Documents*, Volume 15, Allied Pubishers, New Delhi, 1991, pp. 631–8

As directed by the Hon'ble President, Jammu and Kashmir Constituent Assembly a Bill further to amend the Jammu and Kashmir Constitution Act, 1996 is hereby published. The Bill is intended to be introduced in the coming session of the Constituent Assembly.

(Sd.) Hiranand Raina,
Secretary,
Srinagar
3 November, 1952   J&K Constituent Assembly

A Bill Further to Amend the Jammu and Kashmir, Constituent Act, 1996

Be it enacted by the Constituent Assembly as follows:—

1. Short title:—(1) This Act may be called the Jammu and Kashmir Constitution (Amendment) Act, 2009.

(2) It shall come into force on the 17th of November, 1952.

2. Amendment of section 3, Act XIV of 1996:—Clause (c) of section 3 of the Jammu and Kashmir Constitution Act, 1996 (hereinafter referred to as 'the said Act'), shall be omitted.

3. Substitution of section 4, Act XIV of 1996:—For section 4 of the said Act the following section shall be substituted, namely:—

Sadar-i-Riyasat:—4 (1) The Head of the State shall be designated as 'Sadar-i-Riyasat'.

(2) All rights, authority and jurisdiction which appertain or are incidental to the Government of the territories of the State of Jammu and Kashmir shall be exercisable by the Sadar-i-Riyasat on the advice of the Council except in so far as may be otherwise provided by or under this Act, and except in regard to those matters enumerated in List I in the Seventh Schedule to the Constitution of India with respect to which the Parliament of India has power to make laws for the State.

(3) Election and term of office of the Sadar-i-Riyasat and all other matters pertaining to the office of the Sadar-i-Riyasat shall be regulated in accordance with the Resolution of the Constituent Assembly dated: the 21st August, 1952, which Resolution is set out in Schedule I.

4. Amendment of a number of sections by substitution of 'Sadar-i-Riyasat' for 'His Highness' in Act XIV of 1996.—In sections 7, 8, 9-A sub-section (1), 10 sub-sections (1) and (3), 11, 13 sub-section (1) 16, 17, 31 sub-sections (1) and (2), 38, 43 clause (a), 48 sub-section (b), 49, 52, 53, 57, 58, 64 sub-section (1), 67 sub-section (2) and 71 of the said Act, for the words, 'His Highness' wherever occurring, the words, 'the 'Sadar-i-Riyasat' shall be substituted.

5. Amendment of sections 8, 9-A, 53, 71, Act XIV of 1996.—In sections 8, 9-A, 53, and 71, for the word and figure 'Schedule I' wherever occurring, the word, figure and letter 'Schedule 1-A' shall be substituted.

6. Amendment of sections 37 and 43 (c) heading of section 71 and Schedule 1, Act XIV of 1996.—In sections 37 and 43 clause (c) the heading to section 71 and from C of Schedule I (now to be renumbered as I-A) of the said Act for the words, 'His Highness' 'Board of Judicial Advisers' the words, 'Board of Judicial Advisers' shall be substituted.

7. Addition of new section 46-A, Act XIV of 1996.—After section 46 of the said Act the following section shall be added, namely:—

'46-A—Votes on account, Votes of credit and exceptional grants.— (1) Notwithstanding anything in the foregoing provisions of this Act, the Legislative Assembly shall have power:—

(a) to make any grant in advance in respect of the estimated expenditure for a part of any financial year pending the completion of the procedure prescribed in section 45 for the voting of such grant;

(b) to make a grant for meeting an unexpected demand upon the revenues of the State when on account of magnitude or the indefinite character of the service the demand cannot be stated with details ordinarily given in an Annual Financial Statement;

(c) to make an exceptional grant which forms no part of the current service of any financial years.

(2) The provisions of section 45 shall have effect in relation to the making of any grant under sub-section (1) as they have effect in relation to the making of a grant with regard to any expenditure mentioned in the Annual Financial Statement.

8. Amendment of section 55, Act XIV of 1996:—In section 55 of the said Act, the words 'shall run and be in the name and style of His Highness and' shall be omitted.

9. Amendment of section 66, Act XIV of 1996:—In section 66 of the said Act, for the words 'the commands of His Highness' the words 'orders of the Sadar-i-Riyasat' shall be substituted and for the words 'His Highness' where they occur for the second time the words 'the Sadar-i-Riyasat' be substituted.

10. Amendment of section 72, Act XIV of 1996:—In section 72 of the said Act—

(i)   the heading 'Prerogative' to the section shall be omitted; and
(ii) for the words 'prerogative of "His Highness"' the words 'powers of the Sadar-i-Riyasat' shall be substituted.

11. Substitution of new section for section 73, Act XIV of 1996:— For section 73 of the said Act the following section shall be substituted namely:—

Revenues of the Jammu and Kashmir State:—73 All revenues and public monies raised or received by or on behalf of the Jammu and Kashmir Government shall be received for and credited to the account of the Jammu and Kashmir State.

Explanation.—The expression 'revenues' includes:—

(a) all fines and penalties incurred by the sentence or order of any court of justice in the State, and all forfeitures, for crimes, of any movable or immovable property in the State, and
(b) all movable and immovable property in the State escheating or lapsing for want of an heir or successor and all property in the State developing as bona vacantia, for want of a rightful owner.

12. Insertion of a new Schedule in Act XIV of 1996:—Schedule 1 of the said Act shall be renumbered, as Schedule 1-A and before the said Schedule as so renumbered the following Schedule shall be inserted, namely:—

Schedule I (Section 4)

Whereas this Assembly adopted the recommendations contained in the Interim Report of the Basic Principles Committee presented on the 10th of June, 1952.

And whereas by its Resolution, dated the 12th June, 1952, this Assembly directed that the recommendations so adopted be implemented and for that purpose charged the Drafting Committee to submit appropriate proposals:—

Now, therefore, in pursuance of the Resolution dated the 12th June, 1952, and having considered the report of the Drafting Committee this Assembly reserves:—

(i) that the Head of the State shall be the person recognised by the President of India on the recommendations of the Legislative Assembly of the State;

(ii) he shall hold office during the pleasure of the President;

(iii) he may, by writing under his hand, addressed to the President, resign his office;

(iv) subject to the foregoing provisions, the Head of the State shall hold office for a term of five years from the date he enters upon his office:

Provided that he shall, notwithstanding the expiration of his term, continue to hold the office until his successor enters upon his office:

2. that the recommendations of the Legislative Assembly of the State in respect of the recognition of the Head of the State specified in sub-para (i) of paragraph I, shall be made by election;

3. that the method of election to qualifications for and all other matters pertaining to the office of the Head of the State shall be prescribed in the Constitution, and until, these are so prescribed, shall be as set out in the Rules contained in the Schedule annexed to this resolution;

4. that the Head of the State shall be designated as the Sadar-i-Riyasat;

5. that the Sadar-i-Riyasat shall be entitled to such emoluments, allowances and privileges as may be prescribed in the Constitution and pending the framing of the Constitution to such emoluments, allowances and privileges as may be decided by this Assembly by separate resolution;

6. that the Sadar-i-Riyasat shall exercise such powers and perform such functions as may be prescribed in the Constitution to be framed by this Constituent Assembly, and until such Constitution is framed, he shall exercise such powers and perform such functions as have hitherto been exercised by His Highness under the Jammu and Kashmir Constitution Act, 1966, as amended by Act No. XVII of 2008;

7. that in the event of the occurrence of a casual vacancy in the office of the Sadar-i-Riyasat by reason of his death, resignation or otherwise, the powers and functions exercisable by the Sadar-i-Riyasat shall, until the assumption of office by the newly elected Sadar-i-Riyasat in accordance with the procedure laid down in this resolution, be exercised and performed by the person recommended by the State Government for recognition as Officiating Sadar-i-Riyasat to the President of India; and

8. that this Assembly shall in due course provide a suitable remedy in respect of violation of the Constitution or gross misconduct by the person for the time being holding the office of the Sadar-i-Riyasat.

Schedule (Para 3)

1. Qualifications:—No person shall be eligible for election to the office of the Sadar-i-Riyasat, unless he:—

(a) is a State Subject of Class I as defined in the State Subject Definition Notification No. I-L/84, dated 20th April, 1927;

(b) has completed the age of 21 years on the date of filing the nomination paper; and

(c) is not subject to any of the disqualifications specified in rule 4 of the Jammu and Kashmir Constituent Assembly Election (Part I) Rules, 2008, for being chosen as a member of the Constituent Assembly.

2. The Sadar-i-Riyasat shall not be a member of the Legislative Assembly of the State, or if a member of the Legislative Assembly of the State he shall be deemed to have vacated his seat in the House on the date he enters upon his office as the Sadar-i-Riyasat.

3. The Sadar-i-Riyasat shall hold no other office of profit.

4. Method of Election:—(1) When election to the office of the Sadar-i-Riyasat becomes necessary, the Speaker of the State Legislative

Assembly shall fix time and date for the holding of the election and shall cause a notice thereof to be sent to every member.

2. At any time before noon on the date preceding the date so fixed, any member of the State Legislative Assembly many nominate another person for election by delivering to the Speaker or any officer authorised by the Speaker in this behalf, a nomination paper in the form prescribed in the Annexure to this Schedule signed by himself as proposer and by another member as seconder.

3. Any person who has been so nominated may withdraw his candidature in writing addressed to the Speaker at any time before the Assembly proceeds to hold the election.

4. At the time fixed for election under sub-clause (I), the Speaker or in his absence the person presiding shall read out to the Assembly the name of the persons who have been duly nominated and have not withdrawn their candidature together with those of their proposers and seconders, and, if there is only one such candidate, shall declare him to be duly elected. If there is more than one such candidate, the Assembly shall proceed to elect the Sadar-i-Riyasat by ballot.

5. Where there are only two candidates for election, the candidate who obtain at the ballot the larger number of votes shall be declared elected. If they obtain equal number of votes, the Speaker or in his absence the person presiding shall exercise his casting vote and the person in whose favour such vote is cast shall be declared elected.

6. Where more than two candidatures have been nominated and at the first ballot no candidate obtains more votes than the aggregate votes obtained by the other candidates, the candidate who has obtained the smallest number of votes shall be excluded from the election, and balloting shall proceed the candidate obtaining the smallest number of votes at each ballot being excluded from the election, until one candidate obtains more votes than the remaining candidates, or than the aggregate votes of remaining candidates, as the case may be, and such candidate shall be declared elected.

7. Where at any ballot any of three or more candidates obtain an equal number of votes and one of them has to be excluded from the election under sub-clause (6), the determination, as between the candidates whose votes are equal, of the candidate who is to be excluded

shall be by the casting vote of the Speaker or in his absence of the person presiding.

8. The Prime Minister of the State shall communicate the name of the person duly elected by the Assembly as the Sadar-i-Riyasat to the President of India for being recognised as the Sadar-i-Riyasat.

9. Oath:—The Sadar-i-Riyasat shall, before entering upon his office, make and subscribe in the presence of Chief Justice of the State High Court or in his absence any Judge of the High Court available on oath or affidavitation in the following form, namely:—

I, A.B. swear in the name of God/solemnly affirm that I will faithfully execute the office of the Sadar-i-Riyasat, Jammu wa Kashmir and will to the best of my ability preserve, protect, and defend the Constitution of the State as by law established and that I will devote myself to the service and well being of the people of the State.

8. Mirza Muhammed Afzal Beg Moves the Assembly for the Adoption of the Bill on 10 November 1952 (Extracts)

Valmiki Chowdhary (ed.), *Dr. Rajendra Prasad: Correspondence and Select Documents*, Volume 15, Allied Publishers, New Delhi, 1991, pp. 623–44

*Hon'ble M.A. Beg: Mr. President, the Constituent Assembly passed a Resolution on the 21st of August, 1952, in pursuance of which the report of a Committee of the Constituent Assembly wherein proposals regarding future Head of this State were made was adopted. According to this resolution the Constituent Assembly resolved that the future Head of the State shall be elected and that his term of office will be five years. Rules regulating his election and details thereof were passed by the Assembly. The future Head of the State will henceforth be called the 'Sadar-i-Riyasat' instead of Maharaja, and his appointment was to be made by election. At present the Jammu and Kashmir Constitution Act is in force in this State and still the words 'His Highness the Maharaja of Jammu and Kashmir' are there as also his powers. Till the Constituent Assembly frames a new Constitution, the Jammu and Kashmir Con-

stitution Act will continue to be in force in this country. It is, therefore, expedient to amend the Jammu and Kashmir Constitution Act
in pursuance of the Resolution dated the 21st August, 1952. For this
purpose I ask for leave to introduce the Bill to amend the Jammu and
Kashmir Constitution Act and move that it be taken into consideration
(Note: The Bill will be found at the end as Appendix A). The sections
of my Bill are brief. The first section is that the future Head of the State
will henceforth be called the 'Sadar-i-Riyasat' and the present section 4
which reads as under has been repealed.

'The territories for the time being vested to His Highness are governed
by and in the name of His Highness and all rights, authority and jurisdiction which appertain or are incidental to the Government of such
territories are exercisable by His Highness on the advice of the Council
except in so far as may be provided by or under this Act etc.'. According
to the Rule in force all these territories included in the Jammu and
Kashmir State, all powers, jurisdiction etc. relating thereto are vested
in the Maharaja. My amendment is that all these powers prerogative,
privileges and jurisdiction be vested in the Sadar-i-Riyasat exercisable
in consideration with the Council of Ministers. This amendment is in
consonance with the Resolution of 21st August, 1952. My amendment
that all those powers which the Sadar-i-Riyasat will exercise on the
advice of Council of Ministers will be subject to a condition or two. The
first condition is.

[...]

* Hon'ble M.A. Beg: Now I move that this Bill taken into consideration. Pursuant to the Resolution dated 21st August, 1952, some
amendments in the Jammu and Kashmir Constitution Act were necessitated. In regard to amendment of section 4. I may submit that all powers vested in the Maharaja Bahadur under the existing Act be exercised
by the Sadar-i-Riyasat on the advice of the Council of Ministers. Two
conditions have been imposed in this behalf. The first is that all these
powers will be exercisable subject to the Constitution. Under section
45 and 46 relating to Finance, the Legislature has been authorised to
accord or with-hold sanction to any expenditure and no expenditure
can be incurred without the sanction of the Legislature. Thus whatever
is expended will be subject to sanction of the Legislature. After accession

to India, under list 1, Schedule 7, of the Indian Constitution in regard
to the terms in respect of which accession to India has been effected the
Indian Parliament is authorised to make legislation for the Jammu and
Kashmir State. Thus with regard to the item that we have acceded in the
Centre, the Indian Parliament or the President of India can in exercise
of those powers make legislation for our State; and the 'Sadar-i-Riyasat'
shall have to exercise his powers subject to this condition. Both the conditions are necessary. As we have acceded to India in respect of defence,
communications and external affairs, the centre is authorised to make
suitable legislation in respect thereof. Under Schedule 3, section 4, the
procedure for election of the Sadar-i-Riyasat has been defined which
is in conformity with the Resolution dated 21st August, 1952. Now
that the House has passed this resolution, we have proposed an amendment to the effect that the words 'Maharaja' wherever occurring in the
Constitution Act be substituted by the words 'Sadar-i-Riyasat'. Under
section 45 & 46, this House has been authorised to pass the financial
grants; this is an amendment of which this House will take advantage
from time to time. Another thing of importance relates to the Royal
prerogative. Under the old Constitution Act, the Maharaja could repeat
any law, but now under this Constitution the Royal Prerogative will
cease. Besides, taxes and Revenues were collected from the people of
the State in the name of the Maharaja, under the former Constitution.
It is obvious that according to the Resolution of 21st August, 1952,
this theory will not stand now and henceforth all taxes and revenues
will be collected in the name of Government and credited in the name
of the State. As the question of His Highness is no longer there hence
these reformative amendments were necessary to be made in accordance
with the Resolution dated 21st August, 1952. After the election of the
'Sadar-i-Riyasat' it is essential to make these amendments in the Constitution. Keeping in view all these things this Bill has been placed before
the House. I wish to remind the House here that the Resolution of 21st
August envisages that under Article 370 under the sub-heading 'explanation' recognition of the Sadar-i-Riyasat it is essential that Article 370
is suitably amended just as His Highness and Yuvaraj were recognised
by the Union President under Article 370. Similarly Union President
may accord his recognition to the 'Sadar-i-Riyasat' as required under

Article 370. In view of this the first step to be taken is amendment of the Constitution and making provision therein for the 'Sadar-i-Riyasat' in place of 'His Highness' and when powers of the Sadar-i-Riyasat are provided in the Constitution the second step to be taken will be his election which will be made by this House; and under Article 370, the Union President will accord his recognition to it, and from the date the Union President accords his recognition the Sadar-i-Riyasat will commence to function. It is, therefore essential that we proceed to accomplish the different stages in the following order:—

1. Passing of the Bill presented to this House;

2. election of the 'Sadar-i-Riyasat'; and

3. recognition of the 'Sadar-i-Riyasat' by the Union President as required under Article 370; respectively.

Our country, I may submit here, is anxiously awaiting the enforcement of the Resolution of 21st August, 1952. We have placed this Bill before the House keeping in view all these things I would, therefore, request that this amendment Bill be taken into consideration. If postponement of further action or discussion thereon is necessitated due to one reason or the other, this may be done till the day after tomorrow. Election of the Sadar-i-Riyasat will also take place day after tomorrow. So after the consideration Motion other Business be adjourned till that day.

[...]

12 November 1952

[...]

*Hon'ble M.A. Beg: Hon'ble President, I move that the Jammu and Kashmir Constitution Act (Amendment) Bill be passed.

I had stated in this House while making the original motion that the Head of the State shall according to the resolution passed on the 21st August, 1952, be an elected one. It was essential to amend the existing Constitution of the State to bring it in conformity with this resolution. There is no necessity for any further detailed discussion on this amendment Bill. I have submitted that all the powers, privileges and jurisdiction conferred on His Highness by section 4 of the Act will be exercised by the Sadar-i-Riyasat in consultation with the Council. In addition, according to the second amendment, the Sadar-i-Riyasat will exercise the powers, privileges and jurisdiction according to the existing Constitution. Firstly that he will not be absolute in authority like the old Maharajas, but he shall have to act subject to the limitations imposed by the Constitution, that is to say that he cannot himself sanction the budget of this State nor can he Legislate on his own. On the other hand he will exercise powers as a Constitutional Head according to the advice of the Council and the Legislative Assembly.

The second limitation imposed on the Sadar-i-Riyasat is that in addition to the limitations imposed by the Constitution he will be bound by the provisions applicable to the Jammu and Kashmir State in respect of the matters vested in the centre relating to all the matters enumerated in list No. 1 of schedule No. 7 of the Constitution of India about which the Indian Parliament is empowered to make laws.

The second amendment which has been moved relates to the election of the Sadar-i-Riyasat in accordance with the Resolution of the 21st August, 1952. Special changes have also been effected in the remaining section of the constitution through this amendment Bill, and it is proposed to substitute 'Sadar-i-Riyasat' for this Highness. The words 'Orders of the Sadar-i-Riyasat' have been substituted in place of 'Royal prerogative' which were used in the Constitution Act, 1996. The Government which was operating on the basis of old theory based on the conception of Kinghip have ended and in its place appropriate words 'Orders of the Sadar-i-Riyasat' have been proposed.

The last section concerns the Finances of the Jammu and Kashmir State. Previously all the income of the State such as revenue, income tax etc., was credited into the treasury in the name of the Maharaja. Since that theory has changed all the income of the Government and taxes will in future be credited in the name of the Government. In olden days all income was credited into the treasury in the name of the Maharaja but it will be entered henceforth in the name of the Jammu and Kashmir State. Since these amendments were necessary in the Constitution Act, hence this amending Bill. So far as the Indian States are concerned, the Kashmir State has enjoyed the privilege of giving them a lead. Until the Constituent Assembly of the State frames the new constitution it will be necessary to operate the existing constitution during the interim period in accordance with the resolution of the Constituent Assembly. I, therefore, request that the Bill may be adopted with these amendments.

Hon'ble Girdhari Lal Dogra: So far as the Indian States are concerned it has always been the proud privilege of Kashmir to give them a lead. During the days of agitations and popular movements also it had this proud privilege and when the new Constitution is being framed Kashmir alone has the proud privilege of leading them. I do not want to take much time of the House and would only submit that in order to meet the demand of the times and to carry the democratic order forward we should pass the Bill which has been introduced today. Some people are trying to present this Bill in a wrong manner, and give it a wrong colouring. Such people are reactionaries and are appearing with national slogans at times in a communal form and at times in some other form. But such people are neither honest nor the Indian Parliament would have the authority to frame laws on all the items in the Union list for our State also like the remaining States of India.

Hon'ble M.A. Beg: Sir, clause (4) relates to the powers of the Sadar-i-Riyasat on the advice of the Council except in so far as may be otherwise provided by or ended this Act, and except in regard to those matters enumerated in list 1 in the Seventh Schedule to the Constitution of India with respect to which the Parliament of India has power to make laws for the State.

This reference is to be read with list I Schedule 7 read with Article 370, I (i) which makes it abundantly clear that Dominion Legislature can make laws only in respect of specific matters in consultation with Jammu and Kashmir Government. So there should be no doubt about the fact that powers to make laws for the Jammu and Kashmir State is limited in the Dominion Parliament and limitation to that extent is placed on the powers of the Sadar-i-Riyasat to discharge his duties in the territory of Jammu and Kashmir State. It is, therefore, that these amendments have been made in the Constitution of the Jammu and Kashmir State. When the present Constitution is framed and applied to the State, that is, until the Constituent Assembly of the State frames the new Constitution it will be necessary to apply during the interim period, the existing Constitution along with the amendments proposed by the Constituent Assembly. It is, therefore, by request that this Bill may be adopted with these amendments.

Hon'ble President: The question is that the Jammu and Kashmir Constitution (Amendment) Bill be passed.

Note: The motion was adopted.

9. The Constitution (Application to Jammu & Kashmir) Amendment Order No. 39, Dated 20 March 1952

Published with the Ministry of Law, Notification No. SRO 528, Dated the 20th March, 1952, Gazette of India, Extraordinary, 1952, Part II, Section 3, p. 439

CO 39

In exercise of the powers conferred by clause (1) of Article 370 of the Constitution of India, the President, in consultation with the Government of the State of Jammu and Kashmir, is pleased to make the following Order, namely:—

1. (1) This Order may be called the Constitution (Application to Jammu and Kashmir) (Amendment) Order, 1952.

(2) It shall come into force at once.

2. In the Second Schedule to the Constitution (Application to Jammu and Kashmir) Order, 1950, in the entry in third column relating to Part V, after modification (1), the following modification shall be inserted, namely:—

(1A) Articles 54 and 55 shall apply subject to the modifications:—

(2) that the references therein to the elected members of both Houses of Parliament and to each elected member of either House of Parliament shall be deemed to include, respectively, a reference to the representatives of the State in those Houses and to each such representative,

(3) that the references to the elected members of the Legislative Assemblies of the States and to each such elected member shall be deemed to include, respectively, a reference to the members of the Constituent Assembly of the State and to each such member, and

(4) that the population of the State shall be deemed to be forty-four lakhs and ten thousand.

10. The Constitution (Application to Jammu & Kashmir) Second Amendment Order No. 43, Dated 15 November 1952

Published with the Ministry of Law, Notification No. SRO 1903, Dated the 15th November, 1972, Gazette of India, Extraordinary, 1950, Part II, Section 3, p. 915

CO 43

In exercise of the powers conferred by clause (1) of article 370 of the Constitution of India, the President, in consultation with the Government of the State of Jammu and Kashmir, is pleased to make the following Order:—

1. (1) This Order may be called the Constitution (Application to Jammu and Kashmir) Second Amendment Order, 1952.

(2) It shall come into force on the 17th day of November, 1952.

2. At the end of paragraph 3 of the Constitution (Application to Jammu and Kashmir) Order, 1950[1] (hereinafter referred to as 'the principal Order'), there shall be added the words 'and to the modification that all references in the said provisions to the Rajpramukh shall be construed as references in the Sadar-i-Riyasat of Jammu and Kashmir'.

3. In the Second Schedule to the Principal Order:—

    (a) in the entry in the second column relating to Part XIX, after the figures '365' the words, brackets and figures 'and clause (21) of Article 366' shall be inserted; and

    (b) in the entry in the second column relating to Part XXI, for the figures and word '376 and 378' the figures and word '376, 378 and 386' shall be substituted.

---

[1] CO 10, *supra*. Since superseded by CO 48, *infra*.

11. The Constitution (Application to Jammu & Kashmir) Order No. 44, Dated 15 November 1952

Ministry of Law Order No. CO 44, Dated the 15th November 1952

CO 49

On November 15, 1952 Constitution Order No. 44 was made by the President under Article 370: 'In exercise of the powers conferred by this article the President, on the recommendation of the Constituent Assembly of the State of Jammu and Kashmir, declare that, as from the 17th day of November, 1952 the said Article 370 shall be operative with the modification that for the explanation in clause (1) thereof, the following explanation is substituted namely:—

Explanation.—For the purposes of this article, the Government of the State means the person for the time being recognized by the President on the recommendation of the Legislative Assembly of the State as the Sadar-i-Riyasat of Jammu and Kashmir, acting on the advice of the Council of Ministers of the State for the time being in office.

Chapter 6

Sheikh Abdullah's Arrest

9 August 1953

1. Nehru's Letter to Sheikh Abdullah on 27 April 1953

Selected Works of Jawaharlal Nehru (hereafter *SWJN*)
Volume 22, p. 212

New Delhi
April 27, 1953

My dear Shaikh Saheb,

[...]

I am writing to you, however, about a matter, which has been distressing me for some time. This is the very slow progress made by your committees etc., in regard to giving formal shape to the relationship of Kashmir with India, in terms of the agreement arrived at last year. Normally, I would have thought that, in a matter of this kind, there would have been some speed in implementation. It is now about nine months or so since that agreement was arrived at. I know of course the difficulties you have had to face.

[...]

But the fact remains that this continuing trouble is a strain on all of us. We should like to see the end of it. It would no doubt have ended long ago if we could have said definitely that the Jammu and Kashmir Government had finally implemented the agreement arrived at last year. The only thing that keeps going this trouble and agitation is the charge that even the Agreement has not been implemented. We have no reply to that or rather the reply we have given grows more and more stale as time goes on.

[...]

If that is so, then this matter at least should be tackled with speed and settled. I do not mind how long the rest of your Constitution takes. If it is said that this a part of the entire Constitution and must, therefore wait for it, that argument could have equally applied to the change made in the headship of the State. If that can be isolated, so can other matters we had agreed upon.

My own view about the Constitution has all along been that it is always better to have a brief and flexible Constitution. We have made a mistake, I think, in having too long and complicated a Constitution of India and we are regretting it. If I had another chance, I would not repeat this error, because it comes in the way all the time.

The Constitution of Jammu and Kashmir State will necessarily have to fit into the Constitution of India, if Jammu and Kashmir State is a constituent unit of India and is part of the territory of India. But for the moment I am not concerned with the whole Constitution but only with that part which defines the relationship to India. I fear that the longer we delay this, the more difficult the situation becomes.

[...]

Yours sincerely,
Jawaharlal Nehru

2. The National Conference Working Committee's 8-Member Committee on the Future of Kashmir

The Government of Kashmir was oppressed by the uncertainty which had singled out the State in the entire sub-continent. Sheikh Abdullah took his colleagues into confidence and placed the matter before the Working Committee of the J&K National Conference which met in

May 1953 under his Presidentship. The Working Committee, after prolonged discussions came to the conclusion that it was impossible to have internal stability so long as its future was uncertain. It accordingly appointed a Committee consisting of the following eight members to explore avenues of a settlement:

Sheikh Abdullah   G.M. Sadiq
Maulana Masoodi   Sardar Budhsingh
Mirza Afzal Beg   Pandit Girdharilal Dogra
Bakshi Ghulam Mohammed   Pandit Shamlal Saraf

Jawaharlal Nehru who had come to Kashmir when the Working Committee was in session was informed about its deliberations. Here is an extract from the minutes of the Committee's final session held on June 9, 1953:

As a result of the discussions held in the course of various meetings, the following proposals only emerge as possible alternatives for an honourable and peaceful solution of Kashmir dispute between India and Pakistan:

(a) Overall plebiscite with conditions as detailed in the minutes of the meeting dated 4th June 1953 (this apparently was a reference to Maulana Masoodi's suggestion that the choice of independence be offered in the plebiscite).

(b) Independence of the whole State.

(c) Independence of the whole State with joint control of foreign affairs.

(d) Dixon Plan with independence for the plebiscite area.

'Bakshi Saheb was emphatically of the opinion that the proposal (d) above should be put up as first and the only practicable, advantageous and honourable solution of the dispute. Maulana Saeed, however, opined that the order of preference as given above should be adhered to.'

G.M. Sadiq said:

If an agency consisting of India, Pakistan, Afghanistan, Soviet Russia and China could be created to supervise and conduct the plebiscite, I would suggest that we should immediately ask for an overall plebiscite. Failing this, we may ask for a supervision Commission representing all the Members of the Security Council for ensuring free and fair plebiscite in the State.[1]

[...]

In June 1953 Maulana Abul Kalam Azad, Union Minister for Education, visited Kashmir and was apprised of these developments. Early in July 1953, Nehru was informed about the decision.

[...]

Early in August 1953 Sheikh Abdullah called a meeting of the Working Committee of the General Council in the 3rd and 4th weeks in order to review the whole situation. On August 8, 1953, just two days before the scheduled Cabinet meeting, Sheikh Abdullah was arrested at the dead of night, and so were a number of his colleagues.

3. Nehru's Letter to Sheikh Abdullah on 28 June 1953

SWJN, Volume 22, pp. 193–9

New Delhi
June 28, 1953

My dear Shaikh Sahib,

[...]

I have, thus far, kept my mind fairly clear on the Kashmir issue in spite of its difficulties. That did not mean that I had an easy solution up my sleeve, but that did mean that I was clear about the line of activity we should pursue. But lately I have not at all been clear as to what you have been thinking, and naturally that has a powerful effect on my own thinking. The long talk we had in Srinagar during my last visit in May brought no light to me from you and only led me to think that you are yourself not quite clear. I requested you then to keep any decision pending till my return.

[...]

I had till recently a fairly clear idea of what you thought in this matter. I know that during the past three or four years doubts have

---

[1] Quoted by Sheikh Abdullah in his letter from jail to Mr. G.M. Sadiq dated 26 September 1956 published in *Sheikh-Sadiq Correspondence* (August to October 1956), The pamphlet is published by Miss Mridula Sarabhai, New Delhi, p. 18.

arisen in your mind and we have discussed them. We did not agree about some things and, on one or two occasions, I even told you that I did not wish to come in your way if you differed from me in any vital matter. If so, we naturally have to think what our separate courses of action should be. However, we generally agreed about the policy that should be pursued and there the matter rested.

You will remember that when I went to Sonamarg last year, I wrote a note which I sent you analysing the Kashmir problem in the hope that this might lead us to clear thinking. This note was discussed by us in Srinagar later and I gathered from you and your colleagues that you agreed with that analysis and conclusion. Recent developments have, however, led me to think that you have either changed your mind completely or are not clear about your thinking. This necessitates our understanding, as clearly as possible, what we respectively think. If one cannot agree, one should at least know precisely what the difference is. That difference appeared to me considerable when we talked at Srinagar last. But it seems to me that I could not get a grip of what you had in your mind, except negatively. You told me that there were only two courses open for Kashmir: either full integration or full autonomy, whatever that autonomy might mean. I did not agree with you in this, nor do I agree with you even now, because there are many other middle courses. Nobody can guarantee the distant future.[1] [...] We have argued enough and must accept each other's present conclusions and then discuss the future on that basis. If that future unhappily leads to divergence with all its consequences, we fashion our respective courses accordingly.

[1] Abdullah replied:

You have spoken about guarantees. We certainly believed that the terms of the Indian Constitution provided adequate guarantee. ... But I would point out to you the discrepancies that we come to notice from time to time in the attitude of the Government of India in regard to this position. When Article 370 was devised, we felt assured by Sardar Patel that the Instrument of Accession would be the final basis of the Indo-Kashmir relationship. Subsequently, when the Delhi Agreement came up before the Council of States on August 5, 1952. Shri Gopalaswami Ayyangar stated that Article 370 was not a permanent feature of the Indian Constitution and 'when the time was ripe' the provision could be wiped off the Constitution. This clearly shows that even though assurances were given to us ... such assurances came with a good deal of mental reservation.

You know that the question of Kashmir has had not only a logical appeal for me but also a strong emotional one. But I can suppress my emotion, if necessary, if logic demands that. Thus far, I have proceeded on a basis of friendship and confidence in you and have been vain enough to expect the same approach from you. Whether that is justified now or not, it is for you to say. Individual relations should not count in national affairs and yet they do count and make a difference.[2]

To me it has been a major surprise that a settlement arrived at between us should be by-passed or repudiated, regardless of the merits. That strikes at the root of all confidence, personal or international. No treaty would be worth the paper it is written on, if it was to be repudiated soon after. So far as I am concerned, no power in this world could make me go back on the pledge that I gave in that Agreement. If my Parliament or my people in India repudiate that, they repudiate me. That was my approach. Of course, a new situation requires a new approach. But even that new approach would have been for me something following the implementation of that Agreement and not something which upset it. My honour is bound up with my word.

It is because of this that I have been surprised at recent happenings in Kashmir, which seemed to imply that agreement should not be acted upon and should be repudiated.

My Government has stood, as you have so consistently stood, for a secular democracy.[3] I do not know what your feelings are on this subject now.[4] But I fear the tendency in Kashmir is away from it. Unfortunately

---

[2] Abdullah replied: 'I agree that personal relationship between individuals should not be a consideration where larger national interests are involved. Friendship and sentiments are worthy of respect but they should not come in the way of dispassionate appraisals of one another's difficulties.'

[3] Abdullah wrote:

Muslims may rightly feel that in spite of you and many others, the ideals of secular democracy are not much in evidence in so far treatment of Kashmiri Muslims is concerned. I derived my strength from what I supposed was an assurance that the State's accession with India would result in a fair deal to all sections of the people. But unfortunately that goal has not been achieved.

[4] Abdullah retorted: 'May I say, this is an unkind cut. Time alone will prove my faith in the principle for which I have consistently fought all these years. My

that will have its reactions in India as such tendencies in India have their reactions in Kashmir. On my part I am pledged to that ideal and I shall adhere to it to the bitter end, if necessary, and if my people throw me out. It will grieve me that anything is done in Kashmir which tarnishes that ideal and weakens those who stand for it. Whatever we might do, it is the least that we owe each other that we should try to understand each other and then decide on such courses of action as we might deem proper. It is always painful to part company after long years of comradeship, but if our conscience so tells us, or in our view, an overriding national interest so requires, then there is no help for it. Even so we must do it with full understanding and full explanation to each other and not casually.[5]

[...]

I am sending a copy of this letter to Bakshi, as the letter deals with problems and approaches in which he is obviously interested also.

Yours sincerely,
Jawaharlal Nehru

4. Sheikh Abdullah's Letter to Maulana Azad on 16 July 1953

Kashmir's Special Status (in the Light of Agreements), All Jammu and Kashmir National Conference, Srinagar, 1975, pp. 22–4

Srinagar,
July 16, 1953

Respected Maulana Sahib,
Your letter of July 9, reached me yesterday. It appears certain misunderstanding has arisen in regard to the matters raised by me in my letter to Pandit Ji. There are two aspects of the problem of our State: one

idea about secular democracy is not cramped or narrow-minded. I believe in justice for all sections of the people and my attitude is conditioned by realities and not by wishful thinking.'

[5] Abdullah replied: 'I may, however, assure you that whatever lot may be in store for us, never can you expect me to abandon my respect and affection for you.'

concerns the relationship arising out of the signing of the Instrument of Accession and the other is related to settlement between India, Pakistan and the people of the State of the dispute about the future of the State. These two aspects may be called the internal and external aspects of the Kashmir problem. It appears no distinction is drawn between these two aspects in discussions about the dispute.

As is well known to you, the present relationship of the State is based on the document of Instrument of Accession. We, the people of Kashmir, regard the promises and assurances of the representatives of the Government of India, such as Lord Mountbatten and Sardar Patel, as surety for the assistance rendered by us in securing the signatures of the Maharaja of Kashmir on the Instrument of Accession, which made it clear, that the internal autonomy and sovereignty of the Acceding States shall be maintained except in regard to three subjects which will be under the Central Government.

I mention here in this connection, the clear assurances given by Sardar Patel to Indian States on July 5, 1947. He observed: 'We do not want anything more from them than accession in these three subjects, therein lies the good of the entire country. We respect their independence in all other matters'.

At that time it clearly appeared that even handing over to the Centre of Defence, Communications and External Affairs implied no financial liability on the States. You would recall that Lord Mountbatten declared at the time of Independence in 1947 that 'Instrument of Accession enables Indian States to accede to either of two Dominions without financial liability. Moreover, it is clearly stated in one of its clauses that the Central Government has no power under any circumstances to interfere with the internal autonomy and sovereignty of the Indian States'.

Mr. V.P. Menon, whose opinion is considered quite authoritative is respect of Indian States, observes: 'Accession involves no financial obligation on the States. There is no intention to usurp their internal autonomy nor will they be forced to accept the Central Constitution'.

It is regrettable that despite these clear declarations about these matters, the Government of India has tried several times to impose financial obligations on this State. This action of theirs is in clear violation of the assurances given by its responsible representatives. The State acquired such a status as a result of concessions allowed under its Instrument of Accession to India. When the Constituent Assembly of India proceeded to frame the Union Constitution there arose before it the question of the future position of the State. Our representatives took part in the last sessions of the Assembly and presented their point of view in the light of the basic principles on which the National Conference had supported the State's accession to India. Our view-point drew appreciation and Article 370 of the Constitution came into being determining our position under the new Constitution. Sardar Patel again reiterated his assurances: 'In view of the special problems confronting Kashmir we have enacted a special provision to continue the existing relationship between the Union and this State'.

As time elapsed, it began to become clear that this special position was conceded with certain reservations and there arose objections against this 'special treatment'. It is important to note here that responsible representatives of the Government of India themselves gave rise to many doubts by terming this position as provisional, and the ensuing events confirmed us in our belief that the relationship between India and Kashmir arising out of the document of Instrument of Accession was not final. Even the Government of India entertained doubts about this position. During the debate on this important issue in the Constituent Assembly it emerged that apart from the limitations imposed by the Instrument of Accession the very relationship between India and Kashmir entailed certain responsibilities and many letters were exchanged to secure one's position resulting in the Delhi Agreement.

I hope you are not unaware of the fact that even after the Delhi Agreement responsible spokesmen of the Government of India declared that their ultimate objective was to secure the complete merger of the State with India and that they waited for appropriate time and conditions to bring that about. These statements reveal that the Delhi Agreement could not provide a basis to finalise the relationship between India and Kashmir; but that it (Delhi Agreement) provided temporary arrangements to finalise accession. The only difference between the Government of India and different elements in the country on the issue is whether to bring about the merger of the State with India now or after some time.

This sums up the relationship between Kashmir and India. It should not be forgotten that this is a temporary or provisional relationship as the contending parties have yet to settle the future of the State according to the wishes of the people. This temporary relationship—which we had hoped would strengthen our position—gradually underwent a change with restrictions imposed upon the majority community in the State. The finalisation of this relationship between India and Kashmir caused concern among the people here and has given rise to doubts and fears in their mind. I am very happy to hear from you that the Government of India is willing to declare that the special position given to Kashmir will be made permanent and that the Government of India will be bound by it without any conditions. If such a declaration had been made at an appropriate time, it would undoubtedly have strengthened our hands and unified various organisations and public opinion in the State and even if the masses had been asked about accession, a majority of them would have come out in favour of India. But, unfortunately, that was not to be. And the changes effected on several occasions in the relationship between India and Kashmir greatly agitated the public opinion and also weakened our hands to a great extent. Although such a declaration would be welcome, it remains to be seen if it would draw the support of different sections of people in India and parties in Kashmir. You would appreciate that without such support, this declaration would not suffice to dispel the fears that have arisen in the minds of the people of Kashmir. A big party in India still forcefully demands merger of the State with India. In the State itself, Praja Parishad is threatening to resort to direct action if the demand for the State's complete merger with India is not conceded. I do not understand how in the face of this stiff opposition, your proposed declaration would be able to reconcile different points of view that have arisen concerning the issue of Indo-Kashmir relationship. Assuming such an agreed solution to be possible, it is still to be seen if the resultant benefits would accrue equally and fairly to all sections of people in the State.

In my letter of July 4 (copy of which was sent by me to you also) I made it clear to Pandit Ji that a majority of people in the State feel that they have been completely ignored even in respect of matters which have passed under the control of the Central Government. We will have to settle their future administration without loss of time in a practical way. Naturally, only that solution will be satisfactory which is honourable and acceptable to all parties concerned. Today the contending parties are, between themselves and internationally committed to the principle of free and impartial plebiscite. Mixed populace would naturally give rise to many difficulties and real problems. We have carefully weighed the various pros and cons and have reached certain conclusions after careful deliberation over these matters. Bakshi Sahib and Beg Sahib have been directed to convey these decisions to you. It is now up to you and your colleagues seriously to examine them and decide if they lead to fair solution of the problem. If you do not consider these proposals practicable, then you should put forth your own proposal keeping in view the importance of internal and external aspects of the matter. No doubt, we have had close and intimate relations between us for a long time and you and I both have high regard for them, but when we have to decide issues of national importance, regard for our mutual friendship should not be allowed to come in the way of their dispassionate consideration and discussion. I respect your views but wish at the same time that you appreciate my difficulties. I can be a friend and loyal, as a responsible representative of the people, if I keep to the fore the interests of people whose trust and confidence I enjoy. If I fail to gain the confidence of the people here I will not be able to render any service to my friends. I hope you will appreciate my position and accept my real views after careful deliberation'.

Sincerely yours,

Sheikh Mohammed Abdullah

5. Nehru's Note on Abdullah's Arrest Recorded by His Private Secretary M.O. Mathai on 31 July 1953

SWJN, Volume 23, pp. 303–5

The present drift and the resulting confusion cannot be allowed to go on. The policy of Government must be clearly stated to the public. The members of Government should not speak in different voices. In order to remove doubt about this policy, a brief memorandum might be prepared and placed before the Cabinet. In this Government's policy should be precisely stated. Apart from other major issues, there might be some reference in it to certain economic issues also; or, if it is preferred, the economic issues can be stated in a separate note. Among these economic issues might be mentioned the raising of the price of procurement of rice, the removal of the customs barrier, etc., the object of all this being to lessen the burden on the common man.

The main point clarified in the memorandum should be the future of the State which has given rise to so much argument in public recently. Members of Government should be asked to support the policy laid down in its entirety.

If, as is probable, some members of Government do not agree with this policy and this statement, the majority should nevertheless accept that policy. If the minority refuse to abide by it, the continuation of the present Government becomes impossible. The Head of the State should be informed accordingly. He should ask for the resignation of the Government because it cannot function as a team and pursue its contradictory policies. If the resignation is offered, then the Head of the State should call upon another person representing the majority view to form a new Government.

It will be desirable not to allow any marked lapse of time between the demand for resignation and the formation of the new Government. The Head of the State should send for all members of Government and inform them of his decision and ask for their resignations. If the resignations are not forthcoming, he should have an order ready for the dismissal of the Government because it cannot fulfil its functions properly. Immediately he should entrust the formation of the new Government to the other person.

It will be desirable to prepare the ground for this, insofar as considered feasible, with prominent members of the Executive of the Party.

Immediately after the formation of the new Government, the Executive of the Party should meet. Both the new Government and the Party should issue statements to the public stating the facts and indicating their policy, including their economic policy.

Some persons who are notorious for their corrupt activities should be apprehended and steps taken for an inquiry into those activities.

It may be desirable to arrest one or two such persons, who are known to be corrupt, even before the steps indicated above are taken. But this is a matter of judgment.

All necessary steps should be taken for the preservation of law and order. Any persons taking a lead in creating any disturbance should be apprehended. Such assistance as may be considered necessary for the maintenance of law and order should be available. Any action taken should be carefully calculated so as not to exceed the necessities of the situation, and the change-over should be as peaceful as possible.

Immediate first steps afterwards should be the removal of certain well-known corrupt officers, etc., suspension of others whose loyalty is doubted, and an appeal to the people for maintenance of peaceful conditions. The broad outlines of the programme of the new Government should be given and it should be stated that it would be for the people to decide ultimately what political or economic policy has to be adopted—the sole test will be the good of the people and their wishes in the matter.

6. Sadar-i-Riyasat's Letter to Sheikh Abdullah, 8 August 1953

Karan Singh, *Heir Apparent,* **Oxford University Press, Oxford, 1982, p. 161**

Karan Mahal,
Srinagar,
August 8, 1953

My dear Sheikh Abdullah,

You will recall that in the course of our meeting today, I conveyed to you my deep concern at the serious differences which exist in your Cabinet. I impressed upon you the immediate necessity for restoring harmony and unity or purpose among the members of the Cabinet in the execution of its policies. You were, however, unable to assure me that these acute differences could be remedied.

This conflict within the Cabinet has for a considerable time been causing great confusion and apprehension in the minds of the people of the State. The situation has reached an unprecedented crisis with the effect that three or your four Cabinet colleagues have, in a memorandum to you, a copy of which they have sent to me, expressed their complete dissatisfaction with your action and policies, which have lost the present Cabinet and confidence of the people. This document clearly indicates that the divergence with in your Cabinet has reached proportions in which the unity prosperity and stability of the State are gravely jeopardised.

When we met today, I further suggested to you that an emergency meeting of the cabinet should be held at my residence this evening so that we could jointly explore the possibilities of securing a stable, unified and efficient Government for the country. But to my regret you evaded the issue.

Under these conditions, I, as Head of the State, have been forced to the conclusion that the present Cabinet cannot continue in Office any longer and hence, I regret to inform you that I have dissolved the Council of Ministers headed by you. A copy of my order in this connection is attached herewith.

I need hardly add how deeply distressed I was at having to take this action, but the vital interests of the people of the State, which it is my duty to safeguard, leave me no alternative. I trust that this will in no way affect the mutual regard and cordial feelings we have for each other.

Yours sincerely
Karan Singh
Sadar-i-Riyasat

7. Sadar-i-Riyasat's Order of 8 August 1953 Dismissing Sheikh Abdullah as Prime Minister

Karan Singh, *Heir Apparent*, Oxford University Press, Oxford, 1982, p. 161

Whereas for some months I have been noticing with growing concern that there have existed acute differences of opinion between members of the Government on basic issues—political, economic and administrative—affecting the vital interests of the State;

And whereas members of the Government have been publicly expressing sharply conflicting points of view regarding these matters;

And whereas on these fundamental issues the view of a majority of the members the Cabinet are sharply opposed to the view held by the Prime Minister and one of his colleagues;

And whereas efforts to work in harmony and pull together as a team having failed, and the majority in the Cabinet has expressed that, lacking as it does in unity of purpose and action, the present Cabinet has lost the confidence of the people;

And whereas the economic distress of the people has considerably increased which need prompt and serious attention;

And whereas a state has reached in which the very process of honest and efficient administration has become impracticable;

And whereas finally, the functioning of the present Cabinet on the basis of joint responsibility has become impossible and the resultant conflicts have gravely jeopardised the unity, prosperity and stability of the State;

I, Karan Singh, Sadar-i-Riyasat, functioning in the interests of the people of the State, who have reposed the responsibility and authority of the Headship of the State in me, do hereby dismiss Sheikh Mohammad Abdullah from the Prime Ministership of the State of Jammu and Kashmir, and consequently the Council of Ministers headed by him is dissolved forthwith.

8. Sadar-i-Riyasat's Letter of 9 August 1953 Appointing Bakshi Ghulam Mohammad as Prime Minister

Karan Singh, *Heir Apparent*, Oxford University Press, Oxford, 1982, pp. 601–2

Karan Mahal,
Srinagar,
August 9, 1953

My dear Bakshi Sahib,

I have just dissolved the cabinet which functioned till today and have relieved it of the powers and functions of civil administration of the

State. I, however, feel that a new Cabinet should be constituted immediately so as to avoid a political and administrative vacuum.

In the task of forming a new Ministry, I have decided to seek your aid and advice. Will you, therefore, make it convenient to meet me immediately so that we might discuss the formation and composition of the new Cabinet.

I need hardly add that the continuance in office of the new Cabinet will depend upon its securing a vote of confidence from the Legislative Assembly during its coming session.

Yours sincerely
Karan Singh

Chapter 7

Kashmir's Constitution is Framed
1954–6

1. Report of the Basic Principles Committee Presented on 3 February 1954

Jammu and Kashmir Constituent Assembly Official Report Part I, Volume 1, pp. 711–25 (Extracts)

Wednesday, the 3rd February, 1954/22nd March 2010

The Constituent Assembly met in the Assembly Chamber, Grey Hall, Jammu, at eleven of the o'clock.

Mr. President (Hon'ble G.M. Sadiq) in the Chair.

Mr. President: Mr. Mir Qasim.

Mr. Mir Qasim: Sir, I beg to present the report of the Basic Principles Committee.

(Read out the following Report)

Report of the Basic Principles Committee

The Basic Principles of the State Constitution will contain provisions relating to the form of the State, the Executive, the Legislature, the

Judiciary, the Public Service Commission, the Official Language and other ancillary matters. The recommendations of the Committee in regard to these matters are contained below:

The State of Jammu and Kashmir will comprise such territories which formed part of the State on 15th August, 1947. While retaining its autonomous character the State will continue to remain acceded with the Union of India.

The sovereignty of the State resides in the people thereof and shall except in regard to matters specifically entrusted to the Union be exercised on their behalf by the various organs of the State.

The governing features of the State Constitution would be based on democracy, equality and social and economic justice. The guiding principle of the State policy would be to ensure the rebuilding of the State by harnessing all its recources for the purpose of securing a better and prosperous life for its people. In order to achieve that end the entire economic activity of the State will be conducted in accordance with plans envisaged in New Kashmir.

In order to satisfy the urge of the people of the State for an intimate association with administration at all levels the Constitution shall embody suitable provisions to that effect. Suitable provision shall also be made enabling the people to develop their various cultures, languages and scripts and to promote closer association and better understanding amongst themselves.

Based on the decision of the Constituent Assembly for the termination of the Hereditary Rulership in the State, the Head of the State will be a person designated as the Sadar-i-Riyasat whose election and other terms of office will be regulated in accordance with the resolution of the Constituent Assembly dated 21st August, 1952.

The Superintendence, direction and control of the Government will vest in a council of Ministers headed by the Prime Minister who will be appointed by the Sadar-i-Riyasat. The Prime Minister will be the person who enjoys the confidence of the State Legislative Assembly. The Council of Ministers will be collectively responsible to the State Legislative Assembly.

The State Legislative Assembly will be composed of members chosen by direct election who will represent constituencies determined by Law.

The determination of constituencies will be on population basis and on the scale of one member for every 40,000 of the population. Election to the State Legislative Assembly shall be on the basis of adult suffrage that is to say, every male or female who has attained the age of 18 years and is not otherwise disqualified under the constitution or any Law made by the State Legislative Assembly on grounds of non-residence, unsoundness of mind, crime or corrupt or illegal practice shall have the right to vote. The State Legislative Assembly will have powers to make laws for the State, in respect of all matters falling within the sphere of its residuary sovereignty. Its life will be five years. Provision for the rights, powers and privileges of the members and the Committees of the Assembly should be made on the lines of the corresponding provisions of the Constitution of India. The superintendence, direction and control of all elections to the State Legislative Assembly including the appointment of Election Tribunals will vest in a Commission to be appointed by the Sadar-i-Riyasat. Provision will also have to be made for a fixed period to promote with special care the interests of the weaker sections of the people by ensuring their representation in the Assembly.

The Judiciary of the State will be independent of executive. The High Court of Judicature shall consist of the Chief Justice and two or more other judges as the Sadar-i-Riyasat may from time to time appoint. In order to ensure the independent and impartial character of the High Court, a judge of the High Court will not be removed from his office except by an order of Sadar-i-Riyasat passed after an address by the National Assembly supported by a majority of the total membership of the National Assembly and by a majority of not less than two third of the members of the House, present and voting, has been presented to the Sadar-i-Riyasat in the same session for such removal on the ground of proved mis-behaviour or incapacity. Provisions will also have to be made for the terms and conditions of service of High Court Judges commensurate with the independence and dignity of the High Court.

The High Court will be a Court of Record and shall have all the powers of such Court including the powers to punish for contempt of itself. The High Court shall have the same powers and jurisdiction as are exercised by it at present under the Constitution or any other law in force in the State. Provisions in this respect will be modelled on those contained in the existing Constitution of the State and the relevant parts of the Constitution of India. Adequate provisions shall also be made in the Constitution for ensuring independence and integrity of the subordinate Courts.

An appeal shall lie to the Supreme Court of India from a judgement, decree or final order of the High Court in Civil proceedings if the High Court certifies that the amount or value of the subject matter of the dispute in the Court of first instance and still in dispute on appeal was and is not less than 20,000 rupees or that the case is a fit one for appeal to the Supreme Court. Similarly an appeal shall lie to the Supreme Court of India in criminal matters if the High Court has on appeal reversed an order of acquittal of an accused person and sentenced him to death or has withdrawn for trial before itself any case from any subordinate court and has in such trial convicted the accused person and sentenced him to death and lastly if the High Court certifies that the case is a fit one for appeal to the Supreme Court. An appeal shall also lie to the Supreme Court of India in certain civil, criminal or other proceedings if the High Court certifies that he involves a substantial question of law as to the interpretation to the provisions of the Constitution of India which apply to the State under Article 370 of the Constitution. The original jurisdiction of the Supreme Court will extend to disputes between the Centre and States or States inter se as specified in Article 131 of the Constitution of India.

Provisions with regard to the establishment of a Public Service Commission should be made in the Constitution. The appointment of its Chairman and members will be made by the Sadar-i-Riyasat. It will function independent of executive. Its Chairman and other members will be removable from office in the manner provided for the removal of a High Court judge.

The Official Language of the State will be Urdu, but English language may be used for all official purposes for which it is being used at present. The Constitution should also recognise the regional languages of the various cultural units of the State.

Further provisions relating to the transitional and ancillary matters should be incorporated in the Constitution. Necessary provisions should also be incorporated in the Constitution ensuring that an amendment of the Constitution shall be made only by two thirds majority of the total membership of the Assembly.

The State of Jammu and Kashmir having acceded to the Union of India, it becomes necessary to define the relationship of the State with Centre. This relationship was originally based on the instrument of Accession whereby the State of Jammu and Kashmir acceded to the Union of India in matters of Defence, Foreign Affairs and Communication. When the dominion of India became a republic, the relationship of the State with the Union was embodied in Article 370 of the Union Constitution. The State's accession to the Union entails certain responsibilities on the Centre for protecting the interests of the State and also for its social and economic development. In order to enable the Centre to discharge its responsibilities which devolve upon it under the Constitution, those provisions of the Constitution of India which may be necessary for this purpose should be made applicable to the State in an appropriate manner. While preserving the internal autonomy of the State all the obligations which flow from the fact of accession and also its elaborations as contained in the Delhi Agreement should find an appropriate place in the Constitution. The Committee is of the opinion that it is high time that finality in this respect should be reached and the relationship of the State with the Union should be expressed in clear and precise terms. The Committee accordingly recommends:—

(i)   that a directive be issued to the Drafting Committee to bring up appropriate proposals defining the sphere of Union jurisdiction in the State suggesting additions, modifications and amendments wherever necessary in the Constitution (Application to Jammu and Kashmir) order, 1950 to suit requirements of the State;

(ii) that the Drafting Committee should forthwith take up the drafting of the Constitution for the State in the light of the recommendations contained in this report and such other reports as have been or are adopted by this Assembly from time to time.

Mr. President: Mr. Mir Qasim!

Mr. Mir Qasim: Sir, I beg to...

Mr. President: Is the Hon'ble member going to present the report relating to Citizenship and Fundamental Rights?

Mr. Mir Qasim: Yes Sir, I beg to present the report relating to Citizenship and Fundamental Rights?

(Read out the following Report)

Report Relating to Citizenship and Fundamental Rights

The Advisory Committee on Fundamental Rights and Citizenship was set up by the resolution of the Constituent Assembly dated 7th November, 1951, in order to make recommendations as regards qualifications required for Citizenship and the determination of Fundamental Rights of the residents of the State. The Committee was reconstituted by the Constituent Assembly by its resolution dated the 20th October, 1953.

The State having acceded to the Union of India, every State Subject and every person having his domicile in the State is a Citizen of India under the provisions of the Constitution of India. It is however, recognized by the Government of India that this position would not affect the existing State Subject definition. While the Committee adheres to principle underlying this definition, it feels that the definition should be liberalized in keeping with the changed times. The Committee therefore recommends that all the three classes of State subjects provided in the definition be removed and a uniform class of permanent resident be established. Accordingly every person residing in the State who is a State Subject of Class I or Class II or who after having acquired immovable property in the State has been ordinarily residing there for a period of not less than ten years prior to the date of enforcement of this provision shall be a permanent resident of the State.

The power of the State Legislative to define 'Permanent residents of the State' in future in any manner it deems fit and to regulate the special rights and privileges of the permanent Residents of the State should be preserved. A majority of not less than two-thirds of the total membership of the House shall be necessary for the exercise of this power. The Committee is of the opinion that while adequate provisions to that effect should be incorporated at an appropriate place in the Constitution of India the provisions of Part II of the Constitution of India relating to Citizenship should also be made applicable to the State and care should be taken to protect the special position accorded to the State Subjects to be now known as 'Permanent residents of the State' and their special rights and privileges. Necessary modification shall also have to be provided in that Part to enable those Subjects of the State who had migrated to Pakistan in 1947 in connection with the disturbances or in fear of the same to return to the State under a permit for resettlement of permanent return issued under the authority of law that would be made by the State Legislature in due course.

The Committee is of the view that the State Legislature should also be competent to make provisions with respect to acquisition and determination of the status of permanent residents of the State and until the State Legislature enacts provisions in that behalf, the existing Ijazatnama Rules should continue to remain in force and the existing procedure for obtaining a State Subject Certificate should apply for the purpose of securing a certificate as to the status of a permanent resident.

Fundamental Rights

An examination of the Fundamental Rights embodied in the Constitution of some of the more important countries of the world would reveal that while there are certain rights which require positive action by the state and which can be granted only so far as such action is practicable, there are others which require that the State shall abstain from pre-judicial action. It is obvious that the rights of the first type are not normally either capable of or suitable for enforcement by legal action, while those of the second type may be so enforced. Both classes of rights are mentioned together under the head 'Fundamental Rights' in certain Constitutions but in certain other distinction between two forms of rights is clearly recognized. A similar distinction is recognized in Dr. Lauterpacht's 'International Bill of Rights of Man' 1945. The Committee having carefully considered the matter is of the view that it would be useful to separate the two classes of rights; firstly those rights; which shall be enforceable in a Court of law and secondly those which shall be guaranteed by enjoining upon the State to take specified and planned action in the field of social and economic reconstruction of the State. This set of rights shall retain fundamental position in the governance of the State.

The question of evolving Fundamental Rights has been considered and discussed at length by the Committee. It has been recognised by the Government of India that the Fundamental Rights as contained in Part III of the Constitution of India, should not come in the way of Land Reforms already introduced by the State or the reforms that might be undertaken by the State in future. This was particularly necessary in view of the fact that the State has not provided for any compensation for the land expropriated under its Land Reforms.

[...]

Similarly all these Fundamental Rights should be subject to the overriding condition that:—

(i) no law of the State relating to State Subjects to be hereafter called 'Permanent Residents' and regulating their rights and privileges; and

(ii) no law hereafter to be made by the State Legislature defining the permanent residents and conferring on them special rights and privileges in relation to acquisition and holding of property in the State or in matter of employment under the State and imposing restrictions on citizens other than permanent residents for settling within the State should become void on the ground that it is inconsistent with or takes away or abridges any of the rights conferred by Part III of Constitution of India.

[...]

In order to avoid any possibility of conflict of the Fundamental Rights proposed above and those contained in Part III of the Constitution of India the Committee feels that the former rights in so far as they vary in certain respects the provisions of the Fundamental Rights of the Union should be reflected in Part III of the Constitution of India. The Government of India has already agreed to provide appropriate modifications or exceptions in Part III of the Constitution of India to suit the requirements of the State.

[...]

It shall be the obligation of the State to protect every monument or place or object of artistic or historic interest declared by the law of the State to be of national importance, from spoliation, destruction, removal, disposal or export as the case may be, and to preserve and maintain according to the law of the State all such monuments or places or objects.

In the light of the foregoing the Committee recommends that:—

(i)   the Drafting Committee, set up by this House be direct to propose appropriate modifications or exceptions in Part II and Part III of the Constitution of India in their application to the State of Jammu and Kashmir, in the light of the recommendations contained in this report; and

(ii) that the Drafting Committee should, while preparing the Draft Constitution of the State incorporate therein the rights and principals indicated above.

*Mr. Abdul Gani Goni: Sir, I rise on a point of order. My note of dissent to the report presented before the House. [...]

2. Abdul Ghani Goni's Dissent from the Report, 1 February 1954

Jammu and Kashmir Constituent Assembly Official Report Part I, Volume 1, p. 726

The Chairman,
Basic Principles Committee
Jammu

Sir,

I submit my note of dissent to the report relating to Basic Principles Committee:—

(1) I suggest that the right of secession should be provided. For this purpose the following sentence should be added at the end of the third paragraph of the report:—

'The State shall retain the right to secede from the Union of India.'

(2) I object to the application of the jurisdiction of the Supreme Court of India over the State, and suggest that the Judicial Board of the State should function as the highest court of the State, as was proposed by the former Committee.

(3) Right of recall should be provided.

In view of the importance of these matters I desire that of all my points of dissent should be placed before the House along with the report.

Yours faithfully,

A.G. Goni,

Date: 1st February, 1954

Jammu

Member

Basic Principles Committee

3. Report of the Drafting Committee Presented on 11 February 1954

Jammu and Kashmir Constituent Assembly Official Report Part I, Volume 1, pp. 837–48

In pursuance of the directives contained in the Reports of the Basic Principles Committee and the Advisory Committee of Fundamental Rights and Citizenship, as adopted by the House on 6th February, 1954, the Drafting Committee has considered the question as to how best to give effect to the recommendations embodied in these Reports. The task which the committee has to discharge requires action in the following directions:—

1. Preparation of the Draft Constitution of the State.

2. Defining the sphere of Union Jurisdiction in the State and for that purpose suggesting the various provisions of the Constitution of India along with modifications and exceptions subject to which these provisions should apply to the State. These would include appropriate modifications and exceptions in Part II (Citizenship) and Part III (Fundamental Rights) in their application to the State of Jammu and Kashmir in the light of the recommendations contained in the report of the Advisory Committee on Citizenship and Fundamental Rights.

3. Consequential amendments in the Jammu and Kashmir Constitution Act, 1996.

As for the preparation of the Draft Constitution for the State the Committee feels that in view of the importance and magnitude of the work involved, adequate time will be needed for the completion of this task and accordingly recommends that the same may be allowed.

The Annexure to this Report while reflecting the desire of the House for the ratification of the accession of the State with the Union of India, indicates in detail provisions of the Constitution of India which generally correspond to Defence, Foreign Affairs and Communication and such other matters as are considered essential concomitants of the fact of accession. In accordance with the directions contained in the two reports, referred to above, the Committee has endeavoured to clearly demarcate the sphere of Union Jurisdiction keeping intact all along the residual powers of the State. While doing so the Committee has further provided adequate safeguards for preserving the basic policies of the State in respect of the land-reforms and the interests of the permanent residents of the State.

A bill for the purpose of making consequential amendments in the Jammu and Kashmir Constitution Act, 1996 in the light of the Report referred to in the opening paragraph of this Report will be drafted and presented to the House in due course.

Dated: 11 February, 1954
Jammu

(Sd.) G.L. Dogra
" Mir Qasim
" D.P. Dhar
" Ghulam Rasool Renzu
" Harbans Singh Azad
Members Drafting Committee

Annexure to the Report of the Drafting Committee

The provisions of the Constitution of India which, in addition to article 1 and article 370, should be applied in relation to the State of Jammu and Kashmir and the exceptions and modifications subject to which they should so apply will be as follows:—

1. The Preamble.

2. Part I: The article 3, there shall be added the following further proviso, namely:—

'Provided further that no bill providing for increasing or diminishing the area of the State of Jammu and Kashmir or altering the name or boundary of that State shall be introduced in Parliament without the consent of the Legislature of that State'.

3. Part II: (a) This part shall be deemed to have been applicable in relation to the State of Jammu and Kashmir as from the 26th day of January, 1950.

(b) To article 7, there shall be added the following further proviso namely:—

Provided further that nothing in this article shall apply to a permanent resident of the State of Jammu and Kashmir who, after having so migrated to the territory now included in Pakistan, returns to the territory of that State under a permit for resettlement in the State or permanent return issued by or under the authority of any law made by the Legislature of that State, and every such person shall be deemed to be a citizen of India.

4. Part III: (a) In article 13, the references to the commencement of the Constitution shall be construed as references to the commencement of this Order.

(b) In clause (4) of article 5, the reference to Scheduled Tribes shall be omitted.

(c) In clause (3) of article 16 the reference to the State shall be construed as not including a reference to the State of Jammu and Kashmir.

(d) To Article 19 there shall be added for a period of five years from the commencement of this Order the following clause namely:—

(7) The words reasonable restrictions occurring in clause (2), (3), (4) and (5) shall be construed as meaning such restrictions as the appropriate Legislature deems reasonable.

(e) In clauses (4) and (7) of article 22 for the words 'parliament', the words 'the Legislature of the State' shall be substituted.

(f) In article 31, clause (3), (4) and (6) shall be omitted, and for clause (5), there shall be substituted the following clause, namely:—

(5) Nothing in clause (2) shall affect:—

    (a)   the provisions of any existing law; or

    (b)   the provisions of any law which the State may hereafter make:—

        (i)   for the purpose of imposing or leaving any tax or penalty or

        (ii)   for the promotion of public health or the prevention of danger of life or property; or

        (iii)   with respect to property declared by law to be evacuee property.

    (g)   In article 31-A, for sub-clause (a) of clause (2), the following sub-clause shall be substituted, namely:—

        (a)   'estate' shall mean land which is occupied or has been let for agricultural purposes or for purposes subservient to agriculture, or for pasture, and includes:—

            (i)   sites of building and other structures on such land;

            (ii)   trees standing on such land;

            (iii)   forest land and wooded waste;

            (iv)   area covered by or fields floating over water;

            (v)   sites of jandars and gharats;

            (vi)   any jagir, inam, muafi, or mukarrari or other similar grant; but does not include:—

                (i)   the site of any building in any town or town area or village abadior and land appurtenant to any such building or site;

                (ii)   any land which is occupied as the site of a town or village; or

                (iii)   any land reserved for building purposes in a municipality or notified area or cantonment or any area for which a town planning scheme is sanctioned.

    (h)   In article 32, clause (3) shall be omitted; and after clause (2), the following new clause shall be inserted namely:—

(2A) Without prejudice to the powers conferred by clauses (1) and (2), the High Court shall have power throughout the territories in relation to which it exercises jurisdiction to issue to any person or authority, including in appropriate cases any Government with those territories, directions or orders or writs, including writs in the nature of habeas corpus mandamus, prohibition, quo warranto and certiorari, or any of them, for the enforcement of any of the rights conferred by this part.

(i) In Article 35:—

   (i)   references to the commencement of the Constitution shall be construed as references to the commencement of this Order;

   (ii) in clause (a) (i), the words, 'clause (3) of article 16, clause (3) of article 32' shall be omitted; and

   (iii) after clause (b), the following clause shall be added, namely:—

(c) Any law in force immediately before the commencement of the Constitution (Application to Jammu and Kashmir) Order, 1954, in the State of Jammu and Kashmir with respect to any of the matters referred to in clause (7) of article 22 shall continue in force until altered or repealed or amended by the Legislature of that State.

(j) After article 35, the following new article shall be added, namely:—

'35-A. Notwithstanding anything contained in this Constitution no existing law in force in the State of Jammu and Kashmir, and no law hereafter enacted by the Legislature of the State:—

(a) defining the classes of persons who are, or shall be, 'permanent residents of the State of Jammu and Kashmir'; or

(b) conferring on such permanent residents any special rights and privileges, or imposing upon other persons any restrictions, as respects:—

   (i)   employment under the State Government;

   (ii) acquisition of immovable property in the State;

   (iii) settlement in the State; or

   (iv) right to scholarships and such other forms of aid as the State Government may provide.

shall be invalid on the ground that it is inconsistent with or takes away or abridges any rights conferred on the other citizens of India by any provision of this Part.

5. Part V: (a) In articles 54 and 55, the references to the elected members of the House of the People and to each member shall include a reference to the representatives of the State shall be deemed to be forty-four lakhs and ten thousand.

(b) In the proviso to clause (1) of article 73, the words 'or in any law made by Parliament' shall be omitted.

(c) Article 81 shall apply subject to the modification that the representatives of the State in the House of the People shall be appointed by the President on the recommendation of the Legislature of the State.

(d) In article 134, clause (2), after the words 'Parliament may', the words 'on the request of the State' shall be inserted.

(e) Articles 135, 136 and 139 shall be omitted.

(f) In articles 139 and 150, references to the State shall be construed as not including the State of Jammu and Kashmir.

(g) In article 151, clause (2) shall be omitted.

6. Part XI: (a) In article 246, the words 'Notwithstanding anything in clause (2) and (3)' accruing in clause (1) and clause (2), (3) and (4) shall be omitted.

(b) Articles 248 and 249 shall be omitted.

(c) In article 250, for the words 'enumerated in the State List', the words 'not enumerated in the Union List' shall be substituted.

(d) In article 251, for the words and figures 'articles 229 and 250', the word and figures 'article 250' shall be substituted and the word 'under this Constitution' shall be omitted; and for the words under either of the said article', the words 'under the said article' shall be substituted.

(e) To article 253, the following proviso shall be added, namely:—
'Provided that after the commencement of the Constitution (Application to Jammu and Kashmir) Order, 1954, no decision affecting the disposition of the State of Jammu and Kashmir shall be made by the Government of India without the consent of the Government of the State'.

(f) In article 254, the words 'or to any provision of an existing law with respect to one of the matters enumerated in the Concurrent List, then, subject to the provisions of clause (2)' and the words 'or as the case may be, the existing law' occurring in clause (1) and the whole of clause (2) shall be omitted.

(g) Article 255 shall be omitted.

(h) Article 256 shall be renumbered as clause (1) of that article, and the following new clause shall be added thereto, namely:—

(2) The State of Jammu and Kashmir shall so exercise its executive power as to facilitate the discharge by the Union of its duties and responsibilities under the Constitution in relation to that State; and in particular, the State shall, if so required by the Union, acquire or requisition property on behalf and at the expense of the Union, or if the property belongs to the State, transfer it to the Union on such terms as may be agreed, or in default of agreement, as may be determined by an arbitration appointed by the Chief Justice of India.

(i) Article 259 shall be omitted.

(j) In clause (2) of Article 261, the words 'made by Parliament' shall be omitted.

7. Part XII: (a) Clause (2) of article 267, article 273, clause (2) of article 283, articles 290 and 291 shall be omitted.

(b) In articles 266, 282, 284, 298, 299 and 300, reference to the State or States shall be construed as not including references to the State of Jammu and Kashmir.

(c) In article 277, references to the commencement of the Constitution shall be construed as references to the commencement of this Order.

8. Part XIII: (a) In clause (1) of article 303, the words 'by virtue of any entry relating to trade and commerce in any of the Lists in the Seventh Schedule' shall be omitted.

(b) In article 306, references to the commencement of the Constitution shall be construed as references to the commencement of this Order.

9. Part XIV: In article 398 after the words 'First Schedule', the words 'other than the State of Jammu and Kashmir' shall be added.

10. Part XV: (a) Article 324 shall apply only in so far as it relates to elections to Parliament and to the offices President and Vice-President.

(b) Article 325, 326, 327, 328 and 329 shall be omitted.

11. Part XVI: (a) Articles 331, 332, 333, 336, 337, 339, and 342 shall be omitted.

(b) In article 330, references to the 'Scheduled Tribes' shall be omitted.

(c) In article 334 and 335 references to the State or States shall be
construed as not including reference to the State of Jammu and
Kashmir.

12. Part XVII: The provisions of this Part shall apply only in so far as
they relate to:—

(i) the official language of the Union;

(ii) the official language for communication between one State and
another, or between a State and the Union; and

(iii) the language of the proceedings in the Supreme Court.

13. Part XVIII: (a) Articles 356, 357 and 360 shall be omitted.

(b) To article 352, the following new clause shall be added, namely:—

'(4) No Proclamation of Emergency made on grounds only of internal
disturbances or imminent danger thereof shall have effect in relation to
the State of Jammu and Kashmir (except as respects article 354) unless
it is made at the request of or with the concurrence of the Government
of the State'.

14. Part XIX: (a) In article 361, after clause (4) the following clause
shall be added, namely:—

'(5) The proviso of this article shall apply in relation to the Sadar-i-
Riyasat of Jammu and Kashmir as they apply in relation to a Rajprmukh,
but without prejudice to the provisions of the Constitution of that
State'.

(b) Articles 362 and 365 shall be omitted.

(c) In article 366 clause (21) shall be omitted.

(d) To article 367, there shall be added the following clause,
namely:—

'(4) For the purposes of this Constitution as it applies in relation to
the State of Jammu and Kashmir:—

(a) references to this Constitution or to the provisions thereof shall
be construed as references to the Constitution or the provisions
thereof as applied in relation to the said State;

(b) references to the Government of the said State shall be construed
as including references to the Sadar-i-Riyasat acting on the advice
of his Council of Ministers;

(c) references to the High Court of a State shall include references
to the High Court of Jammu and Kashmir;

(d) references to the Legislature or the Legislative Assembly of the said State shall be construed as including references to the Constituent Assembly of the State;

(e) references to the permanent residents of the said State shall be construed as meaning person who, before the commencement of the Constitution (Application to Jammu and Kashmir) Order, 1954, were recognised as State subjects under the laws in force in the State or who are recognised by any law made by the State Legislature as permanent residents of the State; and

(f) references to the Rajprmukh shall be construed as references to the person for the time being recognised by the President as the Sadar-i-Riyasat of the Jammu and Kashmir and as including references to any person for the time being recognized by the President as being competent to exercise the powers of the Sadar-i-Riyasat'.

15. Part XX: To Article 368, the following proviso shall be added namely:—

'Provided further that no such amendment shall have effect in relation to the State of Jammu and Kashmir unless applied by order of the President under clause (1) of Article 370'.

16. Part XXI: (a) Articles 369, 371, 373, clauses (1), (2), (3) and (5) of article 374 and articles 376 to 392 shall be omitted.

(b) In article 372—

    (i) clauses (2) and (3) shall be omitted.

    (ii) references to the laws in force in the territory of India shall include references to Hidayats, Ailans, Ishtihrs, circulars, Robkars, Irshads, Yadashts, State Council Resolutions, Resolution of the Constituent Assembly, and other instruments having the force of law in the territory of the State of Jammu and Kashmir; and

    (iii) references to the commencement of the Constitution shall be construed as references to the commencement of the Constitution (Application to Jammu and Kashmir) Order, 1954.

(c) In clause (4) of article 374, the reference to the authority functioning as the Privy Council of a State shall be construed as a reference to the Advisory Board constituted under the Jammu and Kashmir Constitution Act, 1996 and references to the commencement of this Constitution shall be construed as references to the commencement in this order.

17. Part XXII: Articles 394 and 395 shall be omitted.

18. First Schedule.

19. Second Schedule: Paragraph 6 shall be omitted.

20. Third Schedule: Forms V, VI, VII and VIII shall be omitted.

21. Fourth Schedule.

22. Seventh Schedule: In the Union List:—

(i) for entry 3, the entry '3. Administration of cantonments' shall be substituted;

(ii) entries 8, 9, 33 and 34, the words 'trading corporations including' in entry 43, entries 44, 50, 52, 54, 55, 60, 67, 69, 78 and 79, the words 'inter State migration' in entry 81, and entry 97 shall be omitted;

(iii) for entry 56, the entry 53. Petroleum and Petroleum Products but excluding the regulation and development of oilfields and mineral oil resources; other liquids substances declared by Parliament by law to be dangerously inflammable shall be substituted; and

(iv) in entries 72 and 76, the reference to the State shall be construed as not including a reference to the State of Jammu and Kashmir.

(b) The State list and the Concurrent list shall be omitted.

23. Eighth Schedule.

24. Ninth Schedule: After entry 13, the following entries shall be added, namely:—

14. The Jammu and Kashmir Big Landed Estates Abolition Act (No. XVII) of 2007.

15. The Jammu and Kashmir Restitution of Mortgaged properties Act (No. XVI of 2006).

16. The Jammu and Kashmir Tenancy Act (No. II of 1980).

17. The Jammu and Kashmir Distressed Debtors Relief Act (No. XVII of 2006).

18. The Jammu and Kashmir Alienation of Land Act (No. of 1995).

19. Order No. 6H. of 1951 dated 10-3-1951 regarding resumption of Jagirs and other assignments of Land Revenue etc.

20. The Jammu and Kashmir State Kuth Act (No. 1 1978).

Mr. Mir Qasim: Sir, Having presented the Drafting Committee's report, I now beg to move that the report be taken into consideration.

Mr. S.L. Saraf: Sir, I second the motion.

4. The Constituent Assembly Adopts the Report on 15th February and Gives its Concurrence to the Application of the Constitution of India in the Manner Indicated in the Annexure to the Report

Jammu and Kashmir Constituent Assembly Official Report Part I, Volume 1, pp. 873–4

Kotwal Chuni Lal: Sir, I beg to move the following amendment to the Report of the Drafting Committee:

At page 2 of the annexure to the Report of the Drafting Committee, for sub-clause (d) of clause (4) the following sub-clause should be substituted:

(d) In Article 19, for a period of five years from the application of these provisions to the State;

(i) In clauses (3) and (4) after the words 'in the interests of' the words 'the security of the State or' shall be inserted;

(ii) in clause (5) for the words 'or for of the protection of the interests of any Scheduled Tribe' the words 'or for the purposes only of Sub-clause (d) of the said clause, in the interests of the security of the State' shall be substituted; and

(iii) the following new clause shall be added, namely:—

(7) The words 'reasonable restrictions' occurring in clauses (2), (3), (4) and (5) shall be construed as meaning 'such restrictions as the appropriate Legislature deems reasonable'.

*Sir, the purpose of introducing this amendment is that in this Constitution of ours this basic right of the peoples of the State has been recognized that they can peacefully form different Unions and Organizations in the State for the progress of the people and welfare of the country. This is one of the basic rights recognized in every civilized country. We have, therefore, recognized the right and included it in our Constitution. The primary duty of every citizen here is to save his State from danger and preserve its security.

Sir, in view of special geographical position and present circumstances our State has a special international importance. All imperialist war-mongers are greedily looking to our State. Under these circumstances an important duty crops up for us, the representatives of the people that we should incorporate such clauses in our Constitution which can ensure the security of the State. Keeping it in view it is necessary for us to have such clauses in our Constitution which can curb the disruptive elements lawfully. But, no such clause was present in the Constitution. In view of the security, I, therefore, deem it proper that the Government should be allowed such powers so that none might dare to endanger the security of the State. So, I move this amendment and hope that the House will accept it.

*Mr Ghulam Nabi Lolabi: Sir, I support this amendment.

Mr. Mir Qasim: I accept this amendment.

Mr. President: Mr. Mir Qasim.

*Mr. Mir Qasim: Sir, the report of the Drafting Committee is before the House and has been fully discussed. It needs no explanation that political awakening of the people is the true guarantee for a Consti-tution. When people become politically conscious they honour their Constitution. To-day's Draft forms a part of the Constitution. In view of the Reports submitted by the Basic Principles Committee and the Fundamental Rights Committee this House had directed the Drafting Committee to give them a Constitutional shape in order to make the sections, clauses and chapters of Indian Constitution properly applicable which will ratify the relation between India and Kashmir. Now the Draft is before the House in a constitutional language. Not only does the Draft ratify our accession to India but it contains the chapters and provisions of the Constitution of India which are applicable to our State. You must have seen in the Draft that there are not only a few provisions but it contains full chapters like, 1, 2, 3, 5, 9, 10, 13, 14, 15 etc. etc. also. In short we had recommended the application of all such provisions which were necessary to define the relations of a State with the Centre.

In view of the special conditions prevailing in this State it was necessary to guarantee some privileges. The first question relates to the rights of the permanent residents of the State for which necessary provisions have been made in the Draft. The second privilege relates to the Rights of Citizenship. Every section or clause of the Indian Constitution adopted by us regarding the Citizenship Rights is quite obvious from the Draft. The people of Kashmir can enjoy the same rights as are enjoyed by the citizens of India. Here also we have given the same rights to the Indian citizens with one exception namely that some special privileges have been received for permanent citizens of the State i.e. State subjects.

[...]

*Sheikh Moh'd. Akbar: Sir, I beg to support the resolution moved by Hon'ble Harbans Singh Azad.

Mr. President: The question is that 'the Drafting Committee be authorised to incorporate in clause 24 of the Annexure to the report of the Drafting Committee such other laws as may be found essential in the public interest'.

Note: The motion was adopted.

Mr. President: Mr. Dogra.

*Mr. Girdhari Lal Dogra: Sir, I beg to move the following resolution.

Resolution that (a) having adopted the Report of the Drafting Committee this day, the 15th February, 1954; and (b) having thus given its concurrence to the application of the provisions of the Constitution of India in the annexure to the aforesaid report.

This assembly authorises that Government of the State to forward a copy of the said Annexure to the Government of India for appropriate action.

Sir, it is essential that the Report of the Drafting Committee which the House has passed just now should be got incorporate in the Indian Constitution. In this connection the President of India may possibly issue a decree under Article 4570. This recommendation shall become a part of the Indian Constitution according to the provisions of his decree.

[...]

Sir, what I mean to say is that the Indian people have produced men like Gandhi and Nehru (Cheers). They got their Constitution framed by their own representatives. They did not adopt any foreign Constitution. Sir, this is the guarantee for the finality of our accession. To protect the rights of our people it is essential that these recommendations be sent to Government of India for incorporating them in the Indian Constitution. With these words Sir, I move the resolution in the House. Mr. President. Resolved that:

(a) having adopted the Report of the Drafting Committee this day, the 15th February, 1954 and (b) having thus given it concurrence to the application of the provisions of the Constitution of India in the manner indicated in the Annexure to the aforesaid report this Assembly authorises the Government of the State to forward a copy of the said Annexure to the Government of India for appropriate action.

The resolution was adopted unanimously.
[...]

5. The President's Major Order under Article 370, Dated 14 May 1954, CO No. 48, Entitled The Constitution (Application to Jammu & Kashmir) Order 1954. It is the Basic Order

Ministry of Law

New Delhi, the 14th May, 1954

S.R.O. 1610:—The following order made by the President of India is published for general information.

CO 48
The Constitution (Application to Jammu and Kashmir)
Order, 1954

In exercise of the powers conferred by clause (1) of Article 370 of the Constitution, the President, with the concurrence of the Government of the State of Jammu and Kashmir, is pleased to make the following order:—

1. (I) This Order may be called the Constitution (Application to Jammu and Kashmir) Order, 1954.

(2) It shall come into force on the fourteenth day of May, 1954, and shall there upon supersede the Constitution (Application to Jammu and Kashmir) Order, 1950.

2. The provisions of the Constitution which, in addition to Article 1 and Article 370, shall apply in relation to the State of Jammu and Kashmir and the exceptions and modifications subject to which they shall so apply shall be as follows:—

(1) The Preamble

(2) Part I

To Article 3, there shall be added the following further proviso, namely:—

'Provided further that no Bill providing for increasing or diminishing the area of the State of Jammu and Kashmir or altering the name or boundary of that State shall be introduced in Parliament without the consent of the Legislature of the State'.

(3) Part II

(a) This Part shall be deemed to have been applicable in relation to the State of Jammu and Kashmir as from the 26th day of January, 1950.

(b) To Article 7, there shall be added the following further proviso, namely:—

Provided further that nothing in this Article shall apply to a permanent resident of the State of Jammu and Kashmir who, after having so migrated to the territory now included in Pakistan, returns to the territory of the State under a permit for resettlement in that State or permanent return issued by or under the authority of any law made by the Legislature of that State, and every such person shall be deemed to be a citizen of India.

(4) Part III

(a) In Article 13, reference to the commencement of the Constitution shall be construed as references to the commencement of this Order.

(b) In clause (4) of Article 15, the reference to Scheduled Tribes shall be omitted.

(c) In clause (3) of Article 16, the reference to the State shall be construed as not including a reference to the State of Jammu and Kashmir.

(d) In Article 19, for a period of five years from the commencement of this Order:—

    (i) In clauses (3) and (4), after the words 'in the interests of', the words 'the security of the State of', shall be inserted;

    (ii) in clause (5), for the words 'or for the protection of the interest of any Scheduled Tribe', the words 'or in the interests of the security of the State' shall be substituted; and

    (iii) the following new clause shall be added, namely:—

'(7) The words "reasonable restrictions" occurring in clauses (2), (3), (4) and (5) shall be construed as meaning such restrictions as the appropriate Legislature deems reasonable.'

(e) In clauses (4) and (7) of Article 22, for the word 'Parliament', the words 'the Legislature of the State' shall be substituted.

(f) In Article 31, clauses (3), (4) and (6) shall be omitted; and for clause (5), there shall be substituted the following clause, namely:—

(5) Nothing in clause (2) shall affect:—

    (a) the provisions of any existing law; and

    (b) the provisions of any law which the State may hereafter make:—

        (i) for the purpose of imposing or levying any tax or penalty; or

        (ii) for the promotion of public health or the prevention of danger to life or property; or

        (iii) with respect to property declared by law to be evacuee property.

(g) In Article 31 A, the proviso to clause (1) shall be omitted; and for sub-clause (2), the following sub-clause shall be substituted, namely:—

    (a) 'estate' shall mean land which is occupied or has been let for agricultural purposes or for purposes subservient to agriculture, or for pasture, and includes:—

     (i)   sites of buildings and other structures on such land;

     (ii) trees standing on such land;

     (iii) forest land and wooded waste;

     (iv) area covered by or fields floating over water;

     (v) sites of jandars and gharats;

     (vi) any jagir, inam, muafi or mukarrari or other similar grant; but does not include:—

         (i)   the site of any building in any town, or town area or village abadi or any land appurtenant to any such building or site;

         (ii) any land which is occupied as the site of a town or village; or

         (iii) any land reserved for building purposes in a municipality or notified area of cantonment or town area or any area for which *a* town planning scheme is sanctioned.

(h) In Article 32, clause (3) shall be omitted; and after clause (2), the following new clause shall be inserted, namely:—

(2A) Without prejudice to the powers conferred by clauses (1) and (2), the High Court shall have power throughout the territories in relation to which it exercises jurisdiction to issue to any person or authority, including in appropriate cases any Government within those territories, directions or orders or writs, including writs in the nature of *habeas corpus, mandamus, prohibition, quo warranto* and *certiorari,* or any of them, for the enforcement of any of the rights conferred by this part.

  (i) In Article 35:—

     (i)   references to the commencement of Constitution shall be construed as references to the commencement of this Order;

     (ii) in clause (a) (i) the words, figures and brackets 'clause (3) of Article 16, clause (3) of Article 32' shall be omitted; and

     (iii) after clause (b), the following clause shall be added, namely:—

(c) no law with respect to preventive detention made by the Legislature of the State of Jammu and Kashmir, whether before or after commencement of the Constitution (Application to Jammu and Kashmir) Order 1954, shall be void on the ground that it is inconsistent with any of the provisions of this part, but any such law shall, to the extent of such inconsistency, cease to have effect on the expiration of five years from the commencement of the said Order, except as respects things done or omitted to be done before the expiration thereof.

(j)   After Article 35, the following new Article shall be added, namely:—

35A, Saving of law with respect to permanent residents and their rights:— Notwithstanding anything contained in this Constitution, no existing law in force in the State of Jammu and Kashmir, and no law hereafter enacted by the Legislature of the State:

(a)   defining the classes or persons who are, or shall be, permanent residents of the State of Jammu and Kashmir, or

(b)   conferring on such permanent residents any special rights and privileges or imposing upon other persons any restrictions as respects:—

   (i)   employment under the State Government;

   (ii)   acquisition of immovable property in the State;

   (iii)   settlement in the State; or

   (iv)   right to scholarships and such other forms of aid as the State Government may provide, shall be void on the ground that is inconsistent with or takes away or abridges any rights conferred on the other citizens of India by any provision of this Part.

(5) Part V

(a)   For the purposes of Articles 54 and 55, references to the elected members of the Houses of the People and each such member shall include references to the representatives of the State of Jammu and Kashmir in that House; and the population of the State of Jammu and Kashmir shall be deemed to be forty-four lakhs and ten thousand.

(b)   In the proviso to clause (1) of Article 73, the words 'or in any law made by Parliament' shall be omitted.

(c)   Article 81 shall apply subject to the modification that the representatives of the State in the House of the People shall be appointed by the President on the recommendation of the Legislature of the State.

(d) In Article 134, clause (2), after the words 'Parliament may', the words 'on the request of the Legislature of the State' shall be inserted.

(e) Articles 135, 136 and 139 shall be omitted.

(f) In Articles 149 and 150, references to the States shall be construed as not included the State of Jammu and Kashmir.

(g) In Article 151, clause (2) shall be omitted.

(6) Part XI

(a) In Article 246, the words, brackets and figures 'Notwithstanding anything in clauses (2) and (3)' occurring in clause (1), and clauses (2), (3) and (4) shall be omitted.

(b) Articles 248 and 249 shall be omitted.

(c) In Article 250, for the words 'to any of the matters enumerated in the State List', the words 'also to matters not enumerated in the Union List' shall be substituted.

(d) In Article 251, for the words and figures, 'Articles 249 and 250' the words and figures 'Article 250' shall be substituted, and the words 'under this Constitution' shall be omitted; and, for the words 'under either of the said Articles', the words 'under the said Article' shall be substituted.

(e) In Article 253, the following proviso shall be added, namely:—
'Provided that after the commencement of the Constitution (Application to Jammu and Kashmir) Order, 1954, no decision affecting the disposition of the State of Jammu and Kashmir shall be made by the 'Government of India without the consent of the Government of that State'.

(f) In Article 254, the words, brackets and figure 'or to any provision of an existing law with respect to one of the matters enumerated in the Concurrent List, than, subject to the provisions of clause (2)' and the words 'or as the case may be, the existing law', occurring in clause (1), and the whole of clause (2) shall be omitted.

(g) Article 255 shall be omitted.

(h) Article 256 shall be renumbered, as clause (1) of that Article, and the following new clause shall be added thereto, namely:—

'(2) The State of Jammu and Kashmir shall so exercise its executive power as to facilitate the discharge by the Union of its duties and responsibilities under the Constitution in relation to that State; and in particular, the said State shall, if so required by the Union, acquire or requisition property on behalf and at the expense of the Union, or if the property belongs to the State, transfer it to the Union on such terms as may be agreed, or in default of agreement, as may be determined by an arbitrator appointed by the Chief Justice of India'.

(i) Article 259 shall be omitted.

(j) In clause (2) of Article 261, the words 'made by Parliament' shall be omitted.

(7) Part XII

(a) Clause (2) of Article 267, Article 273, clause (2) of Article 283, Articles 290 and 291 shall be omitted.

(b) In Articles 266, 282, 284, 298, 299 and 300, references to the State or States shall be construed as not including references to the State of Jammu and Kashmir.

(c) In Articles 277 and 295, references to the commencement of the Constitution shall be construed as references to the commencement of this Order.

(8) Part XIII

(a) In clause (1) of Article 303, the words 'by virtue of any entry relating to trade and commerce in any of the Lists in the Seventh Schedule' shall be omitted.

(b) In Article 306, references to the commencement of the Constitution shall be construed as references to the commencement of this Order.

(9) Part XIV

In Article 308, after the words 'First Schedule', the words 'other than the State of Jammu and Kashmir' shall be added.

(10) Part XV

(a) Article 324, shall apply only in so far as it relates to elections to Parliament and to the offices of President and Vice-President.

(b) Articles 325, 326, 327, 328 and 329 shall be omitted.

(11) PART XVI

(a) In Article 330, references to the 'Scheduled Tribes' shall be omitted.

(b) Articles 331, 332, 333, 336, 337, 339 and 342 shall be omitted.

(c) In Articles 334 and 335, references to the State or the States shall be construed as not including references to the State of Jammu and Kashmir.

(12) Part XVII

The provisions of this part shall apply only in so far as they relate to:—

(i) the official language of the Union;

(ii) the official language for communication between one State and another, or between a State and the Union; and

(iii) the language of the proceedings in the Supreme Court.

(13) Part XVIII

(a) To Article 352, the following new clause shall be added, namely:—

'(4) No proclamation of Emergency made on grounds only of internal disturbance or imminent danger thereof shall have effect in relation to the State of Jammu and Kashmir (except as respects Article 354) unless it is made at the request or with the concurrence of the Government of that State'.

(b) Articles 356, 357 and 360 shall be omitted.

(14) Part XIX

(a) In Article 361, after clause (4) the following clause shall be added, namely:—

'(5) The provisions of this Article shall apply in relation to the Sadar-i-Riyasat of Jammu and Kashmir as they apply in relation to a

Rajpramukh but without prejudice to the provisions of the Constitution of that State'.

(b) Articles 362 and 365 shall be omitted.

(c) In Article 366, clause (21) shall be omitted.

(d) To Article 367, there shall be added the following clause, namely:—

'(4) For the purposes of this Constitution as it applies in relation to the State of Jammu and Kashmir:—

(a) references to this Constitution or to the provisions thereof shall be construed as references to the Constitution or the provisions thereof as applied in relation to the said State;

(b) references to the Government of the said State shall be construed as including references to the Sadar-i-Riyasat acting on the advice of his Council of Ministers;

(c) references to a High Court shall include references to the High Court of Jammu and Kashmir;

(d) references to the Legislature or the Legislative Assembly of the said State shall be construed as including references to the Constituent Assembly of the said State;

(e) references to the permanent residents of the said State shall be construed as meaning persons who, before the commencement of the Constitution (Application to Jammu and Kashmir) Order, 1954, were recognised as State subjects under the laws in force in the State or who are recognised by any law made by the Legislature of the State as permanent residents of the State; and

(f) references to the Rajpramukh shall be construed as references to the person for the time being recognised by the President as the Sadar-i-Riyasat of Jammu and Kashmir and as including references to any person for the time being recognised by the President as being competent to exercise the powers of the Sadar-i-Riyasat'.

(15) Part XX

To Article 368, the following proviso shall be added, namely:—

'Provided further that no such amendment shall have effect in relation to the State of Jammu and Kashmir unless applied by order of the President under clause (1) of Article 370'.

(16) Part XXI

(a) Articles 369, 371, 373, clauses (1), (2), (3) and (5) of Article 374 and Articles 376 to 392 shall be omitted.

(b) In Article 372:—
   (i) clauses (2) and (3) shall be omitted;
   (ii) references to the laws in force in the territory of India shall include references to hidayats, ailans, ishtihars, circulars, robkars, irshads, yadashts, State Council Resolutions, Resolutions of the Constituent Assembly, and other instruments having the force of law in the territory of the State of Jammu and Kashmir; and
   (iii) references to the commencement of the Constitution shall be construed *as* references to the commencement of this Order.

(c) In clause (4) of Article 374, the reference to the authority functioning as the Privy Council State shall be construed as a reference to Advisory Board constituted under the Jammu and Kashmir Constitution Act, 1996, and references to the commencement of the Constitution shall be construed as reference to the commencement of this Order.

(17) Part XXII

Articles 394 and 395 shall be omitted.

(18) First Schedule

(19) Second Schedule

Paragraph 6 shall be omitted.

(20) Third Schedule

Forms V, VI, VII, and VIII shall be omitted.

(21) Fourth Schedule

(22) Seventh Schedule

    (a) In the Union List:—

        (i) for entry 3, the entry '3. Administration of cantonments', shall be substituted;

      (ii) entries 8, 9, 33 and 34, the words 'trading corporations including' in entry 43, entries 44, 50, 52, 54, 55, 60, 67, 69, 78, and 79 the words 'inter-State migration' in entry 81 and entry 97 shall be omitted;

     (iii) for entry 53, the entry '53. Petroleum and Petroleum Produces, but excluding the regulation and development of oil-fields and mineral oil resources; other liquids and substances declared by Parliament by law to be dangerously inflammable' shall be substituted; and

     (iv) in entries 72 and 76, the reference to the States shall be construed as not including a reference to the State of Jammu and Kashmir.

    (b) The State List and the Concurrent List shall be omitted.

(23) Eighth Schedule

(24) Ninth Schedule

After entry 13, the following entries shall be added, namely:—

'14. The Jammu and Kashmir Big Landed Estates Abolition Act (No. XVII of Svt. 2007).

15. The Jammu and Kashmir Restitution of Mortgaged Properties Act (No. XVI of Svt. 2006).

16. The Jammu and Kashmir Tenancy Act (No. 11 of Svt. 1980).

17. The Jammu and Kashmir Distressed Debtors Relief Act (No. XVII of Svt. 2006).

18. The Jammu and Kashmir Alienation of Land Act (No. V. of Svt. 1995).

19. Order No. 6-H of 1951, dated 10th March, 1951 regarding Resumption of Jagirs and other assignments of Land Revenue, etc.

20. The Jammu and Kashmir State Kuth Act (No. 1 of Svt. 1978)'.

6. The Constituent Assembly Resolves on 6 April 1955 to Authorise the President to Extend to the State 3 Entries in the Union List

Jammu and Kashmir Constituent Assembly Official Report Part I, Volume 1, pp. 903–4 and 909–10

Mr. G.L. Dogra: Sir, I move that

'This Assembly do accord its concurrence to the application of the following further provisions of the Constitution of India to the State, namely:—

(a) Entry 53 of the seventh schedule—Union List (hereinafter referred to as the Union List) in so far as it relates to the regulation and development of oil fields and mineral oil resources;

(b) Entry 54 of the Union List—Regulation of mines and mineral development to the extent to which such regulation and development under the control of the Union is declared by Parliament by law to be expedient in the public interest;

(c) Entry 67 of the Union List—Ancient and historical monuments and archaeological sites and remains declared by Parliament by law to be of national importance.

This Assembly do further authorise the Government of Jammu and Kashmir to communicate a copy of this resolution to the Government of India for appropriate action'.

Sir, the Hon'ble members of this House in particular and the people of the State in general know that this House has taken some decisions in respect of the application of some provisions and Entries of the Constitution of India to the State. We had made minimum possible Entries applicable to the State but after adopting the Application Order we felt the necessity of seeking help in respect of some Entries from the Central Government. We wanted to secure help from the Centre for the survey of mineral oil resources and mines. The Central Government also showed its willingness to give us such help but the correspondence with the Centre makes it clear that it cannot provide for any such expenditure here because we had not applied certain Entries and part of Entry 53. The difficulty arose because of this. The Application Order did not allow the Centre to incur such expenditure here. As soon as the matter came to our notice we wanted to get concurrence of the House for the application of certain provisions of the Constitution of India to the State. Since we want to develop our country in our own way; we want to spread a network of roads throughout the State; we want to improve our means of communication; we want to industrialize our country, that is why, today, we want to make a proper survey of our country which should be of final nature. The conditions prevailing in the country demand that we should immediately put our country on the path of progress so that poverty and unemployment are eradicated. Therefore, keeping all these things in view we tried to remove the obstacles facing us. As this House is a sovereign body the Central Government cannot apply any new Entry to the State without the concurrence of this House. Besides, the Central Government do not wish to apply any new Entry without our consent. Here the Jammu and Kashmir Government also does not wish to take any such step without the concurrence of this House. That is why the need of putting forth this resolution in the House has arisen.

[...]

Mr. G.M. Sadiq (Hon'ble President): Now the question is:—

'This Assembly do accord its concurrence to the application of the following further provisions of the Constitution of India to the State, namely:—

(a) Entry 53 of the Seventh Schedule:—Union List (hereinafter referred to as the Union List) in so far as it relates to the regulation and development of oil fields and mineral oil resources;

(b) Entry 54 of the Union List:—Regulation of mines and mineral development to the extent to which such regulation and development under the control of the Union as declared by Parliament by Law to be expedient in the public interest;

(c) Entry 67 of the Union List:—Ancient and historical monuments and archaeological sites and remains declared by Parliament by Law to be of national importance.'

'This Assembly do further authorize the Government of Jammu and Kashmir to communicate a copy of this resolution to the Government of India for appropriate action'.

Note: The motion was adopted.

7. The Assembly Amends the State Constitution on 6 April 1955

Jammu and Kashmir Constituent Assembly Official Report
Part I, Volume 1, pp. 911–12

Mr. Girdhari Lal Dogra: I move that the Bill be taken into consideration.

(Note: The text of the Bill has been printed as Appendix I.)

Mr. Assad Ullah Mir: Sir, I second it.

Mr. President: Now the question is that 'A Bill to amend further the J&K Constitution Act, 1946', be taken into consideration.

Note: The motion was adopted.

Mr. G.L. Dogra: Sir, I move that the Bill be passed.

Mr. Assad Ullah Mir: Sir, I second it.

Mr. President: Now the question is that 'A Bill to amend further the J&K Constitution Act, 1946' be passed.

Note: The motion was adopted and the Bill passed.

Mr. President: Mr. G.L. Dogra!

Mr. G.L. Dogra: Sir, I move a motion to amend the rules governing the allowances of members of the Jammu and Kashmir Constituent Assembly 2008 (vide Annexure).

Mr. G.L. Dogra: Sir, so far as the members of the Constituent Assembly were drawing Rs 25/- per diem as their allowance. They got the same rate if they participated in any session of the Assembly or in any committee meeting. This system of paying daily allowance has not been considered proper. Nowhere in India or in any progressive country of the world this system is considered good, because it is said to be a source of mental dissatisfaction which I think is not proper. If at any time the session of the Assembly or a Committee meeting is prolonged for some reason it is said that the Hon'ble members have intentionally prolonged it. If you study the system in vogue in India or elsewhere in the progressive countries of the world you will see that a monthly allowance is granted to the members and whenever they have to attend any Committee meeting or the Assembly session they are paid some more daily allowance. Keeping all these things in view I have tabled this motion before the House to amend the old system and request you to adopt this motion unanimously.

Mr. S.L. Saraf: Sir, I second the motion.

Mr. President: Now the motion to amend the rules governing the allowances of the members of J&K Constituent Assembly, 2008 (as contained in appendix II) is before the House.

Some amendments in respect of the motion have come. I will request Mr. Chuni Lal Kotwal to move this amendment.

Mr. Chuni Lal Kotwal: Sir, I move:

'For the words "and includes in the case of a session only such residence not exceeding one day immediately preceding [...]'

8. The Text of the Amending Bill

Jammu and Kashmir Constituent Assembly Official Report,
Volume I, pp. 915–19

A Bill further to amend the Jammu and Kashmir Constitution Act of 1996.

Be it enacted by the Constituent Assembly as follows:—

1. Short title and commencement:—(1) This Act may be called the Jammu and Kashmir Constitution (Amendment) Act, 2011.

(2) Except as hereinafter provided, the provisions of this Act shall be deemed to have come into force from 14th May, 1954.

2. Insertion of new part after section 5:—After section 5 of the Jammu and Kashmir Constitution Act, 1996 (hereinafter referred to as, 'the said Act') the following new part shall be inserted namely:—

Part I (A)

Permanent Residents

5-A. Every person who is or is deemed to be a citizen of India under the provisions of Part II of the Constitution of India as applied to the State of Jammu and Kashmir under the Constitution (Application to Jammu and Kashmir) Order, 1954, shall be a permanent resident of the State of Jammu and Kashmir if at the date of commencement of the Jammu and Kashmir Constitution (Amendment) Act, 2011, namely the 14th May, 1954;

(a) he was a State Subject of Class II as defined in the State Subject Notification No. I-L/84 dated 20th April, 1927 read with Notification No. 13/L dated 27th June, 1932, or

(b) after having acquired immovable property in the Jammu and Kashmir State in pursuance of an *Ijazatnama* granted under the *Ijazatnama* Rules for the time being in force, he has been ordinarily resident in the territory of the State for not less than ten years prior to the date of such commencement.

Explanation:—All persons who before the commencement of the Constitution (Application to Jammu and Kashmir) Order, 1954 were State Subjects of Class I or Class II as defined in the State Subject Notification No. I-L/84 dated 20th April, 1927, read with Notification No. 13/L dated 27th June, 1932, and who having migrated after the first day of March, 1947, to the territory now included in Pakistan return to the State under a permit for resettlement in the State or permanent return issued by or under the authority of any law made by the State Legislature shall continue to be deemed permanent residents of the State.

Status of permanent residentship of certain juristic persons:—5-B. Notwithstanding anything contained in the foregoing provisions of this Act every Company, which, immediately before the commencement of the Constitution (Application to Jammu and Kashmir) Order, 1954, was recognised to be a State Subject within the meaning of the State Subject Notification No. I-L/84 dated 20th April, 1927 shall be deemed to be a permanent resident at such commencement.

Explanation:—In this section 'Company' shall have meaning assigned to it in the Jammu and Kashmir Companies Act, 1927.

Continuance of the Status of permanent residentship:—5-C. Every person who is or who is deemed to be a permanent resident of the State of Jammu and Kashmir shall subject to the provisions of any law that may be made by the State Legislature, continue to be such permanent resident.

State Legislature to define and regulate the rights of permanent residents by 2/3rd majority:—5-D. The power of the State Legislature to define the term permanent resident of the State and to regulate their special rights and privileges shall be exercisable only by a majority of not less than two third of the total membership of the Legislative Assembly.

State Legislature to make laws respecting the acquisition of the status of permanent resident:—5-E. Nothing contained in the forgoing provisions shall derogate from the power of the State Legislature to make such laws as it thinks fit with respect to the acquision of the status of the permanent residents and until the State Legislature enacts provisions in that behalf the existing *Ijazatnama* Rules shall continue to remain in force and the existing procedure for obtaining a State subject Certificate shall be followed for the purpose of securing the certificate of being a permanent resident of the State.

References to the term State subject:—5-F. Unless the context otherwise requires all references in the existing laws of the State to the expression 'State Subject' shall be construed as references to the permanent residents of the State.

3. Amendment of section 23 Act XIV of 1996:—In section 23 of the said Act for the words 'State Subject' the words 'permanent residents of the State' shall be substituted.

Amendment of section 29 Act XIV of 1996:—Section 29 of the said Act shall be numbered as sub-section (1) of the said section and after sub-section (I) as so renumbered the following sub-section shall be added, namely—

Powers, privileges and immunities of the Legislative Assembly and its members and Committees:—(2) In other respects, the powers, privileges and immunities of the Legislative Assembly and of the Legislative Assembly and of the members and the Committees thereof shall be such as may from time to time be defined by law and until so defined shall be those of the Parliament of India and its Members and Committees.

5. Amendment of section 31, Act XIV of 1996:—In sub-section (3) of section 31 of the said Act for the words 'then become an Act and have the force of law' the words 'become an Act and have the force of law as soon as it is published in either of the aforesaid languages' shall be substituted.

6. Amendment of section 37, Act XIV of 1996:—In section 37 of the said Act for the words 'any member of Board Judicial Advisors' the words 'any judge of the Supreme Court of India' shall be substituted.

7. Amendment of section 43, Act XIV of 1996:—In section 43 the said Act:—

(i) in clause (c) the words 'and the members of Board of Judicial Advisors' shall be deleted; and

(ii) The clause (d) the following new clause shall be inserted, namely:—

'(dd) The salaries and allowances of the Speaker and the Deputy Speaker of the Legislative Assembly'.

8. Amendment of section 54, Act XIV of 1996:—In section 54 of the said Act for the words 'Coat of arms' the words 'State emblem' shall be substituted.

9. Amendment of section 56, Act XIV of 1996:—(i) In sub-section (2) of section 56 of the said Act, for the words 'Rupees ten thousand' the words 'Rupees twenty thousand' shall be substituted.

(ii) This section shall come into force from the date of publication of this Act in the Government Gazette.

10. Omission of section 62, Act XIV of 1996:—Section 62 of the said Act shall be omitted.

11. Insertion of new section after section 62, Act XIV of 1996:—After section 62 of the said Act, the following new section shall be inserted, namely:—

62-A. If the High Court is satisfied that a case pending in a court subordinate to it involves a substantial question of law as to the interpretation of this Act or the Constitution of India as applied to the State by the Constitution (Application to Jammu and Kashmir) Order, 1954, the determination of which is necessary for the disposal of the case, it shall withdraw the case and may:—

(a) either dispose of the case itself; or

(b) determine the said question of law and return the case to the Court from which the case has been so withdrawn together with a copy of its judgment on such question and the said court shall on receipt thereof proceed to dispose of the case in conformity with such judgment.'

12. Insertion of new section 66-A, Act XIV of 1996:—After section 66 of the said Act the following new section shall be inserted, namely—

66-A. If at any time it appears to the Council that a question of law or fact has arisen, or is likely to arise, which is of such a nature and of such public importance that it is expedient to obtain the opinion of the High Court upon it, it may refer the question to that Court for consideration and the Court may, after such hearing as it thinks fit, report to the Council its opinion thereon.

13. Omission of section 71, Act XIV of 1996:—Section 71 of the said Act shall be omitted.

14. Omission of section 75, Act XIV of 1996:—Section 75 of the said Act shall be omitted.

15. Insertion of new section 76-A, Act XIV of 1996:—After Section 76 of the said Act the following new section shall be inserted, namely:—

'Savings as regards Letters Patent—76-A. The provisions of the Letters Patent granted to the High Court on 28th May, 1948 shall continue to remain in force except in so far as these are inconsistent with the provisions of this Act or of any other law for the time being in force.'

16. Amendment of Schedule I-A, Act XIV of 1996:—In form 'C' of Schedule I-A of the said Act the words 'for the members of the Board of Judicial Advisors and' occurring in the long title and the words 'President/a member of the Board of Judicial Advisors', in the text of the oath, shall be omitted.

17. Amendment of Schedule III, Act XIV of 1996:—For the third part of Schedule III of the said Act the following shall be substituted, namely:—

  (i) Such allowances as are admissible to the members of the Con-
       stituent Assembly.
  (ii) This provision shall be deemed to have come into force from
       1st April, 1955.

9. Report of the Drafting Committee is Presented on 10 October 1956

Jammu and Kashmir Constituent Assembly Debates, Official Report, Part II, 10 October 1956, p. 947

*Mr. G.L. Dogra: Sir, I beg to present the report of the Drafting Committee and introduce the draft Constitution as settled by the Committee.

Sir, on 20th October, 1953, this House set up the Drafting Committee. This Committee prepared this Draft keeping in view the report of the Basic Principles Committee and other resolutions adopted by the House from time to time. The fundamental principles on which the draft is based are as follows:—

Parliamentary democracy; responsibility of the Executive to the Legislature; joint responsibility of the Cabinet; separation of the various powers of the State, viz; Executive, Legislative and Judicial; and finally the rule of law.

One basic feature of the Constitution is that we have once again affirmed that the State is an integral and inalienable part of India and will ever remain so. The Constitution lays down that the State will consist of all those territories which were under the sovereignty or suzerainty of the Ruler of the State till 1947. Rights of the permanent residents of the State have been secured while they will also enjoy fully the benefits of the citizenship of India.

[...]

10. The Constituent Assembly Begins Consideration of the Draft Constitution on 22 October 1956

Jammu and Kashmir Constituent Assembly Debates, Official Report, Part II, p. 947

Shri G.L Dogra: Sir, the motion which I want to present before the House is that:—

'The Assembly do proceed to take into consideration the Draft Constitution of Jammu and Kashmir, settled by the Drafting Committee, appointed in pursuance of the Resolution of the Assembly dated: 20th October, 1953'.
[...]

11. The Constituent Assembly Accords its Concurrence on 14 November 1956 to the Application to the State of Certain Provisions of the Constitution of India

Jammu and Kashmir Constituent Assembly Debates, Official Report, Part II, p. 1214

Mr. Mir Qasim: Sir, I move:
'This Assembly do accord its concurrence to the application on the lines herein set out of the following provisions of the Constitution of India to the State, namely:—

(a) Articles 149 and 150 omitting the modifications made by clause (f) of paragraph 5 of the Constitution (Application to Jammu and Kashmir) Order, 1954;

(b) Clause (2) of Article 151 subject to the modification that the reference to the Rajpramukh shall be construed as reference to the person for the time being recognised by the President as the Sadar-i-Riyasat of Jammu and Kashmir; and

(c) Entry 76 in list 1 (Union List) in the Seventh Schedule omitting the modification made by sub-clause (iv) of Clause (a) of paragraph 22 of the Constitution (Application to Jammu and Kashmir) Order, 1954 in so far it relates to this entry.

This Assembly do also authorise the Government of Jammu and Kashmir to communicate a copy of this resolution to the Government of India for appropriate action.

I move that this resolution be passed.'

Mr. Sham Lal Saraf: I second the resolution.

The motion was adopted.

[...]

12. The Constituent Assembly Accords its Concurrence on 14 November 1956 to the Application to the State of the Constitution (Sixth Amendment) Act, 1956 Enacted by Parliament

Jammu and Kashmir Constituent Assembly Debates, Official Report, March 1956, September, November 1956, and January 1957 Sessions, Part II (1956), p. 1215

Mr. President: Mr. Mir Qasim:

Mr. Mir Qasim: Sir, I beg to move: This Assembly do accord its concurrence to the application to the State of the provisions enacted in the Constitution (Sixth amendment) Act, 1956, amending the Constitution of India, except in so far as they relate to the amendment of the State list in the Seventh Schedule.

This Assembly do also authorise the Government of Jammu and Kashmir to communicate a copy of this resolution to the Government of India for appropriate action.

Sir, the idea behind this motion is to get the concurrence of the House to the application of the provisions of Constitution (Sixth amendment) Act, 1956, to our State. Their application will be greatly beneficial to us. The receipts from the interstate Sales Tax are pooled at the Centre. Kashmir State will also be entitled to get its due share from these receipts. There is no idea to impose any new tax. The idea is that in case this State purchase anything from other States that tax is charged from the source. The application of these provisions would enable the State of Jammu and Kashmir to get its share from the amount of tax collected in Central pool.

Mr. Assadullah Mir: Sir, I second the motion.

The motion was adopted.

[...]

13. The Constituent Assembly Adopts on 17 November 1956 the Draft Constitution as Revised

Jammu and Kashmir Constituent Assembly Debates,
Official Report, March 1956, September, November 1956,
and January 1957 Sessions, Part II (1956), p. 1248

Mr. President: The question is:—
   'That the Draft constitution as revised be passed'.
   (Note: The motion was adopted and the constitution passed.)

14. The Constituent Assembly Adopts on 17 November 1956 a Resolution Moved by Mir Qasim that it Shall Stand Dissolved from 26 January 1957

Jammu and Kashmir Constituent Assembly Debates, Official
Report, March 1956, September 1956 and January 1957
sessions, Part II (1956), pp. 1248 and 1249–50

*Mr. Mir Qasim: Sir, I move that:
   'Whereas the Constituent Assembly came into being for framing the
constitution for the State;
   And whereas the Constituent Assembly has enacted and adopted the
Constitution for the State;
   Now therefore, this Assembly resolves that it shall stand dissolved on
the 26th day of January, 1957, which is the date of the commencement
of the constitution'.
   Sir, I would like to make a brief submission with regard to this resolution. The resolution aims at dissolving the Constituent Assembly, by
passing and adopting the constitution which will come into force on
the 26th January, 1957. The Assembly has done its primary and main
function and it is but natural that it should stand dissolved. Legally
it could not have been dissolved by any authority because the people

elected this Assembly for a special object. Now the object having been achieved it is reasonable to dissolve it by way of a resolution. Hence the resolution. This Assembly is not capable of protecting the constitution. It had only the mandate of framing and enacting a constitution for the State and nothing more.

The constitution has set forth the rights of the people. For protection of those rights the judiciary, the legislature and the executive will function independently and has further defined the limits of their powers.

[...]

The reason for our parting with friends in 1953 was that they were trying to impede the work of constitution framing. But we were conscious that our prime duty was to frame a constitution that is why we did not permit them to distract us from the path.

I hope that the future Government will try their best to implement the provisions of this constitution to their best ability without fear or favour. I moreover believe that if the people realize or become aware subsequently they will be in a better position to protect their rights. Present Constituent Assembly's work has come to an end and it has done its duty successfully.

I hope the Hon'ble members will approve of this resolution moved in the House for the dissolution.

*Mr. Piyar Singh: I second the motion, Sir.

Mr. President: The question is:

Whereas the Constituent Assembly came into being for framing the constitution for the State;

And whereas the Constituent Assembly has enacted and adopted constitution for the State;

Now, therefore, this Assembly resolves that it should stand dissolved on the 26th day of January, 1957 which is the date of the commencement of the constitution. (Motion was adopted.)

[...]

The Assembly then adjourned till Monday, the 19th November, 1956 at 11.30 a.m.

15. Mir Qasim's Speech on 25 January 1957

Jammu and Kashmir Constituent Assembly Debates,
Official Report, Part II (1956), p. 1265

Mr. Mir Qasim: President, Sir, The House has today successfully completed the work entrusted to it. [...] It is a well-known fact that in 1950 the National Conference decided to convene a Constituent Assembly for the State. All those people who were desirous to see a prosperous Kashmir backed this decision and they still wish Kashmir well. A few persons have, however, swerved from that decision. At the time when the National Conference decided to set up a Constituent Assembly, the Government of India also stated that the proposed Assembly was to end the autocratic rule and set up a democratic regime in Kashmir and besides this it will also ratify the accession of the State to India already entered into through the instrument of accession which was accepted by Lord Mountbatten, the then Governor-General of India. The Assembly was free to ratify that accession. The late Mr. Gopala Swami Ayyanger said in this connection that the Assembly was free if it chose to continue or not to continue the accession and could decide for Kashmir to secede from the Union. I very well remember the words of the Indian leaders when they said that the Assembly can choose to remain with India or to secede from her. In view of the fact that this Assembly had the right not to confirm the accession. I wonder how can one have the face to say that this Assembly was incompetent to ratify the accession. If it was competent to do one thing it was also competent to do the other. These things were manifest in our election manifesto. Our election manifesto clearly stated that firstly this Assembly will decide the future of hereditary rulership and, secondly, it will decide the question of land compensation to those land-lords whose land was distributed amongst the tillers; thirdly, the Assembly was to frame a constitution for the State and lastly, it was to decide the question of State's accession.
[...]

16. The President of the Constituent Assembly Formally Declares its Dissolution Pursuant to the Resolution of 17 November 1956

Jammu and Kashmir Constituent Assembly Debates, Official Report, Part II (1956), p. 1272

*Mr. President: Today this historic session ends and with this the Constituent Assembly is dissolved according to the resolution passed on 17th November, 1956.

Note: The Clock struck 12 p.m. and the Constituent Assembly was dissolved by the President, Hon'ble G.M. Sadiq, according to the resolution passed by the Constituent Assembly on 17th November, 1956.

Jammu and Kashmir Constituent Assembly Debates,
Official Report, Part II (1956), p. 1272.

Mr President: Honourable members, this the Constituent Assembly is resolved according to the resolution passed on

Chapter 8

The Constitution of Jammu & Kashmir

1. The Constitution

Preamble

We, the people of the State of Jammu and Kashmir, having solemnly resolved, in pursuance of the accession of this State to India which took place on the twenty-sixth day of October, 1947, to further define the existing relationship of the State with Union of India as an integral part thereof, and to secure to overselves—

Justice, social economic and political;

Liberty of thought, expression, belief, faith and worship;

Equality of status and of opportunity; and to promote among us all;

Fraternity assuring the dignity of the individual and the unity of the Nation;

In Our Constituent Assembly this seventeenth day of November, 1956, do Hereby Adopt, Enact And Give To Ourselves This Constitution.

Part I: Preliminary

Short Title and Commencement

1. (1) This Constitution may be called the Constitution of Jammu and Kashmir.

(2) This section and sections 2, 3, 4, 5, 6, 7, 8 and 158 shall come into force at once and the remaining provisions of this Constitution shall come into force on the twenty-sixty day of January, 1957, which day is referred to in this Constitution as the commencement of this Constitution.

Definitions

2. (1) In this Constitution, unless the context otherwise requires:—
    (a) 'Constitution of India' means the Constitution of India as applicable in relation to this State;
    (b) 'existing law' means any law, Ordinance, order, bye-law, rule, notification or regulation passed, made or issued before the commencement of this Constitution by the Legislature or other competent authority or person having power to pass, make or issue such law, Ordinance, order, bye-law, rule, notification or regulation;
    (c) 'Part' means a Part of this Constitution;
    (d) 'Schedule' means a Schedule to this Constitution; and
    (e) 'taxation' includes the imposition of any tax or impost, whether general or local or special, and 'tax' shall be construed accordingly.

(2) Any reference in this Constitution to Acts or laws of the State Legislature shall be construed as including a reference to an Ordinance made by the Sadar-i-Riyasat.

Part II: The State

Relationship of the State with the Union of India

3. The State of Jammu and Kashmir is said and shall be an integral part of the Union of India.

Territory of the State

4. The territory of the State shall comprise all the territories which on the fifteenth day of August, 1947, were under the sovereignty or suzerainty of the Ruler of the State.

Extent of Executive and Legislative Power of the State

5. The executive and legislative power of the State extends to all matters except those with respect to which Parliament has power to make laws for the State under the provisions of the Constitution of India.

Part III: Permanent Residents

Permanent Residents

6. (1) Every person who is, or is deemed to be, a citizen of India under the provisions of the Constitution of India shall be a permanent resident of the State, if on the fourteenth day of May, 1954:—

    (a) he was a State Subject of Class I or of Class II; or

    (b) having lawfully acquired immovable property in the State, he has been ordinarily resident in the State for not less than ten years prior to that date.

(2) Any person who, before the fourteenth day of May, 1954, was a State Subject of Class I or of Class II and who, having migrated after the first day of March, 1947, to the territory now included in Pakistan, returns to the State under a permit for resettlement in the State or for permanent return issued by or under the authority of any law made by the State Legislature shall on such return be a permanent resident of the State.

(3) In this section, the expression 'State Subject of Class I or of Class II' shall have the same meaning as in State Notification No. I-L/84 dated the twentieth April, 1927, read with State Notification No. 13/L dated the twenty-seventh June, 1932.

Construction of References to State Subjects in Existing Laws

7. Unless the context otherwise requires, all references in any existing law to hereditary State Subjects or to State Subject of Class I or of Class

II or of Class III shall be construed as references to permanent residents of the State.

Legislature to Define Permanent Residents

8. Nothing in the foregoing provisions of this Part shall derogate from the power of the State Legislature to make any law defining the classes of persons who are, or shall be, permanent residents of the State.

Special Provision for Bills Relating to Permanent Residents

9. A Bill making provision for any of the following matters, namely:—
   (a) defining or altering the definition of, the classes of persons who are, or shall be, permanent residents of the State;
   (b) conferring on permanent residents any special rights or privileges;
   (c) regulating or modifying any special rights or privileges enjoyed by permanent residents; shall be deemed to be passed by either House of the Legislature only if it is passed by a majority of not less than two-thirds of the total membership of that House.

Rights of the Permanent Residents

10. The permanent residents of the State shall have all the rights guaranteed to them under the Constitution of India.
[...]

Part V: The Executive

The Sadar-i-Riyasat: Head of State

26. (1) The Head of the State shall be designated as the Sadar-i-Riyasat.

(2) The executive power of the State shall be vested in the Sadar-i-Riyasat and shall be exercised by him either directly or through officers subordinate to him in accordance with this Constitution.

(3) Nothing in this section shall:—
   (a) be deemed to transfer to the Sadar-i-Riyasat any functions conferred by any existing law on any other authority; or

(b) prevent the State Legislature from conferring by law functions on any authority subordinate to the Sadar-i-Riyasat.

Election and Recognition

27. The Sadar-i-Riyasat shall be the person who for the time being is recognised by the President as such:
Provided that no person shall be so recognised unless he:—
   (a) is a permanent resident of the State;
   (b) is not less than twenty-five years of age; and
   (c) has been elected as Sadar-i-Riyasat by a majority of the total membership of the Legislative Assembly in the manner set out in the First Schedule.

Term of Office

28. (1) The Sadar-i-Riyasat shall hold office during the pleasure of the President.

(2) The Sadar-i-Riyasat may, by writing under his hand addressed to the President, resign his office.

(3) Subject to the foregoing provisions of this section, the Sadar-i-Riyasat shall hold office for a term of five years from the date on which he enters upon his office:

Provided that he shall, notwithstanding the expiration of his term, continue to hold office until his successor enters upon his office.

Eligibility for Re-election

29. A person who holds or has held office as Sadar-i-Riyasat shall, subject to the other provisions of this Constitution, be eligible for re-election to that office.

Conditions of Office

30. (1) The Sadar-i-Riyasat shall not be a member of either House of Legislature and if a member of either House be elected and recognised as Sadar-i-Riyasat, he shall be deemed to have vacated his seat in the House on the date on which he enters upon his office as Sadar-i-Riyasat.

(2) The Sadar-i-Riyasat shall not hold any other office of profit.

(3) The Sadar-i-Riyasat shall be entitled to such emoluments, allowances and privileges as are specified in the Second Schedule.

(4) The emoluments and allowances of the Sadar-i-Riyasat shall not be diminished during his term of office.

Oath of Office

31. The Sadar-i-Riyasat and every person acting as Sadar-i-Riyasat shall, before entering upon his office, make and subscribe in the presence of the Chief Justice of the High Court or, in his absence, the senior-most judge of the High Court available, an oath or affirmation in the following form, that is to say:—

I, A.B., *do swear in the name of God—solemnly affirm* that I will faithfully discharge the functions of the Sadar-i-Riyasat of Jammu and Kashmir and will to the best of my ability preserve, protect and defend the Constitution and the law and that I will devote myself to the service and well-being of the people of State.

Removal from Office

32. The Sadar-i-Riyasat may be removed from his office by the President if an address by the Legislative Assembly supported by a majority of not less than two-thirds of its total membership is presented to the President praying for such removal on the ground of violation of the Constitution.

Acting Sadar-i-Riyasat

33. When a vacancy occurs in the office of the Sadar-i-Riyasat by reason of his death, resignation or removal or when the Sadar-i-Riyasat is unable to discharge his functions owing to absence, illness or any other cause, the functions of the office shall, until the assumption of office by a newly elected Sadar-i-Riyasat or the resumption of duties by the Sadar-i-Riyasat, as the case may be, be discharged by such person as the President may, on the recommendation of the Council of Ministers of the State, recognise as the acting Sadar-i-Riyasat.

Power to Grant Pardons, Reprieves, etc.

34. The Sadar-i-Riyasat shall have the power to grant pardons, reprieves, respites or remissions of punishment or to suspend, remit or commute the sentence of any person convicted of any offence against any law relating to a matter to which the executive power of the State extends.

The Council of Ministers

Council of Ministers to Aid and Advise the Sadar-i-Riyasat

35. (1) There shall be a Council of Ministers with the Prime Minister at the head to aid and advise the Sadar-i-Riyasat in the exercise of his functions.

(2) All functions of the Sadar-i-Riyasat except those under sections 36, 38 and 92 shall be exercised by him only on the advice of the Council of Ministers.

(3) The question whether any, and if so what, advice was tendered by Ministers to the Sadar-i-Riyasat shall not be inquired into in any court.

Appointment of Ministers

36. The Prime Minister shall be appointed by the Sadar-i-Riyasat and the other Ministers shall be appointed by the Sadar-i-Riyasat on the advice of the Prime Minister.

Ministers' Responsibility to the Legislature

37. (1) The Council of Ministers shall be collectively responsible to the Legislative Assembly.

(2) A Minister who for any period of six consecutive months is not a member of either House of Legislature shall upon the expiry of that period cease to be a Minister.

Deputy Ministers

38. The Sadar-i-Riyasat may on the advice of the Prime Minister appoint from amongst the members of either House of Legislature such number of Deputy Ministers as may be necessary.

Tenure of Office

39. The Ministers and the Deputy Ministers shall hold office during the pleasure of the Sadar-i-Riyasat.

Oaths of Office and Secrecy

40. Before a Minister or a Deputy Minister enters upon his office, the Sadar-i-Riyasat or, in his absence, any person authorised by him, shall administer to the Minister or the Deputy Minister the oaths of office and of secrecy according to the form set out for the purpose in the Fifth Schedule.

[...]

Provision Relating to Pakistan Occupied Territory

48. Notwithstanding anything contained in section 47, until the area of the State under the occupation of Pakistan ceases to be so occupied and the people residing in that area elect their representatives:—
   (a) twenty-five seats in the Legislative Assembly shall remain vacant and shall not be taken into account for reckoning the total membership of the Assembly; and
   (b) the said areas shall be excluded in delimiting the territorial Constituencies under section 47.

[...]

Composition of Legislative Council

50. (1) The Legislative Council shall consist of thirty-six members, chosen in the manner provided in this section.

(2) Eleven members shall be elected by the members of the Legislative Assembly from amongst persons who are residents of the Province of Kashmir and are not members of the Legislative Assembly:

Provided that of the members so elected, at least one shall be a resident of Tehsil Ladakh and at least one shall be a resident of Kargil Tehsil.

(3) Eleven members shall be elected by the members of the Legislative Assembly from amongst persons who are residents of the Province of Jammu and are not members of the Legislative Assembly.

[...]

Breakdown of Constitutional Machinery

Provisions in Case of Failure of Constitutional Machinery in the State

92. (1) If at any time the Sadar-i-Riyasat is satisfied that a situation has arisen in which the Government of the State cannot be carried on in accordance with the provisions of this Constitution, the Sadar-i-Riyasat may by Proclamation:—

 (a) assume to himself all or any of the functions of the Government of the State and all or any of the powers vested in or exercisable by anybody or authority in the State;

 (b) make such incidental and consequential provisions as appear to the Sadar-i-Riyasat to be necessary or desirable for giving effect to the objects of the Proclamation, including provisions for for suspending in whole or in part the operation of any provision of this Constitution relating to any body or authority in the State:

Provided that nothing in this section shall authorise the Sadar-i-Riyasat to assume to himself any of the powers vested in or exercisable by the High Court or to suspend in whole or in part the operation of any provision of this Constitution relating to the High Court.

(2) Any such Proclamation may be revoked or varied by a subsequent Proclamation.

(3) Any such Proclamation whether varied under sub-section (2) or not, shall, except where it is a Proclamation revoking a previous Proclamation, cease to operate on the expiration of six months from the date on which it was first issued.

(4) If the Sadar-i-Riyasat by a Proclamation under this section assumes to himself any of the powers of the Legislature to make laws, any law made by him in the exercise of that power shall, subject to the terms thereof, continue to have effect until two years have elapsed from the date on which the Proclamation ceases to have effect, unless sooner repealed or re-enacted by an Act of the Legislature, and any reference in this Constitution to any Acts of or laws made by the Legislature shall be construed as including a reference to such law.

(5) No Proclamation under sub-section (1) shall be issued except with the concurrence of the President of India.

(6) Every Proclamation under this section shall, except where it is a Proclamation revoking a previous Proclamation, be laid before each house of the Legislature as soon as it is convened.

[...]

Flag of the State

144. The Flag of the State shall be rectangular in shape and red in colour with three equidistant white vertical stripes of equal width next to the staff and a white plough in the middle with the handle facing the stripes.

The ratio of the length of the flag to its width shall be 3:2.

Official Language of the State

145. The official language of the State shall be Urdu, but the English language shall, unless the Legislature by law otherwise provides, continue to be used for all the official purposes of the State for which it was being used immediately before the commencement of this Constitution.

Academy for Development of Art, Culture and Languages

146. The Sadar-i-Riyasat shall, as soon as may be, after the commencement of the Constitution, establish an Academy of Arts, Culture and Languages where opportunities will be afforded for the development of Art and Culture of the State and for the development of Hindi, Urdu and other regional languages of the State specified in the Sixth Schedule.

Part XII: Amendment of the Constitution

Amendment of the Constitution

147. An amendment of this Constitution may be initiated only by the introduction of a Bill for the purpose in the Legislative Assembly, and when the Bill is passed in each House by a majority of not less than two-thirds of the total membership of that House, it shall be presented to the Sadar-i-Riyasat for his assent and, upon such assent being given

to the Bill, the Constitution shall stand amended in accordance with the terms of the Bill:

Provided that a Bill providing for the abolition of the Legislative Council may be introduced in the Legislative Assembly and passed by it by a majority of the total membership of the Assembly and by a majority of not less than two-thirds of the members of the Assembly present and voting:

Provided further that no Bill or amendment seeking to make any change in:—

(a) this section; or

(b) the provisions of sections 3 and 5; or

(c) the provisions of the Constitution of India as applicable in relation to the State;

shall be introduced or moved in either House of the Legislature.

[...]

2. Definition of State Subject

Notification Dated the 20th April, 1927

[1]No. I-L/84:—The following definition of the term 'State Subject' has been sanctioned by His Highness the Maharaja Bahadur (*vide* Private Secretary's letter No. 2354, dated the 31st January, 1927 to the Revenue Member of Council) and is hereby promulgated for general information.

The term State Subject means and includes:—

Class I:—All persons born and residing within the State before the commencement of the reign of His Highness the late Maharaja Ghulab Singh Sahib Bahadur, and also persons who settled therein before the commencement of Samvat year 1942, and have since been permanently residing therein.

Class II:—All persons other than those belonging to Class I who settled within the State before the close of Samvat year 1968, and have since permanently resided and acquired immovable property therein.

[1] The notification is subject to the provisions of section 6 of the Constitution of Jammu and Kashmir 1956.

THE CONSTITUTION OF JAMMU & KASHMIR

Class III:—All persons other than those belonging to Classes I and II permanently residing within the State, who have acquired under a *rayatnama* any immovable property therein or who may hereafter acquire such property under an ijazatnama and may execute a *rayatnama* after ten years continuous residence therein.

[2][Class IV:—Companies which have been registered as such within the State and which, being companies in which the Government are financially interested or as to the economic benefit to the State or to the financial stability of which the Government are satisfied, have by a special order of His Highness been declared to be State Subjects].

Note I:—In matters of grants of the State scholarships, State lands for agricultural and house building purposes and recruitment of State service, State Subjects of Class I should receive preference over other classes and those of Class II over Class III, subject, however, to the Order dated 31st January, 1927 of His Highness the Maharaja Bahadur regarding employment of hereditary State Subjects in Government service.

Note II:—The descendants of the persons who have secured the status of any class of the State subjects will be entitled to become the State Subject of the same class. For example, if A is declared a State Subject of Class II his sons and grandsons will *ipso facto* acquire the status of the same Class (II) and not of Class I.

[3][Note III:—The wife or a widow of a State Subject of any class shall acquire the status of her husband as State Subject of the same Class as her husband, so long as she resides in the State and does not leave the State for permanent residence outside the State].

---

[2] Class IV and Note IV added by Order No. 98-H/39, published in Government Gazette dated 27th Poh, 1996. It said that notwithstanding any law, rule or other order to the contrary, no disability as regards acquisition of any interest in land or other immovable property in the State shall attach to a company which is a State Subject within the meaning of Notification No. I-L/84 dated 20th April, 1927, as amended.

[3] Note III added *vide* Notification No. 51-L/1989 as amended by Notification No. 6-L/1990, published in Government Gazette, dated 8th Baisakh, 1990 and Government Gazette dated the 23rd Bhadon, 1990, respectively.

[Note IV:—For the purposes of the interpretation of the term 'State Subject' either with reference to any law for the time being in force or otherwise, the definition given in this Notification as amended up to date shall be read as if such amended definition existed in this Notification as originally issued].

Notification

(Issued by order of His Highness the Maharaja Bahadur dated Srinagar, the 27th June, 1932/14th Har, 1989. Published in Government Gazette Dated 24th Har, 1989)

[4]*No. 13-L/1989*:—Whereas it is necessary to determine the status of Jammu and Kashmir State Subjects in foreign territories and to inform the Governments of Foreign States as to the position of their nationals in the State; it is hereby commanded and notified for public information, as follows:—

1. That all emigrants from the Jammu and Kashmir State to foreign territories shall be considered State Subjects and also the descendants of these emigrants born abroad for two generations:

Provided that, these nationals of the Jammu and Kashmir State shall not be entitled to claim the internal rights granted to subjects of this State by the laws, unless they fulfil the conditions laid down by those laws and rules for the specific purposes mentioned therein.

2. The foreign nationals residing in the State of Jammu and Kashmir shall not acquire the nationality of the Jammu and Kashmir State until after the age of 18 on purchasing immovable property under permission of an *ijazatnama* and on obtaining a *rayatnama* after ten years continuous residence in the Jammu and Kashmir State as laid down in Notification No. I-L of 1984, dated 20th April, 1927.

3. Certificates of nationality of the Jammu and Kashmir State may, on application, be granted by the Minister-in-Charge of the Political Department in accordance with the provisions of section 1 of this Notification.

---

[4] This Notification is to be read subject to the provisions of section 6 of the Constitution of Jammu and Kashmir and the Jammu and Kashmir Grant of Permanent Resident Certificate (Procedure) Act, 1963 (XIII of 1963).

Chapter 9

The Wreck of Article 370

1. Jawaharlal Nehru on the 'Erosion' of Article 370, Lok Sabha, 27 November 1963

Lok Sabha Debates, 27 November 1963, Volume XII, cols 1231–2

Q. Will the Minister of Home Affairs be pleased to state:

    (a) whether any measures have been taken or proposals mooted since October, 1962 for further integration of the State of Jammu and Kashmir with the rest of the Indian Union;

    (b) if so, the details thereof; and

    (c) whether the repeal of Article 370 of the Constitution is under consideration in consultation with the Jammu & Kashmir State Government?

The Minister of State in the Ministry of Home Affairs (Shri Hajarnavis): (a) and (b). (1) An Order of the President under Article 370 of the Constitution was issued on the 25th September, 1963, applying to Jammu & Kashmir State entry 26 of the Concurrent List (List III) in the Seventh Schedule in respect of legal and medical professions and other consequential provisions of the Constitution.

(2) A proposal to apply to Jammu and Kashmir entry 24 of the Concurrence List, in so far as it relates to welfare of labour in the coal-mining industry, is under consideration.

(3) It has been decided that representatives of Jammu and Kashmir in the Lok Sabha should be chosen by direct election as in other States. Effect will be given to this decision after the termination of the present emergency.

(4) It has also been decided that the Sadar-i-Riyasat and Prime Minister of Jammu and Kashmir should be designated as Governor and Chief Minister respectively. Legislation to give effect to the proposal is expected to be taken up during the next session of the State Legislature.

(c) Article 370 of the Constitution occurs in Part XXI of the Constitution which deals with temporary and transitional provisions. Since this Article was incorporated in the Constitution, many changes have been made which bring the State of Jammu and Kashmir in line with the rest of India. The State is fully integrated to the Union of India, Government are of opinion that they should not take any initiative now for the complete repeal of Article 370. This will, no doubt, be brought about by further changes in consultation with the Government and the Legislative Assembly of Jammu and Kashmir State. This process has continued in the last few years and may be allowed to continue in the same way.

[...]

The Minister of Home Affairs (Shri Nanda): There is no question of either reluctance or resistance. To the extent the public opinion, as the hon. Member points out, favours the movement in that direction, it will certainly be reflected in the attitude of the Government. And no such question as the hon. Member has in mind arises.

[...]

Shri Jawaharlal Nehru: Article 370, as the House will remember, is a part of certain transitional provisional arrangements. It is not a permanent part of the Constitution. It is a part so long as it remains so.

As a matter of fact, as the Home Minister has pointed out, it has been eroded, if I may use the word, and many things have been done in the last few years which have made the relationship of Kashmir with the Union of India very close. There is no doubt that Kashmir is fully integrated. [...]

Shri Hari Vishnu Kamath: Not fully.

Shri Jawaharlal Nehru: No, I repeat that it is fully integrated. The fact that there may be some special matters attached to it does not come in the way of integration at all, and I gave as an instance that in Kashmir citizens of India other than those of Kashmir are not allowed to buy land or own property. That is an old rule coming on, not a new thing, and I think that it is a very good rule which should continue, because Kashmir is such a delectable place that moneyed people will buy up all the land there to the misfortune of the people who live there; that is the real reason and that reason has applied ever since British times and for the last one hundred years or more.

[...]

I am merely giving my opinion that it is a good rule and that in Kashmir there should be strict restrictions on the buying of land by people from outside Kashmir, because otherwise the people who can afford it will buy land very largely, prices will go up tremendously there and the local people will suffer.

The House will remember that we have some such restrictions in regard to NEFA and other places; outsiders cannot buy land. This is so even in other districts, the hill districts of Assam. This is to protect them.

So we feel that this process of gradual erosion of article 370 is going on. Some fresh steps are being taken and in the next month or two they will be completed. We should allow it to go on. We do not want to take the initiative in this matter and completely put an end to Article 370. The initiative, we feel, should come from the Kashmir State Government and people. We shall gladly agree to that. That process is continuing.

[...]

2. Union Home Minister G.L. Nanda on Abrogation of Article 370, Lok Sabha, 4 December 1964

Lok Sabha Debates, 4 December 1964, Volume XXXIII, cols 3449–65

(Omission of Article 370) by Shri Prakash Vir Shastri

Mr. Speaker: The House will now take up further consideration of the following motion moved by Shri Prakash Vir Shastri on the 11th

September, 1964, namely:—'That the Bill further to amend the Constitution of India, be taken into consideration.' Five hours had been allotted for this. 4 hours 47 minutes have already been exhausted. Now, I am calling upon the hon. Minister of Home Affairs to reply.

The Minister of Home Affairs (Shri Nanda): Mr. Speaker, Sir, I am aware of the fact that what we are dealing with here on this occasion is an important question. I am aware of the fact that this question has deeply stirred the minds and hearts of many Members of this House.

[...]

This discussion has given me a great deal of emotional satisfaction whatever else may be the outcome of it. It has brought out clearly that there is practical unanimity among the representatives of all the parties here, and I take it, of the various political parties in this country, in the matter of the approach to the question of Kashmir.

[...]

This discussion also reflects a sense of urgency. I recognise that. I appreciate that.

[...]

Therefore, if I have to urge the Members that at this juncture it may be better to follow a different approach from what has been chalked out in the Bill before the House, I hope I shall not be misunderstood and the plea that I am making will not be taken amiss. I shall explain this plea in two ways, first, in terms of the Constitution, that is, the legal and constitutional arguments that arise in this case and secondly in terms also of certain practical considerations, in view of the interests of the nation.

I shall take up first the arguments relating to the Constitution. I take my stand on the Constitution of India as it is.

[...]

Taking the Constitution as it is, let us understand the role of article 370 and then see what happens, if this article is abrogated, or removed and taken out of the Constitution by an amendment of the Constitution on the lines of this Bill. I have a point to urge regarding the procedure also, that is to say, the procedure adopted about the proposed amendment through this Bill.

The power to amend this Constitution is derived from article 368. If the hon. Member looks at that article, he will find that there is at the bottom a proviso which reads thus; the footnote reads as follows:—

In its application to the State of Jammu and Kashmir, to article 368, the following proviso shall be added:—

'Provided further that no such amendment shall have effect in relation to the State of Jammu and Kashmir unless applied by order of the President under clause (1) of article 370.'

So, my hon. friend will have to take shelter under article 370 itself in order to bring forward an amendment, and certain procedures have to be gone through. I may be corrected if I am wrong. My hon. friend opposite is an expert on constitutional law, and he may correct me if I am wrong. But this is my straight reading of the Constitution. Therefore, as long as we have not taken into consideration to that this qualification or this proviso which excludes the scope of amendments to article 370 without certain steps having been taken under article 370 itself, we cannot amend the Constitution; those steps have not been taken, and, therefore, this Bill will suffer from an inherent disability. This may be taken up later on, if need be and if necessary. But apart from this, if the operation which the Bill visualises, namely, the removal of article 370, is carried out, we are left with a complete void as far as any improvement in the administrative relation with Jammu and Kashmir is concerned hereafter.

There will be a total block in the way of any such further change as we might be intending to make. We have been making changes all the time, every year. I will say something more about that. But any further change on the lines of the extension of the Constitution to Jammu and Kashmir with which we are familiar now, cannot be carried out if we take away article 370. If it is imagined that by the repeal of article 370 all the provisions of the Constitution will automatically apply to Jammu and Kashmir, it is a very erroneous reading of the constitution. As things stand—the impediments in the way of achieving uniformity—it is a question of uniformity in the administrative relations, in the administrative set-up; it is not a question of integration; that should be made clear. It is only about uniformity—the intention to bring about uniformity with the rest of India.—The impediments in the way of uniformity are not created by article 370. These impediments are strewn through the pages of the Constitution. In a hundred places, there are those provisions which take away the force of application of the Constitution to Jammu and Kashmir. What will happen to them? Remove 370. They remain.

That is not all when you take away all these limitations, exclusions dated 4th December. What will happen? The position as it is today gets petrified, frozen. No further progress will be possible.

There is some further point in this connection, and that is important. It is not only a question of the extension of the Constitution through a Presidential Order. It is not that. There is something more which figures. In the text of the articles of the Constitution also there are these qualifications and restrictions. You remove article 370. What happens to those articles? They still remain. This is a sizable chunk of the Constitution. Articles 308 and 152 make special reference to J&K. If we repeal article 370, these references will stand. There is the whole of Part VI, and Part XII relating to services.

I am pointing these out because it does not at all help, whatever be the good intentions of the hon. Mover of the Bill. It does not at all help Jammu and Kashmir or anybody if he ever could succeed in getting this Bill through. We may have a look at Part XXII of the Constitution—article 394. It is here that apart from article 1, for which article 370 itself makes provision, that is, article 370, clause 1, it brings in article 1 of the Constitution so far as Jammu and Kashmir is concerned. After that, is the question of the commencement and in the commencement, 394 says that articles 5, 6 etc. shall come into force at once and the remaining provisions of the Constitution shall come into force on such and such date—the provisos.

Therefore, all these things have been excluded. This simple act of taking away this single article, does not take us any further at all—nowhere at all.

The position is this. While the rest of the contents of the Constitution, to which I have made reference, negate the application of the provisions of the Constitution to Jammu and Kashmir—some of them by extension, others directly—the only avenue of taking the Constitution into Jammu and Kashmir is through the application of the provisions of article 370. That is the only way of bringing back the Constitution to J. and K. That is my reading of the Constitution.

It is article 370 which provides for the progressive application of the provisions of the Constitution to Jammu and Kashmir. What does it actually do? As things are, it only regulates the progressive application; it provides for that and regulates it, affirms it; it does not negate. The negations are elsewhere. It is, therefore, wrong to say that article 370 has outlived its utility.

An hon. Member said that article 370 is a wall between Jammu and Kashmir and the rest of India. With reference to that, another hon. Member, Shri D.C. Sharma, said, it is not a question of a wall, it is a big mountain. At the same time, he happened to mentioned the Banihal tunnel also. May I submit to him and the other friends that article 370 is neither a wall nor a mountain, but that it is a tunnel? It is through this tunnel that a good deal of traffic has already passed and more will.

Shri Alvares (Panjim): Why should we have a tunnel at all?

Shri Nanda: There is no wall between Jammu and Kashmir and India. At the most, you can say it is some kind of moveable partition. We can move it on our own. There is nothing coming in the way.

Shri Alvares: If it is neither a wall nor a mountain, where is the need for a tunnel?

Shri Nanda: I say, if there is any wall, then this is the tunnel.

It may be urged, 'Do not take a narrow, legal stand. What is the political purpose?' I can understand that. But that purpose is not going to be served by this Bill. This Bill at any rate will have to be brushed aside, set aside. It cannot be taken up at all because it will be very wrong and detrimental to the interest that we have in view. Something else may have to be done.

[...]

A much more extensive operation of the Constitution is inevitable. We will have to make a very comprehensive examination of the provisions of the Constitution. It is not a question of making an amendment here or there. There are many things which have to be done. If it is to be done at all, I do not think it is necessary to bring in an amending Bill for amending the Constitution—I do not think it is necessary. If ever it were, it will have to be a very different kind of thing. [...]

Dr. M.S. Auey (Nagpur): Does the hon. Minister maintain that even after full integration, it is necessary to keep this article of the Constitution?

Shri Nanda: If it is the intention to amend, the process of amendment is simpler. The processes are provided in article 370. I think it was beautifully conceived. The normal process of amendment is subject to stringent conditions. The processes of amendment made available to article 370 are very simple.

15 hrs

Shri N.C. Chatterjee (Burdwan): Is the hon. Minister prepared to give this House an assurance that under clause (3) of article 370, the President will take action. It says: 'Notwithstanding anything in the foregoing provisions of this article, the President may, by public notification, declare that this article shall cease to be operative or shall be operative only with such exceptions and modifications and from such date as he may specify:'
Therefore, it is given to the President practically to effectuate. ...

Shri Khadikar (Khed): There is a proviso. You are omitting it.

Shri N.C. Chatterjee: I know. There is nothing in the proviso. It says: 'Provided that the recommendation of the Constituent Assembly of the State referred to in clause (2) shall be necessary before the President issues such a notification.'

The Constituent Assembly is gone. Therefore, the proviso is otiose, and, according to my submission, when the Constituent Assembly is not functioning, the proviso does not operate any more, and the President has got unfettered powers to act under clause (3).

Will the hon. Minister give an assurance to the House that the President will be advised, or he is going to consider that? One thing more. The hon. Minister says that in article 368 some rider has been added. What is the rider?

Mr. Speaker: There, he is not right. I agree with the Member.

Shri N.C. Chatterjee: It only says: 'Provided further that no such amendment shall have effect in relation to the State of Jammu and Kashmir unless applied by order of the President under clause (1) of article 370.'

Mr. Speaker: That we will see afterwards, when the Bill has been passed, whether it should be effected or not.

Shri N.C. Chatterjee: I am only pointing out that there is no impediment to the House passing this Bill. The only thing is that it will come into operation in relation to Jammu and Kashmir by an order of the President. That is a purely executive order.

Shri Nanda: I would not hastily give any assurance. I find that in dealing with the Constitution, so many different views are taken. For example, in regard to clause (3), there is another opinion, that this clause has exhausted itself completely.

Shri N.C. Chatterjee: May I know who has said that?

Shri Nanda: We are not debating this. It may be there is a difference between his view and my view; because there are so many indirect considerations to be taken into account, it may be that article 368, at any rate, by itself is not sufficient. Other things have to be done, and other things are contingent on something else happening. Therefore, by itself it does not suffice.

As to whether clause (3) is available or not. I am not able to say anything. I do not think I would be right in giving any kind of hasty assurance on the subject, because my stand is very different.

What I am saying is that all that is intended to be secured can be more easily secured. There is an easier path available to us, a more handy instrument for us to get the same thing done. Why do we go about bringing in amendments to the Constitution itself with all the processes attendant on that, when article 370 itself enables—not through clause (3) but through clause (1) and (2)—the President to pass orders which will enable any entry in the Lists to be taken and applied to Jammu and Kashmir and any other provision of the Constitution? This is available. What remains there is. ...

[...]

Shri Nanda: I have explained two things. One is that if you just take out article 370, does it remove all the provisos which have entered

into the various clauses in one way or other? Does it also take away
the restrictions and qualifications to the various other articles in the
Constitution, where the Constitution is made applicable to Jammu and
Kashmir? It does not.

[...]

If I am told and I agree that the purpose can be served only by a
Bill, then we can certainly bring in a better Bill, but it is not necessary.
The same purpose can be served fully and properly through the utilisa-
tion of this. There is nothing wrong about this argument, because it is
a fact.

[...]

Who do you want this more elaborate proceedings of bringing in an
amendment to the Constitution? We have got the other way.

The proof of it, the evidence that what I am saying has great substance, is that in the past years article 370 has been so used, has been
availed of, for this purpose. Hon. Members are quite familiar with that
process. This article has not remained static. It is through a dynamic
process, year after year, that the provision in Jammu and Kashmir
has been assimilated in these matters with the rest of India, and this
policy, the policy of steady, progressive erosion, has been reiterated
here several times. This has been the policy, this was the policy laid
before the House several times before by the late Prime Minister and
others, and this policy, apart from other considerations which attach
to it, does not suffer from any kind of inherent limitation, because it
can unfold itself completely. What happens is that only the shell is there.
Article 370, whether you keep it or not, has been completely emptied
of its contents. Nothing has been left in it. We can regulate it, we can
do it in one day, in ten days, ten months. That is entirely for us to
consider.

Shri Hem Barua (Gauhati): May I seek your indulgence for a moment? May I know if the hon. Minister is aware of the fact that the
Plebiscite Front in Kashmir, together with certain communal and political elements within the State are planning to have demonstrations from
tomorrow, 5th December; if so, how does the hon. Minister justify his
stand, what he has stated just now?

Mr. Speaker: Did he say that he welcomes that demonstration?

Shri Hem Barua: He said everything has been regulated there.

Mr. Speaker: That is about a different thing.

Shri Nanda: I referred to regulated extension of the provisions. Some of the hon. Members made an observation, and that is a point which does really deserve consideration. Hon. Members from the State of Jammu and Kashmir and some others said that there are advantages, benefits, available to the rest of India; why should the people of Jammu and Kashmir be deprived of those benefits? Then, other things are mentioned here. There are various forms of beneficiary relations between the Centre and the States.

Shri Ranga: They get so much more.

Shri Kapur Singh: It is one-sided benefit.

Shri Nanda: If they are getting so much more because article 370 is still there, I do not know if...

Shri Sham Lal Saraf (Nominated—Jammu and Kashmir): What the Home Minister refers to is that these things do not apply to the State.

Shri Ranga: We have been subsidising all the time.

Shri Nanda: This result has been brought about, the proper extension of those beneficial arrangements, to the State of Jammu and Kashmir, by progressive and successive stages of application of these provisions, and if anything remains which could be of benefit to the people of Jammu and Kashmir and which today has been kept away from them because any provision of this Constitution has not been applied to them, there need not be any delay about that. Hon. Members coming from Jammu and Kashmir were deeply concerned about it. I think I can say very clearly that almost every month, every two or three months, a review is taken, and some of these provisions are applied. I might therefore, mention something about it. It will give some idea of what has been happening. This would sink into the minds of hon. Members and that is why I am indicating the process which can bring about the same results that process has been very active in the past.

Shri Inder J. Molhotra (Nominated—Jammu and Kashmir): It should be expedited.

Shri Nanda: I can understand that plea that it should be expedited and I do not stand up against that idea.

Shri D.C. Sharma (Gurdaspur): What have you done in the last three months to expedite it?

Shri Nanda: I shall say what has been happening in the last few months. Since the new Government took charge there with Mr. Sadiq as the head of that Government, this process has been accelerated and Presidential orders have been issued applying the constitutional provisions relating to the following subjects—welfare of labour, legal, medical and other professions, trade and commerce in and the production, supply, and distribution of commodities, price control, gold control, enquiries and statistics, regulation of labour and safety in mines, vital statistics including registration of births and deaths, vocational and technical training, and newspapers, books and printing presses. They are also considering applying provisions relating to elections—Members of Parliament to be elected direct rather than in the manner in which the elections now take place. That is going to be done very soon.

[...]

Shri Nanda: A Bill for changing the nomenclature for Sadar-i-Riyasat and Prime Minister of the State has been referred to a select committee by them. Thus, it would be seen that the progress has been significantly accelerated.

I take this opportunity to inform the House that is has been decided to apply the provisions of articles 356 and 357 also to Jammu and Kashmir. Entries 43 and 78 of the Union List and Entries 33 and 34 of the Concurrence List are also being made applicable. This would show the extent to which both the Government of India and the State Government are constantly keeping the situation in view. Therefore, the area of uniformity is being constantly extended and it is being accelerated and expedited and as I said before, the House would certainly understand from what I have said that anything else which has to be done quickly could certainly be considered and some kind of action could be taken on that.

Shri Hem Barua: When you have done so much, why don't you do the rest?

Shri Nanda: Those who have done so much will certainly do the rest ... (*Interruption*) Sir, I have to add one or two more observations.

Shri Ranga: That point is enough.

Shri Nanda: It is all right then. The hon. Member appreciates what I have said. I would say something about the question of the status of Jammu and Kashmir. I do not understand why it has been brought in this context. I believe Article 370 has been given too much importance and some kind of a doubt seems to have crept in for which there is no scope at all. Then seem to think that there is some kind of a deficiency in relation to the status of Jammu and Kashmir, in the matter of the full integration of Jammu and Kashmir with India. It has been repeatedly stated here and statements were made by the hon. Prime Minister and the late Prime Minister and I would like to refer to them because it is very important that there should be no doubt left on that score. Article 370 does not detract from that status. It is not as if it is not quite complete now and if 370 is removed, it will become full. It is not so at all; it is a wrong reading of the situation. The hon. Prime Minister, when he was the Minister without portfolio, stated very clearly the position. He referred to the Security Council proceedings and said that in the Security Council Mr. Chagla has made it absolutely clear, that the accession of Kashmir to India is irrevocable and the present relationship between Kashmir and India must continue. The irrevocability of this position has been stressed there. There was an occasion when I had the privilege to place before this House something about this question of status. I have said then that there are certain facts of history which cannot be undone. [...]

Shri Hari Vishnu Kamath (Hoshangabad): On a point of clarification, Sir. Will the Prime Minister be pleased to tell this House whether there are at the moment any political groups or elements in the State of Jammu and Kashmir who are opposed to fuller integration of that State with India or to the abrogation of article 370, and if it be not so, why this hesitancy?

Shri Nanda: No responsible person in that State is opposed, and particularly the Government of Jammu and Kashmir now is fully helpful in making progress with all these things.

3. The Plebiscite Front's White Paper on Constitutional Relationship of Kashmir with India, 1964

Jammu & Kashmir Plebiscite Front, Srinagar, 1964

Foreword

Since some time past, much is being said about the nature and character of Kashmir's 'accession' with India and about the Article 370 of the Indian Constitution. Protagonists of this 'accession' have been claiming irrevocability and finality about it, and article 370 has often been referred to as 'conferring some special status' on the State. Such expressions are responsible for considerable confusion in the public mind, both about the nature of Kashmir's relationship with India as well as the purport and connotation of provisions of article 370.

The Working Committee of the J&K Plebiscite Front took note of this position in their last meeting held on 27th and 28th June, 1964 and discussed the issue in some detail. Mirza M.A. Beg, the Founder-President, gave a detailed review of the constitutional relationship of the State with India as well as a history of Article 370. As he had happened to be a member of the Indian Constituent Assembly, he was in a position to give the Working Committee first-hand information based on his own experience, about the history of various provisions of the Union Constitution, that relate to Kashmir's relationship with India as well its nature and character.

After taking stock of the whole situation and considering broadly the views expressed in diverse quarters about this issue, the Working Committee directed that a comprehensive White Paper be issued on the subject on behalf of the Plebiscite Front, after a thorough examination of the whole position, legally and constitutionally. The Committee asked some of the prominent party lawyers to lend assistance to the President in the preparation of this White Paper. Accordingly, after appropriate examination of the relevant provisions of the Indian Constitution, this document was prepared which is herewith published for the general information.

I am extremely grateful for the assistance rendered in this behalf by Mr. G.N. Kochak (M.A.L.L.B.), Mr. G.M. Shawl (B.A.L.L.B.), Mirza M.Y. Beg (B.A.L.L.B.), Mr. G.M. Shah (B.A.L.L.B.), Hikim Habibullah (B.A.L.L.B.), Mr. Abdul Ahad Vakil (B.A.L.L.B.) and Mr. G.M. Hamdani (B.A.L.L.B.).

G.R. Kochak
President
J.&K. Plebiscite Front

Srinagar,
23rd June, 1964

1. It has been, of late, contended in certain quarters that the accession of the State of Jammu and Kashmir to the Union of India is 'complete, final and irrevocable,' and, for that reason, it is not permissible to claim secession from the Union, which is not even within the power of Parliament to grant. Having regard to these assertions, the Working Committee of the Plebiscite Front resolved that the entire legal position be reviewed and a White Paper issued as a result thereof.

2. The question of the alleged accession of the State of Jammu and Kashmir to the Union of India was pursuant to this direction of the Working Committee, subjected to a denavo examination and the conclusions arrived at are set forth below:—

3. The examination aforesaid has revealed that the assertions referred to in the first para of this White Paper are without foundation.

4. While, however, concentrating largely on the strict letter of the law, reference will have to be made, though very briefly, to the past history of the case, in so far as it is relevant to us for this very limited purpose.

5. The accession of six hundred and odd princely States to one of the then two newly carved out Dominions did not present any difficulty barring that of some States; namely Junagadh, Manavadar, Talukadri States of Sardargarh, Batva, Sultanabad, Mangrol, Hyderabad and Jammu and Kashmir. In the case of the States of Junagadh, Manavadar etc., and Hyderabad their population was overwhelmingly Hindu but the Rulers thereof were Muslims; and in the case of Jammu and Kashmir the reverse was the case. The view had been expressed that the

Ruler of a State as distinguished from its people was the sole authority competent to accede to one of the two countries aforesaid, and once the Ruler did so, the accession became legal, final and irrevocable and the State could not then 'opt out'. In the case of Junagadh, Manavadar etc., however, the Rulers thereof had offered to accede to the then Dominion of Pakistan and this offer had been accepted unconditionally by the then Dominion of Pakistan. Nevertheless, as history would record, India did not hesitate to repudiate these accessions on the main ground that the population of those States was predominantly Hindu and the partition of India had been effected on the basis of religion and it did not hesitate to annexe these States by force and, thereafter, India at one time even offered to the then Dominion of Pakistan to hold a plebiscite therein to ascertain the will of the people on the question of their accession to one of the two Dominions. It was Sir Gopalaswamy Ayyengar who, as leader of the Indian delegation at the Security Council, gave an assurance to hold a plebiscite in Junagadh under the U.N. auspices which India had never implemented.

6. The argument, therefore, that the accession of a State to one of the two Dominions effected by the Ruler thereof could not be impugned, was, thus not treated as unassailable by India itself.

7. In the case of Hyderabad, the Muslim Ruler of that State was found unwilling to accede to the Dominion of India, and we know that that Dominion launched what was euphemistically termed as a Police action to Force its accession to the Dominion and to annexe it to the Dominion of India eventually. Here again, the treatment meted out to the State of Hyderabad by the Dominion of India in this regard belies the assertion that the Ruler was regarded as the final arbiter by India in such a matter.

8. In the case of Jammu and Kashmir, the Ruler who was a Hindu, under the stress of circumstances which completely vitiated his choice offered to accede to the Dominion of India. Assuming that he was otherwise competent to do so, the surrounding circumstances, in which he had literally to act on the point of the bayonet could not be disregarded. In 1946, on the arrival of the British Cabinet Mission in India, a movement, under the leadership of Sheikh Mohammad Abdullah was launched in the State which was popularly known as 'Quit Kashmir

Movement', aimed at ending the rule of the Maharaja and installing in its place a democratic and popular regime, where the hereditary ruler had no place. This movement owed its genesis to a long period of misrule and oppression perpetrated by these hereditary rulers of Kashmir and that movement gained momentum and strength so as to imperil the very existence of the Maharaja. In Poonch particularly, the population rose in open revolt against the Maharaja's rule and the Maharaja had to promulgate Marshal law there to quell this revolt. This demand for supplanting the Maharaja's rule by a democratic set up and for the abolition of the hereditary office of the Maharaja was also blessed and supported by the then Indian National Congress and its foremost leaders, notably Mahatma Gandhi and Pt. Jawaharlal Nehru. The Maharaja confronted with this movement to end his regime, resorted to most stringent measures and in the process his subjects, mainly Muslims, suffered great ruthlessness and tyranny at his hands. This was followed by a tribal raid which succeeded in shaking the Maharaja's rule to its very foundations, so much so that the Maharaja fled the capital of Srinagar and left the population of the Valley to their fate. He, thus, virtually ceased to exercise authority over the State long before he even offered to accede to the Union of India.

9. On October 24, 1947, Maharaja Hari Singh, on reaching Jammu from the flight from Srinagar, made a request to the Union of India for armed assistance to deal with this situation, without at that time making any offer to accede to the Dominion of India. The Indian Government, however, reacted to this request by averring that troops could not be sent to Kashmir by them unless the State had first offered to accede. The Chiefs of Indian Army, Air Force and Navy were, nevertheless, given directions the same morning 'to examine and prepare plans for sending troops to Kashmir by air and road', and simultaneously Mr. V.P. Menon, the then State Secretary was sent to Srinagar evidently charged with a commission to persuade the Maharaja to sign on the dotted line and Mr. Menon returned to Delhi on October 26, 1947, with an Instrument of Accession executed by the Maharaja the same day. Lord Mountbatten, the then Governor General of India, reiterated the suggestion made at the Defence Committee meeting held on October 25, 1947, that the accession of Jammu and Kashmir should be considered as temporary to

be finalized through a plebiscite, and that the acceptance of the accession, however, was conditional on the will of the people being ascertained as soon as law and order were restored, and 'this principle was at once freely accepted and unilaterally proposed by Mr. Nehru'. In a letter dated 27th October, 1947, conveying his acceptance of the State's accession to India, Lord Mountbatten, the then Governor General of India, wrote to the Maharaja that his Government had decided to accept the accession 'in the special circumstances mentioned by His Highness'. He, however, added that in consistence with 'the policy of his Government, where the issue of accession had been the subject of dispute, the question of accession was to be decided in accordance with the wishes of the people of the State, it was his Government's wish that as soon as law and order had been restored in Kashmir and her soil cleared of the raiders the question of State's accession was to be settled by a reference to the people.' Mr. V.P. Menon in his book entitled, *The Integration of Indian States*, had admitted that the accession of Jammu and Kashmir State to India was accepted as 'conditional and provisional'. Mr. Menon had further stated therein that Sheikh Mohammad Abdullah had agreed to this provisional accession 'subject to a plebiscite'.

10. Even a day before the Instrument of Accession was sent by the Maharaja by hand of Mr. Menon alongwith the letter asking afresh for help, India had sent a cable to Mr. Attlee, the then Prime Minister of England, stating therein that the question of aiding Kashmir in that emergency was not designed in any way to influence the State to accede to India and that India adhered to this view that the question of accession in any disputed territory or State must be decided in accordance with the wishes of the people. A copy of the cable was sent by Mr. Nehru to the then Prime Minister of Pakistan, the next day. On October 28, 1947, Mr. Nehru sent a telegram to the Prime Minister of Pakistan assuring him that India had no desire to intervene in the affairs of the State of Jammu and Kashmir. In regard to accession it had been made clear that that was subject to reference to the people of the State and their decision. In a telegram dated October 28, 1947, to Pakistan, Mr. Nehru, inter alia, stated that they had no desire to intervene in the affairs of Kashmir and that after raiders had been driven away and law and order established they would hold a referendum in the State. It

was further stated therein that the Government of India had no desire to impose any decision and would abide by the people's wishes, but those could not be ascertained till peace and law and order prevailed. The Pakistan Government, however, denounced the accession as having been achieved by fraud and violence. On November 4, 1947, Mr. Nehru in a telegram to the Prime Minister of Pakistan stated that he wished to draw his attention to a broadcast by Mr. Nehru on Kashmir in which Mr. Nehru had stated that his Government's policy was that they had no desire to impose their will on Kashmir but to leave the final decision to the people of Kashmir and that he had further stated in the broadcast that they had agreed on an impartial international agency like the United Nations supervising any referendum. In that broadcast Pt. Nehru had also stated as follows:—

We have declared that the fate of Kashmir is ultimately to be decided by the people. That pledge we have given, and the Maharaja has supported it, not only to the people of Kashmir but to the world. We will not and cannot, back out of it. We are prepared when peace and law and order [sic] been established, to have a referendum under international auspices like United Nations. We want it to be a fair and just reference for people and shall accept their verdict.

11. Lord Attlee, as he now is, while paying a tribute to Mr. Nehru at the time of his passing away and eulogising his great qualities, had publicly stated that he considered that the fact that Mr. Nehru had gone back on his plighted word in regard to the holding of a plebiscite in the State of Jammu and Kashmir was but a blind spot in his otherwise effulgent life.

12. From the above resume of the facts of the case, it would appear that the then Dominion of India had expressly made a counter-proposal to the offer initially made by the Maharaja to accede to the Dominion of India, postulating therein in very clear and un-ambiguous terms that the accession of the State to the then Dominion of India would be subject to ratification by the will of the people freely and fully exercised by them, and this condition had been accepted both by Sheikh Mohammad Abdullah, as the acknowledged leader of the then largest political organisation in the State and the Maharaja himself. The accession, therefore, that thus emerged, was an accession which could not be

regarded as unqualified and un-conditional but was governed by this one stipulation of ratification of the accession by the ascertainment of the will of the people of the State; and the gentleman who made this offer of accession of the State to the Union of India had altogether lost his authority over the State, even before he had signed the Instrument of Accession and who was, soon after, extended from the State with the consent of the Government of India and later completely ousted from it as a result of his hereditary office of the Maharaja having been abolished in the State. The accession was thus effected by a lame-duck Ruler who had been deprived of the capacity and the means to exercise his free will and volition and whose power to bind the State by any of his acts had vanished by reason of his authority and suzerainty over the State having been effectively repudiated by his subjects even before he had offered to accede to the Dominion of India and by his ceasing completely to possess any such authority thereafter.

13. A careful examination of the provisions of the Constitution of India would show that it was this conditional accession which was provided for in the relevant provisions thereof. Let it be stated once that but for article 370 of the Constitution of India there is no provision contained in the Constitution of India which applies per se to the State of Jammu and Kashmir. It appears that this fact has been overlooked by those who clamour that Article 370 should be 'abrogated' in order to complete the integration of the State with India, forgetting as they evidently do 'their stand that the State is irrevocably bound to the Union of India and cannot claim the right to secede from it'. It may be said in passing that these two positions are self-contradictory, as when the accession of the State to the Union of India is claimed to be already completed under the existing provisions of law then it could not be made more complete by the repeal of Article 370. Be that as it may, the point that arises is that Article 370 finds a place in Part XXI of the Constitution of India entitled 'Temporary and Transitional Provisions'. As if this was not enough to indicate the transitory nature of these provisions of Article 370, the head-note of Article 370 contains the words 'Temporary Provisions' with respect to the State of Jammu and Kashmir. The word 'Transitional' connotes what is not permanent, but what exists during a stage which has to change from that state to a

different state. Article 370 itself provides that Article 370 will apply in relation to the State of Jammu and Kashmir and it also provides that the provisions of Article 1 shall apply in relation to the State of Jammu and Kashmir. Article 1 deals with the name and territory of the Union of India, and states that India shall be a Union of States and shall comprise of the territories of the States and by virtue of Article 370 the State of Jammu and Kashmir becomes a part of the Union of India within the meaning of Article 1 of the Constitution of India. The legal position, therefore, is that if Article 370 is abrogated, the State of Jammu and Kashmir will cease to be a part of the Union of India even temporarily under Article 1 of the Constitution of India. This was bound to be so as the future disposition of the State of Jammu and Kashmir had remained un-determined and was yet to be finally settled and Article 1 of the Constitution of India was applied in relation to the State of Jammu and Kashmir by Article 370 which being of a temporary and transient character could itself go lock, stock and barrel.

14. As a matter of fact, Article 1 of the Constitution of India could not provide for a permanent accession of the State of Jammu and Kashmir to the Union of India, as at the time when that provision was adopted, India continued to declare publicly that she was bound morally, legally, constitutionally and internationally by her commitment to hold a plebiscite in the State of Jammu and Kashmir to determine the will of the people on the question of accession, and since the Constitution of India could be made applicable to the State of Jammu and Kashmir by virtue of the Instrument of Accession alone. Article 1 of the constitution of India could not and did not provide for a permanent accession of this State to the Union of India.

15. In this connection, reference may also be made to Article 370, Clause (3) which empowered the President even to declare that this Article shall cease to be operative. The temporary and the transient character of these provisions of Article 370 would become manifest when we consider that power had been reserved under this Article to the President himself to annul this Article itself and assuming that he did so after the conditions laid down therein were satisfied, then no provision whatever contained in the Constitution of India would continue to be applicable to the State of Jammu and Kashmir. We may also in this

context consider some of the other provisions of Article 370 namely, Clause (1) sub-section (b) and (d) thereof. The power of Parliament to make laws for the State of Jammu and Kashmir had been limited to certain matters specified therein. The power of the Union Parliament to make laws for the State was strictly circumscribed by the provisions of the Instrument of Accession. The Union Parliament, therefore, did not enjoy supremacy of plenary powers in the domain of legislation in respect of the State of Jammu and Kashmir. Article 370 being temporary and transitory in character the powers exercisable by the President in virtue of those provisions also acquired a temporary character and, therefore, it could not be contended that any of the provisions of the Constitution of India which applied to the State of Jammu and Kashmir were permanently applicable to the State of Jammu and Kashmir. It was, therefore, not strictly correct to describe Article 370 as conferring any special status on the State of Jammu and Kashmir, as the provisions of this article being temporary in character, the relationship that has come into being between the State of Jammu and Kashmir and Union of India pursuant to this ad hoc arrangement envisaged by and based on the rider added to the accession of the State in the matter of a referendum is also temporary in character and could even be determined or terminated by an order passed by the President of India in that behalf. Once Article 370 disappeared, it could not be open to the Indian Parliament to amend the Constitution of India vis-à-vis the State of Jammu and Kashmir under Article 368 of that Constitution by making other provisions for the State of Jammu and Kashmir as Article 368 was applicable to the State of Jammu and Kashmir in virtue of the provisions of Article 370 itself, let alone the proviso which has been added thereto as being applicable to the State of Jammu and Kashmir namely that no such amendment shall have effect in relation to the State of Jammu & Kashmir unless applied by the order of President under clause (1) of Article 370.

16. We may also here mention that the Constitution Application to Jammu and Kashmir Order 1954 promulgated by the President of India in exercise of the powers vested in him under Article 370 of the Constitution of India specifically provides that Article 1 is applicable to the State of Jammu and Kashmir. This further shows that

Article 1 is made operative in the case of the State of Jammu and Kashmir by the presidential order which itself is of a temporary character. We may also refer to Article 253 of the Constitution of India which gives power to Parliament to make any law for the whole or any part of India for implementing any treaty, agreement or convention with any other country or countries or any decision made at any International Conference, Association or other body and the Constitution Application to Jammu and Kashmir Order, 1954, referred to above makes this Article applicable to the State of Jammu and Kashmir with the addition of the following proviso, namely:

provided after the commencement of the Constitution Application to Jammu and Kashmir Order, 1954, no decision affecting the disposition of the State of Jammu & Kashmir shall be made by the Government of India without the consent of the Government of that State. These provisions also underline the fact that in the case of the State of Jammu and Kashmir the existing relationship between the State and the Union of India could be varied in order to give effect to or implement some agreement or treaty arrived at in respect of the State of Jammu and Kashmir internationally. The view has, therefore, been taken by some legal experts duly finding a place in some publications that

this Article 253 which has a direct bearing on the Kashmir dispute read with Article 246 and the Union List items 10, 12, 13 and 14—would make the accession of Kashmir to India provisional and by implication provide for even her seccession from the Union.

17. The view, therefore, that the State of Jammu and Kashmir could not secede from the Union of India and that even Parliament had not the power to give effect to such a decision and thereby 'de-annexe' the State is not borne out from the provisions of the Constitution of India itself.

18. Some of the provisions contained in the Instrument of Accession would also bear reproduction here as fortifying the view in regard to the temporary nature of the accession of the State to the Indian Union:

5. The terms of this my Instrument of Accession shall not be varied by any amendment of the Act or of the Indian Independence Act, 1947, unless such amendment is accepted by me by Instrument supplementary to this Instrument.

7. Nothing in this Instrument shall be deemed to commit me in any way to acceptance of any future Constitution of India or to fetter my discretion to enter into arrangements with the Government of India under any such future Constitution.

8. Nothing in this Instrument affects the continuance of my sovereignity in and over this State, or, save as provided by or under this Instrument, the exercise of any powers, authority and rights now enjoyed by me as Ruler of this State or the validity of any law at present in force in this State.

9. I hereby declare that I execute this Instrument on behalf of this State and that any reference in this Instrument to me or the Ruler of the State is to be construed as including a reference to my heirs and successors.

19. It would, therefore, appear from the above provisions of the Instrument of Accession that the sovereignity or any part thereof over the State of Jammu and Kashmir had not been parted with in favour of the Union of India; but under the terms of this Instrument of Accession, it continued to vest in the State and that any Constitution of India which might be adopted at any time in future would not bind the State ipso-facto. Reading clauses (7) and (8) of the Instrument of Accession together, it becomes crystal clear that while the sovereignty over the State continued to vest in the State and had not been parted with in favour of the Dominion of India, no provisions to the contrary if found in the Constitution of India could be binding on the State and be valid and effectual so far as that State was concerned. Clauses (8) and (9) of the Instrument of Accession quoted above, read conjointly, would also show that while sovereignty over the State of Jammu and Kashmir continued to vest in the State itself, and had not been surrendered either in whole or in part of India, what these provisions contemplated was the assignment of certain functions exercisable by the Union of India in relation to the State of Jammu and Kashmir which would not and does not derogate from such sovereignty. Even Section 6 of the Government of India Act 1935, as amended in India, has made it abundantly clear that under the Instrument of Accession some 'functions' were to be delegated by an acceding State to the Union of India. Article 1 of the Constitution of India could not and had not, therefore, provided for a permanent accession of Jammu and Kashmir State to the Union of India, and if it did so, it would be void and illegal in view of these

express provisions of the Instrument of Accession. It was for this reason that Article 370 made Article 1 applicable only provisionally to the State Jammu and Kashmir, a view which is further reinforced by the expression used in Article 370 clause (1) viz., 'Notwithstanding anything in this Constitution' which clearly implied that anything found contrary in the Constitution of India to the provisions of Article 370 would not be applicable to the State of Jammu and Kashmir and Article 370 had made Article 1, among other Articles, temporarily and provisionally applicable as a transitional Provision to the State of Jammu and Kashmir and, therefore, Article 1 became applicable to the State of Jammu and Kashmir only temporarily and transitionally within the meaning of Article 370 itself. Article 1 of the Constitution of India not having been assented to by the Ruler of the State within the meaning of clause (7) of the Instrument of Accession at the time of the adoption of the Constitution of India, this fact also would detract from the view that Article 1 provided for a permanent accession of the State to the Union of India.

20. A reference may also be made to a provision contained in the so-called Constitution of Jammu and Kashmir that the State of Jammu and Kashmir is and shall be an integral part of the Union of India. It may be noted that the Constituent Assembly of State was not legally and constitutionally competent to determine the question of the final disposition of the State; and all doubts on that score had been set at rest both on the floor of that House and outside it from different forums; and it is, therefore, not necessary for us to recapitulate those grounds here. It would suffice here to recall very briefly the events which preceded the passing of the so-called Constitution of Jammu and Kashmir. A legal and constitutional Government of the State presided over by Sheikh Mohd. Abdullah was overthrown by a coup d'etat and power forcibly seized by a coterie, now defunct, which to-day stands completely discredited even in the eyes of its erstwhile supporters by its policy of graft, self-aggrandizement, jobbery and nepotism and a reign of hell unleashed by it in the form of mass arrest, detentions without trial of both the leaders and the rank and file, committing atrocities on them and not even sparing their lives. All this was done in the belief that, apart from providing an opportunity to it to amass fabulous wealth,

it would enable it cow down the spirits of the people. It succeeded in its first aim but signally failed in the realisation of second objective. A Constituent Assembly functioning under such auspices when a mere expression of opinion not palatable to the regime entailed most dire consequences in the shape of prolonged incarcerations and concoction of cases, and an assiduous attempt made at decoying, by intimidation, bribe and bluster, ceased to represent the will of the people, who lost no time in disowning it and repudiating the spurious constitution in many diverse ways still open to them under such unfavourable conditions. A Constitution thus hammered out was, therefore, robbed of all its value and sanctity and could not be pitted against them to thwart the declared will of the people and be regarded even on this account as having achieved even a modicum of the fulfilment of the solemn pledges given and the commitments made for holding a plebiscite in the State under the United Nations auspices.

21. It is, however, not without significance that Article 370 of the Constitution of India which was enacted before the Constitution of Jammu and Kashmir was adopted stood un-changed even after the adoption of section 3 of the Constitution of Jammu and Kashmir as if this provision had never been adopted, and, therefore, this provision contained in the Constitution of Jammu and Kashmir became in effect a unilateral declaration which did not evoke a sympathetic or any consequential action on the part of the Union of India. And this was not surprising, when it is remembered that the Security Council had issued an interdiction not to alter the existing status of the State of Jammu and Kashmir unilaterally, and the Government of India had in keeping with the stipulation made by them with regard to the ascertainment of the will of the people at the time of the acceptance by them of the Instrument of Accession executed by the then Ruler and the subsequent pronouncements made by India from time to time from different forums reiterating and confirming this stipulation on their part, given a public assurance that the outcome of the deliberations of the Constituent Assembly convened in the State would not prejudice the final disposition of the State. Moreover, if we close reading to section 3 of the Constitution of Jammu and Kashmir it does not lend support to the view that it had provided that the accession of the State

of Jammu and Kashmir to India was permanent and irrevocable, as there are no express provisions made therein to that effect, and the State could be an integral part of the Union of India even temporarily and for the time being only. Section 1 of the Constitution of Jammu and Kashmir has to be read with the Preamble to that Constitution which while referring to the accession of the State which took place on the 27th of October, 1947, sought to define the existing relationship of the State with the Union of India based on the Instrument of Accession. In other words, this Constitution did not seek to enlarge the scope of the original accession which was subject to the overriding condition of the ratification of the accession by the will of the people, but was seeking merely in view of the Instrument of Accession to define the existing relationship of the State with the Union without prejudice, of course, to the final disposition of the State as determined as a result of the ascertainment of the will of the people.

22. Further, some Jurists have in a printed publication expressed the view that section 3 of the constitution of Jammu and Kashmir is ultra vires the Constitution of India and, therefore, void and illegal as that section 'impinges on matters within the exclusive reserve of the Union of India.'

23. Before we close, we may draw attention to the 'White Paper' on Jammu and Kashmir issued by the Government of India in 1948, which is replete with statements and pronouncements made by the Government of India that the accession of the State of Jammu and Kashmir to the Indian Union was provisional and temporary and that the issue of accession to India or Pakistan was to be decided by a referendum or a plebiscite of the people of Jammu and Kashmir held under the auspices of the United Nations and that even in their first communication to the Security Council seeking to invoke their jurisdiction in regard to Jammu and Kashmir dispute before the Security Council, this position was fully maintained and adhered to by them. These averments made by the Government of India soon after the Instrument of Accession executed by the Maharaja was accepted by them, and even before the Security Council became seized of the matter on the motion of the Government of India itself, operate as an estoppel to any subsequent retraction by them and furnish irrefutable and incontrovertible

evidence as regards the true import and meaning of these provisions of the Instrument of Accession.

24. In this connection we may also with advantage refer to what Mr. M.C. Chagla had stated in his address to the United Nations on May 8, 1964 as supporting our view that the statements made at the time or soon after the event are by far more relevant than any subsequent statement to the contrary as to the real intentions and purport underlying and instrument.

25. Mr. Chagla had also reportedly referred in that address to the Independence Act of 1947. Curiously enough, Mr. Chagla seemed to have overlooked the fact that it was not the Indian Independence Act of 1947 that had provided for an accession of an Indian state to one of the then two newly created Dominions of India and Pakistan as that Act inter alia merely provided for the lapse of paramountcy together with all the treaties, agreements and engagements based thereon. On the other hand, it was the Government of India Act 1935 as adapted by India or Pakistan that provided for such accession but that Act did not apply ipso-facto to an Indian State but only in so far as the ruler of a State agreed by an Instrument of Accession or by a supplementary Instrument of Accession to have it applied to that State. The argument, therefore, advanced by Mr. Chagla as revolving round the provisions of the Indian Independence Act 1947 would, therefore, seem to be untenable.

26. For the foregoing reasons, the accession of the State of Jammu and Kashmir to the Union of India is purely temporary in character and is not complete, final or irrevocable.

Chapter 10

The Governor Replaces
the Sadar-i-Riyasat

1(a). The Constitution of Jammu & Kashmir
(Sixth Amendment) Act, 1965

[10th April, 1965]

An Act further to amend the Constitution of Jammu and Kashmir.

Be it enacted by the Jammu and Kashmir State Legislature in the Sixteenth Year of the Republic of India as follows:—

1. Short Title

This Act may be called the Constitution of Jammu and Kashmir (Sixth Amendment) Act, 1965.

2. Amendment of the Constitution

In the Constitution of Jammu and Kashmir (hereinafter referred to as 'the Constitution') except in Parts XII and XIII for the expressions 'Sadar-i-Riyasat' and 'Prime Minister' wherever they occur the expressions 'Governor' and 'Chief Minister' shall respectively be substituted.

3. Amendment of Section 2

In section 2 of the Constitution, after sub-section (2) the following sub-section shall be inserted, namely:—

'(3) Any reference in this Constitution to the Sadar-i-Riyasat shall, unless the context otherwise requires, be construed as a reference to the Governor'.

4. Substitution of New Section for Section 27

For section 27 of the Constitution, the following section shall be substituted, namely:—

27. Appointment of Governor.—The Governor shall be appointed by the President by warrant under his hand and seal:—

Provided that the person holding office as Sadar-i-Riyasat immediately before the commencement of the Constitution of Jammu and Kashmir (Sixth Amendment) Act, 1965, shall on such commencement be the Governor and shall, subject to the other provisions of this Constitution, continue to hold office as Governor until the remaining period of his term for which he was elected as Sadar-i-Riyasat expires.

5. Substitution of New Section for Section 29

For section 29 of the Constitution, the following section shall be substituted, namely:—

'*29. Qualifications for appointment as Governor.*—No person shall be eligible for appointment as Governor unless he is a citizen of India and has completed the age of thirty years.'

6. Amendment of Section 30

In section 30 of the Constitution, in sub-section (1) for the words 'Elected and recognized' the words 'appointed' shall be substituted.

7. Substitution of New Section for Section 31

For section 31 of the Constitution, the following section shall be substituted, namely:—

31. Oath of office.—The Governor and every person discharging the functions of the Governor shall, before entering upon his office, make and subscribe in the presence of the Chief Justice of the High Court or, in his absence, the senior most Judge of that Court available, an oath or affirmation in the following form, that is to say:—

I, A. B., do $\dfrac{\text{swear in the name of God}}{\text{solemnly affirm}}$ that I will faithfully execute the office of Governor (or discharge the functions of the Governor) of Jammu and Kashmir and will to the best of my ability preserve, protect and defend the Constitution and the law and that I will devote myself to the service and well being of the people of the State.

8. Omission of Section 32

Section 32 of the Constitution shall be omitted.

9. Substitution of New Section for Section 33

For section 33 of the Constitution, the following section shall be substituted, namely:—'*33. Discharge of the functions of the Governor in certain contingencies:*—The President may make such provision as he thinks fit for the discharge of functions of the Governor in any contingency not provided for in this Part'.

10. Amendment of Section 51

In section 51 of the Constitution, for clause (a), the following clause shall be substituted, namely:—(a) 'is a permanent resident of the State, and makes and subscribes before some person authorised in that behalf by the Election Commission of India an oath or affirmation according to the form set out for the purpose in the Fifth Schedule.'
[...]

1(b). The Constitution of Jammu & Kashmir as Amended

Part V: The Executive
The Governor

26. Head of State

(1) The Head of the State shall be designated as the [1]Governor.

(2) The executive power of the State shall be vested in the Governor and shall be exercised by him either directly or through officers subordinate to him in accordance with this Constitution.

(3) Nothing in this section shall

(a) be deemed to transfer to the Governor any functions conferred by any existing law on any other authority; or

(b) prevent the State Legislature from conferring by law functions on any authority subordinate to the Governor.

[1]27. Appointment of Governor

The Governor shall be appointed by the President by warrant under his hand and seal:

Provided that the person holding office as Sadar-i-Riyasat immediately before the commencement of the Constitution of Jammu and Kashmir (Sixth Amendment) Act, 1965, shall on such commencement be the Governor and shall, subject to the other provisions of this Constitution, continue to hold office as Governor until the remaining period of his term for which he was elected as Sadar-i-Riyasat expires.

28. Term of Office

(1) The Governor shall hold office during the pleasure of the President.

(2) The Governor may, by writing under his hand addressed to the President, resign his office.

(3) Subject to foregoing provisions of this section, the Governor shall hold office for a term of five years from the date on which he enters upon his office:

Provided that he shall, notwithstanding the expiration of his term continue to hold office until his successor enters upon his office.

[2]29. Qualifications for Appointment as Governor

No person shall be eligible for appointment as Governor unless he is a citizen of India and has completed the age of thirty years.

---

[1] Substituted by the Constitution of Jammu and Kashmir (Sixth Amendment) Act, 1965, S. 4.

[2] Substituted by the Constitution of Jammu and Kashmir (Sixth Amendment) Act, 1965, S. 5.

30. *Conditions of Office*

(1) The Governor shall not be a member of either House of Legislature and if a member of either House be [3][appointed] as Governor, he shall be deemed to have vacated his seat in the House on the date on which he enters upon his office as Governor.

(2) The Governor shall not hold any other office of profit.

(3) The Governor shall be entitled to such emoluments, allowances and privileges as are specified in the Second Schedule.

(4) The emoluments and allowances of the [5]Governor shall not be diminished during his term of office.

[3] Substituted for 'elected and recognized' by section 6, ibid.

Chapter 11

'Erosion' of Article 370

The Process

1. The President's 47 Orders under Article 370

Published in the Gazette of India, Extraordinary, Part II Section 3, No. 31, Dated the 11th February, 1956.

Ministry of Law: New Delhi, the 11th February, 1956

Published in the Gazette of India, Extraordinary, Part II Section 3, No. 27-A, Dated the 17th January, 1958/ Pausa 27, 1879

S.R.O. 322:—The following order made by the President of India is published for general information.

C.O. 51

The Constitution (Application to Jammu and Kashmir) Order, 1956

In exercise of the powers conferred by clause (1) of Article 370 of the Constitution the President, with the concurrence of the Government of the State of Jammu and Kashmir, is pleased to make the following order:

1. (1) This Order may be called the Constitution (Application to Jammu and Kashmir) Amendment Order, 1956.

(2) It shall come into force at once.

2. In paragraph 2 of the Constitution (Application to Jammu and Kashmir) Order, 1954, in clause (a) under sub-paragraph (22) relating to the Seventh Schedule to the Constitution of India:

(a) Item (ii), the figures '54' and '67' shall be omitted;

(b) for Item (iii), the following item shall be substituted, namely:

'(iii) for entry 67, the entry "67. Ancient and historical monuments, and archaeological sites and remains, declared by Parliament by Law to be of national importance" shall be substituted'.

[No. F. 17(1)/56-G]

Ministry of Law: New Delhi, the 16th January, 1958

Published in the Gazette of India, Extraordinary, Part II Section 3, sub-section (1) No. 13, Dated the 27th February, 1958/Phalguna 8, 1879

S.R.O. 262-A:—The following order made by the President of India is published for general information.

C.O. 55

The Constitution (Application to Jammu and Kashmir) Order, 1958

In exercise of the powers conferred by clause (1) of Article 370 of the Constitution, the President, with the concurrence of the Government of the State of Jammu and Kashmir is pleased to make the following Order:—

1. (1) This Order may be called the Constitution (Application to Jammu and Kashmir) Amendment Order, 1958.

(2) It shall come into force at once.

2. In paragraph 2 of the Constitution (Application to Jammu and Kashmir) Order, 1954:—

(1) in sub-paragraph (7) (relating to part XII), clauses (a), (b) and (c) shall be re-lettered as clauses (c), (d) and (e), respectively, and before

clause (c) as so re-lettered, the following clauses shall be inserted, namely:—

    (a) In Article 269:—(i) in clause (1), after sub-clause (f), the following sub-clause shall be inserted, namely:—(g) taxes on the sale or purchase of goods other than newspapers, where such sale or purchase takes place in the course of inter-State trade or commerce; and (ii) after clause (2), the following clause shall be inserted, namely:—'(3) Parliament may by law formulate principles for determining when a sale or purchase of goods takes place in the course of inter-State trade or commerce'.

    (b) In Article 286:—(i) In clause (1), the Explanation shall be omitted; and (ii) for clauses (2) and (3), the following clauses shall be substituted, namely:—

(2) Parliament may by law formulate principles for determining when a sale or purchase of goods takes place in any of the ways mentioned in clause (1).

(3) Any law of a State shall, in so far as it imposes, or authorises the imposition of, a tax on the sale or purchase of goods declared by Parliament by law to be of Special importance in inter-State trade or commerce, be subject to such restrictions and conditions in regard to the system of levy, rates and other incidents of the tax as Parliament may by law specify.

(2) In sub-paragraph (22) (relating to the Seventh Schedule), in clause (a), after item (iv), the following item shall be inserted, namely:—'(v) after entry 92, the following entry shall be inserted, namely:—'92A. Taxes on the sale or purchase of goods other than newspapers, where such sale or purchase takes place in the course of inter-State trade or commerce.'

Ministry of Law: New Delhi, the 26th February, 1958

Published in the Gazette of India, Extraordinary, Part II
Section 3 (i), No. 19, Dated the 10th February, 1959/
Magha 21, 1880 Saka

G.S.R. 78:—The following order made by the President of India is published for general information.

C.O. 56

The Constitution (Application to Jammu and Kashmir) Second Amendment Order, 1958

In exercise of the powers conferred by clause (1) of Article 370 of the Constitution, the President, with the concurrence of the Government of the State of Jammu and Kashmir, is pleased to make the following Order:—

1. (1) This Order may be called the Constitution (Application to Jammu and Kashmir) Second Amendment Order, 1958.

(2) It shall come into force at once.

2. In paragraph 2 of the Constitution (Application to Jammu and Kashmir) Order, 1954:—

(1) in the opening portion, after the words 'the Constitution', the words, letters and figures 'as in force on the 15th day of February, 1958' shall be inserted;

(2) in sub-paragraph (5) (relating to Part V), clauses (f) and (g) shall be omitted;

(3) in sub-paragraph (6) (relating to Part XI), clause (i) shall be omitted, and clause (j) shall be re-lettered as clause (i);

(4) in sub-paragraph (7) (relating to Part XII), clauses (a) and (b) shall be omitted, and clauses (c), (d) and (e) shall be re-lettered as clauses (a), (b), (c) respectively;

(5) in sub-paragraph (8) (relating to Part XIII), the brackets and letters '(a)' at the commencement and clause (b) shall be omitted;

(6) in sub-paragraph (9) (relating to Part XIV), the existing modification relating to Article 308 shall be omitted, and in lieu thereof, the following modification shall be inserted, namely:—

'In Article 312, after the words "the States", the brackets and words (including the State of Jammu and Kashmir) shall be inserted';

(7) in sub-paragraph (14) (relating to Part XIX):—

(a) in clause (a), for the word 'Rajpramukh', the word 'Governor' shall be substituted;

(b) clause (c) shall be omitted, and clause (d) shall be re-lettered as clause (c);

(c) in clause (c) as so re-lettered, in new clause (4) of Article 367:—
(i) sub-clause (d) shall be omitted, and sub-clauses (e) and (f) shall be re-lettered as sub-clauses (d) and (e) respectively; (ii) in sub-clause (e) as so re-lettered, for the word 'Rajpramukh', the word 'Governor' shall be substituted;

(8) in clause (a) of sub-paragraph (16) (relating to Part XXI), after the figures '371', the figures and letters '372A' shall be inserted, and for the words and figures 'Articles 376 to 392', the words, figures and letters 'Articles 376 to 378A and 392' shall be substituted;

(9) in sub-paragraph (19) (relating to the Second Schedule), the modification relating to paragraph 6 shall be omitted;

(10) in sub-paragraph (22) (relating to the Seventh Schedule), for clause (a), the following clause shall be substituted, namely:—'(a) in the Union List:—
(i) for entry 3, the entry "3. Administration of Cantonments" shall be substituted;
(ii) entries 8, 9 and 34 the words "trading corporation including" in entry 43, entries 44, 50, 52, 55 and 60, the words "and records" in entry 67, entries 69, 78 and 79, the words Inter-State migration in entry 81, and entry 97 shall be omitted; and
(iii) in entry 72, the reference to the State shall be construed as not including a reference to the State of Jammu and Kashmir'.

(11) in sub-paragraph (24) (relating to the Ninth Schedule), for the figures '13', '14', '15', '16', '17', '18', '19' and '20', the figures '20', '21', '22', '23', '24', '25', '26' and '27' shall respectively be substituted.

Ministry of Law: New Delhi, the 9th February, 1959

Published in the Gazette of India, Extraordinary, Part II Section 3 (i), No. 60, Dated April 23, 1959/ Vaisakha 3, 1881

G.S.R. 175:—The following order made by the President of India is published for general information.

C.O. 57

The Constitution (Application to Jammu and Kashmir) Amendment Order, 1959

In exercise of the powers conferred by clause (1) of Article 370 of the Constitution, the President, with the concurrence of the Government of the State of Jammu and Kashmir, is pleased to make the following Order:—

1. (1) This Order may be called the Constitution (Application to Jammu and Kashmir) Amendment Order, 1959.

(2) It shall come into force at once.

2. In paragraph 2 of the Constitution (Application to Jammu and Kashmir) Order, 1954, under sub-paragraph (22) (relating to the Seventh Schedule), in item (ii) of clause (a), the figures '69' shall be omitted.

Ministry of Law: New Delhi, the 23rd April, 1959

Published in the Gazette of India, Extraordinary, Part II Section 3 (i), No. 6, Dated January 20, 1960/Pausa 30, 1881

G.S.R. 513:—The following order made by the President of India is published for general information.

C.O. 59

The Constitution (Application to Jammu and Kashmir) Second Amendment Order, 1959

In exercise of the powers conferred by clause (1) of Article 370 of the Constitution, the President, with the concurrence of the Government of the State of Jammu and Kashmir, is pleased to make the following Order:—

1. (1) This Order may be called the Constitution (Application to Jammu and Kashmir) Second Amendment Order, 1959.

(2) It shall come into force at once.

2. In paragraph 2 of the Constitution (Application to Jammu and Kashmir) Order, 1954, under sub-paragraph (4) (relating to the Part III), in clause (d) and in sub-clause (iii) of clause (i), for the word 'five', the word 'ten' shall be substituted.

Ministry of Law: New Delhi, the 20th January, 1960

**Published in the Gazette of India, Extraordinary,
Part II Section 3 (i), No. 80, Dated June 22, 1960/
Asadha 1, 1882**

G.S.R. 98:—The following Order made by the President of India is
published for general information.

C.O. 60

The Constitution (Application to Jammu and Kashmir) Second Amendment Order, 1960

In exercise of the powers conferred by clause (1) of Article 370 of the
Constitution, the President, with the concurrence of the Government
of the State of Jammu and Kashmir, is pleased to make the following
Order:

1. (1) This Order may be called the Constitution (Application to
Jammu and Kashmir) Amendment Order, 1960.

(2) It shall come into force on the 26th day of January, 1960.

2. In paragraph 2 of the Constitution (Application to Jammu and
Kashmir) Order, 1954:—

(1) in sub-paragraph (5), (relating to Part V), in clause (e), the figures
'136' shall be omitted; (2) after sub-paragraph (5), the following shall
be inserted, namely:—(5A) Part VI.

   (a) Articles 153 to 217, Article 219, Article 221 and Articles 223
      to 237 shall be omitted. (b) in Article 220, reference to the
      commencement of the Constitution shall be construed as refer-
      ences to the commencement of the Constitution (Application
      to Jammu & Kashmir) Amendment Order, 1960. (c) To Article
      222, the following new clause shall be added, namely:—

(2) Every such transfer from the High Court of Jammu and Kashmir
or to that High Court shall be made after consultation with the Sadar-
i-Riyasat;

(3) for sub-paragraph (10) (relating to Part XV), the following shall
be substituted, namely:—(10) Part XV.

   (a) In clause (i) of Article 324, the reference to the Constitution
      shall, in relation to elections to either House of the Legislature

of Jammu and Kashmir, be construed as a reference to the Constitution of Jammu and Kashmir. (b) Articles 325, 326, 327 and 328 shall be omitted. (c) In Article 329, clause (a) shall be omitted, and in clause (b) the reference to a State shall be construed as not including a reference to the State of Jammu and Kashmir.

Ministry of Law: New Delhi, the 22nd June, 1960

Published in the Gazette of India, Extraordinary, Part II
Section 3 (i), No. 53, Dated May 2, 1961/Vaisakha 12, 1883

G.S.R. 721:—The following order made by the President of India is published for general information.

C.O. 61

The Constitution (Application to Jammu and Kashmir)
Second Amendment Order, 1960

In exercise of the powers conferred by clause (1) of Article 370 of the Constitution, the President, with the concurrence of the Government of the State of Jammu and Kashmir, is pleased to make the following Order:—

1. (1) This Order may be called the Constitution (Application to Jammu and Kashmir) Second Amendment Order, 1960.

(2) It shall come into force at once.

2. In paragraph 2 of the Constitution (Application to Jammu and Kashmir) Order, 1954, under sub-paragraph (22) (relating to the Seventh Schedule), in item (ii) of clause (a), the figures '50' shall be omitted.

Ministry of Law: New Delhi, the 2nd May, 1961

Published in the Gazette of India, Extraordinary, Part II
Section 2, sub-section (i), No. 133, Dated September 25, 1963/Asvina 3, 1885

G.S.R. 633:—The following order made by the President of India is published for general information.

C.O. 62

The Constitution (Application to Jammu and Kashmir) Amendment Order, 1961

In exercise of the powers conferred by clause (1) of Article 370 of the Constitution, the President, with the concurrence of the Government of the State of Jammu and Kashmir, is pleased to make the following Order:—

1. (1) This Order may be called the Constitution (Application to Jammu and Kashmir) Amendment Order, 1961.

(2) It shall come into force at once.

2. In paragraph 2 of the Constitution (Application to Jammu and Kashmir) Order, 1954, under sub-paragraph (22) (relating to the Seventh Schedule), in item (ii) of clause (a), the figures '52' shall be omitted.

Ministry of Law: New Delhi, the 25th September, 1963

Published in the Gazette of India, Extraordinary, Part II Section 3(i), No. 47, Dated March 6, 1964/Phalguna 16, 1885

G.S.R. 1567:—The following order made by the President of India is published for general information.

C.O. 66

The Constitution (Application to Jammu and Kashmir) Amendment Order, 1963

In exercise of the powers conferred by clause (1) of Article 370 of the Constitution, the President, with the concurrence of the Government of the State of Jammu and Kashmir, is pleased to make the following Order:—

1. (1) This Order may be called the Constitution (Application to Jammu and Kashmir) Amendment Order, 1963.

(2) It shall come into force at once.

2. In paragraph 2 of the Constitution (Application to Jammu and Kashmir) Order, 1954:—

(1) in sub-paragraph (5) (relating to Part V) clause (b) shall be omitted, and clauses (c), (d) and (e) shall be re-lettered as clauses (b), (c) and (d) respectively;

(2) in sub-paragraph (6) (relating to Part XI):—

(a) for clause (a), the following clause shall be substituted, namely:—
'(a) in Article 246, for the words, brackets and figures "clauses (2) and (3)" occurring in clause (1), the word, brackets and figure "clause (2)" shall be substituted, and the words, brackets and figure "Notwithstanding anything in clause (3), occurring in clause (2) and the whole of clauses (3) and (4) shall be omitted".' (b) clause (f) shall be omitted, and clauses (g), (h) and (i) shall be re-lettered as clauses (f), (g) and (h) respectively;

(3) for sub-paragraph (22) (relating to the Seventh Schedule), the following sub-paragraph shall be substituted, namely:—(22) Seventh Schedule

(a) In the Union List:—(i) for entry 3, entry '3. Administration of cantonments', shall be substituted; (ii) entries 8, 9 and 34 the words 'trading corporations, including' in entry 43, entries 55 and 60, the words 'and records' in entry 67, entries 78 and 79, the words 'inter-State migration' in entry 81, and entry 97 shall be omitted; and (iii) in entry 44, after the words 'but not including universities', the words 'in so far as such corporations relate to the legal and medical professions' shall be inserted; and (iv) in entry 72, the reference to the States shall be construed as not including a reference to the State of Jammu and Kashmir.

(b) The State List shall be omitted.

(c) In the Concurrent List:—(i) for entry 25, the entry '26. Legal and medical professions' shall be substituted; (ii) entries 1 to 25 (both inclusive) and entries 27 to 44 (both inclusive) shall be omitted; and (iii) in entry 45, for the words and figures 'List II or List III, the words "this List"' shall be substituted.

S. Radhakrishnan,
President.
(No. F. 19(1) 63-LL)
S.P. Sen Verma,
Spl. Secy.

Ministry of Law: New Delhi, the 6th March, 1964

Published in the Gazette of India, Extraordinary,
Part II Section 3(1), No. 196, Dated December 21,
1964/Agrahayana 30, 1886

G.S.R. 422:—The following order made by the President of India is published for general information.

C.O. 69

The Constitution (Application to Jammu and Kashmir) Amendment Order, 1964

In exercise of the powers conferred by clause (1) of Article 370 of the Constitution, the President, with the concurrence of the Government of the State of Jammu and Kashmir, is pleased to make the following Order:—

1. (1) This Order may be called the Constitution (Application to Jammu and Kashmir) Amendment Order, 1964.

(2) It shall come into force at once.

2. In paragraph 2 of the Constitution (Application to Jammu and Kashmir) Order, 1954:—

(1) In sub-paragraph (4) (relating to Part III). In clause (d) and in sub-clause (iii) of clause (i), for the words 'ten years', the words 'fifteen years' shall be substituted;

(2) in sub-paragraph (22) (relating to the Seventh Schedule), for clause (c), the following clause shall be substituted, namely:—

(c) in the Concurrent List:—

(i) for entry 1, the following entry shall be substituted, namely:—

'1. Criminal law (excluding offences against laws with respect to any of the matters specified in List I and excluding the use of naval, military or air forces or any other armed forces of the Union in aid of the civil power) in so far as such criminal law relates to offences against laws with respect to trade and commerce in, and the production, supply and distribution and price control of gold'.

    (ii) in entry 24, after the words 'and maternity benefits', the words 'but only with respect to labour employed in the coal-mining industry' shall be inserted.

    (iii) for entry 26, the entry '26. Legal and medical professions', shall be substituted.

    (iv) for entry 33, the following entry shall be substituted, namely:—

'33. Trade and commerce in and the production, supply and distribution of the products of any industry by the Union is declared by Parliament by law to be expedient in the Public interest in so far as such industry relates to gold, and imported goods of the same kind as ssuch products'.

    (v) for entry 34, the entry '34. Price Control of gold', shall be substituted;

    (vi) entries 2 to 23 (both inclusive), entry 25, entries 27 to 32 (both inclusive) and entries 35 to 44 (both inclusive) shall be omitted; and

    (vii) in entry 45, for the words and figures 'List II or List III', the words 'this List' shall be substituted.

The Constitution (Application to Jammu and Kashmir) Second Amendment Order, 1964

C.O. 70

In exercise of the powers conferred by clause (1) of Article 370 of the Constitution, the President, with the concurrence of the Government of the State of Jammu and Kashmir, is pleased to make the following Order:—

1. (1) This Order may be called the Constitution (Application to Jammu and Kashmir) Second Amendment Order, 1964.

(2) It shall come into force at once.

2. In paragraph 2 of the Constitution (Application to Jammu and Kashmir) Order, 1954, in sub-paragraph (22) (relating to the Seventh Schedule):—

(1) in item (ii) of clause (a), for the words and figures 'entries 55 and 60', the word and figures 'entry 60' shall be substituted;

(2) in clause (c):—(a) for item (i), the following shall be substituted, namely:—

1. Criminal law (excluding offences against laws with respect to laws with respect to any of the matters specified in List I and excluding the use of naval, military or air forces or any other armed forces of the Union in aid of the civil power) in so far as such criminal law relates to offences against laws with respect to any of the matters specified in this List.

(b) items (iv) to (vii) shall be renumbered as (v) to (viii) respectively and before item (v) as so renumbered, the following shall be inserted, namely: '(iv) for entry 30, the entry "30. Vital statistics in so far as they relate to births and deaths including registration of births and deaths" shall be substituted';

(c) for item (vii) as so re-numbered, the following shall be substituted, namely:—(vii) entries 2 to 23 (both inclusive), entries 27, 28, 29, 31 and 32, entries 35 to 38 (both inclusive) and entries 40 to 44 (both inclusive) shall be omitted; and.

S. Radhakrishnan,
President.
R.C.S. Sarkar, Secy.
GMGIP ND- TS Wing-51 M of Law (2845)28-09-1964-100.

Ministry of Law: New Delhi, the 21st December, 1964

Published in the Gazette of India, Extraordinary, Part II Section 3 (i), No. 70, Dated May 17, 1965/ Vaisakha 27, 1887

G.S.R. 1839:—The following order made by the President of India is published for general information.

The Constitution (Application to Jammu and Kashmir) Third Amendment Order, 1964

In exercise of the powers conferred by clause (1) of Article 370 of the Constitution, the President, with the concurrence of the Government of the State of Jammu and Kashmir, is pleased to make the following Order:—

1. (1) This Order may be called the Constitution (Application to Jammu and Kashmir) Third Amendment Order, 1964.

(2) It shall come into force at once.

2. In paragraph 2 of the Constitution (Application to Jammu and Kashmir) Order, 1954, in sub-paragraph (13) (relating to Part XVIII), for clause (b), the following clauses shall be substituted, namely:—'(b) in clause (1) of Article 356, references to provisions or provision of this Constitution shall, in relation to the State of Jammu and Kashmir, be construed as including references to provisions or provisions of the Constitution of Jammu and Kashmir. (c) Article 360 shall be omitted'.

Ministry of Law: New Delhi, the 17th May, 1965

G.S.R. 744:—The following order made by the President of India is published for general information.

C.O. 72

The Constitution (Application to Jammu and Kashmir) Amendment Order, 1965

In exercise of the powers conferred by clause (1) of Article 370 of the Constitution, the President, with the concurrence of the Government of the State of Jammu and Kashmir, is pleased to make the following Order:—

1. (1) This Order may be called the Constitution (Application to Jammu and Kashmir) Amendment Order, 1965.

(2) It shall come into force at once.

2. In paragraph 2 of the Constitution (Application to Jammu and Kashmir) Order, 1954, in sub-paragraph (22) (relating to the Seventh Schedule):—

(1) in clause (a), for item (ii), the following shall be substituted, namely:—'(ii) entries 8, 9, 34 and 60, the words "and records" in entry 67, entry 79, the words "Inter-State migration" in entry 81, and entry 97 shall be omitted'.

(2) in clause (c):—(a) items (v) and (vi) shall be omitted; (b) items (vii) and (viii) shall be renumbered as items (v) and (vi) respectively; (c) for item (v) as so re-numbered, the following shall be substituted, namely:—'(v) entries 2 and 3, entries 5 to 10 (both inclusive), entries 12 to 23 (both inclusive), entries 27, 28, 29, 31, 32, 36, 37 and 38 and entries 40 to 44 (both inclusive) shall be omitted; and'.

Ministry of Law: New Delhi, the 24th November, 1965

G.S.R. 1757:—The following order made by the President of India is published for general information.

C.O. 74

The Constitution (Application to Jammu and Kashmir) Second Amendment Order, 1965

In exercise of the powers conferred by clause (1) of Article 370 of the Constitution, the President, with the concurrence of the Government of the State of Jammu and Kashmir, is pleased to make the following Order:—

1. (1) This Order may be called the Constitution (Application to Jammu and Kashmir) Second Amendment Order, 1965.

(2) It shall come into force at once.

2. In paragraph 2 of the Constitution (Application to Jammu and Kashmir) Order, 1954:—

(1) in the opening portion, for the words, figures and letters 'as in force on the 15th day of February, 1958', the words, figures and letters 'as in force on the 20th day of June, 1964' shall be substituted;

(2) in sub-paragraph (5A) (relating to Part VI) for clause (c), the following clause shall be substituted, namely:—(c) in Article 222, after clause (1), the following new clause shall be inserted, namely:—'(1A) Every such transfer from the High Court of Jammu and Kashmir or to that High Court shall be made after consultation with the Governor';

(3) in sub-paragraph (14) (relating to Part XIX):—(a) clause (a) shall be omitted; (b) clauses (b) and (c) shall be re-lettered as clauses (a) and (b) respectively; (c) in clause (b) as so re-lettered, in clause (4) of Article 367:—

(i) for sub-clause (b) the following sub-clauses shall be substituted,
     namely:—

(aa) references to the person for the time being recognised by the President on the recommendation of the Legislative Assembly of the State as the Sadar-i-Riyasat of Jammu and Kashmir, acting on the advice of the Council of Ministers of the State for the time being in office shall be construed as references to the Governor of Jammu and Kashmir.

(b) references to the Government of the said State shall be construed as including references to the Governor of Jammu and Kashmir acting on the advice of his Council of Ministers:—

Provided that in respect of any period prior to the 10th day of April, 1965, such references shall be construed as including references to the Sadar-i-Riyasat acting on the advice of his Council of Ministers;

(ii) for sub-clause (e), the following sub-clause shall be substituted, namely:—

(e) references to a Governor shall include references to the Governor of Jammu and Kashmir:—

Provided that in respect of any period prior to the 10th day of April, 1965, such references shall be construed as references to the person recognised by the President as the Sadar-i-Riyasat of Jammu and Kashmir and as including references to any person recognised by the President as being competent to exercise the powers of the Sadar-i-Riyasat;

(4) in sub-paragraph (16) (relating to Part XXI), in clause (a); after the figures '371', the figures and letters '371 A', shall be inserted;

(5) in sub-paragraph (22) (relating to the Seventh Schedule):—(i) in clause (a):—

(a) in item (ii), the word 'add' shall be added at the end;

(b) item (iii) shall be omitted;

(c) item (iv) shall be re-numbered as item (iii);

(ii) in clause (c):—

   (a) items (ii) and (iii) shall be omitted;

   (b) items (iv), (v) and (vi) shall be re-numbered as items (ii), (iii) and (iv) respectively;

(c) in item (iii) as so re-numbered:—

(A) for the words, figures and brackets 'entries 12 to 23 (both inclusive)', the words, figures and brackets 'entries 12 to 21 (both inclusive)' shall be substituted;

(B) the figures '36', shall be omitted;

(6) for sub-paragraph (24) (relating to the Ninth Schedule); the following sub-paragraph shall be substituted, namely:—

'(24) Ninth-schedule

After entry 64, the following entries shall be added, namely:—

"65. The Jammu and Kashmir State Kuth Act (No. 1 of Svt. 1978)".

66. The Jammu and Kashmir Tenancy Act (No. 11 of Svt. 1980).

67. The Jammu and Kashmir Alienation of Land Act (No. V. of Svt. 1995).

68. The Jammu and Kashmir Restitution of Mortgaged Properties Act (No. XVI of Svt. 2006).

69. The Jammu and Kashmir Distressed Debtors Relief Act (No. XVII of Svt. 2006).

70. The Jammu and Kashmir Big Landed Estates Abolition Act (No. XVII of Svt. 2007).

71. Order No. 6-H of 1951, dated 10th March, 1951 regarding Resumption of Jagirs and other assignments of Land Revenue, etc.'

S. Radhakrishnan,
President.

R.C.S. Sarkar,
Secretary to the Govt. of India

GOVERNMENT OF JAMMU AND KASHMIR (LAW DEPARTMENT)

Published for general information.

T.N. Mattoo,
Secretary to Government.

Ministry of Law: New Delhi, the 29th June, 1966

G.S.R. 1060:—The following order made by the President of India is published for general information.

C.O. 75

The Constitution (Application to Jammu and Kashmir) Amendment Order, 1966

In exercise of the powers conferred by clause (1) of Article 370 of the Constitution, the President, with the concurrence of the Government of the State of Jammu and Kashmir, is pleased to make the following Order:—

1. (1) This Order may be called the Constitution (Application to Jammu and Kashmir) Amendment Order, 1966.

(2) It shall come into force at once.

2. In paragraph 2 of the Constitution (Application to Jammu and Kashmir) Order, 1954:—

(1) In sub-paragraph (5) (relating to Part V), for clauses (a) and (b), the following clauses shall respectively be substituted, namely:—

(a) For the purposes of Article 55, the population of the State of Jammu and Kashmir shall be deemed to be forty-four lakhs and ten thousand.

(b) In Article 81, for clauses (2) and (3), the following clause shall be substituted, namely:—

(2) For the purposes of sub-clause (a) of clause (1):—(a) there shall be allotted to the State six seats in the House of the People; (b) the State shall be divided into single member territorial constituencies by the Delimitation Commission constituted under the Delimitation Commission Act, 1962, in accordance with such procedure as the commission may deem fit; (c) the constituencies shall, as far as practicable, be geographically compact areas, and in delimiting them regard shall be had to physical features, existing boundaries of administrative units, facilities of communication and public convenience; (d) the constituencies into which the State is divided shall not comprise the area under the occupation of Pakistan; and (e) until the dissolution of the existing House of People, the representatives of the State in that House shall be appointed by the President on the recommendation of the Legislature of the State.

(2) in sub-paragraph (10) (relating to Part XV), for clauses (b) and

(c) the following clauses shall be substituted, namely:—

(b) In Article 325, 326, 327 and 329, the reference to a State shall be construed as not including a reference to the State of Jammu and Kashmir.

(c) Article 328 shall be omitted.

(d) In Article 329 the words and figures 'or Article 328' shall be omitted.

S. Radhakrishnan,
President.
(No. F. 19(1)/66.LL)
S.P. Sen Verma, Secretary.

GOVERNMENT OF JAMMU AND KASHMIR (LAW DEPARTMENT)

Published for general information.

(Sd/.) Muftibaha-Ud-Din
Secretary to Government.

Ministry of Law: New Delhi, the 13th February, 1967

G.S.R. 192:—The following order made by the President of India is published for general information.

C.O. 76

The Constitution (Application to Jammu and Kashmir) Amendment Order, 1967

In exercise of the powers conferred by clause (1) of Article 370 of the Constitution, the President, with the concurrence of the Government of the State of Jammu and Kashmir, is pleased to make the following Order:—

1. (1) This Order may be called the Constitution (Application to Jammu and Kashmir) Amendment Order, 1967.

(2) It shall come into force at once.

2. In paragraph 2 of the Constitution (Application to Jammu and Kashmir) Order, 1954, in the opening portion after the words, figures and letters 'as in force on the 20th day of June, 1964', the words, brackets and figures 'and as amended by the Constitution (Nineteenth Amendment) Act, 1966' shall be inserted.

S. Radhakrishnan,
President.
(No. P. *19(2)/67* ID)
S.P. Sen Verma
Secretary.

GOVERNMENT OF JAMMU AND KASHMIR (LAW DEPARTMENT)

Published for general information.

(Sd/-) G.N. Shora,
Under Secretary to Government.

Ministry of Law: New Delhi, the 5th May, 1967

G.S.R. 661:—The following order made by the President of India is published for general information.

C.O. 77

The Constitution (Application to Jammu and Kashmir) Second Amendment Order, 1967

In exercise of the powers conferred by clause (1) of Article 370 of the Constitution, the President, with the concurrence of the Government of the State of Jammu and Kashmir, is pleased to make the following Order:—

1. (1) This Order may be called the Constitution (Application to Jammu and Kashmir) Second Amendment Order, 1967.

(2) It shall come into force at once.

2. In paragraph 2 of the Constitution (Application to Jammu and Kashmir) Order, 1954, in sub-paragraph (22) (relating to the Seventh Schedule), in item (iii) of clause (c) for the words, figures and brackets 'entries 12 to 21 (both inclusive), entries' the words, figures and brackets 'entries 12 to 18 (both inclusive), entries 20, 21,' shall be substituted.

S. Radhakrishnan,
President.
(No. F. 19(3)/66 LI)
S.P. Sen Verma
Secretary.

GOVERNMENT OF JAMMU AND KASHMIR
CIVIL SECRETARIAT LAW DEPARTMENT

Published for general information.

(Sd/-) A.R. Khajuria,
Under Secretary to Government.
Law Department.

Ministry of Law: New Delhi, the 11th August, 1967

G.S.R. 1235:—The following order made by the President of India is published for general information.

C.O. 79

The Constitution (Application to Jammu and Kashmir)
Third Amendment Order, 1967

In exercise of the powers conferred by clause (1) of Article 370 of the Constitution, the President, with the concurrence of the Government of the State of Jammu and Kashmir, is pleased to make the following Order:—

1. (1) This Order may be called the Constitution (Application to Jammu and Kashmir) Third Amendment Order, 1967.

(2) It shall come into force at once.

2. In paragraph 2 of the Constitution (Application to Jammu and Kashmir) Order, 1954, in the opening portion, after the words, brackets and figures 'the Constitution (Nineteenth Amendment) Act, 1966', the words, brackets and figures 'and the Constitution (Twenty-first Amendment) Act, 1967', shall be inserted.

Zakir Husain,
President.
(No. F. 19(6)/67-LI)
S.P. Sen Verma
Secretary.

GOVERNMENT OF JAMMU AND KASHMIR
(LAW DEPARTMENT)

Published for general information.

(Sd/-) B.N. Sharma,
Under Secretary to Government.

Ministry of Law: New Delhi, the 26th December, 1967

G.S.R. 1933:—The following order made by the President of India is published for general information.

C.O. 80

The Constitution (Application to Jammu and Kashmir) Fourth Amendment Order, 1967

In exercise of the powers conferred by clause (1) of Article 370 of the Constitution, the President, with the concurrence of the Government of the State of Jammu and Kashmir, is pleased to make the following Order:—

1. (1) This Order may be called the Constitution (Application to Jammu and Kashmir) Fourth Amendment Order, 1967.

(2) It shall come into force at once.

2. In paragraph 2 of the Constitution (Application to Jammu and Kashmir) Order, 1954, in sub-paragraph (22) (relating to the Seventh Schedule), in item (iii) of clause (c), for the words, figures and brackets 'entries 12 to 18 (both inclusive), entries', the words, figures and brackets 'entries 12 to 15 (both inclusive), entries 17' shall be substituted.

Zakir Husain,
President.
(No. F. 19(10)/67-LI)
V.N. Bhatia
Secretary.

GOVERNMENT OF JAMMU AND KASHMIR (LAW DEPARTMENT)

Published for general information.

(Sd/-) B.N. Sharma.
Under Secretary to Government.

Ministry of Law: New Delhi, the 9th February, 1968

G.S.R. 282:—The following order made by the President of India is published for general information.

C.O. 83

The Constitution (Application to Jammu and Kashmir) Amendment Order, 1968

In exercise of the powers conferred by clause (1) of Article 370 of the Constitution, the President, with the concurrence of the Government of the State of Jammu and Kashmir, is pleased to make the following Order:—

1. (1) This Order may be called the Constitution (Application to Jammu and Kashmir) Amendment Order, 1968.

(2) It shall come into force at once.

2. In paragraph 2 of the Constitution (Application to Jammu and Kashmir) Order, 1954, in sub-paragraph (22) (relating to the Seventh Schedule), for item […] of clause (a), the following item shall be substituted, namely:—

(iii) in entry 72, the reference to the States shall be construed:—

(a) in relation to appeals to the Supreme Court from any decision or order of the High Court of the State of Jammu and Kashmir made in an election petition whereby an election to either House of the Legislature of that State has been called in question, as including a reference to the State of Jammu and Kashmir;

(b) in relation to other matters, as not including a reference to that State.

Zakir Husain,
President.
(No. F.19(2)/67-Ll)
V.N. Bhatia, Secretary.

GOVERNMENT OF JAMMU AND KASHMIR (CIVIL SECRETARIAT LAW DEPARTMENT)

Published for general information.

(Sd/-) B.N. Sharma,
Under Secretary to Government.

Ministry of Law: New Delhi, the 17th February, 1969

G.S.R. 303:—The following order made by the President of India is published for general information.

C.O. 85

The Constitution (Application to Jammu and Kashmir) Amendment Order, 1969

In exercise of the powers conferred by clause (1) of Article 370 of the Constitution, the President, with the concurrence of the Government of the State of Jammu and Kashmir, is pleased to make the following Order:—

1. (1) This Order may be called the Constitution (Application to Jammu and Kashmir) Amendment Order, 1969.

(2) It shall come into force at once.

2. In paragraph 2 of the Constitution (Application to Jammu and Kashmir) Order, 1954.

(1) in sub-paragraph (6) (relating to Part XI), for clause (b), the following clauses shall be substituted, namely:—

(b) For Article 248, the following Article shall be substituted, namely:—

248. Residuary powers of Legislation:—Parliament has exclusive power to make any law with respect to prevention of activities directed towards disclaiming, questioning or disrupting the sovereignty and territorial integrity of India or bringing about cession of a part of the territory of India or secession of a part of the territory of India from the Union or causing insult to the Indian National Flag, the Indian National Anthem and this Constitution.

(bb) Article 249 shall be omitted;

(2) in sub-paragraph (22) (relating to the Seventh Schedule), in clause (a):—

(a) for item (ii), the following item shall be substituted, namely:—
     (ii) entries 8, 9, 34 and 60, the words 'and records' in entry 67,
          entry 79 and the words 'Inter-State migration' in entry 81 shall
          be omitted;
(b) in item (iii), the word 'and' shall be added at the end;
(c) after item (iii), the following item shall be inserted, namely:—
     (iv) for entry 97, the following entry shall be substituted,
          namely:—

97. Prevention of activities directed towards disclaiming, questioning or disrupting the sovereignty and territorial integrity of India or bringing about
cession of a part of the territory of India or secession of a part of the territory
of India from the Union or causing insult to the Indian National Flag, the
Indian National Anthem and this Constitution.

Zakir Husain,
President.
(No. F. 19(10)/69-LI)
V.N. Bhatia
Secretary.

GOVERNMENT OF JAMMU AND KASHMIR
(LAW DEPARTMENT)

Published for general information.

(Sd/-) Ghulam Shah,
Additional Under Secretary to Government,
Law Department.

Ministry of Law: New Delhi, the 31st March, 1969
C.O. 86

*The Constitution (Application to Jammu and Kashmir)
Second Amendment Order, 1969*

In exercise of the powers conferred by clause (1) of Article 370 of the
Constitution, the President, with the concurrence of the Government
of the State of Jammu and Kashmir, is pleased to make the following
Order.

1. (1) This Order may be called the Constitution (Application to Jammu and Kashmir) Second Amendment Order, 1969.

(2) It shall come into force at once.

2. In paragraph 2 of the Constitution (Application to Jammu and Kashmir) Order, 1954, under sub-paragraph (4) (relating to the Part III), in clause (d) and in sub-clause (iii) of clause (i), for the word 'fifteen', the word 'twenty' shall be substituted.

Zakir Husain,
President.

GOVERNMENT OF JAMMU AND KASHMIR (CIVIL SECRETARIAT LAW DEPARTMENT)

Published for general information.

(Sd/-) G.M. Thakur,
Under Secretary to Government
Law Department.

Ministry of Law: New Delhi, the 24th August, 1971

G.S.R. 1218:—The following order made by the President of India is published for general information.

C.O. 89

The Constitution (Application to Jammu and Kashmir) Amendment Order, 1971

In exercise of the powers conferred by clause (1) of Article 370 of the Constitution, the President, with the concurrence of the Government of the State of Jammu and Kashmir, is pleased to make the following Order:—

1. (1) This Order may be called the Constitution (Application to Jammu and Kashmir) Amendment Order, 1971.

(2) It shall come into force at once.

2. In paragraph 2 of the Constitution (Application to Jammu and Kashmir) Order, 1954:—

(1) in the opening portion for the words, brackets and figures 'and the Constitution (Twenty-first Amendment) Act, 1967', the words, brackets and figures, 'the Constitution (Twenty-first Amendment) Act,

1967 and Section 5 of the Constitution (Twenty-third Amendment) Act, 1969' shall be substituted.

(2) in sub-paragraph (4) (relating to Part III), for clause (h), the following clause shall be substituted, namely:—'(h) in Article 32, clause (3) shall be omitted.';

(3) in sub-paragraph (5A) (relating to Part VI), for clause (a), the following clause shall be substituted, namely:—(a) Articles 153 to 217, Article 219, Article 221, Articles 223, 224, 224A and 225 and Articles 227 to 237 shall be omitted.

V.V. Giri,
President.
(No. F. 19(8)/70-LI)
N.D.P. Namboodiripad
Joint Secretary

Ministry of Law: New Delhi, the 8th November, 1971

C.O. 90

Assented on: 5th November, 1971.

The Constitution (Application to Jammu and Kashmir) Second Amendment Order, 1971

In exercise of the powers conferred by clause (1) of Article 370 of the Constitution, the President, with the concurrence of the Government of the State of Jammu and Kashmir, is pleased to make the following Order:—

1. (1) This Order may be called the Constitution (Application to Jammu and Kashmir) Second Amendment Order, 1971.

(2) It shall come into force at once.

2. In paragraph 2 of the Constitution (Application to Jammu and Kashmir) Order, 1954, in sub-paragraph (22) (relating to the Seventh Schedule), in item (iii) of clause (c), for the words, figures and brackets 'and 38, and entries 40 to 44 (both inclusive)' the words and figures '38, 40, 41, 42 and 44' shall be substituted.

V.V. Giri,
President.
N.D.P. Namboodiripad
Joint Secretary to the Govt. of India.

GOVERNMENT OF JAMMU AND KASHMIR (CIVIL SECRETARIAT LAW DEPARTMENT)

Published for general information.

(Sd/-) G.A. Khan,
Assistant Legal Draftsman.

Ministry of Law and Justice: New Delhi, the 29th November, 1971

C.O. 91

The Constitution (Application to Jammu and Kashmir) Third Amendment Order, 1971

In exercise of the powers conferred by clause (1) of Article 370 of the Constitution, the President, with the concurrence of the Government of the State of Jammu and Kashmir, is pleased to make the following Order:—

1. (1) This Order may be called the Constitution (Application to Jammu and Kashmir) Third Amendment Order, 1971.

(2) It shall come into force at once.

2. In paragraph 2 of the Constitution (Application to Jammu and Kashmir) Order, 1954:

(1) in the opening portion for the words, figures and brackets 'and Section 5 of the Constitution (Twenty-third Amendment) Act, 1969', the words, figures and brackets, 'Section 5 of the Constitution (Twenty-third Amendment) Act, 1969 and the Constitution (Twenty-fourth Amendment) Act, 1971' shall be substituted.

(2) in sub-paragraph (15) (relating to Part XX), for the words and figures 'To Article 368', the words, brackets and figures 'To clause (2) of Articles 368' shall be substituted.

V.V. Giri,
President.

GOVERNMENT OF JAMMU AND KASHMIR
(CIVIL SECRETARIAT LAW DEPARTMENT)

Published for general information.

(Sd/-) G.A. Khan,
Assistant Legal Draftsman,
Law Department.

Ministry of Law and Justice: New Delhi, the 24th February, 1972

G.S.R. 90(E):—The following order made by the President of India is published for general information.

C.O. 92

The Constitution (Application to Jammu and Kashmir) Amendment Order, 1972

In exercise of the powers conferred by clause (1) of Article 370 of the Constitution, the President, with the concurrence of the Government of the State of Jammu and Kashmir, is pleased to make the following Order:—

1. (1) This Order may be called the Constitution (Application to Jammu and Kashmir) Amendment Order, 1972.

(2) It shall come into force at once.

2. In paragraph 2 of the Constitution (Application to Jammu and Kashmir) Order, 1954, in sub-paragraph (22) (relating to the Seventh Schedule), in item (ii) of clause (a), for the figures and words, '34 and 60', the words and figures 'and 34' shall be substituted.

V.V. Giri,
President.
(No. F. 19(7)/71-LL.I)
N.D.P. Namboodiripad,
Joint Secretary to the Govt. of India.

Ministry of Law and Justice: New Delhi, the 6th May, 1972

C.O. 93

The Constitution (Application to Jammu and Kashmir) Second Amendment Order, 1972

In exercise of the powers conferred by clause (1) of Article 370 of the Constitution, the President, with the concurrence of the Government of the State of Jammu and Kashmir, is pleased to make the following Order:—

1. (1) This Order may be called the Constitution (Application to Jammu and Kashmir) Second Amendment Order, 1972.

(2) It shall come into force at once.

2. In paragraph 2 of the Constitution (Application to Jammu and Kashmir) Order, 1954:—

(1) in sub-paragraph (6) (relating to the Part XI), for clause (b), the following clause shall be substituted, namely:—

(b) For Article 248, the following Article shall be substituted, namely:—'248. Residuary powers of Legislation: Parliament has exclusive power to make any law with respect to:—

(a) Prevention of activities directed towards disclaiming, questioning or disrupting the sovereignty and territorial integrity of India or bringing about cession of a part of the territory of India or secession of a part of the territory of India from the Union or causing insult to the Indian National Flag, the Indian National Anthem and this Constitution; and (c) taxes on:—(i) foreign travel by sea or air; (ii) inland air travel; (iii) postal articles, including money orders, phonograms and telegrams.

(2) in sub-paragraph (22) (relating to the Seventh Schedule), in clause (a), for item (iv), the following item shall be substituted, namely:—'(iv) for entry 97, the following entry shall be substituted, namely:—

97. Prevention of activities directed towards disclaiming, questioning or disrupting the sovereignty and territorial integrity of India or bringing about cession of a part of the territory of India or secession of a part of the territory of India from the Union or causing insult to the Indian National Flag, the

Indian National Anthem and this Constitution; taxes on foreign travel by sea or air, on inland air travel and on postal articles including money orders, phonograms and telegram.

V.V. Giri,
President.

GOVERNMENT OF JAMMU AND KASHMIR (CIVIL SECRETARIAT LAW DEPARTMENT)

Published for general information.

(Sd/-) G.A. Khan ,
Assistant Legal Draftsman,
Law Department.

Ministry of Law and Justice: New Delhi, the 1st August, 1972

C.O. 94

The Constitution (Application to Jammu and Kashmir) Third Amendment Order, 1972

In exercise of the powers conferred by clause (1) of Article 370 of the Constitution, the President, with the concurrence of the Government of the State of Jammu and Kashmir, is pleased to make the following Order:—

1. (1) This Order may be called the Constitution (Application to Jammu and Kashmir) Third Amendment Order, 1972.

(2) It shall come into force at once.

2. In paragraph 2 of the Constitution (Application to Jammu and Kashmir) Order, 1954:—

(1) in the opening portion for the words, brackets and figures, 'and the Constitution (Twenty-fourth Amendment) Act, 1971', the words, brackets and figures, 'the Constitution (Twenty-fourth Amendment) Act, 1971 and the Constitution (Twenty-sixth Amendment) Act, 1971' shall be substituted;

(2) in sub-paragraph (7) (relating to Part XII), in clause (a), for the words and figures, 'Articles 290 and 291', the words and figures 'and Article 290' shall be substituted;

(3) in sub-paragraph (14) (relating to Part XIX), in clause (a), for the words and figures, 'Articles 362 and 365', the word and figures 'Article 365' shall be substituted;

(4) in sub-paragraph (22) (relating to the seventh Schedule) in clause (c):—

(a) after sub-clause (i), the following sub-clauses shall be inserted, namely:—

'(i-a) for entry 2, the entry '2. Criminal Procedure in so far as it relates to administration of oaths and taking of affidavits by diplomatic and consular officers in any foreign country' shall be substituted;

(i-b) for entry 12, the entry '12. Evidence and oaths in so far as they relate to administration of oaths and taking of affidavits by diplomatic and consular officers in any foreign country' shall be substituted;

(i-c) for entry 13, the entry '13. Civil Procedure in so far as it relates to administration of oaths and taking of affidavits by diplomatic and consular officers in any foreign country' shall be substituted;

(h) in sub-clause (iii):—

(i) for the words and figures 'entries 2 and 3' the word and figure 'entry 3', shall be substituted;

(ii) for the words, figures and brackets 'entries 12 to 15 (both inclusive), entries 17', the words and figures 'entries 14, 15, 17' shall be substituted.

V.V. Giri,
President.
(Sd/-) K.K. Sundaram,
Joint Secretary to the Government of India.

GOVERNMENT OF JAMMU AND KASHMIR (CIVIL SECRETARIAT LAW DEPARTMENT)

Published for general information.

(Sd/-) G.A. Khan,
Assistant Legal Draftsman,
Law Department.

Ministry of Law and Justice: New Delhi, the 10th August, 1972

C.O. 95

The Constitution (Application to Jammu and Kashmir)
Fourth Amendment Order, 1972

In exercise of the powers conferred by clause (1) of Article 370 of the Constitution, the President, with the concurrence of the Government of the State of Jammu and Kashmir, is pleased to make the following Order:—

1. (1) This Order may be called the Constitution (Application to Jammu and Kashmir) Fourth Amendment Order, 1972.

(2) It shall come into force at once.

2. In paragraph 2 of the Constitution (Application to Jammu and Kashmir) Order, 1954, in sub-paragraph (22) (relating to the Seventh Schedule):—(i) in sub-clause (ii) of clause (a), the words and figures 'the words "and records" in entry 67' shall be omitted; (ii) in clause (c) for sub-clause (iii), the following sub-clauses shall be substituted, namely:—

(viii) entry 3, entries 5 to 10 (both inclusive), entries 14, 15, 17, 20, 21, 27, 28, 29, 31, 32, 37, 38, 41 and 44 shall be omitted;

(iii-a) for entry 42, for entry '42. Acquisition and requisitioning of property, so far as regards acquisition of any property covered by entry 67 of List III or entry 40 of List III or of any human work of art which has artistic or aesthetic value', shall be substituted; and.

V.V. Giri,
President.
(Sd/-) K.K. Sundaram,
Joint Secretary to the Government of India.

GOVERNMENT OF JAMMU AND KASHMIR (CIVIL SECRETARIAT LAW DEPARTMENT)

Published for general information.

(Sd/-) G.A. Khan,
Assistant Legal Draftsman,
Bangroo

Ministry of Law, Justice and Company Affairs: New Delhi, the 1st May, 1974

Published in the Gazette of India, Extraordinary, dated May 22, 1974/ 1st Jyai., 1896

The following Order made by the President is published for general information:—

C.O. 97

The Constitution (Application to Jammu and Kashmir) Amendment Order, 1974

In exercise of the powers conferred by clause (1) of Article 370 of the Constitution, the President, with the concurrence of the Government of the State of Jammu and Kashmir, is pleased to make the following Order:—

1. (1) This Order may be called the Constitution (Application to Jammu and Kashmir) Amendment Order, 1974.

(2) It shall come into force at once.

2. In paragraph 2 of the Constitution (Application to Jammu and Kashmir) Order, 1954, under sub-paragraph (4) (relating to Part III), in clause (d) and in sub-clause (iii) of clause (i), for the word 'twenty', the word 'twenty-five' shall be substituted.

V.V. Giri,
President.
K.K. Sundaram,
Secretary.

GOVERNMENT OF JAMMU AND KASHMIR (CIVIL SECRETARIAT LAW DEPARTMENT)

Published for general information.

(Sd/-) G.A. Khan,
Assistant Legal Draftsman.

Ministry of Law and Justice: New Delhi, the 26th June, 1974

Published in the Gazette of India, Extraordinary,
dated July 10, 1974/ 19th Asad., 1896.

G.S.R. 280 (E):—The following Order made by the President is published for general information:

C.O. 98

*The Constitution (Application to Jammu and Kashmir)
Second Amendment Order, 1974*

In exercise of the powers conferred by clause (1) of Article 370 of the Constitution, the President, with the concurrence of the Government of the State of Jammu and Kashmir, is pleased to make the following Order:—

1. (1) This Order may be called the Constitution (Application to Jammu and Kashmir) Second Amendment Order, 1974.

(2) It shall come into force at once.

2. In paragraph 2 of the Constitution (Application to Jammu and Kashmir) Order, 1954:—

(i) in the opening portion for the words, brackets and figures, 'and the Constitution (Twenty-sixth Amendment) Act, 1971', the words, brackets and figures, 'the Constitution (Twenty-sixth Amendment) Act, 1971, the Constitution (Thirtieth Amendment) Act, 1972 and Section 2 of the Constitution (Thirty-first Amendment) Act 1973' shall be substituted.

(ii) in sub-paragraph (5) (relating to Part V), for clauses (a) and (b), the following clauses shall respectively be substituted, namely:—

(a) For the purposes of Article 55, the population of the State of Jammu and Kashmir shall be deemed to be sixty three lakhs; (b) In Article 81, for clauses (2) and (3), the following clauses shall be substituted, namely:—

(2) For the purposes of sub-clause (a) of clause (1):—
   (a) there shall be allotted to the State six seats in the House of the People;
   (b) the State shall be divided into single-member territorial constituencies by the Delimitation Commission constituted under the Delimitation Act, 1972, in accordance with such procedure as the Commission may deem fit;
   (c) the constituencies shall, as far as practicable, be geographically compact areas, and in delimiting them regard shall be had to physical features existing boundaries of administrative units, facilities of communication and public convenience; and
   (d) the constituencies into which the State is divided shall not comprise the area under the occupation of Pakistan.

(3) Nothing in clause (2) shall affect the representation of the State in the House of the People until the dissolution of the House existing on the date of publication in the Gazette of India of the final order or orders of the Delimitation Commission relating to delimitation of parliamentary constituencies under the Delimitation Act, 1972.

   (4) (a) The Delimitation Commission shall associate with itself for the purpose of assisting it in its duties in respect of the State, five persons who shall be members of the House of the People representing the State.
     (b) The persons to be so associated from the State shall be nominated by the Speaker of the House of the People having due regard to the composition of the House.
     (c) The first nominations to be made under sub-clause (b) shall be made by the Speaker of the House of the People within two months from the commencement of the Constitution (Application to Jammu and Kashmir) Second Amendment Order, 1974.
     (d) None of the associate members shall have a right to vote or to sign any decision of the Delimitation Commission.
     (e) If owing to death or resignation, the office of an associate member falls vacant, it shall be filled as soon as may be practicable by the Speaker

of the House of the People and in accordance with the provisions of sub-clauses (a) and (b).

(iii) in sub-paragraph (5) (relating to Part V), clauses (c) and (d) shall be re-lettered as clauses (d) and (e) respectively and before clause (d) as so re-lettered, the following clause shall be inserted, namely:—'(c) in Article 133, after clause (!), the following clause shall be inserted, namely:—

(1A) The provisions of Section 3 of the Constitution (Thirtieth Amendment) Act, 1972, shall apply in relation to the State of Jammu and Kashmir subject to the modification that references therein to 'this Act' 'the commencement of this Act', 'this Act had not been passed' and 'as amended by this Act' shall be construed respectively as references to 'the Constitution (Application to Jammu and Kashmir) Second Amendment Order, 1974', 'the commencement of the said Order', the said Order had not been made' and 'as it stands after the commencement of the said Order'.

(iv) in sub-paragraph (24) (relating to the Ninth Schedule), entries 65, 66, 67, 68, 69, 70 and 71 shall be renumbered as entries 64A, 64B, 64C, 64D, 64E, 64F and 64G respectively.

V.V. Giri,
President.
[No. F. 19(4)/74-LI]
S. Harihara Iyer,
Joint Secretary.

GOVERNMENT OF JAMMU AND KASHMIR (CIVIL SECRETARIAT LAW DEPARTMENT)

Published for general information.

(Sd/-) G.A. Khan,
Assistant Legal Draftsman,
Law Department.

Ministry of Law, Justice and Company Affairs: New Delhi, the 29th June, 1975

Published in the Gazette of India, Extraordinary, dated July 11th, 1975/Asad. 20, 1897

G.S.R. 365 (E): The following Order made by the President is published for general information:

C.O. 100

The Constitution (Application to Jammu and Kashmir) Amendment Order, 1975

In exercise of the powers conferred by clause (1) of Article 370 of the Constitution, the President, with the concurrence of the Government of the State of Jammu and Kashmir, is pleased to make the following Order:—

1. (1) This Order may be called the Constitution (Application to Jammu and Kashmir) Amendment Order, 1975.

(2) It shall come into force at once.

2. In paragraph 2 of the Constitution (Application to Jammu and Kashmir) Order, 1954, in clause (a) of sub-paragraph (13) (relating to Part XVIII), in clause (4) of Article 352, for the words 'unless it is made at the request or with the concurrence of the Government of that State', the following shall be substituted, namely:—

'unless:—(a) it is made at the request or with the concurrence of the Government of that State, or (b) where it has not been so made, it is applied subsequently by the President of that State at the request or with the concurrence of the Government of that State'.

F.A. Ahmed,
President.

GOVERNMENT OF JAMMU AND KASHMIR (CIVIL SECRETARIAT, LAW DEPARTMENT)

Published for general information.

(Sd/-) G.A. Khan,
Assistant Legal Draftsman,
Law Department.

Ministry of Law, Justice and Company Affairs: New Delhi, the 23rd July, 1975

Published in the Gazette of India, Extraordinary, dated July 30, 1975 8th Srav., 1897

C.O. 101

The Constitution (Application to Jammu and Kashmir) Second Amendment Order, 1975

In exercise of the powers conferred by clause (1) of Article 370 of the Constitution, the President, with the concurrence of the Government of the State of Jammu and Kashmir, is pleased to make the following Order:—

1. (1) This Order may be called the Constitution (Application to Jammu and Kashmir) Second Amendment Order, 1975.

(2) It shall come into force at once.

2. In paragraph 2 of the Constitution (Application to Jammu and Kashmir) Order, 1954, in sub-paragraph (15) (relating to Part XX), the existing modification relating to clause (2) of Article 368 shall be re-numbered as clause (a) of that sub-paragraph and after that clause as so renumbered, the following clause shall be inserted, namely:—'(b) After clause (3) of Article 368, the following shall be added, namely:—

(4) No law made by the Legislature of the State of Jammu and Kashmir seeking to make any change in or in the effect of any provision of the Constitution of Jammu and Kashmir relating to:—(a) appointment, powers, functions, duties, emoluments, allowances, privileges or immunities of the Governor; or (b) superintendence, direction and control of elections by the Election Commission of India, eligibility for inclusion in the electoral rolls without discrimination, adult suffrage and composition of the Legislative Council, being matters specified in Sections 138, 139, 140 and 50 of the Constitution of Jammu and Kashmir.

Shall have any effect unless such law has, after having been reserved for the consideration of the President, received his assent.'

Fakhruddin Ali Ahmed,
President.
K.K. Sundaram,
Secretary to the Govt. of India.

GOVERNMENT OF JAMMU AND KASHMIR (CIVIL SECRETARIAT, LAW DEPARTMENT)

Published for general information.

(Sd/-) G.A. Khan,
Assistant Legal Draftsman,
Law Department.

Ministry of Law, Justice and Company Affairs: New Delhi, the 22nd March, 1976

Published in the Gazette of India, Extraordinary, dated March 25th, 1976/5th Chai., 1898

C.O. 103

The Constitution (Application to Jammu and Kashmir) Amendment Order, 1976

In exercise of the powers conferred by clause (1) of Article 370 of the Constitution, the President, with the concurrence of the Government of the State of Jammu and Kashmir, is pleased to make the following Order:—

1. (1) This Order may be called the Constitution (Application to Jammu and Kashmir) Amendment Order, 1976.

(2) It shall come into force at once.

2. In paragraph 2 of the Constitution (Application to Jammu and Kashmir) Order, 1954, in the opening portion, for the words, figures and brackets 'and Section 2 of the Constitution (Thirty-first Amendment) Act, 1973', the words, figures and brackets 'Section 2 of the Constitution (Thirty-first Amendment) Act, 1973 and Section 2 of the Constitution (Thirty-third Amendment) Act, 1974' shall be substituted.

Fakhruddin Ali Ahmed,
President.
[No. F. 19(1)/76-LI]
K.K. Sundaram,
Secretary to the Govt. of India.

GOVERNMENT OF JAMMU AND KASHMIR
(CIVIL SECRETARIAT, LAW DEPARTMENT)

Published for general information.

(Sd/-) G.A. Khan,
Assistant Legal Draftsman,
Law Department.

Ministry of Law and Justice: New Delhi, the 25th May, 1976

Published in the Gazette of India, Extraordinary,
dated June 15, 1976/ 25th Jyai., 1898

C.O. 104

The Constitution (Application to Jammu and Kashmir) Second Amendment Order, 1976

In exercise of the powers conferred by clause (1) of Article 370 of the Constitution, the President, with the concurrence of the Government of the State of Jammu and Kashmir, is pleased to make the following Order:—

1. (1) This Order may be called the Constitution (Application to Jammu and Kashmir) Second Amendment Order, 1976.

(2) It shall come into force at once.

2. In paragraph 2 of the Constitution (Application to Jammu and Kashmir) Order, 1954:—(i) in the opening portion, for the words, figures and brackets 'and Section 2 of the Constitution (Thirty-third Amendment) Act, 1974', the words, figures and brackets, 'Section 2 of the Constitution (Thirty-third Amendment) Act, 1974, and Sections 2, 5, 6 and 7 of the Constitution (Thirty-eighth Amendment) Act, 1975' shall be substituted. (ii) in clause (a) of sub-paragraph (13) (relating to Part XVIII), in new clause (4) of Article 352, for the brackets and figures '(4)', the brackets and figures '(6)' shall be substituted.

Fakhruddin Ali Ahmed,
President.
K.K. Sundaram,
Secretary to the Govt. of India.

GOVERNMENT OF JAMMU AND KASHMIR
(CIVIL SECRETARIAT, LAW DEPARTMENT)

Published for general information.

(Sd/-) G.A. Khan,
Assistant Legal Draftsman,
Law Department.

Ministry of Law and Justice: New Delhi, the 12th October, 1976

Published in the Gazette of India, Extraordinary, dated October 12, 1976/20th Arvina, 1898

C.O.105

The Constitution (Application to Jammu and Kashmir) Third Amendment Order, 1976

In exercise of the powers conferred by clause (1) of Article 370 of the Constitution, the President, with the concurrence of the Government of the State of Jammu and Kashmir, is pleased to make the following Order:—

1. (1) This Order may be called the Constitution (Application to Jammu and Kashmir) Third Amendment Order, 1976.

(2) It shall come into force at once.

2. In paragraph 2 of the Constitution (Application to Jammu and Kashmir) Order, 1954:—

(1) in the opening portion, for the words, figures and brackets 'and Sections 2, 5, 6 and 7 of the Constitution (Thirty-eighth Amendment) Act, 1975', the words, figures and brackets 'Sections 2, 5, 6 and 7 of the Constitution (Thirty-eighth Amendment) Act, 1975, and the Constitution (Thirty-ninth Amendment) Act, 1975' shall be substituted;

(2) in sub-paragraph (10) (relating to Part XV), after clause (d), the following clause shall be inserted, namely:—

'(e) In Article 329A, clauses (4) and (5) shall be omitted'.

(3) in sub-paragraph (24) (relating to the Ninth Schedule), the existing modification shall be numbered as clause (a) of the sub-paragraph and the following shall be inserted as clause (b), namely:—

'(b) Entries 87 to 424, inserted by the Constitution (Thirty-ninth Amendment) Act, 1975, shall be re-numbered as entries 65 to 102 respectively'.

Fakhruddin Ali Ahmed,
President.
11th October, 1976
(Sd/-) S. Harihara Iyer,
Joint Secretary.

GOVERNMENT OF JAMMU AND KASHMIR (CIVIL SECRETARIAT, LAW DEPARTMENT)

Published for general information.

(Sd/-) G.A. Khan,
Assistant Legal Draftsman,
Law Department.

Ministry of Law and Justice: New Delhi, the 31st December, 1976

Published in the Gazette of India, Extraordinary, dated 2nd February, 1977/3rd Magha, 1898

C.O.106

The Constitution (Application to Jammu and Kashmir) Fourth Amendment Order, 1976

In exercise of the powers conferred by clause (1) of Article 370 of the Constitution, the President, with the concurrence of the Government of the State of Jammu and Kashmir, is pleased to make the following Order:—

1. (1) This Order may be called the Constitution (Application to Jammu and Kashmir) Fourth Amendment Order, 1976.

(2) It shall come into force at once.

2. In paragraph 2 of the Constitution (Application to Jammu and Kashmir) Order, 1954, in sub-paragraph (24) (relating to the Ninth Schedule), in clause (a):

(1) entries 64D and 64E shall be omitted and entries 64F and 64G shall be renumbered as entries 64D and 64E, respectively;

(2) after entry 64E as so renumbered, the following entries shall be inserted, namely:—

'64F. The Jammu and Kashmir Restitution of Mortgaged Properties Act, 1976 (Act XIV of 1976).

64G. The Jammu and Kashmir Debtor's Relief Act, 1976 (Act XV of 1976)'.

Fakhruddin Ali Ahmed,
President.

(Sd/-) K.K. Sundaram,
Secretary to the Government of India.

GOVERNMENT OF JAMMU AND KASHMIR (CIVIL SECRETARIAT, LAW DEPARTMENT)

Published for general information.

(Sd/-) G.A. Khan,
Officer Incharge Codification,
Law Department.

Ministry of Law and Justice: New Delhi, the 31st December, 1977

Published in the Gazette of India, Extraordinary, dated March 11, 1978/20th Phal., 1899

G.S.R. 796(E):—The following Order made by the President is published for general information.

C.O. 108

The Constitution (Application to Jammu and Kashmir) Amendment Order, 1977

In exercise of the powers conferred by clause (1) of Article 370 of the Constitution, the President, with the concurrence of the Government of the State of Jammu and Kashmir, is pleased to make the following Order:—

1. (1) This Order may be called the Constitution (Application to Jammu and Kashmir) Amendment Order, 1977.

(2) It shall come into force at once.

2. In paragraph 2 of the Constitution (Application to Jammu and Kashmir) Order, 1954:—

(1) in the opening portion:—(a) after the words, brackets and figures 'the Constitution (Twenty-fourth Amendment) Act, 1971', the words, figures and brackets, Section 2 of the Constitution (Twenty-fifth Amendment) Act, 1971', shall be inserted; (b) for the words, brackets and figures and the Constitution (Thirty-ninth Amendment) Act, 1975, the words, brackets and figures, 'the Constitution (Thirty-ninth Amendment) Act, 1975 and the Constitution (Fortieth Amendment) Act, 1976' shall be substituted;

(2) in sub-paragraph (24) (relating to Ninth Schedule); after clause (b), the following clause shall be inserted, namely:—

'Entries 125 to 188 shall be re-numbered as Articles 103 to 166 respectively'.

N. Sanjiva Reddy,
President.
[No. F. 19(1)/77-LI]
(Sd/-) S. Harihara Iyer,
Joint Secretary.

GOVERNMENT OF JAMMU AND KASHMIR
(CIVIL SECRETARIAT, LAW DEPARTMENT)

Published for general information.

(Sd/-) G.A. Khan,
Officer Incharge Codification,
Law Department.

Ministry of Law and Justice: New Delhi, the 4th June, 1985. No. 234

Published in the Gazette of India, Extraordinary, Part II, Section 3 (i)

G.S.R. 481(E):—The following Order made by the President is published for general information:

C.O.122

The Constitution (Application to Jammu and Kashmir) Amendment Order, 1985

In exercise of the powers conferred by clause (1) of Article 370 of the Constitution, the President, with the concurrence of the Government of the State of Jammu and Kashmir, is pleased to make the following Order:—

1. (1) This Order may be called the Constitution (Application to Jammu and Kashmir) Amendment Order, 1985.

(2) It shall come into force at once.

2. In paragraph 2 of the Constitution (Application to Jammu and Kashmir) Order, 1954:—

(1) in clause (b) of sub-paragraph (6), in Article 248:—

(i) clause (a) shall be re-lettered as clause (aa) and in that clause as so re-lettered, for the words 'prevention of activities', the words 'prevention of other activities' shall be substituted;

(ii) before clause (aa) as so re-lettered, the following clause shall be inserted, namely:—'(a) prevention of activities involving terrorist acts directed towards overawing the Government as by law established or striking terror in the people or any section of the people or alienating any section of the people or adversely affecting the harmony amongst different sections of the people'.

(iii) the following Explanation shall be inserted at the end, namely:—

'Explanation: In this Article, 'terrorist act' means any act or thing by using bombs, dynamite or other explosive substances or inflammable substances or firearms or other lethal weapons or poisons or noxious gases or other chemicals or any other substances (whether biological or otherwise) of a hazardous nature'.

(2) in sub-paragraph (22):—

(i) in sub-clause (iv) of clause (a) (relating to the Union List), for entry 97, the following entry shall be substituted, namely:—

'97. Prevention of activities:—(a) involving terrorist acts directed towards overawing the Government as by law established or striking terror in the people or any section of the people or alienating any section of the people of adversely affecting the harmony amongst different sections of the people;

(b) directed towards disclaiming, questioning or disrupting the sovereignty and territorial integrity of India or bringing about cession of a part of the territory of India or secession of a part of the territory of India from the Union or causing insult to the Indian National Flag, the Indian National Anthem and this Constitution; taxes on foreign travel by sea or air, on inland air travel and on postal articles, including money orders, phonograms and telegrams.

Explanation: In this entry, 'terrorist act' has the same meaning as in the *Explanation* to Article 248'.

(ii) in clause (c) (relating to the Concurrent List), for sub-clauses (ia) and (ib), the following sub-clauses shall be substituted, namely:—

'(ia) for entry 2, the following entry shall be substituted, namely:—

'2. Criminal Procedure (including prevention of offences and Constitution and organization of criminal courts, except the Supreme Court and the High Court) in so far as it relates to:—(i) offences against laws with respect to any matters being matters with respect to which parliament has power to make laws; and (ii) administration of oaths and taking of affidavits by diplomatic and consular officers in any foreign country';

(ib) for entry 12, the following entry shall be substituted, namely:—

'12. Evidence and oaths in so far as they relate to:—

(i) administration of oaths and taking of affidavits by diplomatic and consular officers in any foreign country; and (ii) any other matters being matters with respect to which the Parliament has power to make laws'.

Zail Singh,
President.
[No. F. 19(4)/85-LI)
R.V.S. Peri Sastri,
Secretary.

Ministry of Law and Justice: New Delhi, the 4th December, 1985

Published in the Gazette of India, Extraordinary, Part II

G.S.R. 881(E):—The following Order made by the President is published for general information:

C.O.124

The Constitution (Application to Jammu and Kashmir) Second Amendment Order, 1985

In exercise of the powers conferred by clause (1) of Article 370 of the Constitution, the President, with the concurrence of the Government of the State of Jammu and Kashmir, is pleased to make the following Order:—

1. (1) This Order may be called the Constitution (Application to Jammu and Kashmir) Second Amendment Order, 1985.

(2) It shall come into force at once.

2. In paragraph 2 of the Constitution (Application to Jammu and Kashmir) Order, 1954:—

(a) in sub-paragraph (4) (relating to Part III), clause (b) shall be omitted;

(b) in sub-paragraph (11) (relating to Part XVI):—(i) clause (a) shall be omitted; (ii) clause (b) and (c) shall be re-lettered as clauses (a) and (b), and in clause (a), as so re-lettered, for the figures and word '336, 337, 339 and 342', the figures and word '336 and 337' shall be substituted; (iii) after clause (b), as so re-lettered, the following clause shall be inserted, namely:—

'(c) In clause (1) of Article 339, the words "the administration of the Schedules Areas and" shall be omitted'.

Zail Singh,
President.
(No. F. 19(1)/84-LI)
R.V.S. Peri Sastri,
Secretary.

Ministry of Law and Justice: New Delhi, the 30th July, 1986

Published in the Gazette of India, Extraordinary, Part II

G.S.R. 993(E):—The following Order made by the President is published for general information:

C.O. 129

The Constitution (Application to Jammu and Kashmir) Amendment Order, 1986

In exercise of the powers conferred by clause (1) of Article 370 of the Constitution, the President, with the concurrence of the Government of the State of Jammu and Kashmir, is pleased to make the following Order:—

1. (1) This Order may be called the Constitution (Application to Jammu and Kashmir) Amendment Order, 1986.

(2) It shall come into force at once.

2. In paragraph 2 of the Constitution (Application to Jammu and Kashmir) Order, 1954, in sub-paragraph (6) (relating to Part XI):—

(i) for clause (bb), the following clause shall be substituted, namely:—'(bb) In Article 249, in clause (1), for the words "any matter enumerated in the State List specified in the resolution", the words "any matter specified in the resolution, being a matter which is not enumerated in the Union List or in the Concurrent List" shall be substituted; (ii) clause (d) shall be omitted.'

Zail Singh,
President.
[No. F. 19(5)/86-LI]
S. Ramaiah,
Secretary.

Ministry of Law and Justice: New Delhi, the 7th October, 1989

G.S.R.:—The following Order made by the President is published for general information:

C.O. 142

The Constitution (Jammu and Kashmir) Scheduled Tribes Order, 1989

In exercise of the powers conferred by clause (1) of Article 342 of the Constitution of India, the President, after consultation with the Governor of the State of Jammu and Kashmir, is pleased to make the following Order, namely:—

1. This Order may be called the Constitution (Jammu and Kashmir) Scheduled Tribes Order, 1989.

2. The tribes or tribal communities, or parts of, or groups within, tribes or tribal communities, specified in the Schedule to this Order shall, for the purposes of the Constitution, be deemed to be Scheduled Tribes in relation to the State of Jammu and Kashmir so far as regards members thereof resident in that State.

The Schedule

1. Balti
2. Beda
3. Bot, Boto
4. Brokpa, Drokpa, Dard, Shin
5. Changpa
6. Garra
7. Mon
8. Purigpa

R. Venkataraman,
President.
[No. F. 19(7)/89-LI]
V.S. Rama Devi,
Secretary.

Ministry of Law, Justice and Company Affairs: New Delhi, the 24th February, 1993

G.S.R. 84(E):—The following Order made by the President is published for general information:

C.O. 151

The Constitution (Application to Jammu and Kashmir) Amendment Order, 1993

In exercise of the powers conferred by clause (1) of Article 370 of the Constitution, the President, with the concurrence of the Government of the State of Jammu and Kashmir, is pleased to make the following Order:—

1. (1) This Order may be called the Constitution (Application to Jammu and Kashmir) Amendment Order, 1993.

(2) It shall come into force at once.

2. In paragraph 2 of the Constitution (Application to Jammu and Kashmir) Order, 1954, in sub-paragraph (13) (relating to Part XVIII), after clause (b), the following clause shall be added, namely:—

(bb) in clause (4) of Article 356, after the second proviso, the following proviso shall be inserted, namely:—

Provided also that in the case of the proclamation issued under clause (1) on the 18th day of July, 1990 with respect to the State of Jammu and Kashmir, the reference in the first proviso to this clause to 'three years' shall be construed as a reference to 'four years'.

S.D. Sharma,
President.
[No. F. 19(2)/93-LI)
K.L. Mohanpuria,
Secretary.

Ministry of Law and Justice: New Delhi, the 19th February, 1994

G.S.R. 102(E):—The following Order made by the President is published for general information.

C.O. 154

The Constitution (Application to Jammu and Kashmir) Amendment Order, 1994

In exercise of the powers conferred by clause (1) of Article 370 of the Constitution, the President, with the concurrence of the Government of the State of Jammu and Kashmir, is pleased to make the following Order:—

1. (1) This Order may be called the Constitution (Application to Jammu and Kashmir) Amendment Order, 1994.

(2) It shall come into force at once.

2. In paragraph 2 of the Constitution (Application to Jammu and Kashmir) Order, 1954, in sub-paragraph (13) (relating to Part XVIII), in clause (bb), for the words 'four years' the words 'five years' shall be substituted.

S.D. Sharma,
President.
[No. F. 19(1)/94-LI]
K.L. Mohanpuria,
Secretary.

2. The Supreme Court's Judgements on Article 370

2(a). Prem Nath Koul *vs* State of J&K (1959)

(1959) *Supreme Court Journal* 797

22 March, 1959

Present:—S.R. Das, *Chief Justice*, S.K. Das, P.B. Gajendragadkar, K.N. Wanchoo and M. Hidayatullah, JJ.

[...]

The Judgment of the Court was delivered by

Gajendragadkar, J.—This appeal by Special Leave arises from a suit filed by the appellant in a representative capacity (Civil Suit No. 4 of 2008) against the State of Jammu and Kashmir praying for declaration that the Jammu and Kashmir Big Landed Estate Abolition Act XVII of 2007 (hereinafter called the Act) is void, inoperative and *ultra vires* of Yuvaraj Karan Singh who enacted it and for a further declaration that the appellant was entitled to retain the peaceful possession of his lands.

[...]

The Act was promulgated by Yuvaraj Karan Singh on October 17, 1950. The Preamble to the Act shows that it was promulgated because no lasting improvement in agricultural production and efficiency was possible without the removal of the intermediaries between the tiller of the soil and the State, and so, for the purpose of improving agricultural production, it was expedient to provide for the abolition of such proprietors as own big landed estates and to transfer the land held by them to the actual tiller. The Yuvaraj enacted the law in exercise of the powers vested in him under section 5 of the Constitution Act of 1996 and the proclamation issued by Maharaja Hari Singh on June 20, 1949. The Act consists of 47 sections and purports to carry out its policy of improving the agricultural production of the State by providing for the extinction of the properietor's titles and the transfer of the lands to the tillers, and by setting up a self-contained machinery for the carrying out of the scheme of the Act and for settlement of all incidental disputes arising thereunder.

[...]

The validity of the Act is impeached mainly on the ground that Yuvaraj Karan Singh had no authority to promulgate the said Act. It is this argument which has been urged before us by Mr. Chatterjee in different and alternative forms that needs careful examination. The first attack against the competence of Yuvaraj Karan Singh proceeds on the assumption that at the time when Maharaja Hari Singh conveyed his powers to Yuvaraj Karan Singh by his proclamation of June 20, 1949, he was himself no more than a constitutional monarch and as such he could convey to Yuvaraj Karan Singh no higher powers. Let us first deal with this argument. Prior to the passing of the Independence Act, 1947, the sovereignty of Maharaja Hari Singh over the State of Jammu and Kashmir was subject to such limitations as were constitutionally imposed on it by the paramountcy of the British Crown and by the treaties and agreements entered into between the Rulers of the State and the British Government. It cannot be disputed that so far as the internal administration and governance of the State were concerned Maharaja

Hari Singh, like his predecessors, was an absolute monarch; and that all powers legislative, executive and judicial in relation to his State and its governance inherently vested in him.

[...]

Since Mr. Chatterjee has strongly relied on the application of Article 370 of the Constitution to the State in support of his argument that the Yuvaraj had ceased to hold the plenary legislative powers, it is necessary to examine the provisions of this article and their effect. This article was intended to make temporary provisions with respect to the State of Jammu and Kashmir. It reads thus:

[...]

Having provided for the legislative power of the Parliament and for the application of the articles of the Constitution of the State, Article 370, clause (2) prescribes that if the concurrence of the Government of the State required by the relevant sub-clauses of clause (1) has been given before the Constituent Assembly of Kashmir has been convened, such concurrence shall be placed before such Assembly for such decision as it may take thereon. This clause shows that the Constitution-makers attached great importance to the final decision of the Constituent Assembly, and the continuance of the exercise of powers conferred on the Parliament and the President by the relevant temporary provisions of Article 370 (1) is made conditional on the final approval by the said Constituent Assembly in the said matters.

Clause (3) authorises the President to declare by public notification that this article shall cease to be operative or shall be operative only with specified exceptions or modifications; but this power can be exercised by the President only if the Constituent Assembly of the State makes recommendation in that behalf. Thus the proviso to clause (3) also emphasises the importance which was attached to the final decision of the Constituent Assembly of Kashmir in regard to the relevant matters covered by Article 370.

The appellant contends that the scheme of this article clearly shows that the person who would be recognised by the President as the Maharaja of Jammu and Kashmir was treated as no more than a constitutional Ruler of the State. In regard to matters covered by this article he could not function or decide by himself and in his own discretion. The consultation contemplated by this article had to be with the Maharaja acting on the advice of the Council of Ministers and the concurrence prescribed by it had to be similarly obtained and given, and that brings out the limitations on the powers of the Maharaja. It is also urged that the final decision in these matters has been deliberately left to the Constituent Assembly which was going to be convened for the framing of the Constitution of the State, and that again emphasises the limitations imposed on the powers of the Maharaja.

This argument assumes that under the *Explanation* to Article 370 (1) it is the person recognised by the President as the Maharaja who has to act on the advice of the Council of Ministers in relation to matters covered by Article 370. But, it is possible to take the view that the said clause really indicates that in recognising any person as the Maharaja of the State the President has to act on the advice of the Council of Ministers for the time being in office under the Maharaja's proclamation, dated March 5, 1948. If that be the true construction of the *Explanation* then the argument that, before the Maharaja is consulted or his concurrence is obtained, he must act on the advice of his Ministers would not be valid. We would, however, like to deal with the argument even on the assumption that the construction put by the appellant on the *Explanation* is right.

On the said construction the question which falls to be determined is: Do the provisions of Article 370 (1) affect the plenary powers of the Maharaja in the matter of the governance of the State? The effect of the application of the present article has to be judged in the light of its object and its terms considered in the context of the special features of the constitutional relationship between the State and India. The Constitution-makers were obviously anxious that the said relationship should be finally determined by the Constituent Assembly of the State itself; that is the main basis for, and purport of, the temporary provisions made by the present article; and so the effect of its provisions must be confined to its subject-matter. It would not be permissible or legitimate to hold that, by implication, this article sought to impose limitations on the plenary legislative powers of the Maharaja. These powers had been recognised and specifically provided by the Constitution Act of the State itself; and it was not, and could not have been, within the contemplation, or competence of the Constitution-makers to impinge even indirectly on the said powers. It would be recalled that by the Instrument of Accession these powers have been expressly recognised and preserved and neither the subsequent proclamation issued by Yuvaraj Karan Singh adopting, as far as it was applicable, the proposed Constitution of India, nor the Constitution order subsequently issued by the President, purported to impose any limitations on the said legislative powers of the Ruler. What form of government the State should adopt was a matter which had to be, and naturally was left to be, decided by the Constituent Assembly of the State. Until the Constituent Assembly reached its decision in that behalf, the constitutional relationship between the State and India continued to be governed basically by the Instrument of Accession. It would, therefore, be unreasonable to assume that the application of Article 370 could have affected, or was intended to affect, the plenary powers of the Maharaja in the matter of the governance of the State. In our opinion, the appellant's contention based on this article must, therefore, be rejected.

[...]

2(b). Sampat Prakash vs State of J&K (1968)
AIR 1970 *Supreme Court Journal* 1118

10 October 1968

In view of these activities of the petitioner the District Magistrate of Jammu, on 16th March, 1968, made an order of detention of the petitioner under Sec. 3 of the Jammu and Kashmir Preventive Detention Act No. 13 of 1964 (hereinafter referred to as 'the Act') and, on 18th March, 1968, the petitioner was actually placed under detention. The grounds of detention were served on the petitioner on the 26th March, 1968 and the State Government granted approval to the order of detention on 8th April, 1968. The detention of the petitioner was continued without making a reference to the Advisory Board, as the State Government purported to act under Section 13A of the Act. ...

2. During the preliminary hearing of this petition, Mr. Ramamurthy, representing the petitioner, raised a ground that Section 13A of the Act was ultra vires the Constitution as contravening the provisions of

Article 22 of the Constitution. That question was referred by the Constitution Bench of the Court to a larger Bench and came before the Full Court. On this occasion, the Court held that, in view of Clause (c) of Article 35 of the Constitution introduced in the Constitution in its application introduced in the Constitution in its application to the State of Jammu and Kashmir, the point that had been raised stood answered by the addition of this clause and, unless the clause itself was challenged, the point raised on behalf of the detenu did not arise. In this view, that reference was dissolved and the case has been heard by the Constitution Bench.

3. On the return of the reference, the main point which has been argued on behalf of the petitioner is based on the fact that Article 35 (c) of the Constitution, as initially introduced by the Constitution (Application to Jammu and Kashmir) Order, 1954 (C.O. 48) had given protection to any law relating to preventive detention in Jammu and Kashmir against invalidity on the ground of infringement of any of the fundamental rights guaranteed by Part III of the Constitution for a limited period of five years only. This clause, as introduced in 1954, read as follows:

No law with respect to preventive detention made by the Legislature of the State of Jammu and Kashmir, whether before or after the commencement of the Constitution (Application to Jammu and Kashmir) Order, 1954, shall be void on the ground that it is inconsistent with any of the provisions of this Part, but any such law shall, to the extent of such inconsistency, cease to have effect on the expiration of five years from the commencement of the said Order, except as respects things done or omitted to be done before the expiration thereof.

It was urged that the five years mentioned in the clause expired in 1959, and consequently, the Act, which was passed in 1964, did not get immunity from being declared void on the ground of inconsistency with Article 22 of the Constitution. It, however, appears that for the words 'five years' in Article 35 (c), the words 'ten years' were substituted by the Constitution (Application to Jammu and Kashmir) Second Amendment Order, 1959 (C.O. 59), which was passed before the expiry of those five years and, subsequently, for the words 'ten years' so

introduced, the words 'fifteen years' were substituted by the Constitution (Application to Jammu and Kashmir) Amendment Order, 1964
(C.O. 69). This modification was also made before the expiry of the
period of ten years from the date on which the Constitution (Application to Jammu and Kashmir) Order, 1954 was passed. On these facts,
the point raised on behalf of the detenu was that these two modifications
in 1959 and 1964, substituting 'ten years' for 'five years' and 'fifteen
years' for 'ten years', were themselves void on the ground that orders
making such modifications could not be validly passed by the President under Article 370 (1) of the Constitution in the years 1959 and
1964.

4. Article 370 of the Constitution is as follows:

'370. (1) Notwithstanding anything in this Constitution,

(a) the provisions of Art. 238 shall not apply in relation to the State
of Jammu and Kashmir;

(b) the power of Parliament to make law for the said State shall be
limited to:—

(i) those matters in the Union List and the Concurrent List
which, in consultations with the Government of the State,
are declared by the President to correspond to matters specified in the Instrument of Accession governing the accession
of the State to the Dominion of India as the matters with
respect to which the Dominion Legislature may make laws
for the State; and (ii) such other matters in the said Lists as,
with the concurrence of the Government of the State, the
President may by order specify.

Explanation:—For the purposes of this article, the Government of
the State means the person for the time being recognised by the President as the Maharaja of Jammu and Kashmir acting on the advice of the
Council of Ministers for the time being in office under the Maharaja's
Proclamation dated the fifth day of March, 1948;

(c) the provisions of article (1) and of this article shall apply in
relation to that State;

(d) such of the other provisions of this Constitution shall apply in
relation to that State subject to such exceptions and modifications as the President may by order specify:

Provided that no such order which relates to the matters specified in the Instrument of Accession of the State referred to in paragraph (i) of sub-clause (b) shall be issued except in consultation with the Government of the State:

Provided further that no such order which relates to matters other than those referred to in the last preceding proviso shall be issued except with the concurrence of that Government.

(2) If the concurrence of the Government of the State referred to in paragraph (ii) of sub-clause (b) of clause (1) or in the second proviso to sub-clause (d) of that clause be given before the Constituent Assembly for the purpose of framing the Constitution of the State is convened, it shall be placed before such Assembly for such decision as it may take thereon.

(3) Notwithstanding anything in the foregoing provisions of this article, the President may, by public notification, declare that this article shall cease to be operative or shall be operative only with such exceptions and modifications and from such date as he may specify:

Provided that the recommendation of the Constituent Assembly of the State referred to in Clause (2) shall be necessary before the President issues such a notification.

The first argument was that this article contained temporary provisions which ceased to be effective after the Constituent Assembly convened for the purpose of framing the Constitution of the Jammu and Kashmir State had completed its task by framing the Constitution for that State. Reliance was placed on the historical background in which this Article 370 was included in the Constitution to urge that the powers under this article were intended to be conferred only for the limited period until the Constitution of the State was framed, and the President could not resort to them after the Constituent Assembly had completed its work by framing the Constitution of the State. The background of the legislative history to which reference was made, was brought to our notice by learned counsel by drawing our attention to the speech of the Minister Sri N. Gopalaswami Ayyangar when he moved in the Constituent Assembly Clause 306A of the Bill, which now corresponds with Article 370 of the Constitution. It was stated by him that conditions in Kashmir were special and required special treatment. The special circumstances, to which reference was made by him were:

(1) that there had been a war going on within the limits of Jammu and Kashmir State;

(2) that there was a cease-fire agreed to at the beginning of the year and that cease-fire was still on,

(3) that the conditions in the State were still unusual and abnormal and had not settled down;

(4) that part of the State was still in the hands of rebels and enemies;

(5) that our country was entangled with the United Nations in regard to Jammu and Kashmir and it was not possible to say when we would be free from this entanglement;

(6) that the Government of India had committed themselves to the people of Kashmir in certain respects which commitments included an undertaking that an opportunity would be given to the people of the State to decide for themselves whether they would remain with the Republic or wish to go out of it; and

(7) that the will of the people expressed through the Instrument of a Constituent Assembly would determine the Constitution of the State as well as the sphere of Union jurisdiction over the State.

Learned counsel urged that, in this background, Article 370 of the Constitution could only have been intended to remain effective until the Constitution of the State was framed and the will of the people of Jammu and Kashmir had been expressed and, thereafter, this article must be held to have become ineffective, so that the modifications made by the President in exercise of the powers under this article, subsequent to the enforcement of the Constitution of the State, would be without any authority of law. The Constitution of the State came into force on 26th January, 1956 and, therefore, the two orders of 1959 and 1964 passed by the President in purported exercise of the power under Article 370 were void. It was also urged that the provisions of Cl. (2) of Article 370 support this view, because it directs that, if the concurrence of the Government of the State is given under paragraph (ii) of sub-clause (b) of Clause (1) or under the second proviso to sub-clause (d) of that clause before the Constituent Assembly for the purpose of framing the Constitution of the State is convened, that concurrence has to be placed before such Assembly for such decision as it may take thereon. From this, it was sought to be inferred that the power of the President, depending on the concurrence of the Government of the State, must be exercised before the dissolution of the Constituent Assembly of the State, so that the concurrence could be placed for its decision, and that power must be held to cease to exist after the dissolution of the Constituent Assembly when that course became impossible.

5. We are not impressed by either of these two arguments advanced by Mr. Ramamurthy. So far the historical background is concerned, the Attorney-General appearing on behalf of the Government also relied on it to urge that the provisions of Article 370 should be held to be continuing in force because the situation that existed when this article was incorporated in the Constitution had not materially altered, and the purpose of introducing this article was to empower the President to exercise his discretion in applying the Indian Constitution while that situation remained unchanged. There is considerable force in this submission. The legislative history of this article cannot, in these circumstances, be of any assistance for holding that this article became ineffective after the Constituent Assembly of the State had framed the Constitution for the State.

6. The second submission based on clause (2) of Article 370 does not find support even from the language of that clause which only refers to the concurrence given by the Government of the State before the Constituent Assembly was convened, and makes no mention at all of the completion of the work of the Constituent Assembly or its dissolution.

7. There are, however, much stronger reasons for holding that the provisions of this article continued in force and remained effective even after the Constituent Assembly of the state had passed the Constitution of the State. The most important provision in this connection is that contained in Clause (3) of the article which lays down that this article shall cease to be operative or shall be operative only with such exceptions and modifications and from such date, as the President may specify by public notification, provided that the recommendation of

the Constituent Assembly of the State referred to in Clause (2) shall be necessary before the President issues such a notification. This clause clearly envisages that the article will continue to be operative and can cease to be operative only if, on the recommendation of the Constituent Assembly of the State, the President makes a direction to that effect. In fact, no such recommendation was made by the Constituent Assembly of the State, nor was any order made by the President declaring that the article shall cease to be operative. On the contrary, it appears that the Constituent Assembly of the State made a recommendation that the article should be operative with one modification to be incorporated in the Explanation to Clause (1) of the article. This modification in the article was notified by the President by Ministry of Law order No. C.O. 44 dated 15th November, 1952, and laid down that, from the 17th November, 1952, the article was to be operative with substitution of the new Explanation for the old Explanation as it existed at that time. This makes it very clear that the Constituent Assembly of the State did not desire that this article should cease to be operative and, in fact, expressed its agreement to the continued operation of this article by making a recommendation that it should be operative with this modification only.

8. Further reference may also be made to the proviso added to Article 368 of the Constitution in its application to the State of Jammu and Kashmir, under which an amendment to the Constitution made in accordance with Article 368 is to have no effect in relation to the State of Jammu and Kashmir unless applied by order of the President under Cl. (1) of Article 370. The proviso, thus, clearly requires that the powers of the President under Article 370 must be exercised from time to time in order to bring into effect in Jammu and Kashmir amendments made by Parliament in the Constitution in accordance with Article 368. In view of these provisions, it must be held that Article 370 of the Constitution has never ceased to be operative and there can be no challenge on this ground to the validity of the Orders passed by the President in exercise of the powers conferred by this Article.

9. The next submission made for challenging the validity of the Orders of modification made in the years 1959 and 1964 was that, under sub-clause (d) of Clause (1) of Article 370 of the Constitution,

the power that is conferred on the President is for the purpose of
applying the provisions of the Constitution to Jammu and Kashmir
and not for the purpose of making amendments in the Constitution as
applied to that State. The interpretation sought to be placed was that,
at the time of applying any provision of the Constitution to the State of
Jammu and Kashmir the President is competent to make modifications
and exceptions therein but once any provision of the Constitution
has been applied, the power under Article 370 would not cover any
modification in the Constitution as applied. Reliance was thus placed
on the nature of the power conferred on the President to urge that the
President could not from time to time amend any of the provisions of
the Constitution as applied to the State of Jammu and Kashmir. It was
further urged that the President's power under Article 370 should not be
interpreted by applying Section 21 of the General Clauses Act, because
a Constitutional power cannot be equated with a power conferred by an
Act, rule, bye-law, etc.

10. The argument, in our opinion, proceeds on an entirely incorrect
basis. Under Article 370 (1) (d), the power of the President is expressed
by laying down that provisions of the Constitution, other than article
(1) and article 370 which, under Article 370 (1) (c), became applicable
when the Constitution came into force, shall apply in relation to the State
of Jammu and Kashmir subject to such exceptions and modifications as
the President may by order specify. What the President is required to
do is to specify the provisions of the Constitution which are to apply to
the State of Jammu and Kashmir and, when making such specification,
he is also empowered to specify exceptions and modifications to those
provisions. As soon as the President makes such specification, the
provisions become applicable to the State with the specified exceptions
and modifications. The specification by the President has to be in
consultation with the Government of the State if those provisions relate
to matters in the Union List and the Concurrent List specified in the
Instrument of Accession governing the accession of the State to the
Dominion of India as matters with respect to which the Dominion
Legislature may make laws for that State. The specification in respect of
all other provisions of the Constitution under sub-clause (d) of Cl. (1)
of Article 370 has to be with the concurrence of the State Government.

Any specification made after such consultation or concurrence has the effect that the provisions of the Constitution specified with the exceptions and modifications become applicable to the State of Jammu and Kashmir. It cannot be held that the nature of the power contained in this provision is such that Section 21 of the General Clauses Act must be held to be totally inapplicable.

11. In this connection, it may be noted that Article 367 of the Constitution lays down that, unless the context otherwise requires. The General Clauses Act, 1897, shall, subject to any adaptations and modifications that may be made therein under Article 372, apply for the interpretation of this Constitution as it applies for the interpretation of and Act of the Legislature of the Dominion of India. This provision made by the Constitution itself in Article 367, thus, specifically applied the provisions of the General Clauses Act to the interpretation of all the articles of the Constitution which include Article 370. Section 21 of the General Clauses Act is as follows:

Where by any Central Act or Regulation, a power to issue notifications, orders, rules, or bye-laws is conferred then that power includes a power, exercisable in the like manner and subject to the like sanction and conditions (if any), to add to, amend, vary or rescind any notifications, orders, rules or bye-laws so issued.

This provision is clearly a rule of interpretation which has been made applicable to the Constitution in the same manner as it applies to any Central Act or Regulation.

[...]

12. The legislative history of this article will also fully support this view. It was because of the special situation existing in Jammu and Kashmir that the Constituent Assembly framing the Constitution decided that the Constitution should not become applicable to Jammu and Kashmir under Article 394, under which it came into effect in the rest of India, and preferred to confer on the President the power to apply the various provisions of the Constitution with exceptions and modifications. It was envisaged that the President would have to take into account the situation existing in the State when applying a provision of the Constitution and such situations could arise from time to

time. There was clearly the possibility that, when applying a particular provision, the situation might demand an exception or modification of the provision applied; but subsequent changes in the situation might justify the rescinding of those modifications or exceptions. This could only be brought about by conferring on the President the power of making orders from time to time under Article 370 and this power must, therefore, be held to have been conferred on him by applying the provisions of Section 21 of the General Clauses Act for the interpretation of the Constitution.

13. The next point urged was that Article 368 of the Constitution having been applied to Jammu and Kashmir with a proviso added to it, there now exists a provision relating to amendment of the Constitution as applied to Jammu and Kashmir under this article and, consequently, while such special provision for this purpose exists, we should interpret Article 370 as being no longer applicable for amending or modifying the provisions of the Constitution applied to that State. This argument, in our opinion, is based on a wrong premise. Article 368 has been applied to Jammu and Kashmir primarily with the object that amendments made by the Parliament in the Constitution of India as applicable in the whole of the country should also take effect in the State of Jammu and Kashmir. The proviso, when applying this article, serves the purpose that those amendments made should be made applicable to the State of Jammu and Kashmir only with the concurrence of the State Government and, after such concurrence is available these amendments should take effect when an order is made under Article 370 of the Constitution. Thus, Article 368 is not primarily intended for amending the Constitution as applicable in Jammu and Kashmir, but is for the purpose of carrying the amendments made in the Constitution for the rest of India into the Constitution as applied in the State of Jammu and Kashmir. Even, in this process, the powers of the President under Article 370 have to be exercised and, consequently, it cannot be held that the applicability of this article would necessarily curtail the power of the President under Article 370.

14. It was also urged that the power of making modifications and exceptions in the orders made under Article 370 (1) (d) should at least be limited to making minor alterations and should not cover the power

to practically abrogate an article of the Constitution applied in that State. That submission is clearly without force. The challenge to the validity of Article 35(c) introduced in the Constitution as applied to Jammu and Kashmir on this ground was repelled by this Court in P.L. Lakhanpal v. State of Jammu and Kashmir, (1955) 2 SCR 1101 = (AIR 1956 SC 197). Subsequently, the scope of the powers of making exceptions and modifications was examined in greater details by this Court in Puranlal Lakhanpal v. President of India, (1962) 2 SCR 688 at p. 692 = (AIR 1961 SC 1519 at p. 1521). Dealing with the scope of the word 'modification' as used in Article 370 (1), the Court held:

But, in the present case, we have to find out the meaning of the word 'modification' used in Article 370(1) in the context of the Constitution. As we have said already, the object behind enacting Article 370(1) was to recognise the special position of the State of Jammu and Kashmir and to provide for that special position by giving power to the President to apply the provisions of the Constitution to that State with such exceptions and modifications as the President might by order specify. We have already pointed out that the power to make exceptions implies that the President can provide that a particular provision of the Constitution would not apply to that State. If, therefore, the power is given to the President to efface in effect any provision of the Constitution altogether in its application to the State of Jammu and Kashmir, it seems that when he is also given the power to make modifications that power should be considered in its widest possible amplitude. If he could efface a particular provision of the Constitution altogether in its application to the State of Jammu and Kashmir, we see no reason to think that the Constitution did not intend that he should have the power to amend a particular provision in its application to the State of Jammu and Kashmir. It seems to us that when the Constitution used the word "modification" in Article 370(1), the intention was that the President would have the power to amend the provisions of the Constitution if he so thought fit in their application to the State of Jammu and Kashmir.

Proceeding further, and after discussing the meaning of the word 'modify', the Court held:

Thus, in law, the word 'modify' may just mean 'vary' i.e., amend; and when Article 370 (1) says that the President may apply the provisions of the Constitution to the State of Jammu and Kashmir with such modifications as he may by order specify, it means that he may vary (i.e., amend) the provisions of the Constitution in its application to the State of Jammu and Kashmir. We are, therefore, of opinion that in the context of the Constitution we must give the widest effect to the meaning of the word 'modification' used in Article 370(1) and in that sense it includes an amendment. There is no reason to limit the word 'modifications' as used in Article 370(1) only to such modifications as do not make any 'radical transformation.

This decision being binding on us, it is not possible to accept the submission urged by counsel.

[...]

We have already held that the power to modify in Clause (d) also includes the power to subsequently vary, alter, add to or rescind such an order by reason of the applicability of the rule of interpretation laid down in Section 21 of the General Clauses Act.

3. Indira Gandhi–Sheikh Abdullah Accord: Documents 1974–5

(August 1974–February 1975)

(i) Letter dated 23rd August, 1974 from Sheikh Sahib to Shri G. Parthasarthi.

(ii) Agreed Conclusions signed by Beg Sahib and Shri G. Parthasarthi dated 13th November, 1974.

(iii) Matters reserved for further discussion at an appropriate time signed by Beg Sahib and Shri G. Parthasarthi dated 13th November, 1974.

(iv) Letter dated 13th November, 1974 from Beg Sahib to Shri G. Parthasarthi regarding Article 132 of the Constitution of India.

(v) Letter dated 13th November, 1974 from Shri G. Parthasarthi to Beg Sahib.

(vi) Letter dated 13th November, 1974 from Beg Sahib to Shri G. Parthasarthi.

(vii) Letter dated 13th November, 1974 from Shri G. Parthasarthi to Beg Sahib.

(viii) Letter addressed to the Prime Minister of India by Sheikh Sahib dated 25th November, 1974.

(ix)   Letter from the Prime Minister to Sheikh Sahib dated 16th December, 1974.
(x)   Letter dated 29th December, 1974 from Sheikh Sahib to the Prime Minister.
(xi)   Letter from Sheikh Sahib to the Prime Minister dated 11th February, 1975.
(xii) Letter from the Prime Minister to Sheikh Sahib dated 12th February, 1975.

Confidential

August 23, 1974

My dear Shri Parthasarthi,

Apropos to our talks yesterday and the day before, I hope that I have made it abundantly clear to you that I can assume office only on the basis of the position as it existed on 8th August, 1953.

With regard to the provisions of the Constitution or the Union Laws and Entries applied to the Jammu and Kashmir State after 9th August, 1953, judgement thereupon will be deferred until the newly elected Assembly comes into being.

With kind regards,

Yours sincerely,

(Sd/-) S.M. Abdullah

Shri G. Parthasarthi,
Oberoi Palace Hotel
Srinagar.

Agreed Conclusions

1. The State of Jammu and Kashmir, which is a constituent unit of the Union of India, shall, in its relations with the Union, continue to be governed by Article 370 of the Constitution of India.

2. The residuary powers of legislation shall remain with the State; however, Parliament will continue to have power to make laws relating to the prevention of activities directed towards disclaiming questioning or disrupting the sovereignty and territorial integrity of India or bringing about cession of a part of the territory of India or secession of a part of the territory of India from the Union or causing insult

to the Indian National Flag, the Indian National Anthem and the Constitution.

3. Where any provision of the Constitution of India has been applied to the State of Jammu and Kashmir with adaptations and modifications, such adaptations and modifications can be altered or repealed by an order of the President under Article 370, each individual proposal in this behalf being considered on its merits; but provisions of the Constitution of India already applied to the State of Jammu and Kashmir without adaptation or modification are unalterable.

4. With a view to assuring freedom to the State of Jammu and Kashmir to have its own legislation on matters like welfare measures, cultural matters, social security, personal law, and procedural laws, in a manner suited to the special conditions in the State, it is agreed that the State Government can review the laws made by Parliament or extended to the State after 1953 on any matter relatable to the Concurrent List and may decide which of them, in its opinion, needs amendment or repeal. Thereafter, appropriate steps may be taken under Article 254 of the Constitution of India. The grant of President's assent to such legislation would be sympathetically considered. The same approach would be adopted in regard to laws to be made by Parliament in future under the Proviso to clause 2 of that Article. The State Government shall be consulted regarding the application of any such law to the State and the views of the State Government shall receive the fullest consideration.

5. As an arrangement reciprocal to what has been provided under Article 368, a suitable modification of that Article as applied to the State should be made by Presidential order to the effect that no law made by the Legislative of the State of Jammu and Kashmir, seeking to make any change in or in the effect of any provision of the Constitution of the State of Jammu and Kashmir relating to any of the undermentioned matters, shall take effect unless the Bill, having been reserved for the consideration of the President, receives his assent; the matters are:—

   (a) the appointment, powers, functions, duties, privileges and immunities of the Governor; and

(b) the following matters relating to Elections, namely, the superintendence, direction and control of Elections by the Election
Commission of India, eligibility for inclusion in the electoral
rolls without discrimination, adult sufferage and composition
of the Legislative Council, being matters specified in sections
138, 139, 140 and 50 of the Constitution of the State of Jammu
and Kashmir.

6. No agreement was possible on the question of nomenclature of the
Governor and the Chief Minister and the matter is therefore remitted
to the Principals.

(Sd/-) Mirza Mohammad Afzal Beg   (Sd/-) G. Parthasarthi
New Delhi,
Dated: November 13, 1974.

Matters Reserved for Further Discussion at an Appropriate Time

The following specific questions were left over for further consideration:—

1. What should be the convention with regard to the consultations
with the State Government for the appointment of the Governor under
section 27 of the State Constitution?

2. Whether any modification is called for with regard to the extension
of the scheme of the All India Services to the State?

(Sd/-) M.A. Beg   (Sd/-) G. Parthasarthi
13-11-1974

Camp New Delhi
November 13, 1974

Dear Shri Parthasarthi,
In the course of our discussions, I made a proposal that appeals to the
Supreme Court under Article 132 of the Constitution of India from the
decisions of the High Court of Jammu and Kashmir, should lie only on
a certificate under clause (1) of that Article. After a detailed discussion
on this, you had agreed to the proposed and stated that it can be implemented by an Order under Article 370 making suitable modification to
the modifications made under Article 367.

Kindly acknowledge receipt of this letter.

Yours sincerely,
(Sd/-) Mirza Mohammad Afzal Beg

Shri G. Parthasarthi,
31, Aurangzeb Road, New Delhi.

31, Aurangzeb Road,
New Delhi-11,
November 13, 1974
Phone 615986

Dear Beg Sahib,

I acknowledge receipt of your letter dated 13th November, 1974. The proposal referred to therein was discussed between us at length and agreed to by me. It can be implemented by an appropriate Order of the President in accordance with the procedure prescribed under Article 370.

Yours sincerely,
(Sd/-) G. Parthasarthi

Mirza Mohammad Afzal Beg,
Camp New Delhi.

Camp New Delhi,
November 13, 1974

Dear Shri Parthasarthi,

I have today signed the document containing the points on which we have reached agreement.

2. As you may recall, in the course of discussions we had on the various issues, I made proposals regarding the following matters:—

   (i) The provisions relating to the fundamental rights to be incorporated in the State Constitution.

  (ii) The superintendence, direction and control over elections to the State Legislature by the Election Commission should be removed.

 (iii) Article 356 should be modified to require the consent of the State before an order is issued thereunder, or some similar safeguard should be provided.

After prolonged discussions you did not agree to these proposals.

Yours sincerely,
(Sd/-) Mirza Mohammad Afzal Beg

Shri G. Parthasarthi,
31, Aurangzeb Road,
New Delhi.

31, Aurangzeb Road,
New Delhi-11,
November 13, 1974
Phone 615986

Dear Beg Sahib,
I acknowledge receipt of your letter dated 13th November, 1974, about
the points of agreement and disagreement between us. It is correct to
say that for the reasons I had stated during the discussions, I could not
agree to the proposals referred to in paragraph 2 of your letter.

2. I may add that the fact of our disagreement on theses points are
referred to in this correspondence only for the information of yourself
and Sheikh Sahib. It is clearly understood that these facts should not be
made public without Prime Minister's consent.

Yours sincerely,
(Sd/-) G. Parthasarthi

Mirza Mohammad Afzal Beg,
Camp New Delhi.

Confidential

(Sheikh Mohammad Abdullah)   Phone No. 2178
                                          Mujahid Manzil,
                                          Srinagar (Kashmir),
                                          November 25, 1974

My dear Indira Ji,
Mirza Mohammad Afzal Beg has written to me that he and Shri G.
Parthasarthi have reached the conclusions in regard to constitutional
matters concerning the relationship between Jammu and Kashmir State
and the Union of India. At our instance they had detailed discussions
on these matters and I have received copies of documents from Mr. Beg

containing points on which agreement has been reached between them and those over which no agreement could be reached.

I have several times explained to you my point of view in regard to matters on which the two emissaries have disagreed. I trust you will kindly accommodate our view point to enable me to achieve the main objective.

Some points have been left over for settlement between you and me. I hope that we shall be able to sort out these points satisfactorily when we meet. I feel sure that such a settlement will provide an amicable basis for me and the people of the State to co-operate in cementing Centre-State relationship.

I am awaiting your convenience when we can meet to consider these issues.

I hope you are doing well.

With kind regards,

Yours sincerely,
(Sd/-) S.M. Abdullah

Shrimati Indira Gandhi,
Prime Minister of India,
New Delhi.

Confidential

Prime Minister's House,
New Delhi,
December 16, 1974

Dear Sheikh Sahib,

I have your letter of November 25, 1974. Shri G. Parthasarthi has also given me the documents which he and Mirza Mohammad Afzal Beg have prepared at the conclusion of their talks.

You have referred to matters on which our two representatives have disagreed. As you are aware, these are basic issues on which there have been thorough discussions between them in the course of which Beg Sahib presented your views fully. I doubt whether anything will be gained by our discussing these matters again.

We can discuss the points which have been reserved for our consideration when we meet.

Shri Parthasarthi has told me that you would write to me about the maintenance of those basic features of the State's Constitution which are necessary not only for uniformity but also to give a measure of confidence to the people regarding the democratic functioning of the Government in the State.

I too am anxious to conclude our discussions. I entirely agree with you that political co-operation between us will further strengthen the bond that exists between the State of Jammu and Kashmir and the Union. As you know, I am extremely busy in Parliament these days. We can perhaps meet during the last week of this month on a mutually convenient date.

With regards to you and Begum Sahiba.

Yours sincerely,
(Sd/-) Indira Gandhi

Shiekh Mohammad Abdullah,
10, Maulana Azad Road,
Srinagar, Kashmir.

Confidential

10, Maulana Azad Road,
Srinagar (Kashmir).
December 29, 1974

My dear Indira Ji,

I have received your letter of 16th December, 1974 marked 'Confidential'.

I am sorry to say that your representative should have found it necessary to ask me to write to you about the maintenance of those basic features of the State's Constitution which are necessary not only for uniformity but also to give a measure of confidence to the people regarding the democratic functioning of the Government in the State. It pains me that even after the decades of my sufferings and sacrifices for these very cherished values, I should be called upon to sign an undertaking to stand by them. This attitude clearly shows the lack of trust which continues to exist in the minds of those with whom I may have to deal in the future. I hope you will agree with me that the only way to repair the vast damage done to the Indo-Kashmir relationship by the Arbitrary action of 9th August, 1953 is possible only through complete understanding and mutual trust. If this trust is lacking even in a very small measure, all our efforts to reach an understanding will prove fruitless.

Ordinarily, the broad principles of the partition of the sub-continent might well have taken the State to Pakistan in 1947, but for various reasons, things happened other way. And because of our identity with the basic ideals and fundamental values for which India stood, the Leadership of the National Conference supported the accession of the State to India, on the basis of the instrument of Accession signed by the Maharaja. But in order to make the Indo-Kashmir relationship durable, means had to be devised to have the support of all the sections of the State's population for the Action of the National Conference Leadership. The minorities within the State, no doubt, felt secure once the Leadership of the National Conference decided to throw its lot with India, and their support was, therefore, assured. But what about the Muslim Majority? The Muslims of the State were simultaneously a minority in relation to all India population and a majority within their own State. Therefore, all fears and apprehensions that they would be dominated by all India majority had to be dispelled and they had to be assured that within the State their rights as a majority would be guaranteed. Their fear complex could be dispelled only by ensuring complete internal autonomy of the State as envisaged in the Instrument of Accession signed by the Maharaja. Accordingly, an agreement governing the Centre–State relationship was hammered out by the leaders of the two sides. In evolving this relationship all aspects of the problem and special features of the situation were taken into consideration. The provisions of Article 370 of the Indian Constitution were the result of these efforts.

I have no doubt in my mind that the manner in which the Government of India systematically eroded both the letter and spirit of the special provision of the Union Constitution jeopardised the very foundation of the relationship so laboriously built over years of tireless effort and dedication. I recall with pain and anguish that once a former Home Minister of India publically characterised Article 370 as a 'Tunnel' obviously implying that through it the internal autonomy of Kashmir will be eroded and this exactly was assiduously accomplished behind our back after 9th August, 1953.

Recently, a responsible dignatory of the Government of India was candid enough to tell me that India would not be prepared to throw the minority community of the State, at the mercy of the majority by allowing the fundamental rights to be kept in the State Constitution. I told him that such an attitude of India will completely shatter the trust and confidence of the majority, who, in 1947, put their faith in the declarations of Indian leadership, and gave enough proof, if any was needed, that it was capable of protecting the interests of the minorities, at the most crucial moments even at the cost of its own life. He had no answer.

Myself and the Plebiscite Front Leadership were purposely kept behind the bars or externed from the State at the time of every general election to the State Legislature or the Parliament in the years 1957, 1962, 1967 and 1972. As if this was not enough, large scale rigging in elections was taken recourse to. Obviously these means were adopted so as to bring into being a legislature and Government in the State of a particular choice and keep effective opposition out of the way, thus facilitating the erosion of Article 370—a process which has been going on for over last two decades.

In spite of this all betrayal and sufferings and tribulations that we had to undergo for years on end, I welcomed your desire, which you expressed in 1972, to take a fresh look at the Indo-Kashmir relationship. I made it clear to you and to the public at large that my differences with India were not over the issue of the accession of the State but on the quantum of accession. In my opinion accession and autonomy are inter-dependent. I had agreed to throw in my lot with India on the basis of the Instrument of Accession signed by the Maharaja which guaranteed complete internal autonomy to the State. If this autonomy is taken away, then the very foundation of the relationship is destroyed. I, therefore, pleaded the view that in case you wished me to help in rebuilding the faith and confidence that the majority community in the State has lost in India, I can only start from the point where I left off in August, 1953. For me to take even this position is not going to be without difficulties, and I shall be faced with many a doubting mind. But I would nevertheless give it a try.

You have written in your letter that matters on which our two representatives have disagreed are basic issues and that nothing will be gained by discussing these matters again between ourselves since they have already been thoroughly discussed. If there is no agreement on these basic issues, then what would be the use of discussing issues that are not basic? We consider the matters on which agreement has not been reached equally vital and basic for us and, unless there is agreement on them. I do not think that any useful purpose would be served by prolonging our discussions.

Begum Sahiba sends her respectful regards, I hope you are doing well.

With regards,

Yours sincerely,
(Sd/-) Sheikh Mohammad Abdullah

Shrimati Indira Gandhi,
Prime Minister of India,
New Delhi.

Despatched by hand through Nisar Ahmad on 30th December, 1974.

(Sd/-) S.M.A.

Confidential

3, Kotla Lane,
New Delhi
February 11, 1975

My dear Prime Minister,
I have seen the text of the conclusions reached between Shri G. Parthasarthi and Mirza Mohammad Afzal Beg on the various Constitutional issues concerning the Centre–State relationship between the State of Jammu and Kahmir and the Union of India. I have studied the document and have also had discussion with you. As you are aware, it is my view that constitutional relationship between the Centre and the State of Jammu and Kashmir should be what it was in 1953. Nevertheless, I am happy to say that the agreed conclusions provide a good basis for my co-operation at the political level and for Centre–State relationship.

I appreciate that the main purpose of the dialogue was to remove miasapprehensions on either side to ensure that the bond between the Union and the State is further strengthened and to afford to the people of the State full scope for undertaking social welfare and developmental measures.

The accession of the State of Jammu and Kashmir to India is not a matter in issue. It has been my firm belief that the future of Jammu and Kashmir lies with India because of the common ideals that we share. I hope you would appreciate that the sole reason for my agreeing to co-operate at the political and Governmental levels is to enable the State Government to initiate measures for the well-being of the people of the State which I have always considered as my sacred trust. It will be my constant endeavour to ensure that the State of Jammu and Kashmir continues to make its contribution to the sovereignty, integrity and progress of the Nation. By the same token, I am sure that the Central Government would co-operate with the State Government fully in respect of measures to be undertaken by the State Government to further the progress and welfare of the people of the State as an integral part of India.

The country is passing through a critical period and it is all the more necessary for all of us who cherish the ideals of democracy, secularism and socialism, to strengthen your hands as the leader of the Nation and it is in this spirit that I am offering my wholehearted co-operation.

Yours sincerely,

(Sd/-) Sheikh Mohammad Abdullah

Shrimati Indira Gandhi,
Prime Minister of India,
New Delhi.

Confidential

Prime Minister,
New Delhi.
February 12, 1975

Dear Sheikh Sahib,

I am happy to receive your letter expressing your concurrence with the conclusions reached between Mirza Mohammad Afzal Beg and Shri

G. Parthasarthi on certain constitutional aspects of the relationship of the Centre with the State of Jammu and Kashmir and offering your whole-hearted co-operation at the political and Governmental level to further promote the well-being of the people of the State of Jammu and Kashmir. I am aware of your views on the Centre–State relationship in respect of the State of Jammu and Kashmir. I have already explained to you that the clock cannot be put back and we have to take note of the realities of the situation. I am appreciative of the spirit in which you have expressed your agreement with the terms of the agreed conclusions.

The agreed conclusions have been examined and I am in a position to inform you that such appropriate executive action as may be necessary to give effect to them will be taken. I have been in close touch with the Chief Minister of the State who is in agreement with the approach in regard to political co-operation with you and the understanding reached about the relationship of the State with the Union.

The Central Government would undoubtedly continue to co-operate with the State Government fully in respect of measures to be undertaken by the State Government to further the progress and welfare of the people of that State, which is of equal concern to the Central Government.

As pointed out by you, the country is passing through a critical period and it is a matter of great satisfaction to me that a person of your stature who made an outstanding contribution during the freedom struggle should come forward again to co-operate in the task of strengthening the nation and sustaining its ideals.

Yours sincerely,
(Sd/-) Indira Gandhi

Shiekh Mohammad Abdullah,
3, Kotla Lane,
New Delhi.

3(a). G.A. Lone on Application of Article 249 to the State

Kashmir Times, 20 April 1995

As Secretary to Government, Law Department, it was stunning to discover that during his first stint as Governor in July, 1986 when the State was put under Governor's rule, Mr Jagmohan by sheer manipulation got Article 249 of the Constitution applied to the State. The relevant record in the Law Department bears mute testimony to the fact how the then Secretary Law was made to change his stand on its application under the dictates of the Governor. The proposal itself was initiated on 30.7.1986 in an unprecedented manner on the basis of undisclosed press reports. About the proposal, the Law Secretary pointed out that the application of Article on the concurrence of the Governor acting without the aid and advice of the Council of Ministers is impermissible. The ink of this opinion may have hardly dried up when on the same hour of the day he was made to support the proposal facilitating the granting of the concurrence by the Governor to the application of the aforesaid Article to the State. The whole exercise was completed in a single day and reeks of intrigue to dilute the constitutional status of the State in a highhanded manner. It was indeed a grave constitutional impropriety not only because the manner and method employed in applying the constitutional provision was dubious but also because the Governor in the absence of a Council of Ministers is not competent to grant such concurrence and change the constitutional framework. The concurrence granted was a clear breach and violation of Article 370 of the Constitution.

Chapter 12

Restoring the Autonomy of Jammu & Kashmir

1. Memorandum of the National Conference to the Prime Minister on 4 November 1995

Asian Age, 6 November 1995

In the context of the demand put forth by Jammu and Kashmir National Conference before the Hon'ble Prime Minister of India for restoration of the autonomy to the state of Jammu and Kashmir in terms of Delhi Agreement of June, 1952, we invite a President Order under Article 370 (1) (d). This is consistent with the assurance of the Hon'ble Prime Minister given before Parliament where the Hon'ble Prime Minister rightly and clearly indicated that 'Short of *Azadi*' (Secession), Constitution of India contains scope to permit autonomy to any limit.

The Presidential Order we invite is the means for resolving the political imbroglio in Jammu and Kashmir and is a permissible course under the Constitution of India.

The scope of the powers of the President of India under Article 370 of the Constitution of India to make orders from time to time regarding the application of the provisions of the Constitution to that state has been recognised to be of widest amplitude in several decisions of the Supreme Court of India. Before adverting to those authoritative decisions, certain undisputed position may be noticed:

(i)   Article 368 of the Constitution which provides for 'Powers of Parliament to amend the Constitution and procedure therefore' is not applicable to the state of Jammu and Kashmir;

(ii) The provisions of Article 1 and Article 370 of the Constitution apply to that state:

(iii) The power of Parliament to make laws for the state of Jammu and Kashmir is limited to:—

   (a) Those matters in the Union List and the Concurrent List which are so specific by the President by an order, provided such order is made with the concurrence of the state and such matters correspond to matters specific in the Instrument of Accession governing accession of the state to the dominion of India.

Aforesaid position is summarised in clauses (a), (b) and (c) of sub-Article (1) of Article 370.

Difficulties have arisen as a result of resort made to the provisions of Clause (d) of Sub-Article (1) of Article 370 in the shape of 'Constitutional Application to Jammu and Kashmir Order, 1954,' as amended from time to time.

The question is whether the President can have recourse to Clause (d) of sub-Article (1) of Article 370 for the purpose of reversing the dilution made to the autonomy of Jammu and Kashmir.

This question has been answered in affirmative by two Constitution Bench decision of the Supreme Court. Clause (d) of sub-Article (1) of Article 370 reads as under:—

Such of the other provisions of this Constitution shall apply in relation to that state *subject to such exception and modifications* as the President may by order specify:

Provided that no such order which relates to the matters specified in the Instrument of Accession of the state referred to in paragraph (1) of sub-class (b) shall be issued except in consultation with the government of the state:

Provided further that no such order which relates to matters other than those referred to in the last proceeding proviso shall be issued except with the concurrence of that government.

Way back, on 30 March 1961, a Constitution Bench of the Supreme Court speaking through Justice Wanchoo in Puranlal, vice-president of India (AIR 1961 Supreme Court 1519) construed the key expression 'modification' in Article 370 (1) (d). It would be best to quote from that decision.

Article 370 clearly recognises the special position of the state of Jammu and Kashmir and that is why the President is given the power to apply the provisions of the Constitution to that state subject to such exceptions and modification as the President may by order specify.

The President thus has the power to say by order that certain provisions of the Constitution will be excepted from application to the state of Jammu and Kashmir and on such order being made, those provisions would not apply to that state. Besides this power of making exceptions by which certain provisions of the Constitution were not to apply to that state the President is also given the power to apply the provision of the Constitution with such modifications as he thinks fit to make...

As we have said already the object behind enacting Article 370 (1) was to recognise the special position of the state of Jammu and Kashmir and to provide for that special position by giving power to the President to apply the provisions of the Constitution to that state with such exceptions and modifications as the President might by order specify. We have already pointed out that the power to make exceptions implies that the President can provide that a particular provision of the Constitution would not apply to that state. If, therefore, the power is given to the President to efface in effect any provision of the Constitution altogether in its application to the state of Jammu and Kashmir, it seems that when he is also given the power to make modifications that power should be considered in its widest possible amplitude. If he could efface a particular provision of the Constitution altogether in its application to the state of Jammu and Kashmir, we see no reason to think that the Constitution did not amend a particular provision in its application to the state of Jammu and Kashmir. *It seems to us that when the Constitution used the word 'modification' in Article 370 (1) the intention was that the President would have the power to amend the provisions of the Constitution if he so thought fit in their application to the state of Jammu and Kashmir.*

Thus in law the word 'modify' may just mean 'vary', that is, amend; and when Article 370 (1) says that the President may apply the provisions of the Constitution to the state of Jammu and Kashmir with such modifications as he may by order specify mean of Jammu and Kashmir. We are, therefore, of the opinion that in the context of the Constitution, we must give the wide effect to the meaning of the word 'modification' used in Article 370 (1) and in that sense it includes an amendment. There is no reason to limit the word 'modification' as used in Article 370 (1) only to such modifications as do not make any 'radical transformation'.

The settled position in law, therefore, is that the President's power of modification of the Constitution of India under Article 370 (1) (d) is in effect the power to amend the provisions of the Constitution in their application to Jammu and Kashmir and would include the power to efface a particular provision of the Constitution of India altogether in its application to Jammu and Kashmir. This has further been reiterated by another Constitution Bench decision of the Supreme Court speaking through Justice Bhargava on 10 October 1968 in Sampat Prakash *vs* State of Jammu and Kashmir (AIR 1970 Supreme Court 1118) in the following words:

Article makes Section 21 of the General Clauses Act applicable for the purpose of interpretation of the Constitution. There is nothing in Article 370 which would exclude the applicability of Section 21 when interpreting the power granted by that Article. The President, therefore, can in exercise of power under Article 370 make orders from time to time. The power to modify in Clause (d) of Article 370 (1) also includes the power to subsequently vary, alter, add to or rescind such an order by reason of the applicability of the rule of interpretation laid down in Section 21 of the General Clauses Act.

Article 370 cannot also be so interpreted that the power of making modifications and exceptions in the orders made under Article 370 (1) (d) should be limited to making minor alterations and should not cover the power to practically abrogate an Article of the Constitution applied in Jammu and Kashmir state.

The legislative history of this Article will also fully support this view. It was because of the special situation existing in Jammu and Kashmir that the Constituent Assembly framing the Constitution decided that the Constitution should not become applicable to Jammu and Kashmir under Article 394, under which it came into effect in the rest of India, and preferred to confer on the President the power to apply the various provisions of the Constitution with exceptions and modifications. It was envisaged that the President would have to take into account the situation existing to the state when applying a provision of the Constitution *and such situations could arise from time to time. There was clearly the possibility that, when applying a particular provision, the situation might demand an exception or modification of the provision applied; but subsequent changes in the situation might justify the rescinding of those modifications or exception.* This could only be brought about by conferring on the President the power of making orders from time to time under Article 370 and this power, must, therefore be held to confer on him by applying the provisions of Section 21 of the general Clauses Act for the interpretation of the Constitution ...

Article 370 (1) (d) is not and cannot just be one way stream. It has been brought into existence so as to invest the Constitution with requisite resilience in order to respond to ground situations warranting solution so that the relationship between the state and Union is placed on an even keel in which aspirations of the people of the state would find satisfactory expression. There is no legal impediment, as is evident from the pronouncements of the Supreme Court in reversing the dilution made to the autonomy of the state. Indeed, none can be urged as causes omissus cannot be read into the constitutional text which must be interpreted to give full and wide meaning to its words for it must endure through generations. The issue in that state is not whether elections should be held or not. An election just for the sake of an election will be a farcical exercise which will fail to carry conviction with the people and therefore, not ensure their participation.

It will be another short-sighted step in pursuit of Centre's obduracy in refusing to deal with a political problem in keeping with the principles of secularism, democracy, federalism and solemn obligations under the Delhi Agreement.

2. Report of the State Autonomy Committee (1999) (Extracts)

The State Government set up a Committee to examine the question of restoration of autonomy to the State of Jammu and Kashmir vide

Government Order No. 1164-GAD of 1996 dated 29-11-1996 with the following composition:—

1. Dr. Karan Singh   ... Chairman (resigned 31.7.97)
2. Sh. Mohi-ud-Din Shah   ... Member (Chairman)
3. Sh. Abdul Ahad Vakil   ...   –do–
4. Sh. Abdul Rahim Rather   ...   –do–
5. Sh. Piyaray Lal Handoo   ...   –do–
6. Sh. Bodh Raj Bali   ...   –do–
7. Molvi Iftikhar Hussain Ansari ...   –do–
8. Kushok Thiksay   ...   –do–
9. Shri Teja Singh   ...   –do–

Terms of Reference

The terms of reference of the Committee are as follows:—

(i) To examine and recommend measures for the restoration of autonomy to the State of Jammu and Kashmir consistent with the Instrument of Accession, the Constitution Application Order, 1950 and the Delhi Agreement of 1952.

(ii) To examine and recommend safeguards that be regarded necessary for incorporation in the Union/State Constitution to ensure that the Constitutional arrangement that is finally evolved in pursuance of the recommendations of this Committee is inviolable.

(iii) To also examine and recommend measures to ensure a harmonious relationship for the future between the State and the Union.

Four features of these terms of reference deserve particularly to be noted. First, implicit in the exercise is acknowledgement of the fact that the State's autonomy, guaranteed by Article 370 of the Constitution of India, was eroded in breach of its provisions, of those of the Instrument of Accession to which Article 370 gave full recognition, of the Constitution (Application to Jammu and Kashmir) Order, made under Article 370, by the President of India on January 26, 1950, extending to the State specified provisions of the Constitution of India which had come into force on the same day, and of the Delhi Agreement of July, 1952. It is this erosion which had necessitated 'the restoration of autonomy' to the State. As we shall point out, till now, 94 of the 97 entries in the Union List have been applied to the State. 26 entries in the Concurrent List have also been applied, 6 more with modifications. Even in 1954 the Concurrent List did not apply at all. The process did not cease. It was accelerated. The Constitutional relationship that was established was contrary to and went far beyond the Delhi Agreement.

Secondly, if this exercise is to be worthwhile, it would be necessary to devise appropriate effective constitutional safeguards against any repetition of that unfortunate phase of erosion in future. Any Constitutional arrangement that is evolved to this end must have finality and be 'inviolable'.

Thirdly, the exercise has a definite limit and a clear objective. It seeks in effect the full enforcement of the historic Delhi Agreement concluded between the Prime Minister of India, Pt. Jawahar Lal Nehru, and the Prime Minister (as he was then called) of the State, Sheikh Mohammad Abdullah, the two foremost architects of the State's accession to the Union of India. Implementing their mutual pledges in that Agreement is, at once, the bottom line and the high ideal we have placed before ourselves.

[...]

Regional diversities are reflected in special provisions with respect to the States of Nagaland (Article 371-A), Sikkim (Article 371-F), Mizoram (Article 371-G) and Arunachal Pradesh (Article 371-H) which confer 'special status' on these States. There are other 'special provisions' with respect to some States concerning certain areas within those States, for example, Article 371 relating to the states of Maharashtra and Gujarat. In respect of Nagaland and Mizoram, Parliament is barred not only from altering religious or social practices but also 'customary law and procedure', 'administration of civil and criminal justice' according to such law, and ownership and transfer of land.

[...]

The Maharaja made an order on October 30, 1947 appointing Sheikh Mohammad Abdullah as 'the Head of the Administration with power to deal with the emergency' and appointed a twenty-three member Emergency Council 'pending the formation of the interim Government'. By a proclamation issued on March 5, 1948 the Maharaja decided 'to replace the Emergency Administration by a popular Interim Government and to provide for its powers, duties and functions, pending the formation of a fully democratic Constitution'.

Sheikh Mohammad Abdullah was appointed Prime Minister. The Council of Ministers was to function 'on the principle of joint responsibility'. It was enjoined to convene 'a National Assembly based upon adult suffrage' to frame a Constitution. The Assembly was to submit the Constitution 'through the Council of Ministers for my acceptance.'

This was a reference to a Constitution for the State. Right from the beginning in 1948, there was no doubt in any quarter that, regardless of the arrangements in respect of other former Indian States, the State of Jammu and Kashmir would have its own Constitution as a member of the Indian Union. Uniquely, the State is the only one to have negotiated the terms of its membership of the Union. The negotiations were spread over five months.

Negotiations on the provisions in the proposed Constitution of India that would embody the terms of the State's membership of the Union began when a conference of the leaders of the National Conference and of the leaders at the Centre was held in Delhi on May 15 and 16, 1949. Pt. Jawahar Lal Nehru recorded the issues discussed in a letter to Sheikh Saheb on 18th May. The State was to have its own Constitution and '*it will be for the Constituent Assembly of the state, when convened, to determine in respect of what other subjects the state may accede.*' On May 27, 1949, a member of its Drafting Committee, Sir N. Gopalaswamy Ayyangar moved an amendment to the Assembly's Rules empowering 'the Ruler of Kashmir on the advice of his Prime Minister' to nominate the State's four representatives to the Constituent Assembly of India. The State's legislature, the Praja Sabha, had not met since April, 1947 and was now 'dead'. The National Assembly of the State was yet to be elected. On June 16, 1949 Sheikh Mohammad Abdullah, Mirza Mohammad Afzal Beg, Maulana Mohammad Saeed Masoodi and Moti Ram Baigra took the pledge and signed the Register of Members of the Constituent Assembly of India.

It must be mentioned at the outset in all fairness that the texts of Sheikh Mohammad Abdullah's letters of October 12 and 15, 1949 are not available, whereas those of Mr. Ayyangar and Sardar Vallabhbhai Patel's letter to him and to each other, are. On October 12, Sheikh Saheb complained to Mr. Ayyangar, as he recalled in his letter of 17th October, that the draft Article 306-A (with modifications, the present Article 370) which he had given to Mr. M.A. Beg 'failed to implement the pledges given to us' and was, therefore, unacceptable. Two meetings followed on October 15. After the first, Mr. Ayyangar wrote to Sardar Patel enclosing his draft of the Article. It did not provide a finality to further acquisition of power by the Centre by stipulating that the concurrence of the State Government to such acquisition shall be ratified by the Constituent Assembly.

Mr. Ayyangar presented another draft later on October 15, which drew a protest from Patel and rejection by Sheikh Saheb, both, on 16th October. Mr. Ayyangar prepared yet another draft in consultation with Kashmir's representatives. It was finalized on the afternoon of October 16, 1949. On the assurance that the agreed draft would be moved, Mr. Beg withdrew his own amendment. Sheikh Mohammad Abdullah recorded the agreement in another letter of 16th October and thanked Ayyangar for his pains.

On October 16, 1949 a 'Final Draft' of Article 306-A was settled between Mr. N. Gopalaswamy Ayyangar and Mirza Mohammad Afzal Beg and Mr. M.A. Shahmiri. It read thus:

Final Draft of Article 306-A [Jammu and Kashmir] as settled between the Hon'ble Shri N. Gopalaswamy Ayyangar on the one side and Messers Beg and Shahmiri on the other on October 16, 1949

306-A (1) Notwithstanding anything contained in this Constitution:—

    (a) the provisions of Article 211-A of the Constitution shall not apply in relation to the State of Jammu and Kashmir;

    (b) the power of Parliament to make laws for the State shall be limited to

        (i) those matters in the Union List and the Concurrent List which, in consultation with the Government of State, are declared by the President to correspond to matters specified in the Instrument of Accession governing the accession of the State to the Dominion of India as the matters with respect to which the Dominion Legislature may make laws for the State; and

    (ii) such other matters in the said Lists as, with the concurrence of the Government of the State, the resident may by order specify;

Explanation:—For the purposes of this Article, the Government of the State means the person for the time being recognized by the Union as the Maharaja of Jammu and Kashmir acting on the advice of the Council of Ministers appointed under the Maharaja's Proclamation dated the 5th Mach, 1948.

    (c) the provisions of Article 1 of this Constitution shall apply in relation to the state;

    (d) such of the other provisions of this Constitution and subject to such exceptions and modifications shall apply in relation to the State as the President may by order specify:

Provided that no such order which relates to the matters specified in the Instrument of Accession of the State aforesaid shall be issued except in consultation with the Government of State:—

Provided further that no such order which relate to matters other than those referred to in the preceding proviso shall be issued except with the concurrence of that Government;

(2) If the concurrence of the Government of the State referred to in sub-clause (b) (ii) or in the second proviso of sub-clause (d) of clause (1) was given before the Constituent Assembly for the purpose of framing the Constitution of the State is convened, it shall be placed before such Assembly for such decision as it may take thereon;

(3) Notwithstanding anything in the preceding clauses of this article, the President may, by public notification, declare that this article shall cease to be operative or shall be operative only with such exceptions and modifications and from such date as he may specify:—

Provided that the recommendation of the Constituent Assembly of the State shall be necessary before the President issues such a notification.

This draft was finally agreed on October 16, 1949. What happened next day, October 17, 1949 in the Constituent Assembly was recorded immediately thereafter that very day by Sheikh Saheb in a letter to Mr. Gopalaswamy Ayyangar.

This morning when we expected the final draft, which had appeared in the List of Amendments circulated by the Secretary of the Constituent Assembly, to come up before the Assembly, you and Maulana (Azad) Sahib came to me and asked me if I could accept an important change in the Explanation to Sub-Clause (b) of Clause (1) of the draft Article 306-A, as appearing in the list of Amendments. After careful consideration of the proposed amendment in the Explanation, my colleagues and I told you both in the lobby that it was not possible for us to accept this change in the final draft and you and Maulana Sahib left us while we were still discussing the matter in the lobby amongst ourselves, the draft Article 306-A was moved by you in the Constituent Assembly, and, when part of your speech was over, we were told by someone that the draft Article had been taken up by the Assembly, and, therefore, we took our seats in the Assembly Hall. We could not conceive that any amendment in the final draft, as circulated in the List of Amendments, would be made by you without conveying your final decision in the matter to us, and so we took it for granted that the final draft Article 306-A was presented before the Assembly in the form in which it had our consent; and, therefore, when it was passed by the Assembly, we did not take part in the debate. While Maulana Sahib and you came to us to discuss the matter with us in the lobby, I clearly told you that in the event of any change in the finalized draft Article 306-A, we should be at liberty to move the amendment, of which notice had been given by Mr. Beg and his two other colleagues and which had been withdrawn on the express assurance given by you yesterday. In these circumstances, it was not possible for us to move any amendment and we did not get an occasion to express our views on the matter before the open House.

Sheikh Saheb threatened to resign from the Constituent Assembly. Mr. Ayyangar replied on October 18. He did not deny that the draft had been unilaterally hanged. 'It is true that after having unsuccessfully attempted, along with Maulana Azad, to persuade you to agree willingly to the substitution of the words "for the time being in office" for the word "appointed", I did move the article with that amendment after obtaining the permission of the President to do so.' He argued that it was 'a trivial change' in response to the desire expressed by a large number of the leading Members of the House. The Prime Minister Pt. Nehru was abroad then. Mr. Ayyangar himself recorded that 'the words in the Explanation as agreed to between us are 'Council of Ministers appointed under the Maharaja's Proclamation dated March 5, 1948'. The words appearing in the Article as passed yesterday are 'the Council of Ministers for the time being in office under the Maharaja's Proclamation dated March 5, 1948'. His plea that 'the change of words does not constitute the slightest change in sense or substance' was wrong. Under the agreed Explanation, Sheikh Saheb's dismissal in 1953 would have been a Constitutional impossibility.

In his letter to the Prime Minister Pt. Jawahar Lal Nehru on November 3, 1949 on his return from the United States of America, Sardar Patel also admitted that the draft 'was modified to cover not merely the first Ministry so appointed but any subsequent Ministries which may be appointed under that proclamation.'

The Constituent Assembly adopted the Constitution of India on November 26, 1949 (CAD; Vol. 12, p. 995). It repealed the Government of India Act, 1935. Article 394 provided that most of its provisions would come into force from January 26, 1950. On November 25, 1949 the Maharaja of Jammu and Kashmir made a proclamation declaring that 'the Constitution of India shortly to be adopted by the Constituent Assembly of India shall in so far as it is applicable to the State of Jammu and Kashmir, govern the Constitutional relationship between this State and the contemplated Union of India. ....'[1] On January 26, 1950 the President of India made the first Constitution (Application to Jammu and Kashmir) Order, 1950[2] under Article 370 of the Constitution of India. It conformed strictly to the Instrument of Accession. [...]

The White Paper on Indian States made an important exposition of the Constitutional changes in para 221 at page 113 in Chapter XI entitled 'Indian States under the New Constitution'. Referring to Article 370 it said 'Steps will be taken for the purpose of convening a Constituent Assembly which will go into these matters in detail and when it comes to a decision on them, it will make a recommendation to the President who will either abrogate Article 370 or direct that it shall apply with such modifications and exceptions as he may specify.' Thus, the State's Constituent Assembly's decision was to mark a finality to the exercise of the President's powers under Article 370.

On July 29, 1952 Sheikh Sahib wrote to Pt. Nehru to inform him that the Constituent Assembly proposed to elect the State's Head of

[1] White Paper on Indian States, Government of India, Ministry of States, New Delhi, 1950, p. 371.

[2] See Appendix IV.

the State of August 16, 1952 and he wished that the necessary order under Article 370 should be issued by the President in time to make it possible. [...]

At its fourth session on August 20, 1952 the State's Constituent Assembly passed a detailed Resolution in implementation of its Resolution of June 10, 1952 on the Head of the State.

The President of India persisted with his objections till as late as November 7, 1952 insisting that the Constituent Assembly 'should come to a decision on all matters relating to the State's Constitution. ...'³ The Prime Minister of India was in bind. He had agreed with President's views on the legality but termination of the royal dynasty was also part of the Delhi Agreement. He was under pressure from Sheikh Saheb and his colleagues. Ptandit Nehru, therefore, wrote to the President on the same day, November 7, 1952: 'I can only repeat what I have said above that we have considered every aspect of this question and come to certain conclusions which have to be given effect to now. We cannot reopen six month's discussion'.

Accordingly, on November 15, 1952 Constitution Order No. 44 was made by the President under Article 370:

In exercise of the powers conferred by this article the President, on the recommendation of the Constituent Assembly of the State of Jammu and Kashmir, declare that, as from the 17th day of November, 1952 the said Article 370 shall be operative with the modification that for the explanation in clause (1) thereof, the following explanation is substituted namely:—

Explanation—For the purposes of this article, the Government of the State means the person for the time being recognized by the President on the recommendation of the Legislative Assembly of the State as the Sadar-i-Riyasat of Jammu and Kashmir, acting on the advice of the Council of Ministers of the State for the time being in office.⁴

[...]

It is against this background that the Delhi Agreement was concluded after prolonged discussions; first, from June 14 to 20, 1952 and, next,

³ V. Choudhary, Vol. 20, page 395, footnote 3.
⁴ Ministry of Law Order No. CO 44, dated the 15th November, 1952.

from July 20 to 24, 1952.[5] Its terms were announced by Pt. Jawahar Lal Nehru in Lok Sabha on July 24, 1952[6] and in the Rajya Sabha on August 5, 1952.[7]

The terms of the agreement were explained to the Constituent Assembly of Jammu and Kashmir by the State's Prime Minister Sheikh Mohammad Abdullah on August 11, 1952.[8]

Both leaders provided the background and highlighted the significance of the agreement. Pt. Nehru told the Lok Sabha:

The position since the Constitution was framed is thus contained in the Article 370 and the President's Order following it. Article 370 was obviously of a transitional nature, and it allowed the President to make any additions to it, any variations to it, later on, the object being that if any change or addition was required, we need not have to go through the cumbrous process of amending our Constitution, but the President was given the authority to amend it in the sense of adding subject, part of a subject, whatever, *it was to the other subjects, in regard to Kashmir. But in Article 370 the old principle was repeated and emphasized that all these changes or any change, required the approval of the Constituent Assembly of the Jammu and Kashmir State.*

When this was put down in our Constitution, there was no Constituent Assembly of Jammu and Kashmir State, but we envisaged it. We had envisaged it for a long time. *And if the Constituent Assembly was not there, then it required the consent of the Jammu and Kashmir Government. So that was the position.*[9]

The implication is plain. Additional subjects could be acquired by the Centre only with the approval of the State's Constituent Assembly.

Briefly the Delhi Agreement covered ten points. It was agreed that residuary powers would continue to vest in the State as provided in Article 370; within the ambit of Indian citizenship, the State legislature

[5] S. Gopal (Editor), *Selected Works of Jawahar Lal Nehru*, Vol. 19, p. 211.

[6] Parliamentary Debates, Lok Sabha, Official Report Part II; Vol. III No. 16, Cols 4501–21.

[7] Rajya Sabha Debates, Vol. I; Nos 24–31 (July 28–August 5, 1952), Cols 2970, 2995.

[8] For full text of Sheikh Saheb's Speech see Appendix VI.

[9] For relevant extracts from Pt. Jawahar Lal Nehru's speech in the Lok Sabha on July 24, 1952 see Appendix VII.

would have the power to regulate the rights and privileges of permanent residents or 'State Subjects' as defined in a 1927 State Order, the Fundamental Rights Chapter of the Indian Constitution be applied to the State with modifications and exceptions such as enabling transfer of land to the tiller without payment of compensation; the jurisdiction of the Supreme Court would extend to the State; the State flag would not be a rival to the national tricolour which would occupy a supremely distinctive place in the State, the power to grant reprieve and commute sentences would vest in the President of India; with the abolition of hereditary rulership, the Head of the State of Jammu and Kashmir shall be recognized by the President on the recommendations of the Legislative Assembly of the State; a financial arrangement between the State and the Union be evolved; with regard to emergency powers, Article 352 be modified to provide for its promulgation in case of external aggression but in case of internal disturbance only at the request of or with the concurrence of the State Government; and the Election Commission will conduct elections to Parliament and to the offices of President and Vice-President.

During the course of negotiations, as had become necessary after the presentation of the interim report of the Basic Principles Committee in the circumstances referred to herein before, certain agreements were arrived at, details of which were placed before the House by Janab Sheikh Saheb on 11th of August, 1952. He said:

The Government of India held the view that the fact that J&K State was the Constituent Unit of the Union of India led inevitably to certain consequences in regard to certain matters, namely (a) Residuary Powers (b) Citizenship (c) Fundamental Rights (d) Supreme Court (e) National Flag (f) The President of India (g) The Headship of the State (h) Financial Integration (i) Emergency Provisions and (j) conduct of Election to Houses of Parliament.

Sheikh Saheb informed the House about the agreement arrived at in respect of each of them as follows:

Residuary Powers

It was agreed that while under the present Indian Constitution the Residuary Powers vested with the Centre in respect of all States other than Jammu and Kashmir, in the case of our State they vested in the Article 352. To meet the State's point of view it was therefore decided that Article 352 might be accepted with addition of the following words at the end of the first paragraph: 'But in regard to internal disturbance at the request or with the concurrence of the Government of the State'.

It was also agreed that the whole matter of application of Article 353, 354, 358 and 359 will be further examined.

Conduct of Elections to Houses of Parliament

Article 324 of the Indian Constitution was already applicable so far as it relates to elections to Parliament and to the offices of the President and the Vice-President of India.

This is how the leader of the Constituent Assembly Sheikh Mohammad Abdullah introduced the Delhi Agreement to the Assembly which was adopted unanimously on 19th August, 1952.

Consequent thereupon, the Drafting Committee of the State Constituent Assembly formed to work out and prepare proposals regarding termination of the hereditary rulership in the State presented its report.

Resolution for adoption by the House was introduced in the following words:—

[...]

This resolution was unanimously adopted after a formal amendment of changing the words, President of Union in sub-clause (1) of para 1 of the Resolution to President of India. Bill effecting the change based on this Resolution was introduced and passed on 10th November, 1952. This Act became Jammu and Kashmir Constitution Amendment Act of 2009.

[...]

Constitution (Application to Jammu and Kashmir) Order 1954 and Beginning of Erosion of the State Autonomy

On February 11, 1954 Syed Mir Qasim presented to the Constituent Assembly the report of the Drafting Committee. The annexure to the

Report indicated 'in detail provisions of the Constitution of India which generally correspond to Defence, Foreign Affairs and Communications and such other matters as are considered essential concomitants of the fact of accession.'

On February 15, 1954 the Constituent Assembly adopted the following resolution unanimously: Resolved that

(a) having adopted the report of the drafting committee this day, the 15th February, 1954 and (b) having thus given its concurrence to the application of the provisions for the Constitution of India in the manner indicated in the Annexure to the aforesaid report this Assembly authorise the Government of the State to forward a copy of the said Annexure to the Government of India for appropriate action.

This resolution was defective in form. It was not addressed to the President, as it should have been. But it was a substantial compliance with the requirement of a recommendation to him under Article 370. On May 14, 1954 the President made thereunder C.O. 48 the Constitution (Application to Jammu and Kashmir) Order, 1954. Its preamble says that it was made 'with the concurrence of the Government of the State of Jammu and Kashmir'. Once the Constituent Assembly was convened, the State Government lost the power to accord any such concurrence. However, the order may be said to be valid in so far as it conforms to the Annexure to the report of the Constituent Assembly's Drafting Committee only, and, no further. The Order of 1954 does conform to the Annexure to the Report. This Order superseded the Order of 1950 and has been treated as the parent order to which subsequently amendments were made by Orders by the President under Article 370. [...]

The entries in the Union List-I in the Seventh Schedule as applied to the State by this Order did not, unfortunately, conform strictly to the Instrument of Accession and the Delhi Agreement. However, the State List as well as the Concurrent List were entirely excluded. The State's right to all residuary subjects other than the ones in the Union List which were conferred on the Union was fully accepted. [...]

It will be necessary to see how things had been allowed to go adrift after August 1953 till 1965 and after 1965 till 1975. It will be interesting to note that after inauguration of the Indian National Congress in the State when it substituted the National Conference and made it a branch of the National party with Sheikh Sahib and his colleagues still in jail and later facing alleged cases of conspiracy and treason, how maximum assault was launched upon Kashmir's special position, its autonomous character, its sovereign character and all this only to realise in 1975 that things had gone out of gear and people had lost whatever faith and confidence they had in the democratic relationship. Issues deferred at the time of Delhi Agreement could not be negotiated any further till the Constituent Assembly itself was flawed by putting the real leadership of the people behind the bars arbitrarily and unconstitutionally. Even casual examination of the first Constitution (Application to Jammu and Kashmir) Order, 1954 that came into existence after these traumatic changes of 1953 will show that a path different from the one aspired to be chosen by the people of Kashmir State under the leadership of Sheikh Mohammad Abdullah was far different from the one envisaged by the Instrument of Accession and all that had gone with it. Jurisdiction of Union Parliament was extended from three subjects—Defence, External Affairs and Communications, to almost all the subjects in the Union List. This constituted a first encroachment on the powers of legislation of the State by widening of those of the Union. We have seem the entries of the List 1 of Seventh Schedule which were made applicable by the Constitution Application Order of 1950 and also the entries which were not applicable to the State of Jammu and Kashmir. The Constitution Application Order of 1954 reversed the Order and made Union Parliament capable of legislating in respect of almost all the entries in the List, of course, with some exceptions and modifications. While the 1950 Order made some parts besides Articles I and 370 applicable making exceptions and modifications also, 1954 Order made many more parts applicable with or without modifications. The important Article made thus applicable was Article 3 in which a proviso had been added for its modified application. The proviso required that 'no bill for increasing or diminishing the area of Jammu and Kashmir or for altering the name of boundaries of the State shall be introduced in Parliament without the consent of the Legislature of the State.' Part II of the Constitution of India now became applicable. [...]

We have noticed above that in the eagerness to create an image of cementing closer relations, what followed 1954 is a series of Constitution (Application to J&K) Orders numbering 42 till now which were not conceived at any point of time either in 1950 or in 1952 or even later in May, 1954. Among the changes brought about the most important were in restricting the powers of legislature of the State, extension of powers of the Union Parliament, application to the State of financial provisions of the Constitution of India, provisions relating to emergency, All India Services, superintendence, direction and control of elections of the State Legislature and several other matters.

The position having been so radically altered can be put in the following manner so as to indicate actual State–Union relationship which had emerged as a result of changes brought about:—

(a) Almost all entries in the Union List are applicable to the State of Jammu and Kashmir with the result that Union Parliament's power to legislate extends to matters even beyond the three subjects on which the accession had originally been agreed upon. The list has gone far beyond 20 items of the list attached to the Instrument of Accession or even the Schedules to 1950 Order.

(b) Concurrent List of legislation in essence is applicable even in regard to welfare legislation and essentially local matters.

(c) Most of the provisions about one of the wings of the State namely the Judiciary are now derivable or definable from the Country's Constitution rather than the Constitution of the State.

(d) Provision relating to All India Services is now applicable to the State.

(e) All the matters under Finance, Trade and Commerce are now applicable. Even the rudiments of financial autonomy have completely been swept away.

(f) Even the field of residuary legislation in the matter of law and order has been curtailed so far as the State is concerned and Entry 97 of the Union List too has been made applicable in curiously modified form to the detriment of the principle of political autonomy.

(g) All emergency powers including those in Article 356 and that too in their un-amended form and retrograde shape are applicable to the State and their misuse during the last eight to nine years has proved beyond doubt that apprehensions entertained in 1950's have come out to be true.

(h) Special provisions of Article 249 dealing with the Parliament's power of legislation in the State List have been extended to the State of Jammu and Kashmir quite surreptitiously in a brazen and clandestine manner by misinterpreting and misusing Article 370.

(i) Superintendence, direction and control of local elections now vests with the Central Election Commission.

Besides, some changes of far-reaching consequences including that of altering the mode of appointment of the Head of the State were effected in the Constitution of the State. The extent and the nature of autonomy which has been left with the State as of now can be seen from the following table:—

I. Total No. of Articles	No. of Articles applied	Balance
395	260	135*

*These relate to matters under Part VI of the Constitution of India which pertains to matters concerning the Executive, Legislature and High Courts of States of the Union and provisions whereof are identical to the provisions of the Constitution of Jammu and Kashmir.

II. Total No. of entries In the Union List	Entries applied	Balance
97	94	3*

*Entries 8, 9 and 34 relating to CBI Jurisdiction, preventive detention connected with defence matters, and Courts of wards for the estates of Rulers of Indian States respectively.

III. Total No. of entries in the Concurrent List	Entries applied	Balance
47	26	21*

*Entries 3, 5, 6, 7, 8, 9, 10, 14, 15, 17, 20, 21, 27, 28, 29, 31, 32, 37, 38, 41 and 44.

*Indicates provisions hitherto not applied to the State.

These entries relate mostly to matters of social legislation, charitable institutions, relief and rehabilitation of displaced persons, transfer of property etc.

IV.	Total No. of Schedules	No. of Schedules applied	Balance
	12	7	5*

*Schedule 5	Control of Scheduled Areas and S.T.
Schedule 6	Administration of Tribal Areas.
Schedule 10	Disqualification on grounds of defection except in so far it relates to members of Parliament.
Schedule 11	Powers of Panchayats (new provision of the Indian Constitution vide Seventy-third Amendment Act, 1992).
Schedule 12	Power and responsibilities of Municipalities (new provision of the Indian Constitution vide Seventy-fourth Amendment Act, 1992).

It is abundantly clear, therefore, that from 1953 onwards, especially in sixties, the process of erosion of the State autonomy was so rapid and on such a massive scale that entire Article 370 of the Constitution of India which was supposed to guarantee and preserve the special status of the State in the Indian Union was emptied of its substantive content with the result that the State's jurisdiction over the matters as envisaged by the Instrument of Accession of October, 1947 and the Delhi Agreement of 1952 was gradually diminished and systematically transferred to the Union.

Far from enjoying a special status, as Article 370 envisaged, the State was put in a status inferior to that of other States. One illustration suffices to demonstrate that. Parliament had to amend the Constitution four times, by the 59th, 64th, 67th, 68th Constitution Amendments to extend President's rule imposed in Punjab on May 11, 1987. For the State of Jammu and Kashmir, the same result was accomplished by executive orders under Article 370.

The Union Home Minister, Mr. Gulzari Lal Nanda said on December 4, 1964 that Article 370 could well be used to serve as a

'Tunnel in the wall' in order to increase the Centre's powers. This was diametrically contrary to the clear intent underlying, and the objective of, Article 370.

Another gross case illustrates the extent of misuse of Article 370. On July 30, 1986 the President made an Order under Article 370 extending to the State Article 249 of the Constitution in order to empower Parliament to legislate even on a matter in the State List on the strength of a Rajya Sabha resolution. 'Concurrence' to this was given by the Centre's own appointee, Governor Jagmohan. (*Indian Express*, August 17, 1986).

This is how C.O. 129 was made on July 30, 1986. It said that in Article 249, in clause (1) for the words 'any matter enumerated in the State List specified in the resolution', the words 'any matter specified in the resolution being a matter which is not enumerated in the Union List or in the Concurrent List' shall be substituted. This was made 'with the concurrence of the Government of the State of Jammu and Kashmir' when the State was under Governor's rule and no popular Government existed. This is a clear nullity.

Successive State Governments had in the past accorded their 'concurrence' for various reasons and under various political compulsions. No State would otherwise willingly accept curbs on its autonomy. [...]

Accordingly, it is recommended as under:—

(i) That the word 'temporary' be deleted from the title of part XXI of the Constitution of India; and

(ii) That the word 'temporary' occurring in the heading of Article 370 be substituted by the word 'special'.

Legislative Relations (Part XI)

We have at length described that breath and soul of State Union relationship initially was the Instrument of Accession and later this was replaced by provisions of the India Constitution as and when these became applicable. The Instrument of Accession was to be the basis. The Instrument conceded powers of legislation to the Federal Union in the matter of Defence, External Affairs and Communications and vide clause (3) this Instrument itself specified matters in the 'Schedule' thereto with respect to which the Dominion legislature could make laws for the State of Jammu and Kashmir. These scheduled matters were 20 in number and were grouped under sub-heads.

(a) Defence
(b) External Affairs
(c) Communications
(d) Ancillary

Dominion Legislature, therefore, could legislate with respect to the State of Jammu and Kashmir in respect of matters specified in the schedule to the Instrument of Accession.

Article 1 and 370 became applicable to our State straightway and our State became part of the scheme of distribution of legislative powers enshrined in the Constitution of India. Seventh Schedule to the Constitution itemised the legislative field of operation in the following manner:—

List I   Union List
List II   State List
List III   Concurrent List

With the enforcement of Indian Constitution on 26-1-1950 and simultaneously application of Article 370 to the State of Jammu and Kashmir, Presidential Order of 1950 came to be issued on this very date. With its application relevant Union List items with omissions, exceptions and modifications became applicable from that very date. This was consistent with original terms of accession, conceding powers of legislation to Union Parliament in matters on which State sovereign had acceded to the Union.

The Union thereafter could legislate on items included in the Schedule to 1950 Order. The items which were excluded from the ambit of legislative power of Parliament in respect of the State of Jammu and Kashmir were as under:—

7, 8, 23, 24, 32, 34, 35, 36, 37, 38, 40, 42, to 71, 78 to 92 and 97.

The entries 22 and 76 were applied with modification. A casual examination of these would show that these were rightly not applied being beyond the border line of ceded items of Defence, External Affairs, Communications and Ancillary.

At this stage it would be pertinent to mention that Article 246 in its original form clearly laid down that in relation to the State of Jammu and Kashmir reference to clauses (2) and (3) in clause (1) of the Article and clauses (2), (3) and (4) of the Article shall not apply. This made existence of State and Concurrent Lists only a matter of theoretical interest for our State. All that was yielded in Union List for federal legislation was thus known; rest of the powers were of the State and State alone. Such a decision was quite in keeping with the true spirit and context of federal polity. This is particularly so when application of Articles 248 and 249 was also excluded, the two having been completely omitted from the application to our State.

Their non-application ensured that residuary powers of legislation remained with the State unimpaired and Parliament could not legislate about any State matter even when there would have been a situation envisaged by Article 253.

It is note-worthy that all the entries made applicable particularly the substituted entry 97 read with modified Article 248 were not even remotely connected with Defence, External Affairs and Communications, nor can they in entirety or otherwise be regarded as ancillary to matters covered by these three subjects.

Changes from 1954 onwards, particularly in sixties were so rapid that things started changing even beyond recognition. Encroachment on state jurisdiction was obvious, thereby reducing the State autonomy to a mockery.

Recommendations

In the legislative field, therefore, it is recommended as under:—

(a) Matters in the Union List not connected with the three subjects of Defence, External Affairs and Communications and/or ancillary thereto but made applicable should be excluded from their application to the State.

(b) All modifications made in Article 246 in its application to the State subsequent to the 1950 Order should be rescinded.

(c) Articles 248, 249, 250 and 251 whether applied in original or substituted/modified form should be omitted in relation to the State.

(d) As in 1950 and 1954, List II (State) and List III (Concurrent) of the Seventh Schedule should not be applicable to the State.

(e) Article 254 be restored to the position it had in its application to our State in 1954.

(f) Articles 262 and 263 which were not applicable under 1950 Order but were subsequently extended to the State should cease to apply.

[...]

Part XVIII: Emergency Provisions
(*Articles 352 to 360*)

The following should be added to Clause 6 of Article 352.

Recommendations

(a) 'provided that this request for concurrence of the Government of the State shall be subject to whatever decision the State Assembly may take within two months of declaration of emergency and failing any such decision, the proclamation of emergency shall be deemed to have been revoked.'

(b) Sub-clause (b) of clause (6) of this Article should be deleted.

(c) Articles 355, 356, 357, 358, 359 and 360 should be made non-applicable to the State of Jammu and Kashmir as was the position in 1954.

Part III: Fundamental Rights
(*Articles 12 to 35*)

Recommendations

This Part should be deleted. A separate chapter on Fundamental Rights needs to be included in the Jammu and Kashmir Constitution. Situation where Directive Principles do not apply and Fundamental Rights apply is not a happy one. Directive Principles in the State Constitution apply but in the absence of a provision these can hardly mean anything to Fundamental Rights which are enshrined in the Union Constitution. Fundamental Rights chapter in the State Constitution would add weight and worth to the organic law of the land and give the citizens satisfaction of even testing worth of Directive Principles for Legislation and for governance according to letter and spirit of law.

Part V: The Union *(Articles 52 to 151)*

Very few Articles from this Part were made applicable in 1954 Order but the situation was changed with the passage of Constitution (Application to J&K) Order, 1960 and thereafter. Normally there can be no dispute now with the extended jurisdiction of the Supreme Court over matters in regard to our State, but it has got to be recorded that this aspect of State–Union relationship was not settled at the time of Delhi-Agreement of 1952 and after the events of 1953 quick decisions were forced upon the flawed Constituent Assembly followed by a number of Constitution (Application to J&K) Orders. The position which ultimately has emerged is that the State of J&K has been accorded the same status as the rest of the rest of the States except for the above form of Articles 133 and 134 applied to the State. The judiciary of India has been unitary in character during the British rule and it remained so under the new Constitution of India adopted in 1950. Jammu and Kashmir too became part of it, notwithstanding the fact that strong views to have judicial autonomy were expressed during negotiations for Delhi-Agreement, 1952. In any case divergent views were recorded.

The State had at that time a High Court whose judgements were subject to appeal/review before His Highness, advised in his judicial functions by a Board of Judicial Advisors consisting of eminent jurists/knowledgeable persons. That has not to be and reopening that chapter may not sound appropriate now except, of course, where adopting of provisions of the Union Judiciary for the State have in a way infringed upon the corresponding provisions of the State Constitution in regard to the State High Court.

Recommendations

(a) Article 72 (1) (c), 72 (3), 133, 134, 135, 136, 138, 145 (1) (c) and 151 (2) should be made non-applicable to the State as was the position in 1950 Order.

(b) Article 149, 150 and 151 should apply to the State in the form in which they were in 1954.

Part VI: *(Articles 152 to 237)*

Article 124 (4) of the Constitution of India mandates that a Supreme Court Judge shall not be removed from his office except by an Order of the President passed after an address by each House of Parliament supported by a majority of the total membership of that House and by a majority of not less than two thirds of the members of that House present and voting, has been presented to the President in the same session for such removal on the ground of proved misbehavior or incapacity. Article 218 has in the course of time been applied to the J&K State. The position as it obtained prior C.O. 60 was that under the State Constitution, the removal of a judge of the High Court by the President for proved misbehaviour or incapacity could be on the basis of an address for removal supported by a majority of the total membership of each House of Legislature of the State and by the majority of not less than two thirds of the members present and voting. But after the aforesaid application Order of 1960, the power to pass an address for such removal vests with the Parliament in accordance with Article 124 (4). Part VII of the State's Constitution deals with the State High Court. The Part starts with section 93 (Constitution of High Court) and ends with Section 108 (Officers and Servants of the High Court). Of these, we have Sec. 95 (appointment and tenure of office of judges) and Sec. 99 (Resignation and Removal of a judge of the High Court). The aforementioned provision about removal till 1959 was sub section (2) of section 99 of the State Constitution. The Constitution of Jammu and Kashmir (First Amendment) Act. 1959 vide its section 4 deleted this provision and the question of removal of a judge for proved misconduct or incapacity was left to be taken care of as in the rest of the country by resort to procedure in section 124 Clause (4) thereof. This was so vide Constitution (Application to J&K) Order No. 60 of 1960.

All provisions about High Court having been retained in the State Constitution including one about administrative expenses, salaries, allowances and pensions continuing to remain a charge upon consolidated fund of the State, deletion of the above provision regarding removal by means of an address being the duty, right and obligation of State Legislature and not Parliament in terms of Section 124 (4) is, to say the least, not justifiable. Article 218 conceded this right in respect of other High Courts to Parliament. It is because all other provisions like 93 to 108 of our State Constitution are in their case part of the Union Constitution itself. We would, therefore, recommend the following in this regard:—

Recommendations

(i) Article 218 be omitted in its application to the State. That would enable the State Legislature to re-enact the provisions as they existed in sub section (2) and (3) of Section 99 of the State Constitution before the enforcement of J&K Constitution (First Amendment) Act of 1959.

(ii) Articles 220, 222 and 226 should also be omitted in their application to J&K State.

[...]

Part XIV: Services under the Union and the States (Articles 308–323)

Article 308 excluded application of this Part to our State. There is hardly any federation in the world where such provisions as those contained in Article 312 and legislative enactments thereunder are envisaged. These were not applicable to the State even in 1954 but have been made applicable thereafter.

Notwithstanding seemingly and attractive proposition one can say without any fear of contradiction that it has dwarfed local talent and made it difficult for local youth to aspire to compete for key civil posts on competitive basis. The weak-kneed attempt to organize Kashmir Civil Service is neither here nor there and increasing inflow of All India Services has meant pretty little in the field for which the services were apparently conceived. No imperial model of civil services in central cadre can be or could be a substitute for what the local youth could be expected to have i.e. local patriotic feeling and passionate attachment for the service of those among whom they live. Ever since the application of these provisions of the Indian Constitution to our state the number of direct recruit from the State has been negligible. The problem has attained so unpleasant a shape, even in the national context, that demands of greater number of promotees from local services all over the country have assumed alarming proportions.

Recommendations

It is, therefore, recommended that in Article 312, the brackets and words '(including the State of Jammu and Kashmir)' inserted by the Constitution (Application to J&K) Order 1958 be omitted. [...]
[...]

Part XX

Constitution (Application to J&K) Second Amendment Order, 1975 (C.O. 101) the State Legislature had unfettered powers to amend it. But vide this Order Clause (4) was added to Article 368 of the Indian Constitution in its application to our State which read as under:—

(4) No law made by the Legislature of the State of Jammu and Kashmir seeking to make any change in or in the effect of any provision of the Constitution of Jammu and Kashmir relating to:—

    (a) appointment, powers, functions, duties, emoluments, allowances, privileges or immunities of the Governor; or

    (b) superintendent, direction and control of elections by the Election Commission of India, eligibility for inclusion in the electoral rolls without discrimination, adult suffrage and composition of the Legislative Council, being matters specified in sections 138, 139 and 50 of the Constitution of Jammu and Kashmir shall have any effect unless such law has, after having been reserved for the consideration of the President, received his assent.

The addition of this clause in the Indian Constitution has restricted the power of the State Legislature to amend its own Constitution. This uncalled for clog on the constituent powers of State Legislature needs to be removed lock, stock, and barrel.

Recommendations

It is therefore recommended that:—

    (i) clause (4) of Article 368 added vide C.O. 101 be deleted;

    (ii) clause (2) of Article 368 should apply with the proviso already introduced by 1954 Order and Clause (1) thereof which was not in existence in 1954 and was introduced in 1971 should remain omitted in its application to the State.

Part XXII: *(Schedules First to Twelve)*

The Indian Constitution has 12 schedules only some of which apply to our State with or without modifications relatable to some of the Articles of the Constitution of India. Each Schedule which is applicable to the State of Jammu and Kashmir being fathered by a specific Article in the Constitution of the country will naturally suffer modification, changes/substitution depending upon what that article contains in regard to its application to the State of Jammu and Kashmir.

Seventh Schedule

Seventh Schedule derives its character and quality from what Article 246 of the Constitution reads like. Its corresponding quality in respect of Jammu and Kashmir State naturally will depend upon the form and the content that Article 246 of the Constitution of India will assume in its relation to the State of Jammu and Kashmir. In 1950 Article 246 of the Constitution of India had one character and quality/content in its application to the State of Jammu and Kashmir and that was reflected in the number of entries in the Union List in the Seventh Schedule in their application to the State of Jammu and Kashmir. Later on, this Article suffered changes and consequently various entries in the Union List and the Concurrent List also suffered radical changes.

Recommendations

It is recommended that:—

(a) entries in the Union List which were applied to the State by 1950 Application Order should continue and all other entries made applicable to the State by subsequent orders should be omitted;

(b) Concurrent List was not applicable under 1950 Order and it was also agreed in the Delhi Agreement that this should not apply to the State. Hence all subsequent orders applying various entries from this list should be rescinded.

In sum, it is recommended that consistent with the above, requisite changes as may become necessary consequent upon change in the Articles of the Constitution of India in their application to the State of Jammu and Kashmir as a result of this report be effected in the Schedules concerned.

Changes Required in the State Constitution

In view of what has been stated in Chapter XI ante, this Committee recommends the repeal of:—

   (i) The Constitution of Jammu and Kashmir (First Amendment) Act, 1959 relating to superintendent, direction and control of elections to the State Legislature and provisions relating to the State High Court; and

  (ii) The Constitution of Jammu and Kashmir (Sixth Amendment) Act, 1965 relating to the mode of appointment and nomenclature of the Head of the State and nomenclature of the head of the Executive.

Summary of Recommendations

1. Temporary, Transitional and Special Provisions (Part XXI)

   (i) The word 'Temporary' be deleted from the title of part XXI of the Constitution of India and the word 'temporary' occurring in the heading of Article 370 be substituted by the word 'special'.

2. Legislative Relations (Part XI)

   (a) Matters in the Union List not connected with the three subjects of Defence, External Affairs and Communications and/or Ancillary thereto but made applicable should be excluded from their application to the State.

   (b) All modifications made in Article 246 in its application to the State subsequent to the 1950 order should be rescinded.

   (c) Articles 248, 249, 250 and 251 whether applied in original or substituted/modified form should be omitted from their application to the State.

   (d) As in 1950 and 1954, List II (State) and List III (Concurrent) of the Seventh Schedule should not be applicable to the State.

(e) Article 254 should be restored to the position it had in its application to the State in 1954.

(f) Articles 262 and 263 which were not applicable under 1950 Order but were subsequently extended to the State should cease to apply.

3. Elections (Part XV)

Changes brought about in this Part be reversed and consequential changes in other Articles in this Part be effected.

4. Emergency Provisions (Part XVIII)

(a) The following should be added to C 1.6 of Article 352 in its application to the State:—'Provided that this request for concurrence of the Govt. of the State shall be subject to whatever decision the State Assembly may take within two months of declaration of emergency and failing any such decision, the proclamation of emergency shall be deemed to have been revoked.'

(b) Sub-clause (b) of C.I. (6) of this Article should be deleted.

(c) Articles 355, 356, 357, 358, 359 and 360 should be made non-applicable to the State as was the position in 1954.

5. Fundamental Rights (Part III)

This part should be deleted. A separate chapter on Fundamental Rights be included in the State Constitution.

6. The Union (Part V)

(a) Articles 72 (1) (c), 72 (3), 133, 134, 135, 136, 138, 145 (1) (c) and 151 (2) should be made non-applicable to the State as was the position in 1950 Order.

(b) Articles 149, 150 and 151 should apply to the State in the form in which they were in 1954.

7. The State (Part VI)

(i) Article 218 be omitted in its application to the State and the position as it existed before the J&K Constitution (First Amendment Act) of 1959 restored.

(ii) Articles 220, 222 and 226 should also be omitted in their application to Jammu and Kashmir State.

8. Finance, Property, Contracts and Suits (Part XII)

The matter be discussed between the State representatives and the Union Government as agreed to during the talks in 1952 (Delhi Agreement).

9. Services under the Union and the States (Part XIV)

In Article 312 the brackets and words 'including the State of Jammu and Kashmir' inserted by the Constitution (Application to J&K) Order 1958 be omitted.

10. Special Provisions relating to certain classes (Part XVI)

Application of Articles 338, 339, 340, 341 and 342 to the State should be omitted and corresponding provisions made in the State Constitution.

11. Amendment of the Constitution of India (Part XX)

(i) Clause (4) of Article 368 added vide C.O. 101 be deleted.

(ii) Clause (2) of the Article should apply with the proviso already introduced by 1954 order and clause (1) thereof which was not in existence in 1954 and was introduced in 1971 should remain omitted in its application to the State.

12. Schedules

In the Seventh Schedule entries in the Union List not applied to the State by the Constitution (Application to J&K) Order, 1950 should be omitted. Concurrent List which was not applicable to the State in 1950 but was applied by subsequent orders should cease to apply to the State.

13. Changes in the State Constitution

All amendments in the Constitution of Jammu and Kashmir made vide:—

(i) Constitution of Jammu ad Kashmir (First Amendment) Act, 1959 in so far as they relate to superintendent, direction and control of elections to the State legislature and to the State High Court; and

(ii) Constitution of Jammu and Kashmir (Sixth Amendment) Act, 1965 relating to change of nomenclature of the Head of the State and State Executive, mode of appointment of the Head of the State and other consequential amendments should be repealed and the original provisions of the Constitution of Jammu and Kashmir restored.

To sum up, the provisions of the Constitution of India specified in the Second Schedule and the matters specified in the First Schedule to the Constitution (Application to J&K) Order, 1950 and the matters agreed to by the representatives of the State and the Union vide Delhi Agreement of 1952 should continue to apply to the State subject to the same exceptions and modifications as are specified in the said Order and the Delhi Agreement. All Orders issued thereafter under clause (1) of Article 370 of the Constitution of India by the President, apply in various provisions and matters of the Constitution of India to the state whether in full or in modified form or making any change in the provisions or matters already applied by 1950 Order or agreed to under Delhi Agreement, should be rescinded and the provisions or matters so applied to the State cease to apply.

Also the changes made in the State Constitution vide Constitution of Jammu and Kashmir (First Amendment) Act, 1959 and Constitution of Jammu and Kashmir (Sixth Amendment) Act, 1965 be repealed and the original provisions of the Constitution of Jammu and Kashmir as adopted by the State Constituent Assembly on November 17, 1956 be restored.

Safeguards for Future

[...]

The issue is not one of executive 'functions' but legislative 'powers' apportioned between the Union and the State under two solemn compacts between them, the Instrument of Accession in 1947 and the Delhi Agreement of 1952 to which the President's Order of May 14, 1954 gave constitutional sanction besides, of course, Article 370 itself. To them must we return if popular sentiment is to be respected and resentments assuaged. It is first and foremost a moral issue. It also has important constitutional and political aspects. In the nature of things redress can only be through another compact between the Union and the State. Once the basic principles are agreed, there will be discussion on procedure. Forty years of unconstitutional practice have created a mess. The best course is for the President to repeal all Orders which are not in conformity with Constitution (Application to Jammu and Kashmir) Order, 1950 and the terms of the Delhi Agreement of 1952.

Ever since, Article 370 has acquired a dangerously ambiguous aspect. Designed to protect the State's autonomy, it has been used systematically to destroy it. A compact is necessary between the Union and the State which makes ample redress and finalizes their relationship by declaring a 'Constitutional Understanding' that Article 370 of the Constitution of India can no longer be used to apply to the State of Jammu and Kashmir any other provisions of the Constitution of India beyond the ones extended under 1950 Order and the Delhi Agreement, 1952. This could be embodied in a new Article that specified the agreement as part of the unamendable basic structure of the Indian Constitution.

Such constitutional understandings have been formulated in other democracies. The complexities of our situation render it the best, perhaps the only, course for removing the debris of an unhappy past and building in its place, a relationship between the State of Jammu and Kashmir and the Union of India which reflects the most vital aspect of federalism mutual trust and respect.

(Gh. Mohi-ud-Din Shah)	(Abdul Ahad Vakil)	(Abdul Rahim Rather)
Chairman	Member	Member
(Piyaray Lal Handoo)	(Bodh Raj Bali)	(Molvi I.H. Ansari)
Member	Member	Member
(Kushok Thiksay)	(Mirza Ab. Rashd)	(S. Teja Singh)
Member	Member	Member-Convener

Jammu,
April 1999

3. Debate in the J&K Assembly on the Autonomy Report 2000 and its Resolution Thereon (Extracts)

Assembly Debates on Autonomy Report, 9th Session, 8 and 10 April 2000 and 20, 21, 22, 24 and 26 June 2000, The Jammu and Kashmir Legislative Assembly Secretariat

Mr. P.L. Handoo (Hon'ble Law Minister):—

'The Cabinet discussed the State Autonomy Committee Report and decided that a discussion be raised in the Legislative Assembly along with a proposed resolution to endorse the earlier decision to constitute a Ministerial Committee which would initiate a dialogue with the Government of India on the recommendations of the Report. It was also decided that the aforesaid Ministerial Committee shall visit Delhi and other State Capitals to have discussions at the Ministerial level. It was further decided that an all party meeting would be convened in Srinagar in June, 2000 to discuss recommendations of the Report.'

(ii) 'The Cabinet endorsed the recommendations contained in the Report of the State Autonomy Committee. It was further decided that a special discussion on the Report would be convened in the Legislative Assembly at its next session. At the same time a response to the Government of India may be conveyed regarding the constitution of the Ministerial Committee consisting of the following:—

1. Shri Ghulam Mohi-ud-Din Shah, Minister for Housing and Urban Development.

2. Shri P.L. Handoo, Law Minister.

3. Shri Mohammad Shafi, Education Minister.

4. Shri A.R. Rather, Finance Minister.

5. Shri S.S. Slathia, Minister for Tourism and Youth Services and Sports.

The Government of India would be once again requested to set up a Ministerial Committee in order to initiate a dialogue on the Report' and this House be pleased to approve the same.

Sir, the only correction which I will suggest here is that in the last but one line after the word 'Report' kindly have apostrophy comma as given at the top because that is concluding part of the Cabinet decision. It should not be part of the motion; substantively moved by me. Sir, while I have said in the beginning, I solemnly rise to move this motion for which I feel personally that it will be perhaps the most full of pride occasion for me in my political career. I wish to live long to see this House enacting all the laws as flow from this report. Right now, my esteemed colleagues who are not here, I will have told them what it is? We are not enacting any law, we are not coming forth with any legislative proposal, we are only coming forth with a report submitted to Government of Jammu and Kashmir, field offices, the Government

of India. And Government of India in their eagerness to know what
this report is and to know what opinion of the Government of Jammu
and Kashmir is, addressed a communication seeking the opinion of the
Government of Jammu and Kashmir and seeking also our advice on the
methodology to be followed in the matter of discussion for the legislation and enactment which are bound to flow from this report.
[...]

Jammu and Kashmir Legislative Assembly Secretariat
10th April, 2000 (second sitting)

Hon'ble Speaker: Now we will take up discussion on the State Autonomy Committee Report in respect of which Hon'ble Law Minister
Shri P.L. Handoo has moved a motion. Simultaneously, Mr. Sadiq Ali,
Mr. Mohd. Shafi Bhat and Mr. G.M. Bawan have brought the following amendments on this motion and this will be also a part of the
discussion:—

'This House resolves that the State Autonomy Committee Report
placed on the Table of the House on 13-04-1999 be adopted and
positive steps be taken for its speed implementation'.

Shri Mubarik Gul: Sir, the amendments proposed by some Hon'ble
members reflect the truth that our party has adopted a clear stand on
the State Autonomy Committee Report. Restoration of Autonomy in
the State has been the core item of our election manifesto as a result of
which we got mandate of the people of Ladakh, Jammu and Kashmir in
the elections. The recent statement given by the Union Home Minister
showing his willingness to discuss even pre-1953 position of the State,
has been largely hailed by the Hon'ble members.
[...]

Shri A.R. Rather: Time has come that the situation is reviewed and
the autonomy is restored in its initial and original form. For pleasant
constitutional relations in future, doing this is inevitable. That would
also be in accordance with the spirit of the unambiguous constitutional
decision of the Indian Union, under which the State has been granted a
special status. We also feel it necessary to emphasize that there should be
a credible guarantee system about the constitutional relations between
the Indian Union and State of J&K. I am referring to this fact to make

it clear that National Conference has not raised the issue of autonomy only now, but has always been making the demand. We demanded autonomy in 1994 and declared it as a solution to Kashmir problem when no one in the State could even talk of such a thing. I respect the Hon'ble Member Ashok Sharma and I want to remind him that in 1995 Sh. Narsimha Rao Ji who was the Prime Minister of India then, stated in the Parliament that 'so far as granting autonomy to the State of Jammu and Kashmir is concerned, only sky is the limit. In this context the Constitution of our country has a lot of room and short of Azadi, we are ready to give anything'. The only personality in J&K who reacted positively to this was Dr. Farooq Abdullah. He suggested that the autonomy be restored and 'we are ready to work in the field, ready to work for the country'.

[...]

But it is unfortunate that this sincere offer could not get appropriate response. After this we went to talk to him in Delhi, not once but 10 times we met him and his colleagues. We discussed with them but he did not keep his word. After that the Parliament elections were called and we said we are not participating in these election. We would not go to the Parliament unless you clearly talk about autonomy. Meanwhile, his government went and the United Front came in power. They said they would talk about Kashmir to the leaders of the State, but the leaders of different parties in Kashmir argue that the talks should not be held with National Conference. Negotiations should be conducted with such a party as would prove its representative character and, for that the Assembly elections are necessary. We said that participation in Assembly elections would be possible for us only if the United Front Government stated clearly in its common minimum programme that autonomy would be granted to J&K. They accepted it. Our party accepted the challenge. We went to the people and the first thing we told people was that if they elected us and gave us the power, we would begin with efforts to restore autonomy. On the slogan of autonomy, people gave us two-third majority. I want to remind the people who say today that the people of Jammu or the people of Ladakh are against autonomy, the National Conference got 15 seats in Jammu on the agenda of autonomy. Is there any other party which got 15 seats? We got 3 out of 4 seats in the Ladakh. Who can say that our party did not get a mandate.

[...]

It is also said that granting autonomy to Kashmir would open a Pandora's box and that other States would start making similar demands which cannot be brushed aside. Those who talk like that are ignorant of history. I would advise them to use some time for studying history. They will have to see under what circumstances we established the State's relationship with India.

Please tell me which State other than J&K had negotiated the terms of membership for joining the Union. J&K was the only State which held protracted negotiations with the Centre for achieving a special status. The talks continued for five months. Sher-i-Kashmir and his colleagues started the talks with central leaders on 15th of May, 1949 which concluded on 11th of October, 1949. History is a witness that every line determining the relations between the Centre and the State was discussed even 10 times before finalization. Yesterday, Shah Sahib mentioned Article 306-A which became Article 370 later. The draft Article 370 was changed five times before giving it a final shape. This gives an idea as to how much effort and energy went into the establishment of relationship with the Centre.

[...]

We received 30% of the plan outlay as grant. The remaining 70% was considered as loan whereas other special category States received 90% as grant and 10% as loan. This was a clear discrimination. We cried ourselves hoarse. We tried to convince the central government that this was a very genuine demand. Convince us or get convinced. But they were not satisfied.

[...]

At last, in 1991 the gun convinced them. It is a real misfortune that they listen to the language of gun alone. The gun had its impact and we got the treatment in 1991. Between 1969 and 1991, the 70% loan component of our plan allocations kept increasing as a result of interest chargeable thereon and it became a huge amount. We kept telling successive Governments but no one agreed. Mr. V.P. Singh as the PM did it in 1991. In 1987, when he was the Finance Minister, he said, 'It cannot

be done' but in 1991, perhaps after seeing the gun, he agreed. The debts outstanding against our state are a result of their mistake.
[...]

Thus, Mr. Ayyangar has made it clear that the authority of the Centre can be extended only by the Constituent Assembly of the State.

Pt. Nehru Ji has also expressed similar impressions. As I said earlier the talks between the Central Leadership and Sheikh Sahib and his colleagues started on 15th May 1949. Pt. Nehru communicated the decisions that were taken on May 15 and 16 in his letter to Sheikh Sahib on May 18. It says, 'the State was to have its own Constitution and it will be for the Constituent Assembly of the State, when convened, to determine in respect of what other subjects the State may accede.' It meant that it would be the Constituent Assembly that could decide about additional powers, which could be transferred to the Union. Sheikh Sahib made similar observations in the State Constituent Assembly but in slightly stronger words. On August 11, 1952 while addressing the Constituent Assembly he said, 'I would like to make it clear that any suggestions of altering arbitrarily this basis of our relationship with India would not only constitute breach of the spirit and letter of the Constitution, but it may invite serious consequences for a harmonious association of our State with India.' Today you are seeing that things happened as Sheikh Sahib had apprehended. He had articulated it very clearly. And the reasons for our problems are that commitments were not fulfilled.

After the dismissal and arrest of Sheikh Sahib in 1953, the Centre took concurrence from the so-called Governments of the States, and the autonomy suffered constant erosion. There is no doubt about the fact that the Order of 1954 was issued on the recommendation of the Constituent Assembly. But, on the recommendation of which Constituent Assembly; it was the recommendation of a flawed Constituent Assembly, which did not have Sher-i-Kashmir in it. Neither were his other colleagues and important people around. It was that constituent assembly which accorded approval to the constitutional relationship between the Centre and the State of Jammu and Kashmir. Unfortunately, the entries of Union list in the Order of 1954 are not in conformity with either the Instrument of Accession or the Order of 1950. Therefore, the erosion of autonomy began with that. Still under 1954 Order, the Concurrent List was not applied to the State. Nice, State List was also not made applicable at that time. We had only a Union List and the residuary powers were with us. Article 249 was not made applicable to our State at that time, neither was the Article 356. At that point of time the constitutional provision governing the Central services too had not been extended to our State. All these things happened late and the haste with which all the 'tamashsa' was enacted makes our head bow in shame. What happened sir, after this? We were talking of Instrument of Accession. As many as 260 provisions of the Constitution out of 395 have been extended to our State. Almost the entire Union List is now applicable to J&K—94 out of 97 entries. In 1963, the Concurrent List was also applied—26 entries out of 47. Seven schedules out of twelve were applied. The document on autonomy will guide you about the details of what happened with us.

[...]

The Constituent Assembly of the State framed the Constitution of the State and ceased to exist after that. Even after that, the concurrence of the State Government was obtained for extending the authority of the Union. It was stretched so much that even during the Governor and President Rules, the Governor said that he was the Government and gave concurrence. This was done even as the term 'Government' is clearly defined under Article 370. This Article provides: 'for the purpose of this Article, the Government of State means the person for the time being recognised by the President on the recommendations of the Legislative Assembly of the State as the Sadar-i-Riyasat of Jammu and Kashmir, acting on the advice of the Council of Ministers of the State for the time being in office.'

[...]

When the Governor gave concurrence to it, Mr. Mohd. Shafi and I cried and protested. Mr. Handoo is a witness. I said the Constitution was being torn to shreds. 'What is this happening'? We decided to go to the Court of Law against this order. In this connection, we required a copy of that Presidential Order. I am talking of 1986. We could not get a copy of that order for a full fortnight. If you are trying to apply the Indian Constitution here, do it openly, if the Constitution permits it. But tell the people what you are doing. Why are you surreptitious? It appeared that they had a guilty conscience and that is why we were not given a copy for a long time. Ultimately we filed a writ petition. [...]

Certain quarters are demanding the scrapping of Article 370. It is pure emotion. It is written in Article 370 itself that President can abrogate this Article. But, for that a recommendation of the Constituent Assembly is essential. Since a Constituent Assembly is not in existence now, therefore, there is no question of abrogating Article 370.

Another point that was sought to be made by the friends yesterday, was that Article 370 is a temporary provision. I want to state that the word 'temporary' has a background about it. Article 370 was finalized before November 26, 1949, even though it became a reality on January 26, 1950. The constitutional relationship between the Centre and the State was to be given a final shape by the Constituent Assembly of the State and it had not been convened yet and its recommendations were awaited. Therefore, it was rightly thought that might be the Constituent Assembly makes any amendment or alteration or may be it may recommend the scrapping of Article altogether. That is why this Article was termed temporary. But the Constituent Assembly dispersed without any recommendations on this. Now you yourself can judge whether this Article is permanent or temporary. It is a permanent provision now and no power on earth can change this reality.

Under our Constitution, we used to have a Sadar-i-Riyasat who was elected by this House. We used to have our Prime Minister as well. Our Constitution has a chapter on directive principles. It provides for an independent judiciary. And, another important feature of it is covered under Section 147, which provides the mechanism for amending this Constitution. This provision makes it clear that certain provisions of the Constitution cannot be changed and they constitute its basic pillars. Among the provisions which cannot be amended is Section 3 which says that J&K is a part of India. Nobody can challenge it and the Section cannot be changed. Another unamendable provision is the Section 5. Section 147 can also not be changed under any circumstances. This Section contains the designation of Sadar-i-Riyasat. The Congress activists were very enthusiastic in 1965. Their slogans were, 'Amend the Constitution, amend it wholesale'. At that time they introduced sub clause (3) to Section 2 of the State Constitution which said that wherever the word 'Sadar-i-Riyasat appears in the Constitution, it should be read as 'Governor'. At that time they did not consider the fact that Section 147 is immutable. No amendment can be done to this section. This provision too contains the term Sadar-i-Riyasat. They could not understand that amending the State Constitution would not effect the Constitution of India. The Article 370 of the Constitution of India still contains the word 'Sadar-i-Riyasat' as it could not be changed.

[...]

Mr. Speaker: ...The original motion accompanied by the amend-ments, that has been given by three Hon'ble Members, now, is a substitute motion clubbed together. But the motion before the House is that they have given a substitute motion from the Hon'ble Law & Parliamentary Affairs Minister for the two motions moved on 8th of April, 2000 along with the amendments moved thereto by Hon'ble Mr. Sadiq Ali, Mr. Mohd Shafi Bhat and Mr. G.M. Bhawan.

This House having discussed the report of the State Autonomy Committee placed on the Table of this Hon'ble House on 13th of April, 1999 records its approval of the same and its acceptance of recommendations made therein and further demands of the Union Government and the Government of Jammu and Kashmir to take positive and effective steps for implementation of the same.

[...]

Now I do not need to go through the motion itself. The substitute motion which has already been moved by the Hon'ble Law Minister, Sheikh Abdul Rehman, Leader of B.S.P., Shri Tara Chand Leader of the Congress Party, Lala Shiv Charan Jee, Leader of B.J.P. and the leader of the House had a very lively debate on this report. Now closing the debate I am putting this motion to vote.

Those Hon'ble Members who are in favour of it may say 'Yes' and those who are against may say 'No'.

Voices: Yes, yes.

Note: The Motion was carried by majority vote and the Hon'ble members of BJP, Congress, Panthers Party, Janata Dal and Awami League while opposing, staged a walk out.

[...]

4. Justice Saghir Ahmad's Report, 2009 (Extracts)

The working Group V was set up in implementation of the decisions concerning the establishment of five Working Groups announced by the Prime Minister of India at the Round Table Conference held at Srinagar on 24th & 25th May, 2006.

The issues under the purview of the Working Group V were as follows:—

Strengthening relations between the State and the Centre and to deliberate on

(1) Matters relating to the Special Status of Jammu and Kashmir within the Indian Union;

(2) Methods of strengthening democracy, secularism and the rule of law in the State;

(3) Effective devolution of powers among different regions to meet regional, sub-regional and ethnic aspirations.

The Working Group held five meetings as follows:—

(1) 12th December, 2006 at New Delhi

(2) 03rd February, 2007 at Jammu

(3) 29th March, 2007 at New Delhi

(4) 02nd September, 2007 at New Delhi

(5) 03rd September, 2007 at New Delhi

This report seeks to address the issues that were raised by various members during the deliberations of the Working Group. The members had also submitted written representations and the relevant points therein have also been incorporated in the report. Information was also obtained from the State Government mainly on the issues raised by members and participants/special invitees in the above meetings or through written representations/statements. The same also finds place in the report.

The issues that were raised and discussed in the various meetings and also through written representations are as follows:—

1. Matters relating to the Special Status of Jammu and Kashmir within the Indian Union.

(i) Unity and integrity of the State

(ii) Article 370 of the Constitution of India and other Constitutional provisions

(iii) Central laws extended to the State

(iv) Demand of autonomy by National Conference

(v) Self-Rule proposed by PDP

2. Methods of strengthening democracy, secularism and the rule of law in the State.

(i) Issues regarding democracy, secularism and the rule of law in the State

(ii) Issues relating to Kashmiri migrants

(iii) Issues relating to refugees of 1947, 1965 and later in Jammu region.

3. Effective devolution of powers among different regions to meet regional, sub-regional and ethnic aspirations.

(i) Inter and intra-regional issues between Jammu, Kashmir and Ladakh.

(ii) Development considerations of different areas and local self-governance/regional councils.

(iii) Backward areas and communities within the three regions.

4. Other Issues.

This report is presented in two parts—Part I dealing with the issue No.1 and Part II dealing with the remaining issues.

The Working Group was assisted by Shri Ajit Kumar, Financial Commissioner, Government of Jammu and Kashmir and a group of Officers and Staff from the office of the Principal Resident Commissioner, New Delhi, Government of Jammu and Kashmir.

Justice Saghir Ahmad

Chairman

18-12-2009

Report of the 5th Working Group

At the beginning of the first Meeting of the Group on 12th December, 2006, it was made clear by The Chairman that this Group is not concerned with the dispute between India and Pakistan pertaining to the state of Jammu and Kashmir and, therefore, it will confine itself to the consideration of the question relating to Centre–State Relations within the framework of the Constitution of India. It was also made clear by the Chairman in his letter to the Chief Minister that in the absence of mainstream political parties like the National Conference and All Parties Hurriyat Conference, the deliberations would be of little value.

The National Conference which had not sent its Representative to the first two meetings of the Working Group, however, participated in the 3rd and subsequent meetings and also put forward, rather strongly, its case for restoration of what it called 'Autonomy' of the State of Jammu and Kashmir.

The first three meetings were confined to the consideration of the question of 'Centre–State Relations' with reference to the special status of Jammu and Kashmir under Article 370 of the Indian Constitution, its Autonomy and the erosion of the Autonomy as claimed by the National Conference and PDP. The question of division of J&K State, which was raised specially by one of the Members, namely, Mr. Thupstan Chhewang, who is a member of Parliament from Ladakh, was also discussed and deliberated. In the 3rd and subsequent meetings, National Conference which is the main Opposition Party in Jammu and Kashmir Assembly also participated and was represented by Mr. A.R. Rather Leader of Opposition, who advocated restoration of 'Autonomy'.

Ms. Mehbooba Mufti of the People Democratic Party which is a constituent of the present Coalition Government in Jammu & Kashmir, advocated what she called 'Self-Rule'. In the next meeting, Shri Muzaffar Beg, as a Representative of PDP, orally explained the concept of 'Self-Rule' but the PDP, contrary to its assurances, did not elaborate it in writing.

This Working Group, consists of the representatives of all the National and Regional level Political Parties, active in the State of Jammu and Kashmir. These representatives are the members of this Group and in that capacity they have been participating in all the meetings in which they discussed all the issues including the issues as to why there should be a special status for the State of Jammu and Kashmir in the Indian Constitution, why was Article 370 enacted, why the power of Parliament to make laws for the State of Jammu and Kashmir was restricted to only three items, namely, Defence, External Affairs and Communication referred to in the Instrument of Accession. It was also contended that since 'Accession' has brought about complete integration of the State of Jammu and Kashmir within the Indian Union, there was occasion therefore, no for providing any special status for that State under the Indian Constitution. Most of the Members even submitted their view-points in writing.

[...]

Mr. Muzaffar Hussain Baig on behalf of PDP elaborated the concept of 'Self-Rule' He stated:

In the 'Self-Rule' demand of PDP and the demand of 'Autonomy' of National Conference, there is a difference of approach. Where as Autonomy is essentially a Centre–State Relation, Self Rule has other aspects also as, for example.

1. There is an external dimension between India and Pakistan and there are relevant Constitutional provisions in the Indian and State Constitution. In the State Constitution Section 3 indicates the territory of the State and Section 147 says that Section 3 cannot be amended as such all the territories of J&K including those under Pakistan and China will have to form one single unit and cannot be subdivided.

2. The second aspect is the Centre–State relations within two Constitutions as also the various Presidential Orders issued under the Constitution of India.

3. 'Self Rule' will address itself to Constitutional applications for the people living in PoK and the area of Ladakh under occupation of China also. The State has to recognize that all persons living in these areas including the Northern areas are part of the State.

4. In case the Central Government and Pakistan make for a better rela-tionships between the two countries, border/LoC would become ineffective through joint economic enterprises, Legislative Conferences etc. This aspect will have to be examined.

5. There are a number of regional aspirations and under currents within the State. Many people of Jammu feel that there is Kashmiri dominance and Ladakh also has a sense of discrimination. A model of self governance for Ladakh and some other regions can be examined. So far as the Union territory issue is concerned this will be directly in conflict with section 3 of the State Constitution.

6. There should be a strong United India and similarly a strong union of States with a healthy federal system and this approach has to be for all sections of the society.

Self Rule must benefit all sections of the society and the regions including Doda, Poonch, Rajouri etc. No extreme positions should be taken by any organization but a reasonable middle path should be followed which would be the best course.

So far as the Centre–State relations are concerned, the National Conference has asked for changes with a maximal approach whereas 'self-rule' will ask for minimum changes as illustrated below:—

(a) All legislative matters within the scope of the union under the Instrument of Accession and 1950 Presidential Orders are beyond any debate.

(b) All provisions of the Constitution of India which are necessary for integrity, unity and solidarity must continue.

(c) All provisions permitting democracy, secularism and rule of law should be protected.

(d) All provisions necessary for uniformity among the States to a larger extent has to be protected.

So far as Self Rule is concerned its essential objectives are:—

(i) A reasonable degree of federal structure within the Union.

(ii) Expressed will of the people has to be honoured and not in any way subverted or reduced to the extent that roll back of some provisions may become necessary.

(iii) Any legislative measure which harms the economic interests of the State should be rolled back.

(iv) Article 356 and 367 of the Constitution of India relating to dismissal of the State Government are not necessary as there are safeguards under Article 352 and 355 (emergency provisions which require concurrence of the State in some cases). Besides, under Article 256 and 257 directions can be given to the State Government and therefore, also Article 356 is not necessary.

The issue regarding Art. 368 (Amendment of the Constitution) and part 4 of order No. 101 of the orders issued under Art. 370 restricting amending powers of the State have to be examined.

The Head of the State should be called Sadr-i-Riyasat as earlier and it should be mandatory to be elected/appointed alternatively from Jammu and Kashmir.

The authority of the State is exercised by political leadership and also the administration and hence Art. 312 relating to All India Services is not necessary in respect of the State.

Art. 370 giving powers to the President for certain modifications was examined by the Supreme Court of India in Sampath Prakash case and it was held that this Art. would be of a permanent nature as any modifications could only be made by the Constituent Assembly which however did not take place and as such Art. 370 is to be treated as of permanent nature.

Other items that would be important in the years to come would be the economic relations and trade relations with PoK for which enough scope is there.

The local police have to play a stronger role in internal matters replacing the role of the Central forces including anti militancy operations.

Shri Baig stated that a comprehensive document will be presented by the PDP in due course of time. This has however not been done till date.

In the third meeting, however, Sardar Rafiq Hussain Khan filed a copy of the resolution of the PDP adopted on 11-2-2007. Copies of this document were circulated to all the members of the Working Group. Sardar Rafiq Hussain Khan observed that PDP will pursue its agenda of Self-Rule and try to mobilize public opinion in all the three regions for its acceptance.

The PDP resolution dated 11-2-2007 indicates that the problem of the State has 4 dimensions:—

   (i)   Problems between India and Pakistan
   (ii) Problem between Centre and the State
   (iii) Problems in relations between people living in two parts of the State and
   (iv) Problems of mistrust and discord between the three regions of the State, namely, Jammu, Kashmir and Ladakh.

Mr. A.R. Rather, representing National Conference, advocating question of 'Autonomy' stated:

The views of the National Conference are known about the Centre–State relations. The party after coming to power in 1996 had appointed a Committee which finalized the report on Autonomy. The Report was placed before both the Houses of the Legislative and was adopted.

[Note: Shri Rather presented a copy of the Autonomy Report published by the State Government to the Chairman].

Mr. Rather argued that at the time of the Accession of the State to the Indian Dominion three items namely, External Affairs, Defence and Communications alone were given to the Centre and the rest of the subjects remained with the State. No supplementary Instrument of Accession was signed giving further authority to the Centre.

The demand of National Conference is for restoration of the Autonomy that was already available and has been eroded over a period of time. The erosion of Autonomy is the primary cause of discontent in the State and this fact was accepted at different times. For example, Shri P.V. Narsimha Rao, the then Prime Minister observed 'Sky is the limit and short of independence, the demands can be accepted'. However, the National Conference boycotted the 1996 Parliamentary Elections. Thereafter, Shri Deve Gowda, Prime Minister promised 'maximum autonomy to be discussed with peoples representatives'. The National Conference therefore contested the 1996 Assembly Elections and obtained 2/3rd majority as it had given out in its election manifesto that Autonomy was the prime consideration for the State.

The National Conference got highest number of seats for any party in all the three regions, namely, it got 15 out of 37 in Jammu, 3 out of 4 in Ladakh, and 42 out of 47 in Kashmir. The Committee for Restoration of Autonomy set up by the State Government examined the Autonomy issue with reference to Instrument of Accession, Constitution application order 1950 and Delhi Agreement 1952. The report of the Committee which was duly approved by the J&K Legislature was however, rejected summarily by the Government of India even without any discussions or even detailed examination.

The issues of Accession of the State with the country were discussed by the State representatives with the Government of India in 1949–50 (the negotiations started on 15th May, 1949 and continued up to 16th November, 1949). The discussions were held between Pandit Jawahar Lal Nehru, the then Prime Minister of India and Sheikh Mohammad Abdullah. On 18th May, 1949 the Prime Minister wrote a letter that two major decisions were taken namely that (1) the State will have its own Constitution and (2) it will be for the Constituent Assembly of the State to decide what powers other than those given in the Instrument of Accession, will be given to the Centre. In the background of the above negotiations, the Indian Constituent Assembly enacted and adopted Art. 370 of the Constitution.

Art. 238 of the Constitution of India (which has since been repealed) was not applied to the State of Jammu and Kashmir.

Shri Rather further observed that the agreements of 1949/1950 provided that during the interim period from 1949 to 1951, the Constitutional provisions or laws could be extended to the State with the concurrence of the State

Government and thereafter the same was to be ratified by the Constituent
Assembly of the State which was constituted in 1951. As such the power to
give concurrence was not available to the State Government after 1951 when
the State Constituent Assembly was constituted.

The 'Government of the State' was further defined as the 'Sadar-e-Riyasat as
advised by the Council of Ministers'. However, even after 1951 the concurrence
continued to be given by the State Government and sometime this was done by
the Governor of the State (who exercised the powers of the Government during
the Governor's Rule). The Concurrence given by the Governor extending
certain laws was not, therefore valid.

The Constituent Assembly, after completing its work, was dissolved in 1956
and thereafter 47 Constitution Application Orders were issued which eroded
the original autonomy available to the State, reducing its authority.

Some other provisions of the State Constitution have been now made
permanent and the State Legislature does not have authority to review or
revise the same, for example Section 147 of the State Constitution cannot be
amended and similarly the earlier provisions of elected head of the State was
amended in 1965 which again cannot now be changed.

Shri Rather further stated that the Presidential Orders issued after 1954
were without jurisdiction as they were not ratified by the Constituent Assembly
which had dispersed in 1956 after completing the job of making the Jammu
and Kashmir Constitution. He further stated that Article 370 of the Constitution must be treated as a permanent feature of the Indian Constitution and
the word 'Temporary' used in that Article should be replaced by the word
'Permanent' in consonance with the special provisions made on permanent
basis for other States like Sikkim and few North Eastern States. Shri Rather
stressed that the Report of the Autonomy Committee as adopted by the State
Legislature which was filed before the Working Group today, gives in detail the
manner in which Autonomy could be restored including repeal of certain laws
extended illegally to the State of Jammu and Kashmir after 1954.

Concluding, Shri Rather again stressed that the Report of the Autonomy
Committee as adopted by the State Legislative gives in detail the process by
which Autonomy can be restored to the State by repealing for example, certain
laws extended to the State after 1954.

The continuance or abolition or strengthening of Article 370 of
Constitution of India was, as stated earlier, widely debated and the
views expressed by other Hon'ble Members of this Working Group, are,
briefly, as follows:—

(i)   Shri Saif-ud-Din Soz (Congress): No rigid stand should be taken
      in favour or against Art. 370 and the present position should
      continue. Article 370 should be considered as a permanent
      feature of the Constitution of India.

(ii) Shri Arun Jaitly (BJP): The stand of the Party is that the Article
      370 should be repealed and the State fully integrated with the
      Union as in the case of other States. He also set out in writing
      his Party's stand on Art. 370 (Available in Vol. IV).

(iii) Shri M.Y. Tarigami CPI (M): Article 370 should act as a bridge
      between the Union and the State and the provisions which
      have been eroded in time should be restored.

(iv) Shri Thupstan Chhewang (Leh): Art. 370 of the constitution
      should be abrogated as it hampers the economic development
      of the State.

(v)   Shri Ajay Chrungoo (Panun Kashmir): Art. 370 has hampered
      the smooth functioning of the legal authority in the state and
      hence it should be removed.

(vi) Shri Harish Dev Singh (Panthers Party): Art. 370 should con-
      tinue in the present form with neither going back nor making
      any further change.

(vii) Sheikh Abdul Rahman (Samajwadi Party): Article 370 has
      contributed to certain discrimination against some regions and
      therefore, needs to be suitably modified to protect regional
      aspirations.

(viii) Shri Ashwani Kumar (Jammu Mukti Morcha): Complete in-
      tegration of the State should be done by abolition of Article
      370.

(ix) Shri Yashpal Bhagat (BSP): Art. 370 should be abolished, and
      there should be full integration of the State.

In order to find out an answer to these questions, it would be necessary to delve into the archives of old records which would reveal the
historical and political background of Article 370 of the Constitution
of India.

[...]

In Prem Nath *vs* State of Jammu and Kashmir, AIR 1959 SC 749, the
Supreme Court observed that the Constitution makers were obviously

anxious that the relationship between the Union of India and the State of Jammu & Kashmir should be finally determined by the Constituent Assembly of the State itself. It would thus be seen that the State of Jammu & Kashmir though an integral part of India had the unique position in the Indian Constitution. The Supreme Court, however, took a contrary view in Sampat *v.* State of J&K AIR 1970 SC 1118 (1124): 1969 (2) SCR 365.

[...]

Article 370 (1) (b) (ii) provides that in addition to the matters in the Union List and the Concurrent List as set out in Clause I (b), the Right of Parliament to make laws will also extend to such other matters in that list as with the concurrence of the Government of the State, the President may by order specify. The list of Chief Ministers given above indicates that there was always a popular Government in power and, therefore, the Presidential Orders were apparently issued with the concurrence of that Government.

[...]

It may be stated that on an earlier occasion also while Sheikh Abdullah was the Chief Minister of the State of Jammu & Kashmir, the question had arisen about the erosion in 'Autonomy' available to the State of Jammu and Kashmir on the ground that the Parliament was enacting laws on topics other than Defence, External Affairs and Communication. In order to examine this question, the State Cabinet appointed a Sub-Committee under the Chairmanship of former Deputy Chief Minister, Mirza Mohd. Afzal Beg. Mr. D.D. Thakur, Minister for Finance, Planning & Housing, Mr. A.K. Tikoo, Forest Minister, Mr. G.M. Shah, Transport Minister, Mr. G.N. Kochak, Industry Minister, the Chief Secretary & the Law Secretary were members of the Sub-Committee.

The Committee was constituted to review the Central laws including provisions of the Constitution of India extended/applied to the State of Jammu & Kashmir after 1953 and to report whether the operation of any of the laws was detrimental to the interest of the State.

None of the Members of the Sub-Committee however attended the meetings with the result that the Report could not be prepared within the time fixed by Sheikh Abdullah. On one occasion, therefore,

Sheikh Abdullah had to express his indignation on the Report not being finalized. This prompted Mr. D.D. Thakur to go into the whole question himself and he prepared his Report dated 18th July, 1981 which cannot but be described as a lucid exposition of law. In the first part of his Report Mr. D.D. Thakur himself has stated as under:—

The Hon'ble Chief Minister will kindly recall that the State Cabinet appointed a Cabinet Sub-Committee under the Chairmanship of the former Deputy Chief Minister Mirza Mohd Afzal Beg with Mr. M.K. Tikoo, Forest Minister, Mr. G.M. Shah, Transport Minister, Mr. G.N. Kochak, Industry Minister, the Chief Secretary, the Law Secretary and me as its members, to review the Central laws including the provisions of the Constitution of India extended/applied to the State of Jammu & Kashmir after 1953 and to report whether the operation of any of the laws is detrimental to the interests of the State. The Committee was given time till 5th October, i.e., 15 days from the date of the decision to make a report. The precise terms of reference to the Committee as contained in the Cabinet decision, are reproduced hereunder:—

'The Committee shall examine the Central Laws including the provisions of the Constitution of India extended/applied to the State after 1953 and find out as to the operation of which of them is not beneficial in the interests of the State. The Committee shall submit its report by 5th of October, 1977.'

2. The examination shall be made against the background of:—

(i)   The Instrument of Accession signed by the Maharaja;
(ii) The Delhi Agreement executed between the Centre and the State in 1952;
(iii) Article 370 of the Constitution of India; and
(iv) The Accord entered into between Sheikh Mohd. Abdullah and the Government of India in 1975.'

3. This Cabinet Sub-Committee on the exit of Mr. Beg from the Cabinet was re-constituted vide Cabinet decision No. 851 dated 16.10.1978 under the Chairmanship of the Chief Minister with Mr. G.M. Shah, Mr. G.N. Kochak, Mr. M.K. Tickoo, the Chief Secretary, the Law Secretary and myself as its members. The Hon'ble Chief Minister subsequently vide his order dated 2.1.1979 desired that I should chair the meetings of the Committee.

4. Because of various pre-occupations of the members of the Committee the meetings of the Committee became very difficult with the result that no progress could be made in the matter. On 15.6.1981 the issue came up for discussion in the Cabinet when the Hon'ble Chief Minister expressed his anguish at the delay in the submission of the report to the Cabinet. It was in this

background that I offered to prepare a report which the rest of the members of the Cabinet Sub-Committee could consider and comment upon.

5. I am proceeding to dictate this report after thorough examination of the background material mentioned in the terms of reference. The comments offered and the conclusions drawn are my own and are intended to provide a basis for a more meticulous and in depth examination of the various issues which I have touched in the report.

Mr. D.D. Thakur took into consideration the provisions of Article 370 of the Indian Constitution, Delhi Agreement 1952 and the Kashmir Accord of 1975 besides other relevant documents and circumstances to come to the conclusion that the laws made by Indian Parliament including the laws made on the topics in the Concurrent List of VIIth Schedule which did not apply to the State of Jammu and Kashmir, were properly applied. Mr. D.D. Thakur has given a complete list of laws made by the Indian Parliament till then, including those made on the topics in the Concurrent List. At the end of the Report, Mr. Thakur, inter alia, wrote under:

The Hon'ble Chief Minister to whom I am submitting this report today may consider referring the same to the whole Cabinet for their consideration where the Members of the Cabinet Sub-Committee can also participate or to the Members of the Cabinet Sub-Committee only, if he considers that it is necessary to do so. I would, however, like to be heard in the event of any disagreement on any one of the findings which I have recorded'.

A copy of this Report was sent to Mr. Gulam Nabi Kochak, Minister for Revenue and Forest, who in his Report dated 11th April, 1982 expressed serious reservations with regard to the contents of the Report of Shri D.D. Thakur. It is not clear what happened to these two reports, whether they were placed before the Cabinet or the House and discussed, and, if so, what decision was taken and which Report was accepted and which rejected. A query to this effect was made to the State Government and the Law Department, Government of Jammu & Kashmir vide No. PS/PSL/2009/247 dated 13.5.2009 stated that the Report was never laid on the table of the House.

In 1996, while Dr. Farooq Abdullah was the Chief Minister, the State Government set up a Committee to examine the question of restoration of 'Autonomy' to the State of Jammu & Kashmir under the Chairmanship of Dr. Karan Singh, who, however resigned on July 31, 1997 and the then PWD Minister, Mr. Ghulam Mohi-Ud-Din Shah was appointed as the Chairman. The Committee examined all the aspects of the matter and submitted its Report to the State Government in April, 1999. The Report was placed before the two Houses of the Jammu & Kashmir Legislature on 13.4.1999. It was adopted by the State Legislative Assembly on 26.6.2000 and the State Legislative Council on 27th June, 2000. The State Government submitted the Autonomy Report to the Central Government. But the Central Government refused to consider the matter.

[...]

It would thus be seen from the above, that there is a positive distribution of legislative and administrative powers between the Union and the State. This has been provided with the obvious object of maintaining harmonious relations between the Centre and the State.

In the light of the principles discussed above, it is clear that legislative fields had already been indicated between the Centre and the State in the documents of Accession which was also incorporated in the Indian Constitution in the form of Article 370 and, therefore, the Parliament, to begin with, could make laws for the State of Jammu and Kashmir only on the topics indicated in the Schedule attached with the document of Accession but also on the topics subsequently applied to the State of J&K.

In this connection certain provisions of the Constitution of Jammu and Kashmir may also be noticed. Section 3 of the Jammu and Kashmir Constitution provides as under:—'The State of Jammu and Kashmir is and shall be an integral part of the Union of India'.

... Smt. Indira Gandhi, the then Prime Minister of India, rose to the occasion and agreed that any Provision of the Constitution of India applied to the State of Jammu and Kashmir with adaptations and modifications can be altered or repealed by an order of the President under Article 370.

The question of 'Autonomy' and its demand can be examined in the light of the 'Kashmir Accord' or in some other manner or on the basis of some other formula as the present Prime Minister may deem fit and appropriate so as to restore the 'Autonomy' to the extent possible. This is also a long pending demand which requires to be settled once for all to usher in a brighter relationship between the Centre and the State. The question of appointment of the Governor and dismissal of the popular Government by the Governor may be considered and resolved.

[...]

The Report of Dr. P.B. Gajendragadkar Commission of Inquiry indicates that even in November 1968, that is to say, almost 18 years of the coming into force of the Indian Constitution, there was no recommendation that Article 370 should be abolished. The position remains the same and there has been no material alteration in the circumstances in as much as few voices were raised and are still raised for abrogation of Article 370 while there are other voices which strongly plead for the continuance of this Article. The Gajendragadkar Formula is still relevant and it is for the people of the State of Jammu and Kashmir to decide how long to continue Article 370 in its present form and when to make it permanent or abrogate.

This position has continued since 1950 when the Indian Constitution was enforced. A period of about 60 years is a long period and the Working Group recommends that the question of Article 370 should be settled once for all and the state of uncertainty in respect of this article should be given a final shape.

[...]

5. Draft Article 370: A Proposal

The Constitution (application to Jammu and Kashmir) Order 2009.

In exercise of the powers conferred by clauses (1) and (3) of Article 370 of the Constitution, and in supersession of all the previous orders made under Article 270, the President with the concurrence of the State of Jammu and Kashmir, is pleased to make the following Order:—

1. This Order may be called the Constitution (Application to Jammu and Kashmir) Order, 2011.

2. It shall come into force at once and shall thereupon supersede all the Orders made by the President under Article 370(1).

3. Article 370 shall hereafter be operative as from the date of this Order only with the exceptions and modifications as are specified herein-below and not otherwise.

4. The provisions of Article 1 and of this Article shall apply in relation to that State.

5. The following other provisions of the Constitution shall apply in relation to that State subject to the exceptions and modifications specified herein below: (to be negotiated).

5.1 Parliament shall have exclusive power to make laws for the said State with respect only to the matters enumerated in entries in List I in the Seventh Schedule (in this Constitution referred to as the 'Union List')…. (to be negotiated).

5.2 The legislature of the State of Jammu and Kashmir shall have exclusive power to make laws with respect to all the other matters enumerated in the said Union List and the Concurrent and the State Lists in the Seventh Schedule.

6.1 An amendment to Article 370 shall be initiated either by a Bill for the purpose in either House of Parliament and when the Bill is passed in each House by a majority of the total membership of that House and by a majority of not less than two-thirds of the members of that House present and voting it shall be presented to the President who shall give his assent to the Bill and thereupon the Constitution shall stand amended in accordance with the terms of the Bill.

Provided that if such amendment seeks to make any change in any of the provisions of the Constitution specified in Clauses 4 and 5 as applied to the State, the amendment shall also require to be ratified by each House of the Legislature of the State by resolutions to that effect passed by a total membership of that House and by a majority of not less than two-thirds members of that House present and voting before the Bill making provision for such amendment is presented to the President for assent.

Provided further that any amendment of the Constitution which seeks to apply to the State of Jammu and Kashmir any provision of the Constitution other than the provisions applied under Clauses 4 and 5 it shall be ratified by the State of Jammu and Kashmir only by a resolution passed as aforesaid by its Legislative Assembly first elected after the amendment is passed by Parliament as well as by its Legislative Council in each case by a majority of the total membership of the House and by a majority of not less than two-thirds of the members of each House present and voting.

Provided further that no Bill seeking to make any change in this Article shall be introduced in either House of Parliament.

7. For the removal of doubt, it is hereby declared that Clauses (1) and (3) of Article 370 shall cease to be operative and no orders shall be made by the President hereafter under the said clauses as from the date of this order.

8. The word 'temporary' in the marginal note to Article 370 shall be deleted.

Index

Bakshi Ghulam Mohammed 10, 11,
46, 94–5, 111, 120, 121, 133,
191, 228, 232, 236; appointed as
Prime Minister (9 August 1953)
240–41
Balakrishnan, S. 18
Bali, Bodh Raj 421, 450
Bandhu, Kashapa 46
Baqula, Kashuk 109
Barua, Hem 312–13, 314
Basic Principles Committee 27,
111–13, 116, 117, 121–2, 155,
159, 165–6, 197, 242–50, 251,
262, 283; Interim Report
(10 June 1952) 117–20, 121–2,
176, 186, 191–2, 196, 214, 430
Bawan, G.M. 452, 458
Beg, Mirza M.Y. 317
Beg, Mirza Muhammad Afzal 4,
11, 17, 18, 27, 46, 56, 72, 73,
74, 94, 108, 109, 110, 112, 120,
127–8, 133, 155, 159, 187, 189,
190, 191–2, 217–23, 228, 236,
316, 412, 413, 423, 424–30,
468, 469; and G. Parthasarthi,
correspondence 405–7; signed
agreed conclusions of Indira
Gandhi–Sheikh Abdullah Accord
17, 18, 402–5, 408
Beg, Muzaffar, 461
Bevin, Ernest 200
Bhagat, Yashpal 467
Bharatiya Janata Party (BJP) 21, 22,
458, 467
Bhat, Mohammad Shafi 451, 452,
456, 458

Cabinet Mission 100–01, 318; Plan
150–1, 152; Statement (16 May
1946) 29–30, 44; Memorandum

on Indian States, Treaties, and
Paramountcy 30–32
Chagla, M.C. 315, 330
Charak, Lachman Singh 113
Chatterjee, N.C. 310–11, 388–9
Chhewang, Thupstan 461, 467
Chidambaram, P. 1
Chrungoo, Ajay 467
citizenship issue in Jammu and
Kashmir 53, 54, 77, 108–11,
132, 134–5, 140, 141, 142,
157, 166, 167–8, 183, 246–7,
248, 429
Commission of Inquiry (Justice N.
Rajagopala Ayyangar), Report
(30 June 1967) 11
Commission of Inquiry
(Dr. P.B. Gajendragadkar) 472
Committee for Restoration of
Autonomy 465
communications 161, 433, 437,
438, 439, 446, 452, 462,
464, 468
Concurrent List 7, 20, 23, 52, 60,
62, 64, 79, 162, 208, 256, 260,
269, 274, 303, 345, 346, 384,
393, 398, 404, 422, 424, 432,
434–5, 437, 438, 445, 448, 456,
468, 470
confidence building measures
(CBMs) 21
Constituent Assembly of India 1,
3, 4, 6, 8, 12, 52, 78, 161, 234,
423, 427
Constituent Assembly of Jammu and
Kashmir 4–7, 9, 10, 11, 13,
15–16, 21, 23, 27, 28, 51, 53,
60, 63, 65, 67, 68, 69, 71, 74,
78, 80, 88–122, 123–7, 129,
130–2, 134, 136, 138, 140, 144,

United Nations and Kashmir issue
15, 67, 81, 89, 90–1, 124, 129,
131, 138, 140, 186, 199, 200,
202, 203, 321, 328, 329, 330,
395; Security Council 126, 229,
315, 318, 328, 329
United Progressive Alliance (UPA)
21

Vakil, Abdul Ahad, 317, 421, 450
Venkataraman, R. 18, 385

Wanchoo, Justice K.N. 387, 418

White Paper of the Government of
J&K on the Delhi Agreement,
150–8
White Paper on Jammu and
Kashmir (1948) 329
Working Group V 21, 22, 24, 460,
461–72

Yechury, Sitaram 25

Zakir Husain 356–58, 360–61
Zutshi, J.N. 46